Between
Song and
Story

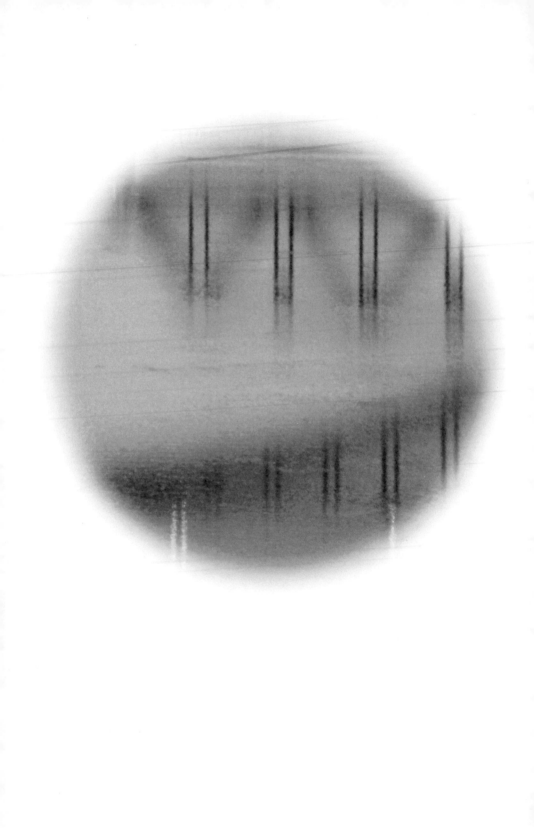

Between Song and Story

Essays for the Twenty-first Century

edited by
Sheryl St. Germain
and
Margaret L. Whitford

PITTSBURGH

"Autumn House" and "Autumn House Press" are registered trademarks owned by
Autumn House Press, a nonprofit corporation whose mission is the publication and
promotion of poetry and other fine literature.

Autumn House Press Staff
Editor-in-Chief and Founder: Michael Simms
Executive Director: Richard St. John
Community Outreach Director: Michael Wurster
Co-Founder: Eva-Maria Simms
Fiction Editors: Sharon Dilworth, John Fried
Associate Editors: Ziggy Edwards, Erik Rosen, Rebecca King
Assistant Editors: Adrienne Block, D. Gilson
Media Consultant: Jan Beatty
Publishing Consultant: Peter Oresick
Tech Crew Chief: Michael Milberger
Interns: Athena Pappas

 PENNSYLVANIA COUNCIL ON THE ARTS

Autumn House Press receives state arts funding support through a grant
from the Pennsylvania Council on the Arts, a state agency, through the
Pennsylvania Partners in the Arts (PPA), its regional arts funding partner-
ship. State government funding depends upon an annual appropriation by
Pennsylvania's General Assembly and from the National Endowment for the
Arts, a federal agency. PPA is administered in the Pittsburgh region by the
Greater Pittsburgh Arts Council.

ISBN: 978-1-932870-50-3
Library of Congress Control Number: 2011900165

Here everything is admissible—philosophy, ethics, divinity, criticism, poetry, humor, fun, mimicry, anecdote, jokes, ventriloquism—all are permitted and all may be combined into one speech.

Ralph Waldo Emerson

Contents

Introduction

Our goal in creating this anthology has been to gather together writings that exemplify the diverse, exuberant, and intrepid forms of the contemporary American essay. We offer here a selection of essays that will serve as models for creative writing students at the graduate and undergraduate levels, but we have also created an anthology that we believe will engage and surprise the general reader. One of the editors (Sheryl) currently directs a Master of Fine Arts program in which she has taught many of these essays; the other (Margaret) is a recent MFA graduate who offers a fresh perspective on what works in terms of nurturing the apprentice essayist.

As a teacher, Sheryl wanted a collection adaptable to multiple teaching situations, in courses, for example, not only devoted to the craft of the essay, but more specifically to explorations of the lyric essay, the formally adventurous (experimental) essay, as well as those focused on nature writing, travel writing, or more nuanced explorations of place. Margaret wanted essays that would challenge her ideas about the form, encourage experimentation, and nourish her own writing. We both wanted a mix of essays that were attentive to diversity in terms of culture, perspective, gender, age, and style. To that end we've included well-known writers as well as emerging writers. And, finally, we both wanted a collection where every essay struck a deep chord in both of us.

We have chosen to use the word *essays* instead of the term *creative nonfiction* in our title because we feel that the word *essay*, from the Old French *essai* (meaning *a trial or an attempt*) best reflects the kind of adventurous spirit the reader will find celebrated in this anthology.

Published writing about the craft of creative nonfiction has focused almost exclusively on the roles fiction and journalism have played in shaping it. The terms "New Journalism," "Immersion Journalism," and "Gonzo Journalism," which emerged out of the mid-sixties, emphasize above all the use of fictional devices in crafting essays. The term "Creative Nonfiction" has gained favor in many academic circles over the last twenty years and owes much to New Journalism. Indeed, Lee Gutkind's widely cited definition of creative nonfiction as presenting or treating information "using the tools of the fiction writer while maintaining allegiance to fact," does not reference the tools of the poet.

We would posit that poetry, or the lyric sensibility, has played an equally important role. We believe our anthology is the first to highlight the ways in which both story (narrative) and song (poetry) inform the essay, thus the title: *Between Song and Story.*

John Biguenet, in "In Between: The Yodeling DeZurik Sisters (or How to Murder a Martian)," writes that the yodel is an expression of "betweenness." The kinds of essays to which we are drawn, like Biguenet's yodel, quaver "between word and sound, between voice and instrument, between man and woman, between despair and exultation, between adult and child, between human and animal, between civilization and nature." Likewise, Linda Hogan, in her essay "The Bats," also evokes the kind of doubleness we find so engaging in the American essay. Bats, she writes, "live in double worlds of many kinds. They are two animals merged into one, a milk-producing rodent that bears live young, and a flying bird." Were we to limit ourselves to only one thing we love about the contemporary essay, it would be its capacity to live between worlds, those of poetry and prose. We have tried to capture that duality in this anthology.

While we have included a good selection of essays in this collection that rely primarily on the techniques of the fiction writer, we are also interested in the transforming role of poetry in shaping the essay form. Of the forty-six essayists in this collection, twenty are also working poets (including one of the editors), a number that suggests the study of poetry—with its intense focus on sound, rhythm, music, imagery, metaphor, and nuance—is good preparation for the writing of essays. Cynthia Ozick writes of the essay, that it is "closer in kind to poetry than to any other form. Like a poem," she writes, "a genuine essay is made of language and character and mood and temperament and pluck and chance." Likwise, John D'Agata writes that the poem and the essay "are more intimately related than any two genres, because they're both ways of pursuing problems, or maybe trying to solve problems . . . ." We maintain that the American essayist is just as likely to use the skills of the poet as she is those of the fiction writer.

Narrative moves us forward in an essay, while poetry stops us; an image, a simile, or a gorgeously tuned phrase makes us pause, gives a piece psychic weight. Many writers who privilege narrative also use the techniques of the poet, often saving poetry for the most intense or epiphanic moments. In "Coming into Language," for example, Jimmy Santiago Baca's narrative essay about his introduction to poetry in prison, he breaks into song at the moment when he finally understands, viscerally, poetry: "Through language I became the grass, speaking its language and feeling its green feelings and black root sensations. Earth was my mother and I bathed in sunshine. Miniscule speckles of sunlight passed through my green skin and metabolized in my blood."

Amanda Leskovac, in "The Presence of Another," her essay about becoming a quadriplegic, takes us into her first visit to the rehabilitation hospital through descriptive detail, scene, and pitch-perfect dialogue, yet when she tries to express what it is like to will her body to feel, she turns to metaphor. "The response," she writes, "is less than nothing. It is nothing wrapped in emptiness, a present I don't want to open." Dorothy Allison uses the same technique in "Privacy Is Not the Issue," a narrative about her development as a writer. To convey how she survived as a child she writes: "I made myself another country. Through most of my adolescence, I lived in that country."

Joy Castro, too, turns to metaphor at the climax of her brief essay, "Grip," when she writes of the bullet-holed paper target that hangs over her child's crib: "It hung there like a promise, like a headboard, like a *No*, like a terrible poem, like these lines I will never show you, shielding you from the fear I carry—like a sort of oath I swore over your quiet sleep." Ending as she does with a series of similes, she is insisting on the comparative thinking that is at the heart of poetry.

For other writers, lyric elements go beyond simile or metaphor. The use of rhythm and repetition in some of the essays hearkens back to song, for example in Brenda Miller's piece, "Season of the Body":

> Think of roasted garlic, Kalamata olives, Asiago cheese. Think of green chilies, poblanos, the snap of red pepper. Think of how your pores open during sex. Think of yourself drunk on good champagne, or the glass of Chardonnay like a bell on your tongue.

Janisse Ray, in "Forest Beloved," turns to music to evoke the spirit of the long-leaf forests: "Rustle, whisper, shiver, whinny," she writes. "Aria, chorus, ballad, chant. Lullaby."

In some instances the poetic sensibility is evident in vivid description, in a finely-tuned attentiveness to language. Melanie Dylan Fox, in "Sustenance," writes of her ambivalence toward the Iowa landscape: "The Plains breathe anonymity and loneliness into everything they touch, are not immediately welcoming." Jo McDougall, writing about her arrival at her grandparents' home in "Villa Augusta," describes the "anemic" cot her grandmother offers her, the "stingy" closet where wire hangers "natter," and the homesickness that "flickers" in her stomach. Writing of her response to Jerusalem, Alicia Ostriker, in "Normal Lives: Israel, Spring 2003," says: "Jerusalem is so beautiful it hurts the bones. It breaks the heart."

So what makes the essays collected here "for the twenty-first century"? First of all, the overwhelming majority have been written within the last twenty years, and most of those (more than half) within the last ten. Several, in terms of the subjects they engage, are timely. In "Whose War," John Edgar Wideman explores the aftermath of the September 11 attacks, examining the risks of what he calls the "one-way gaze of power." Alicia Ostriker in the essay mentioned above, and Naomi Shihab Nye in "Thank You in Arabic," give us two different views of Jerusalem some forty years apart. In "The Idea of a Garden," Michael Pollan tells us "Nature *is* dead, if by nature we mean something that stands apart from man and messy history," and urges us to look to the garden for "the fresh metaphors about nature we need" to confront global environmental problems. Toi Derricotte examines how to address issues of race constructively in "Race in the Creative Writing Classroom." She poses the question: "What happens in the classroom when diversity begins to be expressed?" but her question might also be asked of society as a whole.

Just as importantly, however, never in the history of the essay have we seen so much experimentation with the form. A good selection of essays in this collection push form in new ways, using organizing principles such as segmentation, montage, listing, and collage to break away from straightforward narrative. David Gessner ("Sick of Nature"), Jamaica Kincaid ("The Ugly Tourist"), and Pattiann Rogers ("This Nature") turn to ranting, abandoning the more modulated tones of conventional narrative. Others, like Elizabeth Kirschner ("Wounds and Words") and Barbara Hurd ("Moonmilk") choose to develop their essays lyrically; their essays move, as poems do, in concentric circles. Dinty W. Moore organizes the paragraphs of his essay, "Son of Mr. Green Jeans," by letters of the alphabet, while Debra Marquart borrows her organizational principle from poet Wallace Stevens, in "Thirteen Ways of Looking at the Weather." Michele Morano ("Grammar Lessons: The Subjunctive Mood") organizes her essay according to the rules of the subjunctive; Lawrence Sutin's three small essays riff off of images from postcards, and Ander Monson's "I Have Been Thinking about Snow" incorporates ellipses as design elements and uses repetition of key phrases to evoke the quiet insistence and pattern of falling snow. Tom Varisco in "Let's Pretend," modifies typeface to flood the page with text, evoking the threatening feeling of the flooding waters in New Orleans. Marjane Satrapi's "The Veil" is perhaps the most celebrated example of recent movement into the territory of the graphic essay, as she marries pictures and prose in her memoir about growing up in the midst of Iran's Islamic Revolution.

As early as the beginning of the twentieth century, Georg Lukács suggested that the essay would become the preeminent form of the modern age. Much later, in 1994, Phillip Lopate, in *The Art of the Personal Essay*, noted that we were going through a "cautious revival of the genre"; the essay's tolerance, he wrote, "for the fragmentary and irresolution, make it uniquely appropriate for the present era." What makes the essay such a suitable form for an age of transition such as ours? Perhaps because it is grounded in reality; unlike novels and poems, the essay is assumed to be telling the truth. Perhaps in times of great doubt and change we need reliable narrators who will speak directly and powerfully to us, revealing not only what they think, but what they feel. The form's malleability, its protean qualities, also make it more adaptable to periods of rapid change.

With a couple of exceptions, we have chosen not to print excerpts from larger works unless they were self-contained, as excerpts generally don't serve well as models for full-length essays. Additionally, many wonderful essayists whose work we love will not be found in this collection: Ed Abbey, John D'Agata, Patricia Hampl, Edward Hoagland, Nancy Mairs, Scott Russell Sanders, and David Shields, to name but a few, because many of their essays are already heavily anthologized, and we didn't feel reprinting those essays one more time made much sense. Others who work in longer forms, such as Nick Flynn, Lauren Slater, and Mary Karr, were not easily excerpted. In our Suggestions for Further Reading, the reader will find the works of nonfiction prose writers we admire but whose works are not included here.

In making our selections, we chose to focus on essays written in English by American writers, with the exception of Iranian-born Marjane Satrapi. We included Satrapi's "The Veil" because it is a superb example of a graphic autobiographical essay from a literary comic book, *Persepolis*, that has had wide influence on American writers. In addition, Satrapi writes of a history and place most Americans know little about, even though Iran figures prominently in world affairs.

In "The Greatest Nature Essay *Ever*" Brian Doyle writes that a good essay will make you stop whatever else you are doing so that you might sit down and read, emerging at the end of your reading startled, moved, and somehow changed. We think it's not too much to ask this of all essays, not just ones focusing on nature.

We have included a hefty selection of pieces that might be considered "nature writing" or "writing of place," and in this we find ourselves firmly within the American essay tradition, whose forefathers we take to be Henry David Thoreau and Ralph Waldo Emerson, essayists and nature writers extraordinaire. Within the essays we characterize as nature writing are those that maintain a focus on narrative as well as others that challenge and experiment with the form. The essays of Melanie Dylan Fox, John T. Price, and Michael Pollan, for example, belong to the former group. At the other end of the continuum, we find David Gessner's "Sick of Nature," a rant infused with humor against the constraints of conventional nature writing. He imagines a kegger with nature greats Thoreau, Leopold, Lopez, and Carson, among others: "As usual with this crowd, there's a whole lot of *listening* and *observing* going on, not a lot of merriment," Gessner laments. He owns to hating writing about nature in a quiet and reasonable way, wanting to free himself from the "shackles" of genre. Pattiann Rogers, in "This Nature," provokes us to think in more nuanced ways about nature as she rants: "Bach is nature, and the Marquis de Sade is nature. Florence Nightingale and the Iron Maiden are nature. Michelangelo's Pietà, the swastika, *Penthouse* magazine and solar flares are nature." And in "Against Nature," Joyce Carol Oates explores her "chronic uneasiness with

Nature-mysticism; Nature adoration; Nature-as-(moral)-instruction-for-mankind." Like Gessner and Rogers, she is fatigued by the constraints of genre. We have chosen to publish nature essays that challenge those constraints.

Not surprisingly, considerable overlap exists between essays we characterize as focused on place and those we associate with travel, because meaningful travel involves, of course, an engagement with place—an effort to achieve a degree of intimacy with another geography and culture.

Travel, as several of the essays presented here convey, is frequently uncomfortable and destabilizing. Jane Fishman explores her ambivalent response to Costa Rica in "Country on the Brink" using her singular sense of humor; Derek Green in "Lost in Eden: In Search of the Tree of Life" directs the reader's gaze from Bahrain's ancient burial mounds to an adjacent golf course, juxtaposing the two to highlight the tensions between the old and the new. Robert Isenberg reveals the underside of travel through the eyes of the disadvantaged as he chants, "We are Greyhound."

In some respects, we see the essay itself as the metaphorical equivalent of travel—travel in the sense of a journey into the unknown, one requiring a special kind of permeability to experience. Most essayists we know begin without much of a roadmap or outline. They venture forth, open to possibility, with the capacity to be surprised. Essays are vehicles for discovery, sufficiently generous to allow for the writer's exploration, going wherever the writing takes her intellectually, emotionally, even spiritually. In "War Wounds," for example, Tom Bissell narrates the story of his trip to Vietnam with his elusive father, finding in the journey a catalyst for exploring how the war shaped both his father's life and his own. Ultimately, the personal opens outwards as Bissell recognizes the universal cost of all wars, both for the warriors and those who love them. And John Edgar Wideman, in "Whose War," makes a surprising detour to the linguistic in his meditation on terror: "*Terror*," he writes, "embeds a grab bag of unsettling echoes: tear (as in rip) (as in run fast), terra (earth, ground, grave, dirt, unfamiliar turf), err (mistake), air (terra firma's opposite element), eerie (strange, unnatural), error (of our ways), roar-r-r (beasts, machines, parents, gods)."

Even a trip around a dresser drawer can have surprising implications, as Phillip Lopate demonstrates in "My Drawer." In this brief essay, he writes that he has "an urge to make an inventory of the drawer, in a last attempt to understand the symbolic underpinnings of my character." The essay provides Lopate with the unique flexibility to begin with an object as mundane as a drawer and to arrive finally at reflections about the patterns of his life.

We're pleased to have included pieces that speak for lesser-known places, even some where few would choose to linger. From deep within Baca's prison to the bathroom in Leskovac's hospital room; from ruinous Iowa, the most ecologically altered state in the union, to the empty spaces of Wyoming, Michigan, North Dakota, and Alaska; from the wounded landscapes of New Orleans and New York to Vietnam, our essayists have evoked richly layered senses of place.

Before readers begin traveling through this anthology, we wish to offer a word on its arrangement. We have grouped essays alphabetically by author in our table of contents. Following this listing, we offer an alternative table of contents, or what we prefer to call Other Ways of Reading, where essays are grouped both thematically and by form to facilitate discussions of craft.

We believe this collection tells a rich story about the wealth of experimentation and diversity of approaches in the contemporary American essay. And we also hope that it does what the best of the essays here do: that it sings, and that each reader will find many writers whose voices will echo long after the last word.

Sheryl St. Germain and Margaret L. Whitford

Other Ways of Reading

Janisse Ray (Georgia)
Sheryl St. Germain (New Orleans)
Marjane Satrapi (Iran)
Tom Varisco (New Orleans)
Margaret L. Whitford (Africa)

Race and Ethnicity
Jimmy Santiago Baca
Toi Derricotte
Jamaica Kincaid
Naomi Shihab Nye
Alicia Ostriker
Marjane Satrapi
John Edgar Wideman

Travel
Tom Bissell (Vietnam)
Jane Fishman (Costa Rica)
Derek Green (Bahrain)
Robert Isenberg (United States)
Jamaica Kincaid (Antigua)
Michele Morano (Spain)
Naomi Shihab Nye (Jerusalem)
Alicia Ostriker (Jerusalem)
Margaret L. Whitford (Africa)

Writing
Dorothy Allison
Jimmy Santiago Baca
Toi Derricotte
Brian Doyle
David Gessner
Elizabeth Kirschner
Joyce Carol Oates
Lia Purpura
John Edgar Wideman

War
Tom Bissell
John Edgar Wideman

Weather
John Haines
Debra Marquart
Ander Monson

BY FORM

Adventurous/Experimental
Robert Isenberg
Jamaica Kincaid
Debra Marquart
Ander Monson
Dinty W. Moore
Michele Morano
Joyce Carol Oates
Lia Purpura
Pattiann Rogers
Marjane Satrapi
Lawrence Sutin

Brief
Greg Bottoms
Joy Castro
Brian Doyle
Derek Green
John Haines
Linda Hogan
Elizabeth Kirschner
Phillip Lopate
Jo McDougall
Janisse Ray
Pattiann Rogers
Lawrence Sutin

Humor
Jane Fishman
David Gessner
Lori Jakiela
Amanda Leskovac
Debra Marquart
John T. Price
Marjane Satrapi

Lyric
Joy Castro
Gretel Erhlich
John Haines
Linda Hogan
Barbara Hurd
Robert Isenberg
Elizabeth Kirschner
Brenda Miller
Ander Monson
Joyce Carol Oates
Lia Purpura
Janisse Ray
Pattiann Rogers
Sheryl St. Germain
Lawrence Sutin

Jane Fishman
Melanie Dylan Fox
Derek Green
Lori Jakiela
Amanda Leskovac
Phillip Lopate
BK Loren
Kathryn Miles
Naomi Shihab Nye
Alicia Ostriker
Michael Pollan
John T. Price
Marjane Satrapi
Ruth L. Schwartz
Rhett Iseman Trull
Margaret L. Whitford
John Edgar Wideman

Narrative
Dorothy Allison
Jimmy Santiago Baca
John Biguenet
Tom Bissell
Greg Bottoms

Rants
David Gessner
Jamaica Kincaid
Joyce Carol Oates
Pattiann Rogers

Between Song and Story

Privacy Is Not the Issue

Dorothy Allison

1

As a girl, I was a reader, a bookworm, and secretive—my mother's pride, but no one's prize. There was book-smart and street-smart. I was the first, but not the second. We all agreed on that fact—my sisters and I, my mother and her friends. I remember looking up from one book or another to see how they looked at me, the curiosity in their faces and, now and then, the pity. My sisters would marry, everyone agreed. They would make babies and do what they did. What I would do was unimaginable, or darkly imaginable like the covers of the paperback books on the back racks at the drugstore. I read those books. I searched for myself in them. But somehow the plot turned and nothing came out as I was told it would.

Thirty years past my girlhood, I live in San Francisco with my partner and our child. One thing has not changed. My comfort is still in the bent head and the voice of the text. I read as passionately as I did as a girl, and stockpile books to reassure me that there will always be one to hand no matter how uncertain my everyday life may become. This means that every other week I am in one bookstore or another. In the company of other book lovers, I am at ease, nodding in recognition while shifting a couple of volumes from one arm to the other, running one finger down the stacks of used paperbacks and exclaiming when I find one I had missed.

Max is the guy who handles the cash register at my favorite used bookstore just off Market Street. I have been shopping there since I moved to California more than a dozen years ago. They used to give great trading discounts, so this was where I brought my boxes of review copies. The discounts are no longer as generous, but the turnover on the shelves is steady, and I can usually find half a dozen books I want. It also doesn't hurt that my long-standing account lets me get many of them for less than cover price.

"More of this stuff, huh?" Max says as I pile up my selections. "Damn," he adds. "No one keeps secrets anymore."

I watch him frown balefully at the stack of paperbacks I have put together. They are memoirs mostly, though I have leavened the pile with various poetry chapbooks. He picks up the volume of Mary Karr's poetry, and lets it fall onto *The Kiss* by Kathryn Harrison. We have argued about memoir before. I like them. Max doesn't. He did perversely decide he liked Frank McCourt's *'Tis*, when it got a less than rave review in a local journal, but he says what he is waiting for is for McCourt to try a novel.

"If we don't watch out, people going to quit writing novels," Max complains.

I resist the urge to make excuses for my selections. I don't want to explain that I have assembled this package for a young woman who let me talk to her about what it is like to wake up from a coma. If I tell Max that, he will want to talk about the novel I am writing, and I'm not at a place where that would be easy to do. Worse, Max might get the idea I could be coaxed into teaching a class his girlfriend could attend—something he has been asking about for a long time. I have read two stories by this girlfriend and know I have nothing to teach her. But that, too, is not something I want to explain to Max.

Near the end of my last interview with the coma survivor, she told me she wanted to try to write a true story of her own, about paralysis and despair and recovery—something she knew more about than she could say in a couple of hours of talking to me.

"How do you start to write?" she had asked me when we were finishing up.

"You read," I told her. "You read as much as you can, then you write a little, then you read some more."

"Then what?"

"You do it all over again. You keep at it till you are not ashamed of what you get on the page."

She had laughed at me, but I had been serious. The books were meant to kick start her in the right direction, or just say thank you. I owed her that for letting me look out of her eyes for a few hours.

Max has no way of knowing about my helpful young woman. He just hates memoirs. He is convinced they endanger the novel, and Max loves novels the way I do. It's why he took this job in the first place, why he is always suggesting titles or commenting on the ones you carry up to the cash register. Max is almost a friend—a big burly man, all shaggy-faced with a thick beard and a club of gray-streaked curly hair tied at the back of his collar. I have come to know him a bit over the years, mostly through the comments he has made on books I pile up on his counter. I know he lives with that girlfriend in a rat warren of an apartment building over in the western addition, that he doesn't make much money and doesn't care, and that he loves to read but has no ambition to write. Most importantly, ours is a relationship that deepened, not when my first novel became a best-seller, but when Max saw that I was always buying new copies of old books by Russell Banks and Larry Brown.

"My icons," he told me. "You see a book by either of them here, you know I already got two copies at home—one mint condition and one all soggy with sweat and tears."

"Where are you from, then?" I asked him.

"Oh, hell! Texas. But don't hold that against me. My daddy brought me to California before any of that cowshit stuck. I'm a redneck, but I'm a San Francisco redneck."

I had laughed then. I liked the notion of a guy who looked like Max and wept over *Father and Son* or *The Sweet Hereafter*.

2

I am a not-private person. It is the curse of being a writer, particularly a writer who is believed to have written a biographical novel. It never makes any difference when I insist my first novel, *Bastard Out of Carolina*, was not biography. I always wind up caught in the conflict of acknowledging that I am Southern and an incest survivor. And yeah, the book was about a young girl who grows up in an enormous Southern working-class family that is unable to do anything about the fact that she is being abused and raped by her stepfather.

"Were you raped?" I am asked.

"Yes," I always say, with my matter-of-fact attitude and no secrets implied.

"By your stepfather?"

"Yes." Again, matter-of-fact and bluntly to the point.

"Did your mother know?"

"Now that is complicated," I say, and even as I speak, I feel layers of my skin peeling away, leaving me naked and ashamed before I can begin to explain just how complicated.

I wrote a novel trying to put fully on the page a very complicated story, and I hate to see it made simple. Worst of all, I know there is no winning for me in this discussion. I know how it will go. I will tell the scrupulous truth because I need to for my own sake. I will have no way to control what people will think as I say those things. Most terribly, I will know that we are having this conversation in part because they have not read the book. If they had read the book, I would have made some impact on how they think about rape and poverty and incest and Southern families—not as much as I had hoped, but some. They would not ask me these questions if they had read my book—at least I hope they would not.

I try very hard not to be defensive or strident when I tell people that the novel I wrote was not an autobiography. People always smile at me, a smile that widens when I admit how many of my real experiences got translated in some form into my fiction. That's how it works, I say, and watch people try to be polite. This is not a conversation that can have any easy or ready conclusion.

The reality is that I am not to be trusted. Novelists are liars. That is a fact. We make up stories and try to tell them so well that people will fall under our spell and believe what we say absolutely. We work hard so that the reader will believe our fictional creations, believe all that stuff really happened—had to have happened. How, doing that, can we make so strong a claim to truth? More importantly, how, having written a novel that makes such terrible use of our own reality, can we claim a right to say what about our lives is now off-limits for public discussion? Do we get to hold anything back?

Are we allowed to say what about our lives is now private and not for public discussion? Rarely, it seems, very rarely. Every time we do, there will be someone to argue us down and demand that we explain explicitly and in great detail why we are willing to tell this truth and not that one. I, for one, have never gotten over a conversation I had with a reporter many years ago. I hadn't had much experience with interviewers who did not write for the book pages, and he did not want to talk about books or writing. He wanted to talk about my life.

"You always talk about yourself as a lesbian," the reporter said to me. "You act as if it were the most important thing in the world."

"Some days it is," I told him. It is the most important thing when it is used to dismiss my work or to shore up more contempt for people like me, or to refute what is useful in what I have to say.

"What about your sisters," he asked me. "Are your sisters lesbians?"

No.

"Were they raped as children?"

I was still.

"Like you," he asked. "Did they get fucked like you?"

I remember the feel of the enamel of my teeth, my tongue pressing so hard that an ache seemed to slowly climb from my palate up to behind my eyes. I took my time and looked into his face, into his bland smile. He was wearing a charcoal suit and a gray-blue tie. The suit made his skin look sallow, but it made his eyes seem bright and soft, a brown as golden as a tub of dark honey. Too much honey and your teeth rot, I thought. I kept my mouth closed, my tongue clamped to the back of my teeth.

"Come on." He pushed his little tape recorder across toward me. "Don't you have anything more to say?"

Nothing. Not a damn thing.

They want to get a response, I had been warned. Keep that in mind and always think before you speak. I thought. I wondered if he really believed I would answer him. I wondered if he was talking to me that way because I was a lesbian. I wondered if he had read my book. I wondered why he did not become ashamed as I sat there, not speaking, just looking at him. After far too long, I stood up very carefully. I waited for him to make an excuse, to say he hadn't meant to offend me, but he did not.

He shrugged. He smiled. He said, "I guess we are done."

I said nothing. To say anything would have been to scream.

I have always loved the poetry of Sharon Olds, just as I have loved the very matter-of-fact way she has resisted making any simple or direct links between the events described in her poems and the actual lives of her family. I heard her read once and loved the droll way she replied to questions about a series of poems by saying, "Yes, I have children," and adding nothing more. It was not as if we could resist the notion that the girl in the poem she was describing was her girl, but she was not going to give us any further peek into that girl's life. You don't get everything, her manner seemed to say. You get just this much, this that I made deliberately. But when I made it, I moved it away from the child that I birthed, the life she lives that you are not entitled to intrude upon.

That is the way to do it, I thought. That is the only defense. When I am my strongest self, I can make these distinctions.

Making art is about choosing and constructing, then editing and refining. It is not just giving over everything and letting the audience sort it out. To make a good book, you have to hold back as much as you give over—regardless of whether the book you are making is a memoir, a novel, or a cycle of poems. This is true even though the position the writer takes in addressing the art is entirely about fearlessness, self-revelation, and telling a true story. Maybe it is even most true in that situation. In our long happy discussions of Russell Banks and Larry Brown, Max and I have agreed that what we most passionately adore is the way they make men we know real on the page.

"Sonsabitches!" Max would boom. "The real deal."

That is the key. We want the real on the page—the true, what we know that we want the world to know. I want my uncles. Max wants his dad. More than that, I want my stepfather and Max wants himself—what we know and fear and try with our whole soul to sort out.

"Large as life," I told Max once. Large as life and twice as heartbreaking would barely do justice to the people we have known. Nor does the fact that they might not recognize themselves have much impact on the worth of the story. I have put Max into three stories and one novel, and he seems to have no inkling that is the case. Of course, I deleted the beard, the girlfriend, and the bookstore. Like I have tried to explain, I don't write biography. I tell lies.

3

What is the thing that must remain secret and private?
What is the thing that you find shameful?
What would you never tell?

I have a talent that goes far beyond the ability to write. It is the gift to which I can credit everything I have done in my life. Both my survival and my education have been based upon it. I can make a quiet inside my head. I can shut the world out and be still inside. It is a genius. It may be the only kind of genius I truly believe we need to have to write. It is the quality that makes some of us able to think and work in the middle of confusion, violence, uncertainty, and upheaval. That gift is a quality of privacy, a sense of being safe and intact inside. It was the only kind of privacy I had as a girl, and it was entirely a matter of what I was able to make in my own head.

There was always noise in our house, noise and violence and confusion. If no one was shouting, then music was playing or the television was booming. Often both the radio and television were playing at the same time—one in the living room, one in the kitchen—almost never turned off and only rarely turned down. People were always talking. My sisters and I argued passionately and angrily. My mama would retell what had happened while she was at work. My stepfather cursed—us, Mama, the fools he had to face at work, the newsman on the television—everyone. Normal conversation was at high decibels, violent and full of shouted threats.

When there was quiet it was terrifying.

SHUT UP! SHUT UP! SHUT UP!

My stepfather would storm through the house like a bantam rooster with spurs out. We would be directed to shut up and sit down, to sit in a line on the couch or get the hell out of the living room. Go clean the kitchen. Go clean the bathroom, the bedrooms, pick up the trash in the yard. *I want you to get down on your knees and pick up every rock in that grass. If I find a stone when I go to cut that yard, you'll wish you'd never been born.* He would strut, back and forth, arms up, fists tight. Sometimes his rage would spill out. Sometimes we would be dragged up the halls. Sometimes we would be pushed away and he would glare up at the ceiling as if he wanted to get a grip on God. He would flail and sputter, call our names and curse. He would strike out at anything near, anything that dared his temper. He had a habit of kicking doors. The cheap pasteboard doors in our rented houses would split or crack. The next day my sisters and I would try to peel the edges out and tape them to disguise the damage. My stepfather's black eyes would slip over the cracks as if he had nothing to do with them.

One more thing I got to pay for! Goddamn it, one more thing!

Making a quiet inside was my path to sanity. I buried myself in books and stories. I was never without a book in my hand. *What the hell are you doing? Get your head out of that damn book and go help your mother!* I would jump up, run, and then go back to the book as soon as it was safe to do so. I pretended I lived in the stories I read, or I told myself stories in which I could live. At some point the roar around me receded. I could do nothing about it, do nothing with it—there was, after all, no real way of pleasing my stepfather or changing the poverty in which we lived. I could only do one thing. I could put my stepfather, my sisters, even my beloved mother—all of it—aside. I could shut out the noise.

I developed my talent so early and gradually that I cannot pinpoint the date at which it became my reality. Early on, very early on, I simply developed a skill for going deaf to everything that was around me. I could bury myself in a book and not see or hear anything that did not actually slap me in the face or dump me onto the floor. It was a lifesaving ability, and I suspect that it preceded my other invention—the storytelling, though that is hard to say for sure. What is certain is that they fed each other. Going away in my head gave me time and distance to make up stories. Making up stories gave me a reason to pull back up into my head.

4

Everyone recognizes storytellers. They are great baby-sitters, engrossing gossips, artists of the anecdote. I was all of those from an early age, but I was also one other thing and that was a thing I tried hard to obscure. It seemed to me dangerous to have people know how much I was not present in my own life, how far I disappeared into the story in my head. The one thing I had to keep safe and private was that, how much I lived in my head. For my mother's sake, I did not want her to know how much I hated our life. For my own, I did not want to admit it.

This too is a complicated story, not one that has an obvious plot, no simple, easily explainable cause-and-effect factor. There is not one cause. There are endless effects.

An insomniac from an early age, I would lie in bed with my sisters and listen to the night noises. There was snoring from my parents' bedroom, and sometimes grunts or unintelligible mutters. There were the whispered and hoarse sounds of sex, the creak of the mattress springs, or the thud that might have been the bed frame against the wall and might have been something worse. There was the swish of the omnipresent fans in summer, and the clank-clanking furnace in winter, or my stepfather's angry, "Goddamn it, turn that down!"

We lived in close quarters, my sisters and I, for many years in one bed, for almost my entire childhood—one bedroom. Living close is noisy and never private. If you wiggle, someone feels you move. If you sigh or sob, you do so in company. My sisters and I developed a capacity for pretending we were not lying close, for not hearing what we did not want to have to acknowledge. If my sister was squirming, I would not sit up and ask her what she was doing. She might tell me. If my other sister was crying quietly, I might roll over and try to comfort her, but it was all too likely that she would push me away.

Anyone who has lain in bed sure she would die before morning knows what that was like. What astonishes me is the many people I meet who know exactly what that was like—even people who were never slapped in daylight or screamed at by someone who was supposed to take care of them. I meet those people all the time, and they tell me about their own nights of living nightmare—lying rigid on the mattress waiting for madness to come through the door. Even if the door is never forced open, even if the madman never comes storming into the room, you are defined by that fear.

You have to do something to save yourself. You cannot lie awake every night of your childhood waiting for your own destruction. Was that when I learned to go away? Was that when I began to tell myself a story so engrossing or distracting that I would forget that I was afraid and disappear into the story itself? What if there was a staircase in the closet? What if we could go down and into a land where children have their own nation—not a safe place, but one where the dangers were somehow more bearable, less life-threatening, or just less monstrous. I imagined there was such a place. I made myself another country. Through most of my adolescence, I lived in that country.

I don't think this is entirely what is meant by the storytelling impulse—at least not that impulse that is so often mentioned in writing manuals or workshops. I am sure the country I made in my imagination was a place where I could go to be safe. However, the existence of that imaginary territory made me implicitly less safe in the world. There is something wrong, I feared, with people who lived more in their heads than in the real world. Was I told that or did I figure it out on my own? There is no way to know, but it was something that became more and more of a concern to me as I got older. That private place I had created in my mind became a matter of concern to my family and neighbors.

"She lives in her head," they said of me.
"She almost ain't here."
"Earth to Dorothy, come in, Dorothy."

I would come back, but reluctantly, embarrassed to be re-awakened to the mundane reality of dishes to be washed, trash to be hauled out, or questions to be answered in school. What was truly embarrassing was the implied weirdness. Living in your head was a sign of being crazy. Too much daydreaming was evidence of something wrong at home, and the fact that there were terrible things wrong in my home was no comfort. It was perfectly obvious to me as a girl that there was no rescue outside the circle of my mama's family. We were people who had to take care of our own problems, not go to outsiders for help. We were people who had to hold to the myth of self-sufficiency, to blend in and protect one another from the dangerous attentions of the outside world—the sheriff or child welfare. The child of a waitress who wanted to go to college had better not stand out too much or in the wrong way. It was better to seem absentminded than abused, to appear a parody of the bright bookish shy girl.

"Not tied too tightly, is she?" people would say to my mama with a laugh. Mama would smile, as if it were all a familiar joke. It was a joke we all acknowledged, though I knew she was genuinely frightened. What I could not talk about was how much I suspected there was to fear.

Could a person go away in their imagination so often that they didn't come back? Was that what it meant to be crazy? I think everyone who learns to live in their head—upstairs, I used to call it—knows that concern. Maybe you're crazy. Or maybe this is how you manage not to be crazy. What is fearful is thinking that "normal people" are fully present in their own lives, and you are not normal. Maybe "normal people" tell stories, maybe they even tell themselves stories. What I could not know was if "normal people" fell into the stories so deeply that they fell out of their everyday lives. What I wondered was did other people wait for the moments when they could finally have some peace and quiet, to get away and retreat into their imaginary world? Did they keep a running narrative going for months?

In time, I decided there was a kind of negotiated silence about all this stuff—it was not to be talked about. Perhaps everyone had an alternative life in their heads where they retreated when their daily lives became either unendurable or simply boring. There was Thurber's Walter Mitty after all, and the way people talked about daydreaming. It would be humiliating or worse to have one's daydreaming exposed, and I was smart enough to imagine what people would say about my stories.

Imagine me in my daydreams, in an alternate life. There I might be an orphan in a nation of orphans, maybe even a mutant with the ability to read minds—or maybe not. Imagine I broke into an old abandoned house and discovered it was full of books and stuff I never had in my real life. Imagine that every time I lay down, I went to that house, decorated it, wandered its halls, met others like me who had also sneaked away. Maybe I had sex there, or did not and it did not matter. Maybe I was beautiful there, or was not but it did not matter. Say that every time I was alone for a moment, I resumed the unbroken narrative or replayed earlier inventions with new variations. I could be happy there in ways I could not be in my daily life. Would that not be wonderful? Would it not be terrible to imagine having that exposed or stolen? The fantasy was infinitely precious, and completely fragile. It had to be kept safe, and secret.

Where have you been, did you not hear a word I said?
No mama, I didn't.
I swear I don't know what's wrong with you!

If anyone ever penetrated my secret world, looked into my mind the way I imagined looking into theirs, they would see how small and desperate I was.

Teachers, doctors, and ministers, with the best intentions in the world, would try to help me. They would shake me out of my daydreams. They would drag me back into my unendurable daily life—the one I dared not let them know too much about. How would I survive if I had to be fully awake and present in my stepfather's house? It would be impossible. For the sake of my own survival I had to hide my imaginary world. I had to pretend in order to shield my true self.

Did I begin to write stories to have a justification for living in story? When did writing the stories become more what I did than dreaming up the stories? When did obscuring the origins of those stories begin to shape the kinds of stories I could tell? These are the questions I ask myself now. These are the puzzles that shape how I look at my own construction as a storyteller and a writer.

5

I sometimes imagine that I crawled out of my childhood like a baby turtle pulling myself out of the sucking mud, astonished at my fortune and in love with the natural world I see around me. Of course, I pulled a few things along with me out of that mud. I learned to use my storytelling talent but never to entirely trust what had produced it.

I know that normal is a construct. I know that average is an invention. I also know that the imagination is a complicated and deeply layered territory, and that most of my sense of shame and fear about my girlish fantasies were baseless. Yes, I dreamed lesbian dreams, a whole planet of girls like me. Yes, I daydreamed love and sex, and passionate escapes. But most of my narratives were stunningly commonplace—a house where no one shouted, a secret place where I was not afraid, or not alone, a place where I could do things people had told me I could not do—nothing so extraordinary as elaborate erotic adventures, just everyday simple things like read books for hours, or learn to play music, or sing, or wrestle happily with people I could trust. Of course, sometimes there were elaborate erotic adventures. Perhaps that is the origin of some of the uncertainty people feel about confessing daydream narratives—the sexual content, or the humiliating details. It is hard to translate one's secret fantasies into acceptable public narratives. Some details must always be obscured, or hidden completely. We know what we risk. The secret story is a window into the soul. The story reveals us in ways we are not always prepared to acknowledge.

From my adult perspective, all my girlish fears have assumed different proportions. Nothing I daydreamed was as scary as I imagined it, or as humiliating. Some things, however, would have put me at risk if I had revealed them in full.

For example, I daydreamed my stepfather's murder. Perhaps it was my Baptist influences that made me attribute his death to accident or the intervention of some other person. In my stories, someone was always killing him for me. It was, it seemed, hard for me to admit even to myself that I wanted him dead. From my perspective all these years down, I now believe it was only reasonable that I dreamed the man dead. That I did not try to kill him in my real life is another issue. Sometimes I tell myself that the sane thing to do when you are being slowly murdered is to fight back or run away. Then I have to admit to myself that I did neither. I merely endured.

Why?

All these years later, I look back and think that the girl I was did the right thing. I play the imaginary game of What If and I see all the ways she could have gone mad or died or been destroyed. She took a lot of damage but came out of it a person capable of recovery. She dreamed survival and managed it. Perhaps that is enough to have accomplished.

Madness is real, there is no other way for me to explain my childhood, to explain to myself a man who would beat and rape a child. Having known genuine evil, I am both less afraid of my imagination and more careful of it. This secret private country in my head is very precious, and evidence that I need a place to hide and recover. It makes no difference that I created it when I was a child in genuine danger, subject to my violent stepfather's bullying contempt. The private sanctuary of my own mind was both a sustaining necessity and a secret respite—a place I needed to keep secret.

I wonder sometimes if those who were never beaten as children, who never retreated "upstairs" to avoid an unendurable present, have the same quality of daydreams as those of us who retreated to save our lives? Might that not be the thing we were given in compensation? Of course, to believe that I would have to believe in a rational system of horrors, cause and effect on some scale I prefer to remain immeasurable.

I have made peace with not being normal. I have made myself a life that does not tolerate shame or denial. I am who I am, and I tell people that rather flatly. Yes, I am a lesbian. You got that right. Don't know what made me this way and don't particularly care. It is true, my stepfather could put you off men forever, but I don't choose to credit him with the whole of my identity. Maybe I would be who I am now even if he had never been in my life. For me the issue is how I live my life now. Having been so frightened as a girl, I have worked hard to be not so frightened as an adult, to be peaceable and matter-of-fact about my choices.

Doesn't everyone want to come to a place of acceptance? Doesn't everyone have deep and complicated issues to resolve in the process of growing up and building a life they can enjoy? I think they do, even if they have never believed themselves outside the norm. Certainly the evidence I have from those I love indicates that is so—my sisters with their multiple marriages and hard-loved children, my cousins scattered across every corner of this nation, and all my old girlfriends who check in every few years with stories more astonishing all the time. It's interesting being this particular kind of adult—a lesbian woman at midlife who genuinely believes that her sexual preference is not the most exotic or dangerous thing about her, a writer who wants most of all to put on the page versions of the people I have most loved, most feared, and had to work the hardest to understand.

6

I am never matter-of-fact about the people I create on the page. About this I do not lie. I create my family over and over, and I know it. It is where the sweat is for me, the terror and the passion. Women staggering with exhaustion but going on anyway, girl-children with no notion of how they will survive, men who despise themselves and struggle valiantly to not be what they have been made, and always the unique and embattled emotional lives of the working poor—disenfranchised, queer, and desperate. These are my people. This is my subject. I take them seriously, and God knows, I tell a mean story.

"Nobody's going to quit writing fiction," I tell Max at the bookstore. "And people still keep secrets, lots of secrets."

"Only the dangerous ones," he says. He drags my stack of books to his side of the counter. "You know, secrets like the ones get you sent to jail, or get you sued. Everything else they tell. It's become a Goddamned telling society." He snorts through his beard and shoots a quick glance out at the sidewalk. Last year there was some trouble about a man who slipped and fell at the entrance. There had been a few weeks there when Max had complained endlessly about lawyers and insurance and how small bookstores barely survive as it is. Now he tallies my purchases and checks the total off against my credit slip. When Max slides the receipt across the counter, he looks at me directly for the first time. His eyes startle me. Usually hazel dark, they are suddenly a peculiar muddy green.

"What?" he asks me. "What would you never tell?"

I think about it.

There are a number of things I would never tell Max. I would never say to him that his girlfriend can't write a lick. I would never tell him that his beard always smells to me like salty peanuts and marijuana. Most of all, I would never tell him that he reminds me of one of the few men I ever found genuinely sexually interesting. It would change everything if I admitted that fact was also part of what has made our conversations about Larry Brown so poignant. Now only one of those is secret because it might be dangerous. The other two are simply rude. All are private. They reveal more about me than Max.

"I don't know," I say to him.

Max shakes his head at me. "You know." He nods emphatically. "You know and you won't say. That's what I like about you."

I am completely taken by surprise, so much so that I leave without arguing with him, though I find myself arguing with him for days afterward—every time I imagine again the expression on his face when he got me so completely wrong. The fact is that I will say anything, tell anything, and have done so in essays, poems, and fiction perhaps most of all. But then I read memoirs like novels—as windows into other people's lives. There is so much that I do not know and want passionately to understand, so much that I am sure is misrepresented, lied about, or hidden. I want to know it all, and I want a world in which it is safe to know it all. That is why I try so hard to be matter-of-fact about the hard truths of my own life. That is why I so rarely speak of the private or the unspeakable. I have never felt that I had a right to name anything unspeakable, to declare any part of my life as private.

As I finish up these notes, I can look over and see the stack of books Max hated. I have added another pile to the ones I got from him, assembling an argument of sorts for myself as much as for the young woman to whom I first planned to give them. On top I have put Mark Doty's *Firebird* (a poet's memoir) and below that Michael Patrick MacDonald's *All Souls* (a family history that explores the origins of violence in South Boston). I am going to add a copy of June Jordan's *Soldier* (a wonderful book in which she explores how her father's life shaped her poet's story). I have already written a letter to accompany the books, a letter in which I explain how much I like the way poets approach the understanding of culture.

What I did not say in my letter is that I am working on something else by putting all these books together. I am planning a way to talk to Max again, to try to get him to think about what it is that our lived experience has to do with our imagination. I am beginning with what is dangerous in separating our secrets, lies, and revelatory truths.

For some of us, the most fearful landscape we can portray is the one in which we were made—our own families and those like our own. I chose to write fiction rather than memoir because it is easier for me to do so. Writing a fiction, I am not bound by the real, or my own sense of responsibility to leave nothing out. A novel leaves a lot out. In a good novel, it doesn't matter if what is being told ever really happened in the "real" world. I have read far too many "true" narratives that I did not believe for a minute, or couldn't finish at all.

What other people seemed to me to have, I have had to work to acquire—a sense of worth. This is the great secret of my life, and no secret at all.

Coming into Language

Jimmy Santiago Baca

On weekend graveyard shifts at St. Joseph's Hospital I worked the emergency room, mopping up pools of blood and carting plastic bags stuffed with arms, legs, and hands to the outdoor incinerator. I enjoyed the quiet, away from the screams of shotgunned, knifed, and mangled kids writhing on gurneys outside the operating rooms. Ambulance sirens shrieked and squad car lights reddened the cool nights, flashing against the hospital walls: gray—red, gray—red. On slow nights I would lock the door of the administration office, search the reference library for a book on female anatomy and, with my feet propped on the desk, leaf through the illustrations, smoking my cigarette. I was seventeen.

One night my eye was caught by a familiar-looking word on the spine of a book. The title was *450 Years of Chicano History in Pictures.* On the cover were black-and-white photos: Padre Hidalgo exhorting Mexican peasants to revolt against the Spanish dictators; Anglo vigilantes hanging two Mexicans from a tree; a young Mexican woman with rifle and ammunition belts crisscrossing her breast; César Chávez and field workers marching for fair wages; Chicano railroad workers laying creosote ties; Chicanas laboring at machines in textile factories; Chicanas picketing and hoisting boycott signs.

From the time I was seven, teachers had been punishing me for not knowing my lessons by making me stick my nose in a circle chalked on the blackboard. Ashamed of not understanding and fearful of asking questions, I dropped out of school in the ninth grade. At seventeen I still didn't know how to read, but those pictures confirmed my identity. I stole the book that night, stashing it for safety under the slop-sink until I got off work. Back at my boardinghouse, I showed the book to friends. All of us were amazed; this book told us we were alive. We, too, had defended ourselves with our fists against hostile Anglos, gasping for breath in fights with the policemen who outnumbered us. The book reflected back to us our struggle in a way that made us proud.

Most of my life I felt like a target in the cross hairs of a hunter's rifle. When strangers and outsiders questioned me I felt the hang-rope tighten around my neck and the trapdoor creak beneath my feet. There was nothing so humiliating as being unable to express myself, and my inarticulateness increased my sense of jeopardy, of being endangered. I felt intimidated and vulnerable, ridiculed and scorned. Behind a mask of humility, I seethed with mute rebellion.

Before I was eighteen, I was arrested on suspicion of murder after refusing to explain a deep cut on my forearm. With shocking speed I found myself handcuffed to a chain gang of inmates and bused to a holding facility to await trial. There I met men, prisoners, who read aloud to each other the works of Neruda, Paz, Sabines, Nemerov, and Hemingway. Never had I felt such freedom as in that dormitory. Listening to the words of these writers, I felt that invisible threat from without lessen—my sense of teetering on a rotting plank over swamp water where famished alligators clapped their horny snouts for my blood. While I listened to the words of the poets, the alligators slumbered powerless in their lairs. Their language was the magic that could liberate me from myself, transform me into another person, transport me to other places far away.

And when they closed the books, these Chicanos, and went into their own Chicano language, they made barrio life come alive for me in the fullness of its vitality. I began to learn my own language, the bilingual words and phrases explaining to me my place in the universe. Every day I felt like the paper boy taking delivery of the latest news of the day.

Months later I was released, as I had suspected I would be. I had been guilty of nothing but shattering the windshield of my girlfriend's car in a fit of rage.

Two years passed. I was twenty now, and behind bars again. The federal marshals had failed to provide convincing evidence to extradite me to Arizona on a drug charge, but still I was being held. They had ninety days to prove I was guilty. The only evidence against me was that my girlfriend had been at the scene of the crime with my driver's license in her purse. They had to come up with something else. But there was nothing else. Eventually they negotiated a deal with the actual drug dealer, who took the stand against me. When the judge hit me with a million-dollar bail, I emptied my pockets on his booking desk: twenty-six cents.

One night in my third month in the county jail, I was mopping the floor in front of the booking desk. Some detectives had kneed an old drunk and handcuffed him to the booking bars. His shrill screams raked my nerves like a hacksaw on bone, the desperate protest of his dignity against their inhumanity. But the detectives just laughed as he tried to rise and kicked him to his knees. When they went to the bathroom to pee and the desk attendant walked to the file cabinet to pull the arrest record, I shot my arm through the bars, grabbed one of the attendant's university textbooks, and tucked it in my overalls. It was the only way I had of protesting.

It was late when I returned to my cell. Under my blanket I switched on a pen flashlight and opened the thick book at random, scanning the pages. I could hear the jailer making his rounds on the other tiers. The jangle of his keys and the sharp click of his boot heels intensified my solitude. Slowly I enunciated the words . . . p-o-n-d, ri-pple. It scared me that I had been reduced to this to find comfort. I always had thought reading a waste of time, that nothing could be gained by it. Only by action, by moving out into the world and confronting and challenging the obstacles, could one learn anything worth knowing.

Even as I tried to convince myself that I was merely curious, I became so absorbed in how the sounds created music in me and happiness, I forgot where I was. Memories began to quiver in me, glowing with a strange but familiar intimacy in which I found refuge. For a while, a deep sadness overcame me, as if I had chanced on a long-lost friend and mourned the years of separation. But soon the heartache of having missed so much of life, that had numbed me since I was a child, gave way, as if a grave illness lifted itself from me and I was cured, innocently believing in the beauty of life again. I stumblingly repeated the author's name as I fell asleep, saying it over and over in the dark: Words-worth, Words-worth.

Before long my sister came to visit me, and I joked about taking her to a place called Kubla Khan and getting her a blind date with this *vato* named Coleridge who lived on the seacoast and was *malias* on morphine. When I asked her to make a trip into enemy territory to buy me a grammar book, she said she couldn't. Bookstores intimidated her, because she, too, could neither read nor write.

Days later, with a stub pencil I whittled sharp with my teeth, I propped a Red Chief notebook on my knees and wrote my first words. From that moment, a hunger for poetry possessed me.

Until then, I had felt as if I had been born into a raging ocean where I swam relentlessly, flailing my arms in hope of rescue, of reaching a shoreline I never sighted. Never solid ground beneath me, never a resting place. I had lived with only the desperate hope to stay afloat; that and nothing more.

But when at last I wrote my first words on the page, I felt an island rising beneath my feet like the back of a whale. As more and more words emerged, I could finally rest: I had a place to stand for the first time in my life. The island grew, with each page, into a continent inhabited by people I knew and mapped with the life I lived.

I wrote about it all—about people I had loved or hated, about the brutalities and ecstasies of my life. And, for the first time, the child in me who had witnessed and endured unspeakable terrors cried out not just in impotent despair, but with the power of language. Suddenly, through language, through writing, my grief and my joy could be shared with anyone who would listen. And I could do this all alone; I could do it anywhere. I was no longer a captive of demons eating away at me, no longer a victim of other people's mockery and loathing, that had made me clench my fist white with rage and grit my teeth to silence. Words now pleaded back with the bleak lucidity of hurt. They were wrong, those others, and now I could say it.

Through language I was free. I could respond, escape, indulge; embrace or reject earth or the cosmos. I was launched on an endless journey without boundaries or rules, in which I could salvage the floating fragments of my past, or be born anew in the spontaneous ignition of understanding some heretofore concealed aspect of myself. Each word steamed with the hot lava juices of my primordial making, and I crawled out of stanzas dripping with birth-blood, reborn and freed from the chaos of my life. The child in the dark room of my heart, that had never been able to find or reach the light switch, flicked it on now; and I found in the room a stranger, myself, who had waited so many years to speak again. My words struck in me lightning crackles of elation and thunderhead storms of grief.

When I had been in the county jail longer than anyone else, I was made a trustee. One morning, after a fist fight, I went to the unlocked and unoccupied office used for lawyer-client meetings, to think. The bare white room with its fluorescent tube lighting seemed to expose and illuminate my dark and worthless life. And yet, for the first time, I had something to lose—my chance to read, to write; a way to live with dignity and meaning, that had opened for me when I stole that scuffed, second-hand book about the Romantic poets. In prison, the abscess had been lanced.

"I will never do any work in this prison system as long as I am not allowed to get my G.E.D." That's what I told the reclassification panel. The captain flicked off the tape recorder. He looked at me hard and said, "You'll never walk outta here alive. Oh, you'll work, put a copper penny on that, you'll work."

After that interview I was confined to deadlock maximum security in a subterranean dungeon, with ground-level chicken-wired windows painted gray. Twenty-three hours a day I was in that cell. I kept sane by borrowing books from the other cons on the tier. Then, just before Christmas, I received a letter from Harry, a charity house samaritan who doled out hot soup to the homeless in Phoenix. He had picked my name from a list of cons who had no one to write to them. I wrote back asking for a grammar book, and a week later received one of Mary Baker Eddy's treatises on salvation and redemption, with Spanish and English on opposing pages. Pacing my cell all day and most of each night, I grappled with grammar until I was able to write a long true-romance confession for a con to send to his pen pal. He paid me with a pack of smokes. Soon I had a thriving barter business, exchanging my poems and letters for novels, commissary pencils, and writing tablets.

One day I tore two flaps from the cardboard box that held all my belongings and punctured holes along the edge of each flap and along the border of a ream of state-issue paper. After I had aligned them to form a spine, I threaded the holes with a shoestring, and sketched on the cover a hummingbird fluttering above a rose. This was my first journal.

Whole afternoons I wrote, unconscious of passing time or whether it was day or night. Sunbursts exploded from the lead tip of my pencil, words that grafted me into awareness of who I was; peeled back to a burning core of bleak terror, an embryo floating in the image of water, I cracked out of the shell wide-eyed and insane. Trees grew out of the palms of my hands, the threatening otherness of life dissolved, and I became one with the air and sky, the dirt and the iron and concrete. There was no longer any distinction between the other and I. Language made bridges of fire between me and everything I saw. I entered into the blade of grass, the basketball, the con's eye and child's soul.

At night I flew. I conversed with floating heads in my cell, and visited strange houses where lonely women brewed tea and rocked in wicker rocking chairs listening to sad Joni Mitchell songs.

Before long I was frayed like a rope carrying too much weight, that suddenly snaps. I quit talking. Bars, walls, steel bunk and floor bristled with millions of poem-making sparks. My face was no longer familiar to me. The only reality was the swirling cornucopia of images in my mind, the voices in the air. Mid-air a cactus blossom would appear, a snake-flame in blinding dance around it, stunning me like a guard's fist striking my neck from behind.

The prison administrators tried several tactics to get me to work. For six months, after the next monthly prison board review, they sent cons to my cell to hassle me. When the guard would open my cell door to let one of them in, I'd leap out and fight him—and get sent to thirty-day isolation. I did a lot of isolation time. But I honed my image-making talents in that sensory-deprived solitude. Finally they moved me to death row, and after that to "nut-run," the tier that housed the mentally disturbed.

As the months passed, I became more and more sluggish. My eyelids were heavy, I could no longer write or read. I slept all the time.

One day a guard took me out to the exercise field. For the first time in years I felt grass and earth under my feet. It was spring. The sun warmed my face as I sat on the bleachers watching the cons box and run, hit the handball, lift weights. Some of them stopped to ask how I was, but I found it impossible to utter a syllable. My tongue would not move, saliva drooled from the corners of my mouth. I had been so heavily medicated I could not summon the slightest gesture. Yet inside me a small voice cried out, I am fine! I am hurt now but I will come back! I am fine!

Back in my cell, for weeks I refused to eat. Styrofoam cups of urine and hot water were hurled at me. Other things happened. There were beatings, shock therapy, intimidation.

Later, I regained some clarity of mind. But there was a place in my heart where I had died. My life had compressed itself into an unbearable dread of being. The strain had been too much. I had stepped over that line where a human being has lost more than he can bear, where the pain is too intense, and he knows he is changed forever. I was now capable of killing, coldly and without feeling. I was empty, as I have never, before or since, known emptiness. I had no connection to this life.

But then, the encroaching darkness that began to envelop me forced me to re-form and give birth to myself again in the chaos. I withdrew even deeper into the world of language, cleaving the diamonds of verbs and nouns, plunging into the brilliant light of poetry's regenerative mystery. Words gave off rings of white energy, radar signals from powers beyond me that infused me with truth. I believed what I wrote, because I wrote what was true. My words did not come from books or textual formulas, but from a deep faith in the voice of my heart.

I had been steeped in self-loathing and rejected by everyone and everything—society, family, cons, God and demons. But now I had become as the burning ember floating in darkness that descends on a dry leaf and sets flame to forests. The word was the ember and the forest was my life.

I was born a poet one noon, gazing at weeds and creosoted grass at the base of a telephone pole outside my grilled cell window. The words I wrote then sailed me out of myself, and I was transported and metamorphosed into the images they made. From the dirty brown blades of grass came bolts of electrical light that jolted loose my old self; through the top of my head that self was released and reshaped in the clump of scrawny grass. Through language I became the grass, speaking its language and feeling its green feelings and black root sensations. Earth was my mother and I bathed in sunshine. Miniscule speckles of sunlight passed through my green skin and metabolized in my blood.

Writing bridged my divided life of prisoner and free man. I wrote of the emotional butchery of prisons, and of my acute gratitude for poetry. Where my blind doubt and spontaneous trust in life met, I discovered empathy and compassion. The power to express myself was a welcome storm rasping at tendril roots, flooding my soul's cracked dirt. Writing was water that cleansed the wound and fed the parched root of my heart.

I wrote to sublimate my rage, from a place where all hope is gone, from a madness of having been damaged too much, from a silence of killing rage. I wrote to avenge the betrayals of a lifetime, to purge the bitterness of injustice. I wrote with a deep groan of doom in my blood, bewildered and dumbstruck; from an indestructible love of life, to affirm breath and laughter and the abiding innocence of things. I wrote the way I wept, and danced, and made love.

In Between: The Yodeling DeZurik Sisters (or How to Murder a Martian)

John Biguenet

In his droll travelogue, *A Tramp Abroad*, Mark Twain neatly summarizes the jaundiced response of many music lovers to yodeling: ". . . and during the remainder of the day [we] hired the rest of the jodelers, at a franc apiece, not to jodel any more."

Twain's attitude seems to have prevailed today, but during the first half of the twentieth century, a mania for yodeling seized America, catapulting its greatest practitioners to national celebrity. Though yodelers once numbered among America's best-known vocalists, with the exception of Jimmie Rodgers and a few movie cowboys, their names have faded from public memory.

Arkansas-native Elton Britt, for example, who was unofficially known as "The World Champion Yodeler" after triumphing in a yodeling competition in New York organized by horse-opera film star Tom Mix, became the first country singer to earn a gold record for his million-selling 1942 patriotic hit "There's a Star-Spangled Banner Waving Somewhere." Though Britt was billed as "The World's Highest Yodeler" when he performed at the White House for President Franklin Roosevelt (and when he later ran for the presidency himself in 1960), little of his recorded music is available today.

Britt may have reached the highest notes as a yodeler, but neither he nor any other vocalist of the period approached the range of sounds coaxed from the human voice by two girls from a farm just outside Royalton, Minnesota. Among the first female country singers to appear on stage without husbands or fathers, the DeZurik Sisters always appeared as a duet, amazing audiences with their rapid, high-pitched yodels that often spiraled into animal sounds. In fact, so convincing were their chicken yodels that the act was renamed the Cackle Sisters when they joined the Ralston Purina Company's *Checkerboard Time* radio program as regulars from 1937-1941.

Though presented as a novelty (on one transcription, a *Checkerboard Time* announcer introduces the sisters, who only cackle in response to his questions, as "That fine feathered pair of songsters with their trick vocal stunts"), the DeZuriks' animal imitations actually sprang from the very nature of the yodel and its origins in agrarian culture. The period of its popularity in the U.S., however, coincided—perhaps not so surprisingly—with the rapid transformation of an agricultural America into an industrial and urbanized modern state.

The yodeling craze may have been, in fact, more nostalgia for a passing way of life than celebration of thriving folkways.

But then, yodeling was the perfect music to serve as threshold between a world that had already begun to disappear and the one that would replace it. For what is a yodel except an expression of betweenness?

Between—isn't that where the yodel warbles as it rapidly alternates from low moan to vertiginous falsetto shriek and back again, emphasizing the transition from one to the other with its distinctive break between those opposing registers? As the dean of yodeling studies, Bart Plantenga, defines it in his fascinating and informative survey of the art, *Yodel-Ay-Ee-Oooo: The Secret History of Yodeling Around the World*, "The yodel, simply put, is most distinguishable from other types of vocalizations by its characteristic emphasis on the noise, that jolt of air, that occurs as the voice passes from bass or low chest voice to high head voice or falsetto—and vice versa.... Other vocals may tinker with falsetto, trill, and vibrato, but it's that abrupt, almost rude, leap across the cavern of pitch that makes the yodel *yodel*."

The yodel quavers between word and sound, between voice and instrument, between man and woman, between despair and exultation, between adult and child, between human and animal, between civilization and nature. It reminds one of the cracking voice of a boy on the verge of manhood, of a woman fighting back tears, of a mute struggling for language to express—what? Something melancholy, something quivering between bruised experience and disappointed innocence.

Perhaps that's why the yodel almost always erupts in the midst of a sad story. Caught between desire and rejection, faithfulness and betrayal, love and loss, the balladeer abandons language all together to express the outraged heart in a "barbaric yawp," as Walt Whitman describes the articulation of that which is "untranslatable" into words.

One cannot prove, of course, that yodeling is older than speaking, but its origins are likely ancient. Plantenga hypothesizes that it is rooted in the domestication of animals, noting similarities in yodels to the lowing and calls of local creatures. Examining types of yodeling among groups all over the world, including the Pygmies of Central Africa, the natives of Papua New Guinea, and the Brazilian Bororo Indians, he documents the first notation of Alpine yodels in 1545 and finds similar yodeling practiced from "northern Sweden to the Caucasus, down into Romania."

Though one might assume nineteenth-century Germanic and Scandinavian immigration to the United States accounts for the introduction of yodeling into American popular culture, another kind of betweenness may have been its source. In *Where Dead Voices Gather*, his revelatory study of the career of Emmett Miller, Nick Tosches traces the rise of yodeling to the tradition of minstrel shows: "That tradition, which dominated American music and show business from the middle of the nineteenth century until after the turn of the twentieth, was—simply, bizarrely, inexplicably—a form of stage entertainment in which men blackened their faces, burlesqued the demeanor and behavior of Southern blacks, and performed what were presented as the songs and music of those blacks."

He establishes that by 1925 yodeling was "a routine aspect of blackface performance," and then goes on to note that the most enduring of all yodelers, Jimmie Rodgers, spent the 1924-1925 season working "blackface in a traveling medicine show." Tosches, however, makes a persuasive case that it was not Rodgers but Emmett Miller, a white Georgian in blackface, who transformed the yodel from novelty to "something plaintive and disarming, something that would become . . . an expressiveness pure and free."

If Tosches is right, the yodeling craze that began in the late twenties depended upon another kind of betweenness, the divide between races, and it was the mad song of a white man with a black face, swooning from the falsetto to the guttural and back again, that had toes tapping across America as the Great Depression approached.

The DeZurik Sisters, although fresh-faced Midwestern farm girls rather than blackface Southerners, brought to their Nashville performances at the *Grand Ole Opry* something more authentic to the rural South than the racist parodies of minstrel shows. In their evocation of a natural world in which the human was at home, the two girls hearkened back to the very origins of yodeling with their gift for imitating barnyard animals. The granddaughters of Slovakian immigrants, Mary Jane and younger sister Carolyn grew up to the music of nature. As Carolyn explains, "We listened to the birds and tried to sing with the birds and yodel with them, imitate them. And that is how we got into all the bird stuff and animal sounds, and we would include them in our songs. That was quite a joke to us too."

How did they sound? An article from the late 1930's in *The Prairie Farmer* provided readers a succinct introduction to the sisters' musical style: "They specialize in trick yodels including Hawaiian yodel, the cackle trill, German, Swiss and triple tongue yodel." Though usually accompanying themselves on guitar, the DeZuriks often used their wordless vocalizations as instrumental bridges between verses. Their repertoire of yodeled sounds eventually extended to chime bells, trumpets, muted trombones, Hawaiian guitars, mandolins, and even musical saws. But their signature animal yodels, too, were more instrumental sound effects—almost sonic illustrations of animals referenced in their songs—than expressive plaints or cris de coeur.

Though their yodeling is astonishing and sometimes exhilarating as they rise to shattering heights together, it is in their beautifully matched voices, where one barely shadows the other, that the extraordinary quality of their music becomes apparent.

The simplicity and authenticity of those voices are still evident in the reminiscences of the duet's surviving sister. In an interview with Christoph Wagner published as liner notes for Trikont's 2003 compilation CD entitled *Flowers in the Wildwood: Women in Early Country Music*, Carolyn recounts how their career began:

> This is 1934. In our town they had a band every Wednesday night. My uncle played in a band and the band leader was everybody's dentist out there. Jane and I were out in the field cutting rye. We saw this truck coming up the road and that was my Uncle Frank. He walked over to us with big grins on his face, and he asked us if we would like to sing at the band concert tonight. We said, "What? We are not good enough yet." But he insisted. He pushed us into it. We knew only three songs well. We were nervous. We almost froze on the spot. So we sang our three songs. We didn't have a microphone. When we finished the first song, they screamed, they howled. It was a big success. After that we started in amateur contests and we won all of them but one.

When a unit from WLS (the call letters of the Sears-Roebuck Agricultural Foundation radio station, standing for the "World's Largest Store") came to the fairgrounds at Little Falls, Minnesota, to stage two days of performances, the DeZurik sisters arrived at the end of the second day and sang two songs to wild audience reaction. Eventually persuaded by a WLS program director to audition, they moved to Chicago—despite their distaste for the city—when they were offered a spot on *National Barn Dance* in 1936.

Their trick yodeling eventually landed them a recording contract with the Vocalion label in 1938. Two years later, Carolyn married Ralph "Rusty" Gill, a WLS staff guitarist from East Texas who would become known for his cowboy songs and mountain ballads; less than a month after her sister's wedding, Mary Jane married WLS staff accordionist Augie Klein. That same year, 1940, the DeZuriks starred in a Republic Pictures movie, *Barnyard Follies*, singing five of their distinctive songs. But the sisters went into temporary retirement the next year (except for radio performances and commercials) in anticipation of the birth of their first children.

In 1943, Carolyn joined the Sonja Henie Ice Review. The former Olympic gold medalist skated to Carolyn's yodels for two seasons.

Mary Jane returned from retirement in 1944, and the Cackle/DeZurik Sisters began recording transcriptions for Purina's *Checkerboard Funfest* broadcasts around the country as well as appearing regularly on the *Eddy Arnold Show* and the *Grand Ole Opry*. "But," Carolyn explains, "we had to commute by train from Chicago to Nashville every Friday to be there on Saturday. That was pretty hectic, because that was during the war and the trains were very crowded with soldiers and sailors. The engineers were very good to us because they knew who we were. And they put us on the train before anybody else. Put us in the ladies' room and locked the door so nobody else could get in. Then he put a sign on the door: Out of order! So we were pretty safe. People got pretty rowdy on those long trips."

Following a serious automobile accident in 1947, Mary Jane retired the next year, but a third sister, Lorraine, took her place, appearing with Carolyn from 1949-1950 on NBC's televised *Midwestern Hayride*. Their partnership ended soon after, and Carolyn became the female vocalist for the Prairie Ramblers, her husband's country band that performed some of the campfire songs Rusty had learned as a horseman in East Texas. Eventually joining the ABC television affiliate in Chicago in 1954, the band was featured on *Chicago Parade*, a popular daily program.

Then, in 1956, the Prairie Ramblers gave up country yodeling for polka tunes. As Wayne W. Daniels writes of their transformation in his liner notes for the American Gramophone cassette tape of thirty-eight DeZurik Sister songs, "They swapped their cowboy hats and boots for Bavarian costumes, . . . changed their name to the Polka Chips with Carolyn DeZurik, and became one of the polka sensations of Chicago."

Uniting the two styles of music for which she was known, Carolyn ended her career as the yodeling trademark for Busch Bavarian Beer. When she finally retired from show business in 1963, yodeling was already disappearing from the musical scene. The once-famous "World Champion Yodeler" Elton Britt would have one last solo hit, "The Jimmie Rodgers Blues," in 1968, but no revival of the ancient art of yodeling would follow that song.

Perhaps American culture in the following decades simply lost its taste for in betweenness. Instead of music that celebrated uncertainty, verging, and becoming, we preferred songs that asserted unwavering confidence in something or other, whether it was an emotion or an opinion. Divorced from nature, we were divorced, too, from its bleat and howl and, yes, cackle; the only sounds we recognized were the sounds we made ourselves. And so the yodel became the quaint artifact of a lost world, worthy only of our disdain.

Oh, it is easy enough to point to exceptions. For example, Jewel, the pop singer, yodeled as a child and occasionally performs a rock version of the bluegrass yodeling tune "Chime Bells" in her concerts. And Bart Plantenga catalogues a wide range of occasional yodelers from Bobby McFerrin to Bruce Springsteen to Dave Matthews to K.D. Lang. But the general attitude today toward yodeling is perhaps best expressed by filmmaker Tim Burton.

His 1996 film *Mars Attacks!* offers yodeling not as music but as an alternative to disease as a means of conquering an invading army of Martians. The military is useless since its bullets bounce off the spaceships from Mars without effect, and the Martians have a little vacuum cleaner that sucks up nuclear radiation when we fire missiles at them. Burton certainly can't kill them with the common cold or some other virus, because that's how H. G. Wells did it. So what's left? How about Slim Whitman singing "Indian Love Call"? We never quite get an explanation of how it works—maybe it's the resonant frequency of his yodeling—but once the scrappy humans figure out that's all it takes to turn the evil creatures into green goo inside their space helmets, we wipe them out in about thirty seconds.

If it wasn't so funny, it would break your heart—the way the Martians can't take the yodeling at the end of the movie. Of course, is there anything more melancholy than a good yodeler? All that yearning that just can't quite make it out of the throat as words. Maybe that's what killed the Martians: their green hearts bursting with sadness in those scrawny little chests.

War Wounds

Tom Bissell

In the beginning was the war. Many children of Vietnam veterans, when they look back on their adolescence, feel this with appropriately biblical conviction. *In the beginning was the war.* It sits there, in our fathers' pasts, a dying star that annihilates anything that strays too close. For the growing-up children of many vets, the war's remoteness was all but impossible to gauge because it had happened pre-you, before you had come to grasp the sheer accident of your own placement in time, before you recognized that your reality—your bedroom, your toys and comic books—had nothing to do with the reality of your father. Despite its remoteness, however, the war's aftereffects were inescapably intimate. At every meal Vietnam sat down, invisibly, with our families.

My mother, who divorced my father when I was three, and whose father, a Marine Corps bird colonel, had introduced them, eventually could no longer handle the nightmares, the daymares, the never knowing which husband she would be experiencing at any given moment. My mother descends from a long medaled procession of military men. She understood men who had been to war. It was what men *did*. Whatever shadows war threw across the minds of its survivors—and it did, of course it did; she knew that—were to be borne stoically. But the war hero she married was capable of only fitful stoicism. This place he had returned from was not Normandy but a country that throughout the early years of their marriage became a tacit synonym for failure, savagery. Wars were supposed to end. And yet her war hero remained at war.

When I was a boy, I would dread the evenings my father had too much to drink, stole into my bedroom, woke me up, and for an hour at a time would try to explain to me, his ten-year-old son, why the decisions he made—decisions, he would mercilessly remind himself, that got his best friends killed—were the only decisions he could have made. Other nights he would remember fondly the various women he had courted in Vietnam, of which there seemed an extraordinary number, bringing to my still unformed imagination bizarre images of myself as an Asian boy. With my school friends I would tell elaborate stories about my father. How he single-handedly fought off an entire garrison of "gooners." The day he got lost rafting down a river and survived a waterfall plunge. The time he was wounded and how a heroic black soldier dragged him to safety. Some were true; most were not. The war had not ended for him, and now it was alive in me.

Sometimes it feels as though Vietnam is all my father and I have ever talked about; sometime it feels as though we have never really talked about it. My father trained as an officer at Quantico with the writer Philip Caputo, with whom he has remained close and who ultimately became my literary mentor. My father even makes a brief appearance in Phil's *A Rumor of War*, which is commonly regarded as one of the finest memoirs of the conflict and was the first Vietnam book to become a major bestseller. When in *A Rumor of War* Phil learns of the death of his and my father's friend Walter Levy, who survived all of two weeks in Vietnam, he remembers a night in Georgetown when he, Levy, and some others went to a bar "to drink and look at girls and pretend we were still civilians." And then this: "We sat down and filled the glasses, all of us laughing, probably at something Jack Bissell said. Was Bissell there that night? He must have been, because we were all laughing very hard and Bissell was always funny." I still remember the first time I read that sentence and how my heart had convulsed. Here was the man of whom I had never had as much as a glimpse, whose life had not yet been hewn by so much darkness, the man I did not find in bluish 2:00 A.M. darkness drinking wine and watching *Gettysburg* or *Platoon* for the fortieth time. In *A Rumor of War* I saw the still normal man my father could have become, a man with the average sadnesses.

When I was young, I used to stare at his framed purple heart ("the dumb medal," he calls it) and, next to it, a photo of my father from his training at Quantico. BISSELL is stenciled across his left breast. Friendly Virginia greenery hovers behind him. He looks a little like a young Harrison Ford and is smiling, holding his rifle, his eyes unaccountably soft. I wanted to find that man. I believed I could find him in Vietnam, where he had been made and unmade, killed and resurrected. When over the phone I told my father I had tickets, we could leave in a few months, he was quiet, as quiet as I had ever heard him. "Gosh," he said.

We have been driving for several hours, down the coast, along surprisingly well-maintained roads, through what feels like lush green tunnels of Vietnamese countryside. My father is making satisfied little mouth noises as he pores over a copy of the *Viet Nam News* he picked up in Ho Chi Minh City's airport, where we spent a few hours upon our arrival before lighting off for Hué in central Vietnam.

"Interesting article?" I ask.

His head lifts with birdlike alertness, and he looks over at me. "I'm just enjoying this cultural exchange." When he finishes memorizing the contents of the *Viet Nam News*, he peppers our translator, Hien, with questions such as, "Is that a pigeon?" "Are those tea farmers?" "Is that sugarcane?" "When was this road built?" "Do the Vietnamese use much solar power?"

"So how do you feel?" I ask him, after Hien has debriefed him on the overall impact of rice exports upon the Vietnamese economy.

"Marvelous," he tells me. "Super. I'm having a ball."

"You're sure you're up for seeing some of your old stomping grounds?"

He fixes upon me a crumply eyed look, his mouth cast in the same emotionally undecided frown that I have noticed, with increasing frequency, in recent photographs of myself. "It was a long time ago. I'll be fine."

We pass through the rural sprawl of several villages. I see women wearing conical peasant hats, huge vase-shaped wicker baskets full of rice, all the stage-dressing clichés of the Vietnam War. Yet these are not VC women, and no GI will be along to bayonet the rice baskets in search of hidden ordnance. The clichés mean nothing. They are not even clichés but rather staples of Vietnamese life. I have discerned already that the war informs much here but defines little, and it suddenly seems very strange that we refer to the Vietnam War, a phrase whose adjectivelessness grows more bizarre as I ponder it. It manages to take an entire nation and plunge it into perpetual conflict.

"Where are we?" I ask after a while.

"We are nearing the Hai Van Pass," Hien says, pointing ahead to where the bus-clogged road corkscrews up into the Truong Son mountain range. To our left the wall of thick, long-needled pine trees suddenly breaks to reveal a steep drop. Beyond the cliff's edge is the blue infinity of the South China Sea, a whitecapped chaos so astonishingly choppy I half expect to see the face of Yahweh moving across it.

At the top of the pass we are stopped in a mild traffic jam, and my father gets out of the car to take pictures. I follow him. It feels cold enough up here to snow, the clouds soppingly low. When he wants some photos of himself he hands me his camera.

I stare at this relic, called a Yashica FX-7.

"I had that camera with me," he announces proudly, "the first time I came to Vietnam."

"*This* is the camera you took all those slides with?" The John C. Bissell Vietnam Slide Show was a staple of my Michigan childhood. "Dad, this camera is thirty-eight years old!"

He looks at me. "No it isn't." His hand lifts and bats about frivolously. "It's . . . what? Thirty-two years old."

"It's thirty-eight years old, Dad. Almost *forty*."

"No, it's not, because 1960 plus forty years is 2000. I arrived in 1965, so—"

"So 2005 minus two is today."

My father is silent. Then all at once his color goes. "Oh my God. Holy shit."

"Kinda incredible, isn't it?"

"I didn't know I was that old until just now."

He is worriedly touching his face as I line him up in the viewfinder.

On the other side of the Hai Van Pass, Vietnam grows more tropical, a great rotting chromatic extravagance of jungle and rice paddies. A thick mist hovers above these calm, endless reaches of standing water. Water buffalo the size of small dinosaurs are sunk to their flanks in the mud nearby, while rice farmers wearing condomlike body bags wade through chest-deep water holding bundled nets above their heads.

After a while we stop, at my insistence, at the Son My Memorial, which is a few miles outside the city of Quang Ngai. Son My is a subdistrict that is divided into several hamlets, the most famous of which is My Lai. It was in a part of My Lai where, in 1968, the most notorious U.S. war crimes against Vietnamese villagers took place: Anywhere between 150 and 570 unarmed civilians were butchered with astonishingly versatile brutality. My father did not want to come here, for various reasons, some easily grasped, others less so. One of the "less so" reasons is my father's somewhat unaccountable friendliness with Captain Ernest Medina, who commanded Company C, the unit within the 11th Brigade, 23rd Infantry Division, responsible for the majority of the My Lai killings. Medina, a Mexican-American whose promising military career was garroted by My Lai, eventually wound up settling in northern Wisconsin, and my father would see him occasionally. My father maintains that Medina is a "great guy" who claims to have given no order for what happened and has no explanation for it. On the way here my father grumpily said that what I did not understand was that things like My Lai happened all the time, only on a much smaller scale. I looked at him, astonished. I knew what he meant, and he knew that I knew what he meant, but to hear him say those words—their buried tolerance for murder—was very nearly too much. I could have asked, and almost did: *Did you ever do anything like that?* But I did not ask, because no father should be lightly posed such a question by his son. Because no father should think, even for a moment, that his son believes him capable of such a thing. Because I know my father is not capable of such a thing. So I am telling myself as we pull up to Son My.

Two tour buses are already parked here, both decorated with a splashy porpoise motif. I walk up to a large wooden sign that lists "The Regulations of Son My Vestige Area": "Visitors are not allowed to bring explosive powder, flaming, heating substances, poison or weapons into the museum. Also you should inform and stop any anti-attitudes toward this historical relic." The grounds are marked by a series of tall, wind-hissing palm trees, cobbled paths, and cubically sheared evergreen hedges and statuary, harrowing statuary: staggering gut-shot peasant women, beseeching children, defiant raised fists. These are the first instances of Communist sculpture that I have ever seen that do not produce an instant impulse to have at them with a jackhammer. Meanwhile my father is studying a headstone that lists the names and ages of some Son My victims.

"What don't you see?" he asks me as I join him.

One column of victims' ages works out like this: 12, 10, 8, 6, 5, 46, 14, 45. Most are women. "I don't see any young men."

"That's because none of the young men were around. This was a VC village."

"Dad. *Dad.*"

"It's just an observation. This whole thing was probably a revenge mission. Actually, I know it was. They probably said, 'We're gonna teach 'em a lesson,' so they massacred everyone. Which is a slight violation of every rule and regulation both moral, written, military, and civilian."

As we walk over to the museum, I notice that the palm trees are marked with little plaques to denote the still visible bullet holes the soldiers fired into them during the massacre. ("Kill some trees!" was, among American soldiers in Vietnam, the equivalent of "Fire at will!") "Good Christ," my father says quietly, stopping to finger one palm tree's spiderwebbed bullet hole. His face is suddenly spectral. "Five hundred people . . . "

The museum is filled with tourists, most of them older Europeans, all of whom are walking around, looking at the exhibits, with something like cosmic dread splashed across their faces. I look at a photo of a man who has been thrown into a well, his shiny brain visible through the hole in his skull, and feel that same dread take up residence upon my own face. More photos: a skinny man cut in two by machine-gun fire, a woman with her brains neatly piled beside her. In an adjacent room is a rogues' gallery of My Lai perpetrators, huge blowups of badly Xeroxed photocopies, the pixels as big as dimes. Let their last names stand: Calley, Hodges, Reid, Widmer, Simpson, and Medina, at his court-martial, at which he was acquitted. (Most of the men directly responsible for the My Lai massacres had been discharged by the time the story broke; the arm of military justice is particularly short, and they were never brought to trial at all.) There are also photos of Lawrence Colburn and Hugh Thompson and Herbert Carter. The former two were helicopter crewmen who managed to maintain a grip on their humanity and choppered out a handful of civilians during the slaughter. The latter is said to have pumped a round into his own foot during the massacre to avoid taking part—the operation's only casualty. Colburn's and Thompson's Soldier's Medals for heroism are also on display here, though far less conspicuously.

I see my father ducking out with Hien, both of them gray and punched-looking, and I begin to follow after them when behind me I hear a heavily accented German voice declaim, "I have been to Auschwitz, and it is moving, but this is so much *more* moving, *ja?*" I turn. The people this German woman is speaking to are Canadians.

"Excuse me?" I less say than hear myself saying. She looks at me unapologetically. She is wearing a chunky jade necklace I have seen being sold on the streets. "More moving. Because of the life. The life around this place." She is waving her hands, which are long and thin skeleton hands, while the Canadians stealthily take their leave.

Although I am fairly sure this constitutes some form of "anti-attitude," I do not report her. I do not say anything and stalk off outside. I find Hien and my father standing by the ditch in which many of the victims of the My Lai massacre were dumped. Nearby is a *Guernica*-style mural with death-spraying choppers and wicked-faced American soldiers looming over defenseless Vietnamese women and children. The ditch itself is not very big, long, or wide and is largely grown over with scrub.

"Why would one man," Hien is saying, "like Calley, kill, while another man, like Colburn, try to prevent it? What is the difference?"

My father is staring into the ditch. "It's just . . . war," he tells Hien. Hien nods, but I know he is not satisfied by this. I am not satisfied by this. Neither, it seems, is my father. "I guess what it comes down to," he goes on, searchingly, "is discipline." After Hien leaves, my father rubs his chest through his shirt. "My heart hurts."

"Yeah," I say.

"I've seen American Marines take revenge, but they just killed men, not women and children. It's horrible. When I came here, we were . . . we were like crusaders! We were going to help people. We were going to make their lives better, give them democracy. And the way we did it was so morally . . ." He sighs, rubs his mouth, shakes his head, all the willful gestures of sense-making. My Lai happened two years after my father left Vietnam. The Vietnam War of 1966 was not the Vietnam War of 1968, which had by then scythed down whole fields of men and goodwill, including that of the war's own planners and originators. Kennedy, McNamara, Johnson: By 1968 all had fallen. I think about the story my father once told me about how he had been asked to transport a Vietcong prisoner by helicopter to the village of Tam Ky. He described this prisoner as "a little guy who's terrified, frightened to death, tied up, but still bucking and heaving. And he fought and he fought and he fought for forty-five minutes. He knew he was going to be thrown out of the helicopter. He *knew* that. So we arrived in Tam Ky, and they asked me, 'What'd you learn?' I said, 'I learned that this little guy wants to kill me because he thought I was going to pitch him out of the helicopter!' And goddamnit, at one point I was about to." We had both laughed, grimly. War stories. My father would not have been capable of throwing a bound man from a helicopter, under any circumstances. But I imagine him—I imagine myself—here in My Lai during those first moments of that day's terrible momentum, the evil freedom of the trigger availing itself upon the minds of friends and comrades, and I do not like the range of possibilities that I see.

My father suddenly looks up across this miserable ditch into a verdant neighboring pasture. "I wish Hien were here." Did he have, finally, a better answer for him as to why only some men kill while others think to save? No, actually. He wants to know if that is corn or wheat growing over there or what.

"What does your father do?"

A question young men are asked all the time. Women in particular ask it of young men, I suppose in the spirit of a kind of secular astrology. Who will you be in ten years, and do I want to be involved? The common belief is that every young man, like the weeping Jesus of Gethsemane, has two choices when it comes to his father: rejection or emulation. In some ways my father and I could not be more different. While I have inherited his sense of humor, his love of loyalty, and his lycanthropically hairy back, I am my mother's child in all matters of commerce and emotion. I am terrible with money, weep over nothing, and typically feel before I think. I can anticipate my mother because her heart is mine. My father remains more mysterious.

What does my father do? I have always answered it thus: "My father is a Marine." This typically results in a pinch-faced look of sympathy. But the truth is, my father and I get along. We have not always gotten along—I maintained a solid D average in high school, he viewed my determination to be a writer (at least initially) as a dreamer's errand, and marooned in our history are various wrecked Chevys and uncovered marijuana caches—but we have always been close. As I get older, I have noticed the troubles many of my friends have with their fathers: the animosities and disappointments, held so long in the arrears of late adolescence, suddenly coming up due on both ends. But my father and I, if anything, have gotten closer, even as I understand him less and less.

My father is a Marine. But how poorly that captures him. He is not a tall man, but he is so thin he appears tall. His head is perfectly egg-shaped, which accounts for my brother's and my nickname for him: Egghead. (Although nothing explains his nicknames for us: Ringworm and Remus.) His duck-like gait, a strange combination of the goofy and the determined, sees his big floppy feet inclined outward at forty-five-degree angles. (I used to make fun of him for this until a girlfriend pointed out to me that I walk precisely the same way.) My father, then, was no Great Santini, no Knight Templar of bruising manhood. During the neighborhood basketball games of my childhood, which were played in our driveway, my father, for instance, unforgivably shot granny-style free throws. "Hugs and kisses" is how he used to announce that he was putting me to bed. I unselfconsciously kissed my father until I was in high school, when some friends busted me for it: "You kiss your *dad?*" But we fought all the time. I do not mean argue. I mean we *fought*. I would often announce my presence by punching him hard on the shoulder, whereupon he would put me in a full nelson until I sang the following song, which for years I believed he had made up: "Why this feeling?/Why this joy?/Because you're near me, oh you fool./Mister Wonderful, that's you." The torment was not just physical. When I was very young, my father would tell me he invented trees and fought in the Civil War and would laugh until he had tears in his eyes when my teachers called home to upbraid him. In return my brother and I simply besieged the poor man, pouring liquid Ex-Lax into his coffee before work, loading his cigarettes with tiny slivers of treated pine that exploded after a few drags. One went off in a board meeting at his bank, another while he was on his way to church, sending him up onto the curb. He always got us back. In high school I brought a date over and was showing off with my smart-aleckry, only to be knocked to the floor by my father and held down while he rubbed pizza all over my face and called our dogs over to lick it off. There was, needless to say, no second date.

But my father is a Marine. He could be cruel. After a high school party that left his house demolished and our Christmas presents stolen, I sought him out to tell him I was sorry, that I loved him. "No," he said, not even looking at me as he swept up the glass from a broken picture frame. "I don't think you do." We owned a large stuffed diplodocus named Dino, which became a kind of makeshift couch we used to prop ourselves against while watching television, for my father was the kind of father who got down on the floor with his children. Once, resting against Dino while we watched *Sands of Iwo Jima*, I asked my father what it felt like to get wounded. He looked at me, grabbed the flesh of my forearm, and pinched me so hard sudden tears slickened my eyes. I returned fire by callously asking him if he had ever killed anyone. I was ten or eleven, and my cold, hurt little stare drilled into his, sheer will being one of the few human passions ungoverned by age. He looked away first.

He is a Marine. To this I attributed much of the sheer insanity of growing up with him. He once shot a flaming arrow into his brother's front door, just for instance. Every July Fourth he would take it upon himself to destroy his neighbor's garbage cans by filling them with fireworks and a splash of gasoline, always igniting the concoction by daintily tossing in a cigarette smoked down to its filter. Another neighbor deposited half a dozen garter snakes into our bathtub; my father responded by taking the snakes over to the neighbor's house and calmly stuffing them under his bedspread. Once, at dinner, Phil Caputo recounted a story of my father drunkenly commandeering a tour bus in Key West, Florida, flooring it across a crowded parking lot while his passengers, about seventy touring seniors, screamed. Only later did I realize that Phil did not live in Key West until the early 1980s—which would have made my father a forty-year-old bus thief.

I joined the Peace Corps after college and quickly washed out. The mansion of my father's disappointment had many rooms, and even now I cannot much stand to reread the letters he sent me as I was preparing to come home. They are loving, they are cruel, they are the letters of a man who fiercely loves his son and whose own past is so painful he forgets, sometimes, that suffering is a misfortune some of us are forced to experience rather than a human requirement. But what have I done with my life? I have become a writer greatly interested in sites of human suffering. And lately it occurs to me that this has been my own attempt to approximate something of what my father went through.

During the war in Afghanistan, I got stuck in Mazar-i-Sharif with dangerously low funds and one friend, Michael, a Danish journalist I had followed into the war. Even though I had all the proper credentials, the Uzbek border-patrol turned us back three times in a row. We had brought only enough money for a few days, and, at fifty dollars a cab ride from Mazar to the border, we were running out of options. I called my father on the borrowed satellite phone of an Associated Press journalist. It was Christmas Eve in Michigan, and he and my stepmother were alone, probably waiting for my brother or me to call. He had no idea I was in Afghanistan, since I had promised I was going to stay in Uzbekistan. My father picked up after one ring, his voice edged with joy.

"Dad, please listen because I don't have much time. I'm stuck in Afghanistan. I don't have any money. I may need you to make some calls. Did you hear me?"

The link was quiet but for a faint, cold static.

"Dad?"

"I heard you," he said quietly.

At this, at hearing him, my eyes went hot. "I'm in trouble, I think."

"Have they hurt you?"

In a moment I went from boyishly sniveling to nearly laughing. "No one's hurt me, Dad. I'm just worried."

"Are you speaking code? Tell me where you are." His panic, preserved perfectly after its journey through cloud and space and the digital guts of some tiny metal moon, beamed down and hit me with all the force of an actual voice.

"Dad, I'm not a *captive*, I'm—" But he was gone. The line was silent, the satellite having glided into some nebula of link-terminating interference. I chose not to ponder the state in which my father would spend the remainder of his Christmas, though I later learned he spent it falling apart. And for a short while, at least, the unimaginable had become my life, not his. I was him, and he was me.

My father and I make our way down a bright beach in the city of Qui Nhon. The previous night we drank gallons of Tiger beer, and I find myself comparing my constitution to his. My father imbibes a fraction of what he used to, but he still possesses the iron disposition every alcoholic needs if he or she seeks to make a life out of it. I look and smell as though I have endured a night in a halfway house urinal, whereas he looks and smells as though he has just slept fifteen hours in some enchanted flowerbed. I am reminded of the various times I had, while growing up, seen my father triumphantly insensate after a bottle of Johnnie Walker Red, wearing only underwear and a winter jacket, off to do some 3:00 A.M. snow shoveling. Mere hours later he would be rosy pink and whistling as he knotted his tie before work. Constitutionally, I am not this man's spawn, and here on the beach he pats my back as I dry heave into some bushes.

Qui Nhon is where my father washed ashore with a thousand other Marines in April 1965, one month after the deployment, in Danang, of the first American Marines sent to Southeast Asia explicitly as combat troops. The April battalions were dispatched at the bidding of General William Westmoreland, who sought to bring the war to the Vietcong. Marines would no longer stand impotent guard beside airports and radio towers and hospitals but would hunt down and kill Vietcong insurgents. (This plan did not work. One estimate holds that almost 90 percent of the skirmishes that resulted from search-and-destroy tactics were initiated by enemy troops.) Many expected a quick victory, since everyone knew the VC and North Vietnamese Army could not withstand America's superior firepower. Others braced themselves for a long, ugly fight. My father, like nearly all young Marines of the time, possessed the former belief.

It takes us fifteen minutes' worth of beachcombing to find the site of his landing: A thin stand of coastline palm trees, miraculously unaltered since 1965, hardens his memory into place. We stand looking out on the endless sea in a black grid of shadows cast by the cranes and scaffolds of the resort being built a few dozen yards away. I begin asking him questions, but very gently he asks if I might not give him a moment. Instantly I realize my error. He cannot talk right now, and he stares out at the ocean in both confusion and recognition. I fall silent. This is where the man I know as my father was born. It is as though he is looking upon himself through a bloody veil of memory.

"They told us this was going to be a combat landing," he says after a while. "To expect the very worst. The ships we were in flooded themselves, and the landing craft and amphibious vehicles swam off. We came ashore, heavily armed, locked, cocked, ready to go to war. We had tanks and trucks and Ontos."

"Ontos?"

"Lightly armored vehicles mounted with six recoilless rifles. They shot all kinds of ammunition. Armor-piercing. Antipersonnel ammunition. Willy

Peter, which is white phosphorus, one of the most deadly things you could ever get hit with. When the shell explodes, it sprays white phosphorus, and if you put water on it, it flares right up. It's oxygen-fed, and you have to take mud and smother it. Lovely weapon."

"How old were you with all this at your disposal?"

"I was twenty-three years old. A platoon leader. But I was also the company commander, and I had all of the infantry and supply people under me. I was probably one of the youngest company commanders in Vietnam—if not the youngest." Of this, I can tell, he is still proud. "Everyone was cheering us. It was glorious. That's my biggest frustration when I talk to people who weren't here. They'll say, 'Nobody really wanted us to come to Vietnam.' Well, they sure as hell welcomed us with open arms."

"When did it start to go bad?"

He points to the hills beyond Qui Nhon—an arcadia of rough, beautiful triangles of fuzzy jade and sharp spurs of exposed white rock, a few white waterfalls pouring sparklingly down the hills' faces. "Those look beautiful, but the VC were there, as we found out. It took only two days before we were fired on. We were so inexperienced, we were shooting ourselves at first. One guy, tragically, fell asleep on watch and turned himself around in his foxhole. He woke up, saw people, and opened fire. Killed the rest of his fire team."

In Vietnam, and especially during the war's opening innings, American soldiers experienced chaotic fighting unlike any they had ever seen before. There was no land to take, no front to hold, and few opportunities to glory in the routing of the enemy. All-out battles were few and far between, and enemy combatants perpetually melted away into the forest only to reappear, in the minds of increasingly (and understandably) jittery American soldiers, in the form of putatively innocent villagers.

As we drive on to the village of Tuy Phuoc, I ask my father about this severance between the kind of fighting he was trained to do and the kind of fighting the VC forced him to engage in. "The VC," he says, "would not close with us. They didn't have the firepower. And we knew that if they made a stand against us, they would lose ass, hat, and fixtures. So they would pick on our patrols." He is agitated now and stares with cool determination out his window. Tuy Phuoc, the village we are headed to, is where my father was wounded.

He points out the window at the railroad track that runs contiguous to the road, found on an elevated mound of packed sod perhaps eight feet high. "See that? That's what we used to hide behind, as a fortified position." At this he enjoys a chuckle.

"How many firefights were you in?"

"A dozen, twenty. They would last anywhere from ten seconds to two hours. Then the VC would break off and disappear. We lost a tremendous number of people trying to save our wounded and retrieve our bodies. And they knew it. They knew we would. That's how Walt Levy died, you know: trying to haul someone out of a rice paddy who was wounded."

"I'm sensing some anxiety here. You're sweating."

"Really?" He touches his temple, a lagoon of perspiration. He quickly wipes his fingers on his shirt. "Well, maybe a little."

"How do you feel about the Vietcong now?"

He looks at his camera as he turns it over in his hands. "We were all soldiers. They suffered terribly, you know, compared to us. Brave people. Committed. To their country. We sort of . . . lost that."

"I'm sorry," I say, surprising myself.

"Yeah," he says. "Me too."

Tuy Phuoc is less a village than a series of islands spread across a large plain now completely flooded by the seasonal rains. We ride among these islands along a long straight road that clears the greedy waterline by only a few inches. Each island is a little node of Swiss Family Robinson-type existence: a modest house, a collapsing wooden fence, a damp sandy yard, a small dock, a wooden boat tied up to it. Plastic bags and limp old bicycle-tire linings hang with obscure meaning from the branches of several trees. My father mentions that forty years ago all of these houses were thatched huts. Hien jumps in to say, with some pride, that the government has been building and modernizing all of Vietnam's villages since the war ended in 1975.

The road is narrow and crammed with pedestrians; above, the sky seems a spacious gray cemetery of dead clouds. The surrounding floodwater is tea-colored where it is deep and green where it is shallow. "Vietcong villages," my father suddenly says, looking around at Tuy Phuoc's islands. "All of these." We finally park when the road is too flooded out to continue and stand next to the car. My father was wounded, he thinks, perhaps a hundred yards ahead of where we have been forced to stop. He is visibly rattled and lights up a cigarette to distract himself. On either side of the road stands a crowd of Vietnamese. They call to one another across the water, waving and laughing. Every few minutes some brave soul mounts a scooter charge through the flood, the water parting before his tires with Mosaic instantaneity.

Tuy Phuoc, I gather, is not much of a tourist town, and for the most part we are left alone. But nearly everyone is looking at us. The people of Tuy Phuoc are short and damp and suntanned in a vaguely unhealthy way. The women smile, the men nod civilly, and the children rush at us before thinking better of it and retreat behind their mothers' legs.

"You want to tell me what happened?" This is mostly a courtesy, since I know what happened. My father was shot—in the back, buttock, arm, and shoulder—at the beginning of a roadside melee and was dragged to safety by a black soldier. One of the things I had long admired about my father was his absence of racial animosity—a fairly uncommon trait among the men of rural Michigan. I always attributed this to the black Marine who saved his life. I identically credited my youthful stridency on racial matters—I was forever jumping down the throats of my parents' dinner guests or high school friends whenever the word "nigger" made its unlovely entrance from stage right—to this same mysterious savior.

"We were on a search-and-destroy mission," my father explains. "We entered Tuy Phuoc in a convoy. After twenty minutes of driving we found the road was cut by a huge earthen mound. The VC obviously knew we were coming, so we were all very suspicious. I was at the head of the convoy and called up the engineers. They were going to blow up the mound and rebuild the road so we could continue. About fifteen men came up, and I turned around to talk to the gunnery sergeant from the lead infantry company, and the mound exploded. Inside the dirt they'd packed a bunch of steel and shrapnel. The only reason I'm here is that I turned around to speak to the gunnery sergeant. I remember saying, 'Gunny, I'll go back and get some more equipment.' You know, shovels, stuff like that. The bomb caught Gunny in the face, and I went flying through the air. Then I tried to get up. Couldn't. There were people lying all over the place. I think fifteen were wounded. Gunny was the only guy killed. My platoon sergeant hauled me into a ditch, and they field-dressed me and jammed me full of morphine and then flew in the choppers. I was very fucked up, in total shock. I had two hundred separate wounds. They counted 'em. My left arm caught the brunt of the blast. I thought they were going to have to take it off. So that ended my war for a while."

"Wait a minute," I say. "I thought you were shot."

"No, I never got shot. Which is fine by me."

"But that's not the story you told me."

He looks at me. "I don't think I ever told you that story."

"Then why do I remember you being shot and a black Marine dragging you to safety?"

"I have no idea."

"Was the sergeant who pulled you into the ditch black?"

"I don't think so. I honestly don't remember."

My father's sleeve is rolled up, and I am now looking at his left arm. Incredibly, I have never before noticed the scoring of crosshatched scar tissue running up and down his forearm or how thinner his left arm seems compared with his right. I have, however, many times noticed the bright, pink nickel-sized scars on his bicep and his shoulder blade, the small keloidal lightning bolt on his neck. When I was young, I used to stare at these obvious wounds and, sometimes, even touch them, my tiny fingers freshly alive to their rubbery difference in texture. But I have to admit, now, that I do not actually remember my father ever telling me he was shot or that a black man had saved his life. I remember telling that story myself, but I do not remember being told that story. At some point the story simply appears in my mind. Why did I create this story? Because it made my father heroic? In the emergency of growing up, we all need heroes. But the father I grew up with was no hero to me, not then. He was too wounded in the head, too endlessly and terribly sad. Too funny, too explosive, too confusing. Heroes are uncomplicated. *This* makes them do *that.* The active heroism of my imaginary black Marine made a passive hero of my father; they huddled together, alongside a road in the Vietnam of my mind, shrouded in nitroglycerin, the cordite of gallantry. The story made sense of the senseless. But war does not make sense. War senselessly wounds everyone right down the line. A body bag fits more than just its intended corpse. Take the 58,000 American soldiers lost in Vietnam and multiply by four, five, six— and only then does one begin to realize the damage this war has done. (Project outward from the two million slain Vietnamese and see, for the first time, an entire continent of loss.) War, when necessary, is unspeakable. When unnecessary, it is unforgivable. It is not an occasion for heroism. It is an occasion only for survival and death. To regard war in any other way only guarantees its inevitable reappearance.

I look at my father, who is still smoking and peering around. Suddenly he appears very old. He does not look bad. He is in fact in better physical shape than I, but he is older-looking than I have ever seen him before. His neck has begun to give up and sag, his eyes are bigger and more yellowy, the long wolfish hair at the base of his throat is gray. I am twenty-nine, six years older than my father was when he was wounded. Can I really know the young man who went flying through the air, ripped apart by a booby trap? Can I even know this man, still flying, and in some ways still ripped apart? Ultimately our lives are only partially ours. The parts of our lives that change most are those that intrude with mythic vividness into the lives of those we love: our parents, our children, our brothers and sisters. As these stories overlap they change, but we have no voice in how or why. One by one our stories are dragged away from us, pulled into the ditches of shared human memory. They are saved, but they are changed. One day my father will be gone except for the parts of him I remember and the stories he has told me. How much else about him have I gotten wrong? How much of him have I not properly understood? What have I not asked? And looking at him I want him never to go. I want him always to be here. There is too much left for us to talk about.

At last, a lone Vietnamese man shoelessly wanders over to say hello. His hairless legs and arms are so thin and brown they look made of teak. As he and my father shake hands and (with Hien's assistance) chat, I realize that this man is around my father's age. It is in fact not at all beyond possibility that this man personally wired the booby trap that nearly killed my father. But his solar friendliness is not feigned, and beneath its insistent emotional heat I can see my father's discomfort soften and wilt. Within moments the man and my father are laughing over something together.

I listen to my father and his new Vietnamese friend talk respectfully around the small matter of having taken up arms against each other as young men: Yes, my father *has* been to Vietnam before; no, the Vietnamese man did not always live in the south. Their conversation slides into a respectful silence, and they nod and look at each other. With a smile, the man suddenly asks my father what brings him to Tuy Phuoc, since it is so far away from anything of note. For a long time my father thinks about how to answer, looking up at the low gray clouds, a few small trapezoids of blue showing through. To Hien he finally says, "Tell him . . . tell him that, a very long time ago, I got hurt here."

Once, while hunting partridge, which I did not like to do, my father abandoned me after I maintained I was not going another step until he gave me a granola bar. He refused, I stopped, and off he went. I was probably twelve years old. It was a cold fall day, witchy orange-yellow leaves blew all around me, and, as the moments turned to minutes and the minutes to hours, I sat down on a log and began to despair. Trees grew taller, the air colder; the forest was an endless organic mirror of my fear. I do not remember how long I was alone. After the sky had darkened, after I had turned up my collar and drawn myself into a defenseless ball on the forest floor, my father burst through some bushes on a different path than that by which he had left me and gathered me up into his arms. He was crying. He had gotten "turned around," he said quickly. Not lost. My father never got lost. He was a Marine. He said nothing else; neither did I. I held him, and he held me, and he carried me out of the forest.

Bulldog

Greg Bottoms

The one time I saw the dog—I was eleven and had just met Mark—she had nearly hanged herself, in her maniacal aggression, from a stout oak tree.

Mark and I stood outside of the chain-link fence, in his father's narrow side-yard, watching. The grass was winter-brown; it crunched under our shoes. A jet from the nearby Air Force base, where my mother was at work, roared over us, writing a thick chalk line of exhaust across the sky.

We looked up, at each other, back at Bulldog balanced on her hind legs at the end of the taut leash, tongue out, hopping, gagging, her pink chest forward, exposed. She was short, bulky, white with large brown spots, one encircling her left eye. The leash was wrapped several times around the trunk. Every fourth or fifth inhale was a panicked, gasping snort, her breath pluming out like a cartoon dialogue bubble.

"I told you," Mark said, in that petulant, contorted-face way he had. His parents were in the middle of the divorce at this time; there was name-calling, a custody battle. "She's insane. She does this every time she sees me. She bit someone in my mom's neighborhood, so my mom told my dad he had to keep her here until they could sell her. My mom says my dad drinks and that's why the dog is wild. She's like, 'Stop drinking and pay some attention to the dog.' And then he's like, 'I don't drink.' And then she's like, 'I can't talk to you. Why do you lie? Why do you lie? It's over and you're still lying.' I hate my parents, man. I wish my mom would die sometimes."

"Who's going to buy a dog like that?" I asked.

"She's a purebred." He put his chapped hand on the top bar of the fence. "So you have to find like a dog person, you know, a purebred person. My mom and dad bought her when they were trying to keep everyone in one house. At least they didn't have a baby. Christ."

Bulldog's eyes bulged; her rage sent a tingle like someone's fingers across my scalp.

"Come on," Mark said. "Watch this." He jumped the fence.

The dog became wilder, hopping much higher than before, baring her teeth, slobbering soapy foam. I was sure she'd either strangle herself or get loose and tear him to shreds.

I jumped the fence. I was eleven. My new friend did it. I had to.

I stood fifteen feet or so from Bulldog, whose anger was a magnetic field. I felt it in my back and neck, heat down in my legs. I could hardly breathe.

Mark picked up a rusty hatchet from beside the woodpile. "Come on!" he yelled at the dog. "Come on!"

He wound up, hand cocked high over his head. He threw it.

My whole body blinked. My hands curled like claws, my shoulders flinched up toward my ears.

After I opened my eyes, he turned toward me, laughing, the hatchet still in his hand, a tormentor playing a joke for my enjoyment.

Did the dog yelp and briefly cower? I don't know. In the close-up shot my memory supplies I see only Mark's face, and the hatchet blade, brown from corruption.

What I do remember clearly—what happened next, the image organizing these words—is how Bulldog lunged at him then, the feral, almost otherworldly sound of her, the way she pulled hard against the leash, stretching her leather and metal collar until it was about to break, willing, like the rest of them, to be hanged there by her own truculence if that's what it took to get revenge.

Grip

Joy Castro

Over the crib in the tiny apartment, there hung a bullet-holed paper target, the size and dark shape of a man, its heart zone, head zone, perforated where my aim had torn through: thirty-six little rips, no strays, centered on spots that would make a man die.

Beginner's luck, said the guys at the shooting range, at first. *Little lady*, they'd said, until the silhouette slid back and farther back. They'd cleared their throats, fallen silent.

A bad neighborhood. An infant child. A Ruger GP .357 with speed-loader.

It's not as morbid as it sounds, a target pinned above a crib: the place was small, the walls already plastered full with paintings, sketches, pretty leaves, hand-illuminated psychedelic broadsides of poems by my friends. I masking-taped my paper massacre to the only empty space, a door I'd closed to form a wall.

When my stepfather got out of prison, he tracked my mother down. He found the city where she'd moved. He broke a basement window and crawled in. She never saw his car, halfway up the dark block, stuffed behind a bush.

My mother lived. She wouldn't say what happened in the house that night. Cops came: that's what I know. Silent, she hung a screen between that scene and me. It's what a mother does.

She lived—as lived the violence of our years with him, knifed into us like scrimshaw cut in living bone.

Carved but alive, we learned to hold our breath, dive deep, bare our teeth to what fed us.

When I was twenty-one, my son slept under the outline of what I could do, a death I could hold in my hands.

At the time, I'd have denied its locale any meaning, called its placement coincidence, pointing to walls crowded with other kinds of dreams.

But that dark torn thing did hang there, its lower edge obscured behind the wooden slats, the flannel duck, the stuffed white bear.

It hung there like a promise, like a headboard, like a *No*, like a terrible poem, like these lines I will never show you, shielding you from the fear I carry—like a sort of oath I swore over your quiet sleep.

Race in the Creative Writing Classroom

Toi Derricotte

Baring/Bearing Anger

A few weeks ago I got angry at a student in one of my creative writing classes who complained that I was talking too much about race. She said there were people in the class who were tired of hearing about it. I have heard that complaint from white students before, and in the past, I have been patient, tried to listen and clarify my purposes in a more tolerant manner. This time, however, I found myself tired and lashing out. "If you don't like it, you don't have to stay." She looked devastated. I thought about calling her that night and apologizing, but I didn't. It isn't that I didn't feel sorry for her pain, and it wasn't that I felt completely justified, but I wanted to give us both time to think, and I wanted her to consider the seriousness of what I was trying to do. Sometimes anger can get one's attention.

That night I anguished about my behavior, but I'm sure I didn't feel the vulnerability that my student must have felt. Because of the dynamics of power, I am in a totally different position now in the classroom as a professor than I was as a student.

For many years, not looking black and being the only black student in a traditional graduate English literature department, I never spoke about my race. Partly I didn't speak about it because there didn't seem to be an appropriate time, and partly it was because I felt, never having read a black author all the way through high school, college, and graduate school, that revealing my race might somehow endanger my fragile ambition to be a writer. Once I had asked a professor why we hadn't read any black writers in his class. "We don't go down that low," he had explained. I was too shocked to ask him what he meant. How would his opinion of my papers have changed if I had revealed I was black, or even if I had questioned him about his statement? I thought for a long time about going back to talk to him, but I didn't. It wasn't just that I thought my professors regarded the writings of blacks as inferior, the damage was even more corrosive: I thought that many of them felt black people themselves were incapable, either because of our minds, experiences, or language, of writing "real" literature.

The next day I called my student and we met for coffee. She told me how afraid she had been that she would lose our relationship. She had studied with me for three semesters and I had always been supportive. This was the first time she had seen me angry. I assured her that my anger had passed quickly. But I wanted her to know that, given the history of racism, at least as far as I was concerned, no relationship between blacks and whites will be genuine unless it can bear and bare anger, that bearing and baring anger is the real test of whether a relationship can last.

One of the writing assignments I give new writing students is based on a quote by Red Smith. "There is nothing to writing; all you have to do is sit down and open up a vein." We talk about the pain of revealing ourselves, of getting out what is inside. Later I may ask students to write a letter of unfinished business to someone from their past. Often the first important poems we write, our "breakthrough" poems, are angry. There's something about anger that motivates, that gets us over our "stuckness," over our fear. Often poems seem to burst out whole from some storeroom in the body/mind as if they had been sitting around waiting for years. But there is a danger in anger for black students. White students often write "breakthrough" poems about their childhood. Often called "brave" by the other poets in the class, these poems are frequently painful reassessments of their parents. Black students, however, often don't go back to childhood. They have clear angers that are more weighty right here in the present. There is always a "last straw." Writing about the past is not threatening to others in the class, but writing about what is happening in the classroom here and now is. For the black writer breaking silence, breaking restraint is a frightening step. The person who was the catalyst for the angry poem, unaware of the long history of oppression and internalized rage, takes it as a personal insult. Some students side with the white student, some with the black, but most students remain silent, afraid to go in either direction. In any event, the black student may lose a few of his or her best supporters, people who can tolerate poems about race as long as they don't make anybody feel too uncomfortable. I have had people give me "gifts" after reading a poem of mine, quotations from the Bible or other calming and inspirational words suggesting ways to find love and inner peace. As Cornelius Eady says, presenting one's emotional truth is difficult enough. But unlike white writers, black writers are also expected to solve the problems they present in their work.

What happens in a classroom when diversity begins to be expressed? It would be nice if suddenly everything got better, but in reality this does not happen. There's a very dangerous moment when feelings, real feelings, start to emerge. The reactions of white students to the writings of the one or two writers of color in my undergraduate and graduate writing classes vary, but often an entirely different state of receptivity is in effect. Often they feel isolated, excluded, bombarded by experiences and words they don't understand. They have described a feeling of distance from the poems, feeling defensive and determined not to be made to feel guilty, responsible, or ashamed. Some students say that they listen in spite of these difficulties because it helps them to understand what it means to be black. An easy way out of seriously examining a poem may be to romanticize it, to say it must be "a black thing."

A student complained that he was tired of reading books by black writers and having "the race thing rubbed in my face." A black student asked him, how many books have you read? Four or six? The black student said that he had read thousands of books by white writers and felt it unjust that his writing was read through so many layers. When he picks up a book, he never expects a white writer, for example, to educate him about what it means to be white.

Perhaps teachers of creative writing should encourage students to read texts that give basic information about race and racism in order to help fill in the gaps caused by the common lack of education. It is useful to talk about race before it comes up specifically in reference to students' work. More important, providing information may remove the burden on black students to be the primary sources of information about blackness and let them get on with their own work. For its facts, figures, and readability, I suggest Andrew Hacker's *Two Nations: Black and White, Separate, Hostile, Unequal.* A provocative video about images of blacks in the media, *Ethnic Notions*, should stimulate useful dialogue. Of course, teachers should include writers of color in their lists of required reading.

Hayes Davis, a student in my senior seminar, wrote this poem in response to a white student's complaints.

Black Writers

I don't really give a rat's ass
if you're tired of reading black poets,
but I do, really, and I couldn't help
but think, if I want to write
for this class any more, I have to
start editing myself a little now
and I'm angry about that
and I'm not going to let
you edit me through myself,
or are you really tired of me?
Are you tired of me, or Huie, or Cassandra,
are you tired of Toi?
Why the fuck are you in the class,
or are we acceptable black poets,
or were you thinking there wouldn't
be any black poets in the class?
Are we not really black poets?

Poets that happen to be black
ya know, but not really like black, ya know?

Race is a scary subject. Discussions about it in a diverse community are fraught with dangers. People walk on eggs. My husband uses flip charts when he makes presentations in the corporate world. Being the only black person in the room most of the time, he feels people hear him better when they aren't looking at his face. But we as writers are told to reveal ourselves.

Michele Elliot wrote very sparingly during her two years as a graduate student, and what she wrote she was careful about sharing. Though she had shared little in class, she had made many comments to me about her discomfort as one of two black students in the class, of her sadness that classmates—even people she respected and liked—lacked understanding of the most basic aspects of racism and made comments about her poems that completely missed the boat. Finally, something triggered the release of many years of anger.

Perhaps you will never be able to experience these lines, perhaps you will dismiss me as absurd, inflexible, acting difficult as an unruly child. Maybe you will never feel the colonization of your own mind, notice the weight of its chains. You're defensive and you don't even realize it. You're asking me questions you've already created the answers for, formed hypotheses, collected data and published the results. What would happen if the world split open and you were forced to face the scared, uncomfortable you, the unlistened to, unrecognizable you, unable to put your feet down, orient yourself. The rules are gone, no walls to hide behind, left on the plantation without a gun. You can't shut it down, package it, contain it. It's exploding everywhere. The gaps are too big to bridge. In it you can hear the violence of your own words, see the consequences. Language has left you alone, lonely. You're without an agenda, a place to be. Everything is at stake, raw and unbearable.

For Ms. Elliot the most violent and revengeful fantasy she could imagine was for the tables to be turned, for the one who has privilege to walk the line between worlds, to see with double vision from the eyes of the "other." A white woman in one of my classes, Kristen Herbert, wrote a collection of poems titled *White Space* in which she interrupted the normal lines of the poem with cutouts, so that you could open up the flaps and read what was underneath, what was inside the white space. Whiteness has to be examined, addressed, not taken as "normal." White people have to develop a double consciousness, too, a part in which they see themselves as "other." We are all wounded by racism, but for some of us those wounds are anesthetized. When we begin to feel it, we're awake.

I want to talk about anger, about how important it is as a part of the process of coming to one's voice, about how it is inevitable in a diverse classroom. I want to talk about how powerful it is, how dangerous it is, how mysterious, about how suddenly real feelings start to emerge. If we don't recognize anger, if we don't allow for it, if we're not ready, if we don't, in fact, welcome it as a creative force, then I think we're going to end up blaming and dividing people even more. We hesitate to allow it to happen, though anger is a part of life. (So often "life" is not allowed in the classroom.)

At the same time that we move toward clarity about our differences, it is also possible to move toward clarity about what makes us human, the same. The edges of the workshop are ragged. But I have seen a few black and white students bare and bear their own raw truths.

Grad Class

Last week, at a panel on teaching creative writing in a diverse classroom, I read an essay I had written about an incident that had happened several years ago in a graduate class I was teaching.

> Some of the white students in my class are very angry. They feel that they are being attacked, not listened to, silenced. It hurts. It makes them angry. And they don't know what to do.
>
> Some of the black students in my class are very angry. They feel that they have been attacked, not listened to, silenced. It hurts. It makes them angry. They have tried for years to be silent. But finally it is coming out.
>
> Some of the gays, some of the straights, some of the men, some of the women, some of everybody is walking on a tightrope, and I am the teacher. What am I responsible for? For "educating" them to new material? For allowing them to speak? For encouraging them to dig deeper? For saying "put it all in your work?" For being quiet? For talking? For telling my own personal truth?
>
> Everything one says can be misunderstood, used against one, piled up as evidence, used to support something one did not intend. Everything one does not say can cause a vacuum in which much destructive force can appear.
>
> I saw it happen once, in a course I was teaching. During the semester a black man began flirting with a white woman. You could see he was very attracted, and the woman seemed not to be attracted, but something slightly more. She was conversational when he approached, but at the same time pulled away. There was a kinetic energy between them that seemed to be based on something more than their personal likes and dislikes. He was affronted. He was a

beautiful, strong-looking man who, I sensed, was not accustomed to rejection. This was his first semester away from home, one black man in a group of strangers, and in the school he had come from, a black school, he had been a powerful and known entity. I sensed his pain at realizing that what our society had, on the one hand, taught him was most useful about himself—his body—was at the same time power-less to get what he had been taught was the most desirable thing—a beautiful blonde. He could only get so far. And he wasn't willing to accept that.

She, on the other hand, I couldn't figure out. I resented her because he seemed to want her. A white woman. A beautiful blonde. I felt jeal-ous for the black girls who weren't wanted. I felt jealous for myself, who I feel had never been able to attract such a beautiful black man. Maybe I wanted him. Or wished I had been so wanted by some black man. My father? Or was it my own desire and inability to touch that so confused me?

I could feel him aggressively positioning himself and she defensive-ly responding. There seemed to develop an unspoken wall between them, and they both began doing things that seemed to mean the op-posite of what was apparent, so that when she smiled, it seemed she most wanted to get away, and when he pursued her, it was as if he was really ignoring her, ignoring her block.

His male assertiveness seemed to change into aggression, and her self-containment into patronization. It frightened me. I've known men and women enter into mortal combat like that, with terrible repercussions for everyone in their path. I wanted to stop the escala-tion. I especially feared the man's anger. My father was an angry man. When I challenged him, I feared for my life. And I did challenge him. But often, at the thought of confronting an escalating anger, I bowed to it, rolled over and played dead. This woman wasn't playing dead. She was more determined. And he was more in her face. I feared for him, too. And for me. I felt called forth to take a side, to be loyal. Just as much as I resented what I perceived to be her arrogance, I was equally afraid of what I perceived to be his assertion of entitlement. In a way, I wanted him to fight. But no. How could I want him to fight for something so wrong to fight for? A white woman? A blonde? And what about the right of any woman for any reason to say no?

Once they were standing together, and I felt something so alive between them. I wanted them to go to bed with each other, to make love, for all of us. I wanted them to be the most beautiful couple at the ball, for black assertion to win and white resistance to give in, for male desire to change the frightened heart that wanted to shield itself. There was something that I wanted to stop, yet it was like watching an oncoming collision, hoping that, at the last moment, what looked like a dangerous confrontation would somehow turn, not into an unbreachable distance or a deadly fight, but into the joining of whatever we have been trained to keep apart by instinct.

It didn't happen that way. At that very moment when I was hoping, she raised her hand, feeling or patting or petting his hair. He felt that moment as an invasion—how dare she touch his head?—and it brought up the nearly instinctual rage at the "good-luck" rub—white people who had said for generations that you can get good luck by rubbing a black boy's head. Why had she touched his head? We never found out. But, saying he had felt "raped" by that touch, he wrote an enraged poem in which he raped a woman. Which engendered her saying that his poem was a public humiliation to her and screaming that she had been raped in actuality when she was young and nobody could do this to her in a poem.

People were moved and sorry for her, and he was soon isolated, except for the few blacks in the class. Some people claimed, on his behalf, that a rape in a poem is not the same as a rape in life. And he said the person raped in the poem was not her. But he didn't back down from his isolation and rage, and he didn't say he was sorry.

Who was wrong? Who right? Most of us tried to settle the confrontation by taking sides. In a way, I think both of them were reacting to something much larger, and neither had the wisdom to make us comfortable by saying so. It made us all, poor poets who probably have receded into poetry precisely because we want nothing to do with such out-and-out confrontation, show our worst side.

The day after I read this, I got a call. Editors from a major magazine wanted to publish it. I am afraid. Will I make people I love angry and hate me for revealing their "dark" secrets? Do I have the right? Is this a "true" story? Or just my sick need to see always, as my mother said, "the bad"?

I had decided to publish and be damned, because "the truth" has to be told by somebody: Racism isn't out there, it's in here, within our families and the community we most love and want to love us. How can we tell the truth about the people we love without hurting them and breaking our needed connection? How can we do it without accomplishing a terrible thing—putting in the place of that unrealized hope for connection, that continuous and painful longing, this "necessity," which feels cold and hard, violent, this withdrawal, a choice that puts in my soul a danger—emptiness, loneliness, a stuckness behind an untranslatable puzzle, a cold spot, a detachment that I "bear" with dignity because I am to "blame," either unconsciously, because of my human flaws, or because I have chosen the "brave" route.

The choice feels so lonely that I want to die, tell whatever truth and then die, perhaps kill myself rather than live with that hopeless sense of violence to those I love, and that pain so impossible to bear, that they will never trust me, that I can never trust myself, and that I cannot say I'm sorry, because, as my father said, it's too late. Sorry never helps.

My father chose coldly like that. He said he'd never apologize; he said you mustn't be weak, never say you're sorry. What he did he did. Perhaps, locked in his house, unable to get out because of his leg, in his seventies, having, in his youth, driven away his mother, driven away my mother, and his second wife, he sat alone in that upstairs window with his police radio and his speakers turned up, which were connected to the outside so he could hear his neighbors' goings and comings—the sound of crackling paper as they lifted grocery sacks—perhaps he felt that painful inability to connect.

A woman I recently met spent the night with me. This morning she said, "I want to talk to you about that story you wrote. I see it's important to you. That story is really about you and me, it's about how we are attracted to each other and yet you pull away." And she said, wisely, "What you must do is show how that story is really about you, about your story, about your struggle and need to heal. That's what you haven't shown, and it puts an entirely different light on the story."

I said, "Then it makes it personal, and I don't want it to be merely personal."

And she said, "Oh no. It's much more than about gender or race, it's about being human, and even more than being human, it's about being human at the end of the twentieth century. That's what you have to put back in."

For so long I struggled to eviscerate the personal. I thought I was following Eliot's dictum to let the metaphor speak. I thought I was proving, like the victim at a trial who sticks to the facts, that my "story" is "real."

What I realize is that I am always mixing up the world with my own soul, so that when I see these two people coming close and moving away, really, it is not about the world at all—or, as my friend said, it is about the world, about the human condition, but the metaphor is not something that one finds in the world. Eliot was wrong. The metaphor is me, and not acknowledging the self, pretending there is no self, or only a thread of self, one portrays falsely. One does not see the metaphor out there as if one were focusing on a movie, the only way into understanding is to put in the self, the most "juicy" part.

Four months ago, in January, I went out with a man in his sixties. I have lived apart from my husband for eight years, and this was my first "date." We held hands and, that night, after a year and a half of seeing him at public places and having sporadic conversations with him on the phone, I let him kiss and touch me on the inside. It was the first time in twenty-seven years that I have let anyone touch me like that except my husband. Why did you do it? my new friend asked. And I said because I wanted to see if I would die, if I would go crazy. I started weeping as I told her, because I had felt nothing. I had felt detached, but I was glad I had done it, glad to see that I wouldn't die.

I had hung a Peruvian rug over the window. I suppose I hadn't wanted anyone to see inside. He didn't stay overnight, but I left the rug up, and the next morning, when the sun shone through its dark patterns, it looked as if streaks of wet, bloody skin were hanging at the window, as if the light were shining through raw skin.

Fearful desire. Dangerous longing.

How can I publish these words when they come so much out of my own sickness? Without answers, do I cause more harm? Shams threw Rumi's book down a well and said, "If you want, I can pull it up with every sheet dry, or you can follow me." I want to burn the book until the sickness dies in *me*.

Before I had read the piece, I had thought about how it "spills the beans" on people I long not to hurt, offend, people I love. I looked out over the audience and tried to decide what to do. I realized my fearful tendency to do something impulsive and regret it. I had brought something "safe" to read. And yet, as often happens, the "safe" piece just didn't seem right.

I saw the face of a woman I love, Alicia Ostriker, a great poet and lover of poets, a white woman who I know would have wanted me to read that work. I knew she was one who, even if I had pointed out to her something she had done that hurt me, wouldn't have abandoned our friendship.

I looked around the room again. There were people in the room who knew the people I had written about. I knew my story would get back and that, though the point of the story was totally the opposite, people would take sides, find reasons to bolster their own points of view.

Then, in the middle of my shaky fear, I remembered my present graduate class, who had come to the reading. There was a whole row of them, the second row, so close to me. I could sense them through my downturned eyes, sitting with a kind of exactness and tension in their bodies, a readiness to receive. I felt an opening of my heart that happens, like everything of wonder always does, in a great wave of surprise—love coming in the middle of my fear. And that inspired me to feel my place in my work, my home. I read what I read because of those I love and who love me, and somehow, that is a part of my braveness.

Later, at dinner, the white woman sitting across from me told me how much she was moved by what I had read. She said that several people had remarked that the story made them cry. She talked about the part where the young black man and white woman had come together, how I wished that they could make love for all of us. She told me about her own blond daughter and the young black man whom she kissed and nuzzled in the backyard of the house that had opened onto the world. The relationship didn't last, and now she has a beautiful, dark grandchild, an eight-year-old who said to her last week, "Gramma, I wish I was white."

She told me how inadequate she felt when her grandchild had said that. What could she, a white woman, know of her grandchild's feelings? What could she say? She kept saying to her grandchild, "Why do you wish that? You're beautiful just as you are. You're beautiful." But she looked at me as if she was accusing herself of what mothers always accuse themselves of, of never getting it right.

I told her how important it was that her grandchild could speak to her, how, sometimes, I couldn't go to black women, how sometimes, no, not sometimes, but for many, many years, it was white women whom I poured my soul out to, white women I wasn't afraid would hate me or leave, it was white women, maybe precisely because they didn't have the same agony about race, who could still trust me, listen. Perhaps their generosity was based on naïveté, ignorance, on their own prejudice—wouldn't it be nice to have one black friend to take under one's wing? Whatever the motive, my need made myself available to it.

I have laid my soul bare to Mady, to Camille, to Marilyn, to Sarah, to Alicia, to Sharon, to Mary Jane, to Nancy, to so many strangers I have met at workshops, so many women like this woman sitting across the table, I have trusted as I didn't trust my family, my oldest friends. Maybe, somewhere in all that, love comes in a mysterious way, the way I came upon the faces of my students at the reading and suddenly knew I loved them.

What has happened between black people is sometimes so intense that a certain kind of sharing is too frightening. All those years when I had to say the most horrible thing—that, yes, I felt deep conflicts about who I am and who I want to be, that I often felt a shock of distance when I saw a person on the street with dark skin—it was white women I could say this to. I was afraid to say these things to the ones whose love and understanding I most longed for.

At that moment I thanked all the white women who have listened, who have befriended me, who have made a net over which I walked somewhat safely, the ones who were there for me to speak my self-doubt to, my justified angers, the ones willing to meet me more than halfway. I told her not to worry, that she was a great blessing to her granddaughter, whose longings and fears make clear the deepest shadows of the heart.

We shared pictures of our grandchildren, and she pointed out how ironic it is that I have a blond grandchild, a child who could be white, whereas she has a dark grandchild. A black woman sitting across from a white woman talking about race, while the most significant and dramatic thing is happening out of our conscious control—our genetic selves are changing, the white woman's self turning darker and the black woman's self turning whiter.

Perhaps "race" isn't something that locks us into separate groups. Perhaps it is a state that floats back and forth between us, equally solid and unreal, as if our body and soul were kept apart and, like a kind of Siamese twins, joined only by the thin cord of desire.

The Greatest Nature Essay *Ever*

Brian Doyle

. . . would begin with an image so startling and lovely and wondrous that you would stop riffling through the rest of the mail, take your jacket off, sit down at the table, adjust your spectacles, tell the dog to lie *down*, tell the kids to make their own sandwiches for heavenssake, that's why God gave you *hands*, and read straight through the piece, marveling that you had indeed seen or smelled or heard *exactly* that, but never quite articulated it that way, or seen or heard it articulated that way, and you think, *Man, this is why I read nature essays, to be startled and moved like that, wow.*

The next two paragraphs would smoothly and gently move you into a story, seemingly a small story, a light tale, easily accessed, something personal but not self-indulgent or self-absorbed on the writer's part, just sort of a cheerful nutty everyday story maybe starring an elk or a mink or a child, but then there would suddenly be a sharp sentence where the dagger enters your heart and the essay spins on a dime like a skater, and you are plunged into waaay deeper water, you didn't see it coming at *all*, and you actually shiver, your whole body shimmers, and much later, maybe when you are in bed with someone you love and you are trying to evade his or her icy feet, you think, *My God, stories do have roaring power, stories are the most crucial and necessary food, how come we never hardly say that out loud?*

The next three paragraphs then walk inexorably toward a line of explosive Conclusions on the horizon like inky alps. Probably the sentences get shorter, more staccato. Terser. Blunter. Shards of sentences. But there's no opinion or commentary, just one line fitting into another, each one making plain inarguable sense, a goat or even a senator could easily understand the sentences and their implications, and there's no shouting, no persuasion, no eloquent pirouetting, no pronouncements and accusations, no sermons or homilies, just calm clean clear statements one after another, fitting together like people holding hands.

Then an odd paragraph, this is a most unusual and peculiar essay, for right here where you would normally expect those alpine Conclusions, some Advice, some Stern Instructions & Directions, there's only the quiet murmur of the writer tiptoeing back to the story he or she was telling you in the second and third paragraphs. The story slips back into view gently, a little shy, holding its hat, nothing melodramatic, in fact it offers a few gnomic questions without answers, and then it gently slides away off the stage, it almost evanesces or dissolves, and it's only later, after you have read the essay three times with mounting amazement, that you see quite how the writer managed the stage-craft there, but that's the stuff of another essay for another time.

And finally the last paragraph. It turns out that the perfect nature essay is quite short, it's a lean taut thing, an arrow and not a cannon, and here at the end there's a flash of humor, and a hint or tone or subtext of sadness, a touch of rue, you can't quite put your finger on it but it's there, a dark thread in the fabric, and there's also a shot of espresso hope, hope against all odds and sense, but rivetingly there's no call to arms, no clarion brassy trumpet blast, no website to which you are directed, no hint that you, yes you, should be ashamed of how much water you use or the car you drive or the fact that you just turned the thermostat up to seventy, or that you actually have not voted in the past two elections despite what you told the kids and the goat. Nor is there a rimshot ending, a bang, a last twist of the dagger. Oddly, sweetly, the essay just ends with a feeling eerily like a warm hand brushed against your cheek, and you sit there, near tears, smiling, and then you stand up. Changed.

———

The Solace of Open Spaces

Gretel Ehrlich

It's May and I've just awakened from a nap, curled against sagebrush the way my dog taught me to sleep—sheltered from wind. A front is pulling the huge sky over me, and from the dark a hailstone has hit me on the head. I'm trailing a band of two thousand sheep across a stretch of Wyoming badlands, a fifty-mile trip that takes five days because sheep shade up in hot sun and won't budge until it's cool. Bunched together now, and excited into a run by the storm, they drift across dry land, tumbling into draws like water and surge out again onto the rugged, choppy plateaus that are the building blocks of this state.

The name Wyoming comes from an Indian word meaning "at the great plains," but the plains are really valleys, great arid valleys, sixteen hundred square miles, with the horizon bending up on all sides into mountain ranges. This gives the vastness a sheltering look.

Winter lasts six months here. Prevailing winds spill snowdrifts to the east, and new storms from the northwest replenish them. This white bulk is sometimes dizzying, even nauseating, to look at. At twenty, thirty, and forty degrees below zero, not only does your car not work, but neither do your mind and body. The landscape hardens into a dungeon of space. During the winter, while I was riding to find a new calf, my jeans froze to the saddle, and in the silence that such cold creates I felt like the first person on earth, or the last.

Today the sun is out—only a few clouds billowing. In the east, where the sheep have started off without me, the benchland tilts up in a series of eroded red-earthed mesas, planed flat on top by a million years of water; behind them, a bold line of muscular scarps rears up ten thousand feet to become the Big Horn Mountains. A tidal pattern is engraved into the ground, as if left by the sea that once covered this state. Canyons curve down like galaxies to meet the oncoming rush of flat land.

To live and work in this kind of open country, with its hundred-mile views, is to lose the distinction between background and foreground. When I asked an older ranch hand to describe Wyoming's openness, he said, "It's all a bunch of nothing—wind and rattlesnakes—and so much of it you can't tell where you're going or where you've been and it don't make much difference." John, a sheepman I know, is tall and handsome and has an explosive temperament. He has a perfect intuition about people and sheep. They call him "Highpockets," because he's so long-legged; his graceful stride matches the distances he has to cover. He says, "Open space hasn't affected me at all. It's all the people moving in on it." The huge ranch he was born on takes up much of one county and spreads into another state; to put 100,000 miles on his pickup in three years and never leave home is not unusual. A friend of mine has an aunt who ranched on Powder River and didn't go off her place for eleven years. When her husband died, she quickly moved to town, bought a car, and drove around the States to see what she'd been missing.

Most people tell me they've simply driven through Wyoming, as if there were nothing to stop for. Or else they've skied in Jackson Hole, a place Wyomingites acknowledge uncomfortably because its green beauty and chic affluence are mismatched with the rest of the state. Most of Wyoming has a "lean-to" look. Instead of big, roomy barns and Victorian houses, there are dugouts, low sheds, log cabins, sheep camps, and fence lines that look like driftwood blown haphazardly into place. People here still feel pride because they live in such a harsh place, part of the glamorous cowboy past, and they are determined not to be the victims of a mining-dominated future.

Most characteristic of the state's landscape is what a developer euphemistically describes as "indigenous growth right up to your front door"—a reference to waterless stands of salt sage, snakes, jack rabbits, deerflies, red dust, a brief respite of wildflowers, dry washes, and no trees. In the Great Plains the vistas look like music, like Kyries of grass, but Wyoming seems to be the doing of a mad architect—tumbled and twisted, ribboned with faded, deathbed colors, thrust up and pulled down as if the place had been startled out of a deep sleep and thrown into a pure light.

I came here four years ago. I had not planned to stay, but I couldn't make myself leave. John, the sheepman, put me to work immediately. It was spring, and shearing time. For fourteen days of fourteen hours each, we moved thousands of sheep through sorting corrals to be sheared, branded, and deloused. I suspect that my original motive for coming here was to "lose myself" in new and unpopulated territory. Instead of producing the numbness I thought I wanted, life on the sheep ranch woke me up. The vitality of the people I was working with flushed out what had become a hallucinatory rawness inside me. I threw away my clothes and bought new ones; I cut my hair. The arid country was a clean slate. Its absolute indifference steadied me.

Sagebrush covers 58,000 square miles of Wyoming. The biggest city has a population of fifty thousand, and there are only five settlements that could be called cities in the whole state. The rest are towns, scattered across the expanse with as much as sixty miles between them, their populations two thousand, fifty, or ten. They are fugitive-looking, perched on a barren, windblown bench, tagged onto a river or a railroad, or laid out straight in a farming valley with implement stores and a block-long Mormon church. In the eastern part of the state, which slides down into the Great Plains, the new mining settlements are boomtowns, trailer cities, metal knots on flat land.

Despite the desolate look, there's a coziness to living in this state. There are so few people (only 470,000) that ranchers who buy and sell cattle know one another statewide; the kids who choose to go to college usually go to the state's one university, in Laramie; hired hands work their way around Wyoming in a lifetime of hirings and firings. And despite the physical separation, people stay in touch, often driving two or three hours to another ranch for dinner.

Seventy-five years ago, when travel was by buckboard or horseback, cowboys who were temporarily out of work rode the grub line—drifting from ranch to ranch, mending fences or milking cows, and receiving in exchange a bed and meals. Gossip and messages traveled this slow circuit with them, creating an intimacy between ranchers who were three and four weeks' ride apart. One old-time couple I know, whose turn-of-the-century homestead was used by an outlaw gang as a relay station for stolen horses, recall that if you were traveling, desperado or not, any lighted ranch house was a welcome sign. Even now, for someone who lives in a remote spot, arriving at a ranch or coming to town for supplies is cause for celebration. To emerge from isolation can be disorienting. Everything looks bright, new, vivid. After I had been herding sheep for only three days, the sound of the camp tender's pickup flustered me. Longing for human company, I felt a foolish grin take over my face; yet I had to resist an urgent temptation to run and hide.

Things happen suddenly in Wyoming, the change of seasons and weather; for people, the violent swings in and out of isolation. But good-naturedness is concomitant with severity. Friendliness is a tradition. Strangers passing on the road wave hello. A common sight is two pickups stopped side by side far out on a range, on a dirt track winding through the sage. The drivers will share a cigarette, uncap their thermos bottles, and pass a battered cup, steaming with coffee, between windows. These meetings summon up the details of several generations, because, in Wyoming, private histories are largely public knowledge.

Because ranch work is a physical and, these days, economic strain, being "at home on the range" is a matter of vigor, self-reliance, and common sense. A person's life is not a series of dramatic events for which he or she is applauded or exiled but a slow accumulation of days, seasons, years, fleshed out by the generational weight of one's family and anchored by a land-bound sense of place.

In most parts of Wyoming, the human population is visibly outnumbered by the animal. Not far from my town of fifty, I rode into a narrow valley and startled a herd of two hundred elk. Eagles look like small people as they eat car-killed deer by the road. Antelope, moving in small, graceful bands, travel at sixty miles an hour, their mouths open as if drinking in the space.

The solitude in which westerners live makes them quiet. They telegraph thoughts and feelings by the way they tilt their heads and listen; pulling their Stetsons into a steep dive over their eyes, or pigeon-toeing one boot over the other, they lean against a fence with a fat wedge of Copenhagen beneath their lower lips and take in the whole scene. These detached looks of quiet amusement are sometimes cynical, but they can also come from a dry-eyed humility as lucid as the air is clear.

Conversation goes on in what sounds like a private code; a few phrases imply a complex of meanings. Asking directions, you get a curious list of details. While trailing sheep I was told to "ride up to that kinda upturned rock, follow the pink wash, turn left at the dump, and then you'll see the water hole." One friend told his wife on roundup to "turn at the salt lick and the dead cow," which turned out to be a scattering of bones and no salt lick at all.

Sentence structure is shortened to the skin and bones of a thought. Descriptive words are dropped, even verbs; a cowboy looking over a corral full of horses will say to a wrangler, "Which one needs rode?" People hold back their thoughts in what seems to be a dumbfounded silence, then erupt with an excoriating perceptive remark. Language, so compressed, becomes metaphorical. A rancher ended a relationship with one remark: "You're a bad check," meaning bouncing in and out was intolerable, and even coming back would be no good.

What's behind this laconic style is shyness. There is no vocabulary for the subject of feelings. It's not a hangdog shyness, or anything coy—always there's a robust spirit in evidence behind the restraint, as if the earth-dredging wind that pulls across Wyoming had carried its people's voices away but everything else in them had shouldered confidently into the breeze.

I've spent hours riding to sheep camp at dawn in a pickup when nothing was said; eaten meals in the cookhouse when the only words spoken were a mumbled "Thank you, ma'am" at the end of dinner. The silence is profound. Instead of talking, we seem to share one eye. Keenly observed, the world is transformed. The landscape is engorged with detail, every movement on it chillingly sharp. The air between people is charged. Days unfold, bathed in their own music. Nights become hallucinatory; dreams, prescient.

Spring weather is capricious and mean. It snows, then blisters with heat. There have been tornadoes. They lay their elephant trunks out in the sage until they find houses, then slurp everything up and leave. I've noticed that melting snowbanks hiss and rot, viperous, then drip into calm pools where ducklings hatch and livestock, being trailed to summer range, drink. With the ice cover gone, rivers churn a milkshake brown, taking culverts and small bridges with them. Water in such an arid place (the average annual rainfall where I live is less than eight inches) is like blood. It festoons drab land with green veins; a line of cottonwoods following a stream; a strip of alfalfa; and, on ditch banks, wild asparagus growing.

I've moved to a small cattle ranch owned by friends. It's at the foot of the Big Horn Mountains. A few weeks ago, I helped them deliver a calf who was stuck halfway out of his mother's body. By the time he was freed, we could see a heartbeat, but he was straining against a swollen tongue for air. Mary and I held him upside down by his back feet, while Stan on his hands and knees in the blood, gave the calf mouth-to-mouth resuscitation. I have a vague memory of being pneumonia-choked as a child, my mother giving me her air, which may account for my romance with this windswept state.

If anything is endemic to Wyoming, it is wind. This big room of space is swept out daily, leaving a bone yard of fossils, agates, and carcasses in every stage of decay. Though it was water that initially shaped the state, wind is the meticulous gardener, raising dust and pruning the sage.

I try to imagine a world in which I could ride my horse across uncharted land. There is no wilderness left; wildness, yes, but true wilderness has been gone on this continent since the time of Lewis and Clark's overland journey.

Two hundred years ago, the Crow, Shoshone, Arapaho, Cheyenne, and Sioux roamed the intermountain West, orchestrating their movements according to hunger, season, and warfare. Once they acquired horses, they traversed the spines of all the big Wyoming ranges—the Absarokas, the Wind Rivers, the Tetons, the Big Horns—and wintered on the unprotected plains that fan out from them. Space was life. The world was their home.

What was life-giving to Native Americans was often nightmarish to sodbusters who had arrived encumbered with families and ethnic pasts to be transplanted in nearly uninhabitable land. The great distances, the shortage of water and trees, and the loneliness created unexpected hardships for them. In her book *O Pioneers!*, Willa Cather gives a settler's version of the bleak landscape:

> The little town behind them had vanished as if it had never been, had fallen behind the swell of the prairie, and the stern frozen country received them into its bosom. The homesteads were few and far apart; here and there a windmill gaunt against the sky, a sod house crouching in a hollow.

The emptiness of the West was for others a geography of possibility. Men and women who amassed great chunks of land and struggled to preserve unfenced empires were, despite their self-serving motives, unwitting geographers. They understood the lay of the land. But by the 1850s the Oregon and Mormon trails sported bumper-to-bumper traffic. Wealthy landowners, many of them aristocratic absentee landlords, known as remittance men because they were paid to come West and get out of their families' hair, overstocked the range with more than a million head of cattle. By 1885 the feed and water were desperately short, and the winter of 1886 laid out the gaunt bodies of dead animals so closely together that when the thaw came, one rancher from Kaycee claimed to have walked on cowhide all the way to Crazy Woman Creek, twenty miles away.

Territorial Wyoming was a boy's world. The land was generous with everything but water. At first there was room enough, food enough, for everyone. And, as with all beginnings, an expansive mood set in. The young cowboys, drifters, shopkeepers, schoolteachers, were heroic, lawless, generous, rowdy, and tenacious. The individualism and optimism generated during those times have endured.

John Tisdale rode north with the trail herds from Texas. He was a college-educated man with enough money to buy a small outfit near the Powder River. While driving home from the town of Buffalo with a buckboard full of Christmas toys for his family and a winter's supply of food, he was shot in the back by an agent of the cattle barons who resented the encroachment of small-time stockmen like him. The wealthy cattlemen tried to control all the public grazing land by restricting membership in the Wyoming Stock Growers Association, as if it were a country club. They ostracized from roundups and brandings cowboys and ranchers who were not members, then denounced them as rustlers. Tisdale's death, the second such cold-blooded murder, kicked off the Johnson County cattle war, which was no simple good-guy-bad-guy shoot-out but a complicated class struggle between landed gentry and less affluent settlers—a shocking reminder that the West was not an egalitarian sanctuary after all.

Fencing ultimately enforced boundaries, but barbed wire abrogated space. It was stretched across the beautiful valleys, into the mountains, over desert badlands, through buffalo grass. The "anything is possible" fever—the lure of any new place—was constricted. The integrity of the land as a geographical body, and the freedom to ride anywhere on it, were lost.

I punched cows with a young man named Martin, who is the great-grandson of John Tisdale. His inheritance is not the open land that Tisdale knew and prematurely lost but a rage against restraint.

Wyoming tips down as you head northeast; the highest ground—the Laramie Plains—is on the Colorado border. Up where I live, the Big Horn River leaks into difficult, arid terrain. In the basin where it's dammed, sandhill cranes gather and, with delicate legwork, slice through the stilled water. I was driving by with a rancher one morning when he commented that cranes are "old-fashioned."

When I asked why, he said, "Because they mate for life." Then he looked at me with a twinkle in his eyes, as if to say he really did believe in such things but also understood why we break our own rules.

In all this open space, values crystalize quickly. People are strong on scruples but tenderhearted about quirky behavior. A friend and I found one ranch hand, who's "not quite right in the head," sitting in front of the badly decayed carcass of a cow, shaking his finger and saying, "Now, I don't want you to do this ever again!" When I asked what was wrong with him, I was told, "He's goofier than hell, just like the rest of us." Perhaps because the West is historically new, conventional morality is still felt to be less important than rock-bottom truths. Though there's always a lot of teasing and sparring, people are blunt with one another, sometimes even cruel, believing honesty is stronger medicine than sympathy, which may console but often conceals.

The formality that goes hand in hand with the rowdiness is known as the Western Code. It's a list of practical do's and don'ts, faithfully observed. A friend, Cliff, who runs a trapline in the winter, cut off half his foot while chopping a hole in the ice. Alone, he dragged himself to his pickup and headed for town, stopping to open the ranch gate as he left, and getting out to close it again, thus losing, in his observance of rules, precious time and blood. Later, he commented, "How would it look, them having to come to the hospital to tell me their cows had gotten out?"

Accustomed to emergencies, my friends doctor each other from the vet's bag with relish. When one old-timer suffered a heart attack in hunting camp, his partner quickly stirred up a brew of red horse liniment and hot water and made the half-conscious victim drink it, then tied him onto a horse and led him twenty miles to town. He regained consciousness and lived.

The roominess of the state has affected political attitudes as well. Ranchers keep up with world politics and the convulsions of the economy but are basically isolationists. Being used to running their own small empires of land and livestock, they're suspicious of big government. It's a "don't fence me in" holdover from a century ago. They still want the elbow room their grandfathers had, so they're strongly conservative, but with a populist twist.

Summer is the season when we get our "cowboy tans"—on the lower parts of our faces and on three fourths of our arms. Excessive heat, in the nineties and higher, sends us outside with the mosquitoes. In winter we're tucked inside our houses, and the white wasteland outside appears to be expanding, but in summer all the greenery abridges space. Summer is a go-ahead season. Every living thing is off the block and in the race: battalions of bugs in flight and biting; bats swinging around my log cabin as if the bases were loaded and someone had hit a home run. Some of summer's highspeed growth is ominous: larkspur, death camas, and green greasewood can kill sheep—an ironic idea, dying in this desert from eating what is too verdant. With sixteen hours of daylight, farmers and ranchers irrigate feverishly. There are first, second, and third cuttings of hay, some crews averaging only four hours of sleep a night for weeks. And, like the cowboys who in summer ride the night rodeo circuit, nighthawks make daredevil dives at dusk with an eerie whirring sound like a plane going down on the shimmering horizon.

In the town where I live, they've had to board up the dance-hall windows because there have been so many fights. There's so little to do except work that people wind up in a state of idle agitation that becomes fatalistic, as if there were nothing to be done about all this untapped energy. So the dark side to the grandeur of these spaces is the small-mindedness that seals people in. Men become hermits; women go mad. Cabin fever explodes into suicides, or into grudges and lifelong family feuds. Two sisters in my area inherited a ranch but found they couldn't get along. They fenced the place in half. When one's cows got out and mixed with the other's, the women went at each other with shovels. They ended up in the same hospital room but never spoke a word to each other for the rest of their lives.

After the brief lushness of summer, the sun moves south. The range grass is brown. Livestock is trailed back down from the mountains. Water holes begin to frost over at night. Last fall Martin asked me to accompany him on a pack trip. With five horses, we followed a river into the mountains behind the tiny Wyoming town of Meeteetse. Groves of aspen, red and orange, gave off a light that made us look toasted. Our hunting camp was so high that clouds skidded across our foreheads, then slowed to sail out across the warm valleys. Except for a bull moose who wandered into our camp and mistook our black gelding for a rival, we shot at nothing.

One of our evening entertainments was to watch the night sky. My dog, a dingo bred to herd sheep, also came on the trip. He is so used to the silence and empty skies that when an airplane flies over he always looks up and eyes the distant intruder quizzically. The sky, lately, seems to be much more crowded than it used to be. Satellites make their silent passes in the dark with great regularity. We counted eighteen in one hour's viewing. How odd to think that while they circumnavigated the planet, Martin and I had moved only six miles into our local wilderness and had seen no other human for the two weeks we stayed there.

At night, by moonlight, the land is whittled to slivers—a ridge, a river, a strip of grassland stretching to the mountains, then the huge sky. One morning a full moon was setting in the west just as the sun was rising. I felt precariously balanced between the two as I loped across a meadow. For a moment, I could believe that the stars, which were still visible, work like cooper's bands, holding together everything above Wyoming.

Space has a spiritual equivalent and can heal what is divided and burdensome in us. My grandchildren will probably use space shuttles for a honeymoon trip or to recover from heart attacks, but closer to home we might also learn how to carry space inside ourselves in the effortless way we carry our skins. Space represents sanity, not a life purified, dull, or "spaced out" but one that might accommodate intelligently any idea or situation.

From the clayey soil of northern Wyoming is mined bentonite, which is used as a filler in candy, gum, and lipstick. We Americans are great on fillers, as if what we have, what we are, is not enough. We have a cultural tendency toward denial, but, being affluent, we strangle ourselves with what we can buy. We have only to look at the houses we build to see how we build *against* space, the way we drink against pain and loneliness. We fill up space as if it were a pie shell, with things whose opacity further obstructs our ability to see what is already there.

Country on the Brink

Jane Fishman

A week after returning from Costa Rica I'm still trying to figure out a clever, pithy answer to: "Well, how was it? How was the trip?" You have to be quick when you get that question. There's a lot competing for our attention. Because while you've been lucky enough to get out of the country, fingering new money, trying to figure out which way is east or how to say *bathroom* in Spanish, other people have been busy, too. Life just doesn't stop because you left town. I go for brevity.

"Fantastic. Beautiful. No Army! Same size as West Virginia. Monkeys with white faces. Crocodiles, lounging around with their mouths open. Real scarabs in the cloud forest—gold and silver—that look like fake jewels only they're alive. They're bugs."

I try to talk fast. But I'm losing them. I can tell. They check their watches or are glancing down for a text message. Plus, it's not as if everyone doesn't travel these days. Especially to Costa Rica. Costa Rica is the new "it" place. On a recent plane ride I counted two families, both with young children, who were just returning.

Can this be good for a country?

Just last year one man I know, very successful in Savannah real estate, moved to Costa Rica with his partner. A few days ago I heard of another Savannah entrepreneur who sold her house, joined a travel agency and moved to San José, the capital.

Part of me wished to go somewhere more exotic. But when a trip to Costa Rica was offered through my graduate program, I said, "Sign me up." Then the day came. On May 1, my 63rd birthday, I would join 12 other students, most just a third of my age, on a 16-day excursion to a place that half the world—or so it seemed—had already discovered. I was ready for the worst. Americans—and condos—at every turn. A bunch of whiney slackers. Group think.

"Just don't sound too much like an English teacher," a 17-year-old daughter of friends emailed me. "Don't start talking about the old days."

"You mean I shouldn't talk too much about the backpacking trips we took to Europe in the '60s after 18-hour trips aboard the questionable Flying Tigers airlines when there was no cell phone, no email connection, no money, no phone calling cards, no ATM, no ice, no advance reservations? When all we traveled with were our traveler's checks and a Eurail pass?"

"Yep. That's what I'm talking about," she said.

A lot to remember, I thought, jamming Glucosamine, calcium, Vitamin C, and Advil into my pack. But while those battles against age may be new, other things aren't. I still don't know Spanish or the metric system. I still haven't taken the time to familiarize myself with the country's currency ahead of time, which happens to be *colones*, named after the peripatetic Christopher Columbus.

So an hour after we arrive in San José and I've scooted off to the Super Mercado for toothpaste (mine was confiscated at the airport), there I stand, across from the clerk and the cash register, fumbling with these strange bills, trying not to look at them as if they were funny money, looking all the while like the quintessential ugly American.

Make that North American. Our Costa Rica liaison, Priscilla, made that very clear. Costa Ricans, or Ticos, are also Americans. So are people from Guatemala, Ecuador, and Brazil. We, from the States, are North Americans. Even before Homeland Security, journeying alone or with a group—whether to a popularized, trendy Costa Rica, shaped like a squished Italy, or to a place less known—is not easy. It's not supposed to be. You want easy, stay home.

Because even though every day feels like Saturday when you travel, there is a lot of getting on and getting off of buses. There are bug bites, diesel fumes, bumpy roads, lumpy pillows, skinny towels, polyester sheets. There are sore shoulders from carrying bags, drivers who pay no attention to stop signs, guides who don't shut up. And what is it with people who speak Spanish? They seem to talk forever. What do they talk about?

As if that's not bad enough, in Central America or anywhere so close to the equator, the day loses its light way too early. Six-thirty, if you can believe it. No lingering summer days. Not much chance to sleep either if the early morning light, which shows up around 3:30, bothers you. Or the cheerful, jaunty tones of the ubiquitous clay-colored robin, Costa Rica's national bird.

There are mildewed rooms, rooms with no hot water, rooms with a drizzle for a shower. There is a shady thing with electricity. Something to do with rain. One bank we visited, faced with diminished electrical power, had to choose between computers and air conditioning. They chose computers.

Yes, there are computers. But where is the ampersand? What about the dash? And why can't we use it until 7 a.m.? And what's with this dial-up? Come on! We're in a hurry. Except that's the deal with travel. That's the drill with traveling to a foreign country, traveling in a group, no matter what age. You can't be in a hurry.

Which is the beauty of the occasional guided excursion. Silently, I protested all the scheduled activities of our pending trip. Much better to wander through the barrio, to pick up, as if by osmosis, the essence, the pith, the marrow of a country. My one night off by myself I found a Chinese restaurant in

San José. Quite comfortably I sat eating my egg roll next to a Chinese couple—surely the owners—playing backgammon, making those backgammon noises. Two tables over three men, glued to the tube, watched the soccer game du jour. No one paid any attention to a couple, glued to each other, or to me.

But this was before I met our Costa Rican guides, each one more engaging, knowledgeable, amiable, charming, and good-looking than the last, trained guides who were to lead us through rain forests, cloud forests, secondary forests, tropical forests, creeks, rivers, highways, museums, small towns, volcano sites. Armed with well-worn bird books stuck in their back pockets (and an encyclopedic knowledge of the book's interior—"an orange-bellied trogan, page 45, plate 13") and combination binoculars/tripods slung over their shoulders, they led us into the woods to teach us the original meaning of shock and awe.

On one night hike in Monteverde we saw the following: a set of raccoon eyes high up in a tree; a dangling puddle of froth where a spittle bug laid its eggs; then an improbably motionless hummingbird, asleep. Hours earlier, the same hummingbird was flying backwards and upside down, flapping its wings some 15-to-80 times a second. We also saw an orange-kneed tarantula, which had crawled to the front of a hole in a limestone wall, formerly a bird's nest; a wolf spider; an inchworm; a golden scarab beetle; a walking stick.

The guide was the youngest son of one of Monteverde's original settlers. They arrived with a group of Quaker families from Fairhope, Alabama, who did not believe in war. In the late 1940s, this intrepid, improbable collection of Southern peaceniks relocated to Costa Rica, which had also decided to ditch its Army.

During another excursion, this time a morning hike in Tortuguero, where we stayed at a rustic jungle lodge, we took a boat across the Pacuare River and started walking. Twenty minutes into the hike we spotted our first howler monkeys, big bruisers, aptly named, high in the trees. I had heard them early that morning. I mistook their barking whoops for a pack of dogs. Our guide, quick to notice any movement in the trees or the slightest sound, stopped abruptly, put out his hand for quiet and emitted an otherworldly grunt. Without any warning, his sound, primitive, singular, deep-throated, produced a response from the monkeys, who answered in unison. I felt the woods rumbling. On other hikes, the guide, sensitive to the slightest of vocalizations, would repeat the sound of a bird by placing his fingers to his lips or making smooching sounds with his mouth. Call and response. Call and response.

"Why is it the smallest birds make the biggest sounds?" someone remarked.

The guides, who could probably speak to plants if asked, were tireless and almost childlike in their enthusiasm over hearing a particular bird or seeing a particular bug. Any possibility thrilled them. One, Guillermo Canessa, a native Tico who spent several years at the University of Michigan's forestry school, read Kurt Vonnegut to improve his English ("I had to have the dictionary very close"), and reads John Grisham for fun, made numerous forays from the bus to try to find red cellophane to put over his flashlight for our midnight trip to watch the leatherback turtle, the largest in the world, lay her eggs. Even the stops were instructive. In Siquirres, where he found the cellophane, we watched kids play a different level of soccer and we learned about a group of Chinese-Jamaicans. They came to work for the Banana Fruit Company.

"But because they were so dark-skinned (in a country that really favored light-skinned people with ties to Spain) they couldn't leave town," Guillermo said.

That was not the first time I wondered about the brown-skinned people and when and where they will be in charge of their own country.

The nighttime trek to find the leatherback turtle was no guaranteed excursion. It's not like because you pay your money you get to see turtles. It was work getting there, too. After a short boat ride, we walked along the lumpy masses of the Caribbean Sea's black sand until we got the signal from the experienced guide. Big mama, some six-feet long and three-feet wide with seven deep ridges down her back, tears in her eyes, and the look of some ancient, mythical, primordial creature, had been spotted, burrowed in the sand, doing the same thing her ancestors have done for millions of years. She appeared oblivious to the crowd of paparazzi surrounding her and the volunteer lying on his belly, removing each of her 103 golf ball-size eggs the second she deposited them. Quickly, efficiently, he dispatched them to another volunteer who stacked them in an ordinary blue-and-white plastic shopping bag.

"Go ahead," said a male volunteer with a French accent and a ponytail. "Touch them."

So I did. They felt like marshmallows.

There we remained, squatting, standing, sitting under the Southern Cross, a constellation we can't see in North America. I wasn't prepared for the spray of sand from her flippers. She was making snow angels in the sand. She was trying to cover her eggs.

But they weren't there. The eggs were headed for the incubation station, safe from the friggin' frigates, the marauding profiteers. I felt bad. We had deceived her. It was for the best, right? Even if no one had taken her eggs she would have done the same thing. She would rest, then head back to the sea to get ready for two or three more birthings in the next few months. Mama turtles never see their offspring. Even on Mother's Day.

But at least they won't be sold for meat. At least she gave birth. Many never make it that far. They get tangled up in nets from shrimp boats. They can't find a wide enough beach. They get confused by the lights from new condos and can't find the beach. They die after mistaking plastic bags for jellyfish, their favorite food. After that I returned to the lodge and had a drink. Imperial Beer is cheap in Costa Rica, 700 *colones*, a dollar something. Smokes, less than two dollars a pack.

I was tired. I should have gone to bed. Yet I felt conflicted about standing around the mama turtle and not doing anything. This wasn't supposed to be a moral issue. I felt the same way when I watched dozens of varieties of hummingbirds flock toward the red plastic containers filled with sugar water, ignoring the nearby lush heliconias, cannas, passion flowers, and bromeliads. What are we doing to this country?

Earlier we learned that when Columbus did not find enough minerals, jade or gold to satisfy his colonizing and greedy king and queen in Spain, he got his marching orders to move on to places like Guatemala, which was fine with the Ticos.

But can they duck the limelight a third time? Can this tiny, Central American country, an isthmus bordered on both sides by water, a connector between two larger land masses, retain its natural beauty in the face of foreign money, big investors, greedy developers? It's true there are still people like the crunchy granola turtle volunteers who come every year to help. But is that enough?

Between my two sets of Savannah friends who made their money in real estate and business and hightailed to Costa Rica for more of the same, the millions of tourists who visit and/or buy second (or third) homes each year, and the eagerness of locals to sell property for big bucks, the country is poised to kill off its main resource—the forests. Extinction, we heard more than once, is forever.

I wondered if this acquiescence is a national trait. Are they pushovers or just sweet people? "We will make a decision when the clouds disappear," they say.

But maybe all this commercialism is a wake-up call. There does seem to be a new attention to eco-tourism, a new appreciation by natives of their country's natural beauty. There is an impressive and rigorous system of guide preparation—some three years and four months in school. At least one guide spoke of a heightened awareness of fair trade, a return to organic farming, and stricter enforcement of land use.

I want to think positively about Costa Rica's future. With all those orchids—more than anywhere in the world (and we can only get to something like five percent because most are too high in the tree canopy to reach); all those bromeliads, iguanas, birds, and varieties of ginger lilies, many of which are only in Costa Rica—I don't want to feel that by visiting or even writing about it, I'm contributing to its demise.

I'd like to think I could return to Costa Rica and still see the old man by the banana processing plant selling coconut juice, dangling his pet rhino beetle at the end of a stick. That the algae in Manuel Antonio will stop spreading. That the monkey population will not keep shrinking (no trees, no monkeys). That something of the coral reef will remain. That towns will still have electricians ("We just lost our last one," said Dulce Wilson, coordinator of the Monteverde Cloud Forest Biological Preserve. "Now he thinks he's a guide. Everyone's trying to cash in.")

Clearly, the balance is being challenged. It is shifting.

In the past, a Costa Rica tourist fit the adventurous profile, someone hauling a backpack into the rain forest, looking for simple accommodations. These days the country's visitors require more creature comforts. "It's like they want to bring their own home to Costa Rica," one of the guides said.

Luxury condos, à la Cancun, Mexico, are popping up everywhere. Developers, local and foreign, lean on banks for loans and get them. Then they pay off another person, bend a few laws regulating the approved number of hotel units and put up another complex. Gated communities and package deals, where the front desk person clamps a plastic, colored bracelet on your wrist when you check in, are not uncommon. Ours was green. If we took it off the guards wouldn't let us back to our rooms, the waiters wouldn't seat us. We wouldn't get the Wednesday night buffet dinner.

So there I sat in the dining room, with my own compatriots in green, next to another party of North Americans in white, listening to elevator music or muzak, soft string renditions of "Three Coins in the Fountain" or, even more ironic, "The Girl from Ipanema." *Qué Va!* I said to myself. No way!

One morning during our comfortable stay in Monteverde I woke up and thought, "Hey, I'm in Snowmass, outside of Aspen, right?" It had that look—cute little chalets, a vast expanse of manicured grass, self-conscious rows of hibiscus and croton, carefully placed ginger lilies, gigantic in the wild. Just like Florida, I thought. Rip out all the original trees, build condos, level plants for parking lots, haul in new palms.

I'm remembering this when people ask about Costa Rica. But I don't say too much. I don't complain. Instead, I gush about the bird of paradise, the poinciana tree, the red hot poker, the fishtail palms where the hummingbirds nest, the agapanthus, the bottle brush tree, the beautiful jacaranda tree that people want to eradicate.

But I'm withholding. I say Costa Rica has a literacy rate of ninety percent. I don't say I didn't see any libraries, any bookstores, or hardly anyone with a book in their hand. I leave out how few written records archeologists have found. I say there's no Army, but I don't tell them our hotel in San José was named after the owner's great-uncle who was a general, that the red in the flag stands for blood.

Instead, I talk about the fair-trade coffee plantation we visited, a manageable farm tucked into the hills at a high elevation near Monteverde. The farm, part of a regional coffee cooperative, is operated by one man, one committed, dedicated, impassioned farmer. This man, introduced as Victor, took us through the life of a coffee bean, which takes nine months to ripen. He started from the beginning. With pride and care, he bent down to show us his germination bed—a row of three-inch seedlings planted in small plastic *copitas* (small cups) in sand from the river ("fewer fungi")—that won't produce beans for three to five years.

I was sorry we missed the coffee plants' flowering season, the month before. The blooms, I am told, resemble in smell and color the jasmine blossom. The beans turn red in November.

In more than four decades, I've probably bought and ground 14,000 pounds of coffee beans—which are really the seeds or "coffee berries" of the plant—and consumed 14,000 cups. Coffee is my habit of choice. My other habit is gardening. I've probably started twenty gardens. I study plants. I draw them, transplant them, trade them, write about them, read about them, observe them. I grow banana trees. I grow sugar cane.

But I have never seen a coffee plant up close and personal. I never knew how beautiful and shiny the leaves could be, how the beans are handpicked. I did not know how much the minerals from the frequent volcanic eruptions helped the soil. I didn't know that farmers like Victor plant orchids to attract bees, that bees (followed by hummingbirds) germinate plants, that the proximity of mangoes, papayas, and avocados help to distract monkey interest in coffee plants. When Victor's grandfather started the plantation, the whole family participated. Coffee kept the family together. Children learned to read by reciting, "Coffee is good for you. I drink coffee everyday."

But people are human. When Costa Ricans started selling land to foreigners for big bucks, farmers began wondering if it might be time for them to cash in, too. They began adding chemicals to the land to boost production. They sold off acreage to cattle farmers, which meant more coffee plants had to be jammed into a smaller space. In the process, they lost their shade; they encouraged erosion, they introduced new insects.

But then, some at least started changing their ways. They saw what was happening to the soil. They saw what the world would pay for fair-trade, organic coffee. And they went back to their original methods, even knowing it will take 10 years to reverse the quality of the soil and almost as long to gain proper organic certification.

When Victor was showing us his coffee farm and telling us—through a translator—how his grandfather used the leaves of the plantain trees to stuff cots and as an occasional substitute for toilet paper, I looked over to Victor's daughter. Was she embarrassed? Did she think he was cool or not? I couldn't tell.

Now they use California red worms to reduce the amount of coffee pulp, formerly the No. 1 river water polluter in the area. Members of the cooperative stack the pulp, add the worms and water for three months. When the old pulp is ready to be used for fertilizer, the farmers haul in a new batch of pulp and in twenty to thirty hours the worms have found the new stash.

"We never find worms in fertilizer," our guide told us.

Will she think that's cool, too? Or a waste of time? Will she pay a dollar to get her picture taken next to a farmer and his oxcart? Will she know that farmers with oxcarts used different wind chimes so people would know by their sound who was coming?

What about our guide Guillermo's nostalgia for the days when locals in Alajuela, the country's second largest city, would head to the town square to sit under the mango tree, to gossip and do business. Or when people in San Jose would walk along Central Avenue, now deserted, to shop and gossip with friends.

Would that be cool?

Still, coffee is important. To a lesser degree, so is tobacco. As Costa Rica's first crop, it was exchanged for taxes with Spain. Today, it's starting to make a comeback now that more Cuban expatriates are moving to Central America.

Unlike the banana and pineapple industries—considered imperialist crops since eighty percent are owned by foreigners—the coffee industry, historically a product of pride for Costa Rica, is locally owned. The first plants came from Cuba as ornamentals. The British, who brought bricks to Costa Rica, used the beans, the only weight they could find, as ballast for their return trip home.

Nicaragua, a country to the north, is also an issue for the Ticos. Nicaraguans are not quite so steeped in democracy or peace. They have a very active army. And they're sneaking across the border to do jobs Costa Ricans no longer want to do, like hauling banana out of the fields, then standing for long hours in front of water troughs preparing them for market. They're our Mexicans, I think. Panamanians, we're told, are too comfortable, too rich to leave their country. Guatemalans are arrogant. They think they're better than anyone else.

When people ask about Costa Rica I mention cashew trees, how the nut grows on the end of a fruit. I talk about traveling with the under-30 crowd. How they walk in pairs and wear their clothes tight and take a lot of showers. How they talk about younger siblings, stepsisters and brothers. How much money they owe in student loans.

The worst part is when I try to compare our jungle lodge in Pacuare with "The African Queen," Katherine Hepburn and Humphrey Bogart ("Huh? Who?"), when I say our guide Priscilla reminds me of the movie, "The Adventures of Priscilla, Queen of the Desert," with a campy Terence Stamp and his Veronica Lake hairdo. ("Terence Stamp? Who's Veronica Lake?").

The best part is that we are all visiting a place like Costa Rica, listening for birds, watching leaf cutter ants carry leaves three times their own weight, learning about fair-trade coffee, being around people who don't understand English no matter how loudly or clearly we speak, seeing Quiznos, KFC, and Tommy Hilfiger.

No matter our age, as tourists we are figuring and refiguring the relationship between beauty and exploitation, greed and development, some for the first time, some for the umpteenth. Some of us remember traveling when we had to eat local food, when there were no McDonalds or TCBY or Mail Boxes, Etc. For all of us, finite has taken on a new meaning. But where will it go from here? What will we do with what we learn?

"Hey, look at this," one of the younger set said at the Super Mercado, the night before we headed back to Pittsburgh. She was standing in the potted plant section, making a connection between what she had seen in the rain forest, nudged between two limbs of an ancient ficus tree, and what she had spotted in the world of commerce, one aisle over from produce, not too far from the packaged and precooked pork.

"An orchid for sale. Two thousand *colones*. Four dollars. Not bad."

"For whom?" I asked. "Not bad for whom?"

Sustenance

Melanie Dylan Fox

One day past the autumnal equinox. The sky this morning is the color of dirty chalk. It reaches past my living room, past the turn-of-the-century farmhouses of this small town. It stretches farther, past the hypnotic, even rows of brittle, brown cornfields ready for harvest. The sky tautens, wraps itself around faint, almost unnoticeable remnants of these indigenous Iowa prairies.

I stare out the window at the carefully planted rows of elms and maples that line my street. Most of them have not yet begun to turn stunning colors of crimson, orange, gold. The trees are full, fertile, with lush green leaves as if it were still summer. Only a few months ago I was still standing in the fields, planting sunflowers.

So often here, I hope that staring long enough, hard enough, at the plain Midwestern landscape will transform it. By the strength of desire alone the flat earth might twist upward, growing steeper, until it reaches the sharp edges of mountains. I would see serpentine manzanita bushes, dusty trails winding through granite boulders, spiny Douglas fir trees. And beyond, the Pacific Ocean. The landscape would become a familiar one. The one I've left behind in California's Sierra Nevada Mountains of Sequoia National Park, and the one I still occasionally dream about late at night.

The relentless drizzle becomes snow. In September. I watch the heavy, dense flakes. They fall slowly at first. I see one out of the corner of my eye, then another. Until soon I can no longer see the outline of the trees and the entire world is covered in unexpected whiteness. The snow is just the kind I drew as a child, waxy round crayon dots on rough vanilla-colored paper. The flakes are too saturated with moisture to last—they melt as they meet the warm, gray concrete.

I run outside without reaching for my coat, and stand on the front porch, looking up, as if the falling snow could teach me how to relate to this dark Midwestern soil. The snow seeps through my shirt, wet and warm, leaving large droplets on my face, in my eyelashes.

The sunflowers I've planted in the yard bend and sway in the wet wind. They stand seven feet tall, spiny shadows towering over me. They only bloomed a few weeks ago—hundreds of tiny, mustard-colored flowers. I watched them all summer, touching the unopened buds as I left the house each morning, waiting for them to open. I stand in the midst of the first snow of the season and wonder how long it will be before the sunflower petals drop to the ground, and the trees along the street are empty and bare.

Last summer, in the relentless July humidity, I leaned against my shovel and rested. The sun was intense. No matter how much water I consumed, my thirst was unquenchable, and rivulets of sweat collected in the tangles of hair at the back of my neck. I couldn't keep up with the other employees. Most of them were native Iowans who had spent their entire lives on their families' farms. They'd gotten up before dawn to milk cows, bale hay till their hands were callused and no longer bled from the sting of labor, working till nightfall during each season's harvest.

I'd known that I wasn't strong enough for this job. My only calluses were from gripping the pen to grade my college students' composition papers each semester. But this was the last chance I would have to feel a part of this landscape. To look at acres of fields I'd helped plant with my own hands.

I worked for the North Central Regional Plant Introduction Stations. A cooperative venture between Iowa State University and the United States Department of Agriculture, Plant Introduction grew and harvested hundreds of diverse plants and vegetables. This wasn't unusual in Iowa, where crop production makes up much of the state's economic livelihood. But this was different. This project was about seed, nothing more. In the main building, a refrigerator the size of a small warehouse contained hundreds of thousands of seed in glass jars, from every imaginable country, all to fulfill the mission of conserving "genetically-diverse crop germplasm and associated information."

The plants themselves, grown large, ripe, and luscious after a summer of sunshine and warmth, were useless. At summer's end, we'd harvest the seeds from each plant, leaving the fruit behind, abandoned. None of the seedlings we planted all summer held any aesthetic or intrinsic value; only what the plants contained was precious.

I'd been assigned to the Sunflower Crew. For three months we built enormous metal and mesh screen cages, and replanted thousands of sunflower seedlings. My back ached. I put the shovel aside and knelt on the ground. I dug in the clumps of hard, black earth, gently making sure each plant stood upright and straight toward the sun.

I planted fifteen seedlings in each rectangular plot inside the cage. Any extra plants we transported to the fields were supposed to be dumped outside the cages. We shook the soil from their roots and left them to burn and wither. Despite their best efforts, their roots would never have the chance to take hold. These plants would never know summer wind, rain, and tornadoes. It occurred to me that, until this very moment, I had felt much the same way. I had spent most of my two years in Iowa trying, and failing, to plant roots. The act itself, the effort I would make, of tethering myself to this temporary, unfamiliar place had become what mattered, overshadowing whatever beauty I might find in the plains and plowed fields.

While hoeing the sunflower fields, I often encountered field bindweed, or creeping Jennie as I learned to call it, a weedy perennial whose tangled mats of narrow vines stretch out along the rich soil of cultivated Iowa fields. Its complex, intertwined root system sprawls stubbornly far and deep underground. Each time I struck a plant's primary, fleshy root, I uncovered more and more. Despite how forcefully I cut and scraped, more roots always emerged from the ground, as deeply embedded as the first, burrowing deep into a place I couldn't see, one I couldn't reach completely.

And always as I would struggle and cut I could think only of the mountains of California, of the trees and meadows of Sequoia National Park. Like the creeping Jennie, my connection to that landscape couldn't be severed completely. It was as if I'd managed to cut only the parts I could see. But the unseen roots were still there, still growing far beneath the forest ground. And still there were my friends, my brother, nearly every person I truly cared about in the world. The decision to leave, to choose another path, was mine. But it felt like some intangible part of myself held back, still lingered like a ghost in the forest, unable to move forward.

One afternoon I asked my supervisor, Sam, if I could take home some of the unplanted sunflowers. I wanted to plant the leftover seedlings in my front yard. Sam looked at me, puzzled for a moment, not understanding why anyone would do such a thing. Many of the varieties of sunflowers we planted appeared on the State of Iowa's list of "most noxious weeds"; they were important for preserving ecological diversity, but still considered an economic nuisance to farmers' crops. "Go ahead," he said, laughing and shaking his head.

At the end of the day, I carried as many as I could back to my car. The seedlings stayed outside for a long time, black plastic flats leaning against my house, waiting for clear weather. As soon as my upstairs neighbors saw the seedlings outside, they approached me. Did I really plan to put those things in the yard, they asked. Did I know that, once planted, the sunflowers would drop hundreds of tiny seeds in that same place, every, single year? From that summer on, my sunflowers would keep coming back, keep growing next to the front porch, long after I was gone. Certainly no one would mind, I responded, didn't everyone like sunflowers?

It was impossible to explain that this sense of constancy was what I wanted. The very quality that made Sam and the people here consider these plants weeds was the same one that made them so sympathetic to me. Ecologist Neil Evernden describes a peculiarly human tendency, a common desire borne primarily out of aesthetics, for having a "sense of place, a sense of knowing and of being a part of a particular place . . . what it feels like to be home, to experience a sense of light or smell that is inexplicably right." Planting the sunflowers would be a permanent gesture, a sense of knowing I now more needed than wanted—their reappearance each year a reminder that part of me belonged here, now.

By the time the summer rains ended I'd finally placed the sunflowers in the ground, spacing them evenly so each seedling had a clear, sunny place to grow. I planted stem after stem, my back aching. But this time I didn't mind; the sunflowers were mine, and planting them would help settle my transient life. In three decades, I'd moved twenty-three times, fifteen of those in just a five-year period. Eight different states. Four different countries. Summers working in Sequoia National Park, winters spent wherever I happened to find myself through circumstance. But always to return to the Sierra Nevada mountains each springtime. If I could have put all the time together in a straight and continuous line, Sequoia was the one place I'd lived the longest since childhood. It was the landscape I knew more intimately than any other, a comfortable, familiar place with the power to evoke a sense of belonging in me.

Such seasonal work is emotionally and physically exhausting. At the end of each season, just as I had grown attached, the yearly closing of the park's facilities uprooted me. The separation would last until the next season, when I had to relearn the subtleties of the forest. And after years of constant movement, redefining and reinventing home and self, I had learned to resist attachments to people or places—they were only temporary. This habit of creating distance followed me across the country to Iowa.

But this time I wanted some physical sign of my connection to this new place, one that symbolized change, difference. When the sunflowers bloomed, I would look out my window and know that this was my home now, that I belonged here, for however brief a time. I would appreciate their simplicity, their ability to remain rooted, to grow tall each summer.

The waist-high, murky water is numbing, and there is no hint left of yesterday's snowfall. I stand in a bend of the South Skunk River and stare at the next fifty-yard stretch along the right riverbank. My carefully chosen layers of fleece clothing are inappropriate and inadequate as my shirt clings, sticky and cold, to my stomach, and the water flows slowly in and out of my expensive waterproof hiking boots.

I inhale, letting the autumn air fill my lungs. The water smells like only a river in the Midwest does—musty like the scent of wet, rotten leaves, and dying animals. I compare the smell to the one I remember of the Pacific Ocean—bitter, salty, and clean.

The day is unusually clear, the sky an intense, opaque blue like a plastic candy-filled Easter egg. Throughout the morning and most of the afternoon we've been traversing the Iowa countryside as part of an undergraduate biology field trip. We stop our van at three different locations along the river, near home.

We are looking for freshwater mussels. At one time these bivalve mollusks were plentiful in every river in the United States, including this one. Most freshwater mussels are in trouble, with over seventy North American species listed as endangered, threatened, or of special concern. Although mollusks are extremely resilient and belong to the second largest phylum of animals (about 550 million years old), freshwater mussels are rapidly disappearing. We're looking for them because they are a critical indicator species. Easily injured by pollution and habitat destruction, these small creatures can reveal the quality of a watershed and offer insight into the health of an entire landscape. Mussels form countable bands of calcium deposits, much like the rings inside a sequoia tree, which not only reveal their age—some species have life spans up to 100 years—but also represent an entire life history of the river.

Now, these animals' habitats have been devastated by water pollution, soil erosion from agriculture, and forcibly dammed waterways. Over-harvesting by the pearl industry also continues to threaten freshwater mussels. In Asia, mussel shells imported from the U.S. are sliced and shaped into perfectly rounded beads, inserted into marine oysters, and eventually become pearls. I'm overwhelmed to discover that about fifty million dollars' worth of shells are shipped yearly to Japan, with the U.S. buying millions of dollars of pearls in return. Our purpose on this field trip is to determine if any populations of mussels still survive in these dark, damaged waters.

Three distinct types of mussels may still live in the South Skunk River. *Actinonaias ligamentina*, or muckets, are small, smooth-shelled, and pale. Three-ridge mussels, *Amblema plicata*, are larger, with wavy ridges across the top of each of the animal's valves. And *Potamilus alatus*, pink heel splitters, are the largest we hope to find—bumpy, mud-colored mussels with a rough edge on their dorsal surface. If I accidentally stepped on one, barefoot or in flimsy shoes, the sharp ridge could cut through to layers of wet skin. All three species are considered threatened.

The professor who directs this trip insists that enough remnants of these populations still exist to warrant our presence here. As I shiver in the semi-warmth of the early afternoon sun, I'm still not sure. After a half-day's search, we've found nothing.

I shuffle through the water to the next stretch of river. Unlike the students, for whom this trip is mandatory, I've volunteered my day to help collect this data. The trip director's father and teenage daughter are the other two members of my team. The company of people who are also less-knowledgeable strangers among the others is comforting. The daughter, Nicole, is quiet. Her expression hasn't changed—a defiant and passive scowl, as if this really is the last place she cares to be on a Saturday.

Nicole's grandfather, John, smiles the same, faint smile he has had all day. He reminds me of my own grandfather. John keeps up easily with my quick pace as we hike through dense woods to get to the edge of the river. The thick, closely knotted trees are an unanticipated change in landscape, one I appreciate.

Driving toward my new home here a few summers ago, I fixed on the miles of fields blurring by through the car window and tried to remember the word for the opposite of claustrophobia, tried to let myself be embraced by this landscape. The Plains breathe anonymity and loneliness into everything they touch, are not immediately welcoming. They had seemed to spread out in front of me, becoming the edge of the earth, dropping off into emptiness. There is something about the introspection such a landscape encourages that hints at clarity, insight, self-understanding. In open spaces we can find ourselves, fill ourselves. And the disappointment was overwhelming when I first sensed that there was nothing unpredictable about the Iowa landscape. When I finally leave this place, what I'll remember most distinctly is the lack of trees, the wide, empty spaces that look so much alike.

Earlier this morning when John stopped along the trail to point out the names of unfamiliar trees and plants to me, I realized that I'd stopped looking for the unexpected here, taking for granted that it's always the same. Spending many years in the sequoia forest was the same way—I didn't take the time to notice the unexpected there until it was far away from me.

A blue rubber bag on the riverbank marks the next research area. We collect the data in random, one-square-meter sections, which I learn are called quadrants. I'm in charge of measuring these sections for my team. The quadrant marker is made of lightweight PVC pipe sections fitted together to form a perfect square. With each forward step the dark water grows shallower and I can nearly see the river bottom. A fish nips behind my knee with a brief, unsettling tug.

I stand in the only patch of sunlight along the bank, and close my eyes. We need to preserve the randomness of the data. I take the quadrant from around my neck and throw it, far ahead of me. Perhaps this time we will find something.

John and Nicole follow me and we bend down toward the water. I've begun to dry off, just a little. At first, the cold water on my arms makes me flinch, as I would at the unwanted touch of an estranged lover. We reach our arms into the water, searching the river bottom with our hands inside the plastic quadrant, feeling for mussels.

The silt is soft and smooth beneath the water. Something sharp stings my hands. I pull the object to the surface, into the light. It's a large, square-shaped rock that only vaguely resembles a mussel. I toss it into the water behind me and listen to the deep, hollow splash. I start to reach into the water again. Nicole just shakes her head at me. "Nothing."

"Look at that," John says. "You're covered in dragonflies and damselflies." Looking up from the water I see a dozen, brilliantly colored insects swarming around my head, hovering above my arms and my back. They are an indescribable, bright green, a color that has never before existed. The wings of the dragonflies are transparent, nearly invisible, with finely woven strands. The dragonflies and damselflies move as if they share a common rhythm, soothing and hypnotic.

Dragonflies aren't unusual; we've seen them all day, skimming the cloudy waters. But for a moment I'm standing in the midst of something unexpected. I think of Diane Ackerman's words: "The essence of natural beauty is novelty and surprise . . . our sense of community widens—we belong not just to one another but to other species, other forms of matter." Last summer, or even yesterday, I probably wouldn't have paid attention to these flashes of color moving around my eyes. But in this moment, I am changed.

"Over here," Nicole calls. "It's not in the quadrant, but I found one." John and I exchange smiling glances. We wade over to the place where Nicole points to a shiny, pale mussel on the shallow river bottom.

I look down into the water. This mussel, a mucket, is much smaller than I had imagined. All freshwater mussel shells, made of calcium, consist of two halves held together by a strong dorsal ligament which acts as a hinge, allowing the halves to open and close. They are uncomplicated creatures, with no eyes, no ears, no outer appendages. Their shells contain only muscle tissue, reproductive organs, and an intestinal tract. Simple, straightforward, honest.

Mussels are usually found upright—their shells vertical in the water with the open edge reaching out, filtering food by siphoning water through the digestive tract. This one lies on its side. It may be dying. I'd like to pick it up, replace it so that it stands tall and upright in the water, the way it belongs. But it's not my place to interfere.

The mussel itself isn't beautiful, not much different from the rocks I've pulled out of the river all day. In the reflection of the faintly flowing water, it had looked shiny and bright. When Nicole holds it in her hand now, the surface is not as smooth as it had appeared. I can see imperfections, tiny fractures and ridges along its shell. As the mussel dries in the sunlight, its glow fades and dulls. It reminds me of handfuls of desert sand, bleached into hundreds of almost unnoticeable colors. The way you don't notice the desert's distinctive beauty until you think about the sheer difficulty of survival in such a place, the adaptations of plants and animals. Many species of mussels can actually change as their environments change; many have the ability to fasten themselves firmly to solid objects, holding fast, letting go only to find food in a new place. And most mussels spend their entire lives in a single river or stream, never knowing another home, never needing to.

What is beautiful about the mussel is its singular presence here, along the riverbed. The mussel survives through all the river's changes, in spite of a home that no longer sustains it completely. The Midwest landscape may also never sustain me completely. In many ways I will probably always equate it with absence—of mountains and sequoia trees, meadows overflowing with plants. But I learn. How to adapt to its changes, how to take nourishment from what I do have, how to appreciate its intricate, subtle colors.

The sun is warm and the trees seem part of a dense forest. The tallest trees here in Iowa stand small and unremarkable next to the ones still in my memory of California. But it doesn't matter. After living in a place like Sequoia for so long, it is easy to believe that nature is supposed to be huge and awe-inspiring. That it must leave us breathless and without words. Perhaps my struggle to understand and take root in this landscape means I haven't been looking closely, in simple places like this still river next to the endless cornfields.

I breathe deeply and try to memorize the river. I want to remember these trees and the exact scent of Iowa water, instead of the too-predictable postcard cornfields. I'll leave Iowa next summer, long before my sunflowers bloom. But they will. Shallow roots have, without my knowing, taken hold in this Midwestern soil. My ambivalence subsides. Belonging has less to do with this exact place than with recognizing its shape and meaning: appreciating a sunflower for more than the seed it provides, and admiring the changing nature of a single, freshwater mussel. In the mountains, when I stand again beneath the sequoia trees, I'll know the rightness of this Midwestern landscape, and that it is also a part of me.

Sick of Nature

David Gessner

I am sick of nature. Sick of trees, sick of birds, sick of the ocean. It has been almost four years now, four years of sitting quietly in my study and sipping tea and contemplating the migratory patterns of the semipalmated plover. Four years of writing essays praised as "quiet" by quiet magazines. Four years of having neighborhood children ask their fathers why the man down the street comes to the post office dressed in his pajamas ("Doesn't he work, Daddy?") or having those same fathers wonder why, when the man actually does dress, he dons the eccentric costume of an English bird watcher, complete with binoculars. Four years of being constrained by the gentle straightjacket of genre; that is, four years of writing about the world without being able to say the word "shit." (While talking a lot of scat.) And let's not forget four years of being the official "nature guy" among my circle of friends. Of going on walks and having them pick up every leaf and newt and turd and asking "what's this?" and, when I (defenseless unless armed with my field guides and even then a bumbler) admit I don't know, having to shrug and watch the sinking disappointment in their eyes.

Worse still, it's been four years of living within a genre that, for all its wonder and beauty, can be a little like going to Sunday School. A strange Sunday School where I alternate between sitting in the pews (reading nature) and standing at the pulpit (writing nature). And not only do I preach from my pulpit, I preach to the converted. After all, who reads nature books? Fellow nature lovers who already believe that the land shouldn't be destroyed. Meanwhile my more hardnosed and sensible neighbors on Cape Cod are concerned with more hardnosed and sensible reading material (*People, Time, Playboy*—not a quiet magazine in the house), when occasionally resting from the happy exertion of gobbling up what's left of our neighborhood, selling and subdividing. Being honest (one of the nature writer's supposed virtues), I have to admit that an essay is a much less effective way of protecting the land than a cudgel. In other words, I have to admit to impotence.

Which isn't much fun. Today, the morning after yet another legislative defeat for conservation on Cape Cod, I find myself feeling particularly pessimistic about the possibility of affecting change. The original land bank bill, which marked my first minor foray into volunteer politics, was a modest and sensible proposal for putting aside some money to spare the remaining undeveloped land on the Cape, a still beautiful place that's quickly going the way of the Jersey Shore. But because that money would come from the profits of the sellers of real estate (one percent on sales over $100,000), conservatives (is there a more tediously ironic word in the language?) decided that the time was ripe for another Boston Tea Party. The real issue was that developers and realtors and builders wanted to keep on developing and realting and building, but of course they couldn't come right out and say that. So they pooled a big pile of money and called in a big telemarketing firm from Washington that proceeded to reframe the debate entirely in terms of that highly original catchphrase "no new taxes" (while also, just for the fun of it, scaring the bejesus out of the Cape's substantial elderly population).

The standard response to this unfairness of things is to curse and wave our little fists at the wicked telemarketers, but today I have a different reaction. I marvel at their effectiveness. Had the pro-land bank forces called in a team of essayists, what would we have done to help? Assembled, we'd have looked like a reunion of Unabombers: solitary, hollow-eyed, scraggly-bearded characters ranting against progress. Likely our strategy would have been to abandon the phone lines and take to the beaches to wander, alone and aimless, in search of terns and profundities. Not only that, but had we somehow—despite ourselves—won, the victory party wouldn't exactly have been a barrel of laughs. You can bet you wouldn't find a single lampshade-wearing party guy in the group.

Which is part of the problem, or, at least, part of my current problem. Throw an imaginary kegger and fill the room with nature writers throughout history and you'll get the idea. Henry Beston, looking dapper if overdressed, alternates tentative taco dabs at the cheese dip with Aldo Leopold; Barry Lopez sits in the corner whispering to Thoreau about the sacredness of beaver dams; Joseph Wood Krutch stands by the punch bowl and tells Rachel Carson the story of how he first came to the desert as Carson listens earnestly. In fact, everything is done earnestly; the air reeks with earnestness. As usual with this crowd, there's a whole lot of *listening* and *observing* going on, not a lot of merriment. Writers from earlier times drift off alone to scribble notes, modern ones talk into microcassette recorders. You might think Ed Abbey could spark the party to life, but until the booze to blood ratio rises he remains painfully shy. Everyone else merely sips their drinks; buffoonery is in short supply; no one tells bawdy anecdotes. In short, the party is a dud.

Perhaps in real life these writers wouldn't restrict their discussions to the mating habits of the roseate spoonbill (*Ajaia ajaja*). In my present state of mind, I'd like to imagine them talking about anything other than nature. Sex maybe. Certainly sex must have played at least a minor role in all their lives, even Thoreau's. Perhaps one reason for the retreat to Walden, unexplored by most critics of American Romanticism, was to have more time and freedom for masturbatory binges. We'll never know. We do know that Thoreau exalted in that most underrated aspect of nature appreciation: pissing outside. "I have watered the red huckleberry, the sand cherry and the nettle tree," he wrote. Hell, maybe Thoreau himself would be just the man to break the ice at my party. "Water is the only drink for the wise man," he said piously, but since I'm imagining I'll imagine having someone, Abbey maybe, spike his water. Perhaps for one night, throwing off his teetotaling ways, he could sing and dance, putting folks at ease by showing that even the great stuffy father figure could tie one on. And with Thoreau—Thoreau of all people, the one they respect the most, their God!—acting the buffoon, the rest of them could let their hair down and start to drink and talk about normal party things like lust or the score of the Celtics game.

I, a relative neophyte, wouldn't have merited an invitation to the big shindig, but, along with the rest of the Corps of Junior Nature Writers, I'd watch Thoreau's wild-man antics through the window. And maybe, just maybe, Henry would stumble out and bullshit with me late at night, and together, just two drunk guys, we could water the sand cherry.

The preceding scenario may suggest that I am losing my grip (on this essay as well as my mind). Maybe so. Not long ago I moved from Colorado to Cape Cod to live in Thoreauvian isolation, and for a while I was convinced solitude was driving me insane. (I'll admit that, unlike Thoreau, I had a wife with me, but we still felt isolated together.) Since coming back, I have been a literary Euell Gibbons, subsisting on a diet of pure nature reading as well as writing. Assuming the mantle of genre, I began my adventure determined to deepen my connection to the natural world, inscribing the front of my journal with Henry Beston's words: "A year in outer nature is the accomplishment of a tremendous ritual." But at some point I cracked. I started writing pieces like this one, tossing aside the stage craft of birds and bugs and beaches, and focusing on what I really cared about—*me*. Usually I rate about a 7.3 on the narcissism scale, but suddenly, finding myself with long hours to contemplate an empty beach and my own deep thoughts, my rating shot off the charts. Working at a job in the city, it's easy to dream of the rustic life, but actually living it entails dangers. It's not just nature that abhors a vacuum. Deprived of its usual gripes, the imagination creates elaborate dissatisfactions and paints masterpieces of hypochondria. There's a reason Cape Cod, our seaside paradise, has such high suicide and alcoholism rates. Though it isn't fashionable to admit, I wouldn't have made it through the fall without television. ("Our only friend," my wife called it.) As the sages have long reminded us, when we get away from it all we still bring our minds along.

As I turned inward, I forgot about the beautiful world outside. Nature became, if not a malevolent presence, at least an irritating one. Gulls shat on my back deck, raccoons rummaged through the trash cans, and the powder post beetles (close cousin to the termite) drilled into the beams day and night with a sharp *tcckkk tcckk tcckk* noise that made me feel as if they were burrowing into the meat of my temples. And then, suddenly, I realized that I hated nature, or at least hated writing about it in a quiet and reasonable way. Why? Because the whole enterprise struck me as humorless, which in turn struck me as odd, given that comedy often draws on a strain of wildness. Gary Snyder wrote that those who are comfortable in wilderness are often comfortable in their own subconscious. And it seemed to me that those who are comfortable with the uncertainty of nature should also be comfortable on the same shaky ground of humor. Why was it, then, that so often love of nature seemed to breed earnestness?

And then there was this: With only a couple of obvious exceptions, the modern nature writer is most often praised for his or her "restrained" voice. Restrained as in shackles, it seemed to me. "Quietly subversive," is the phrase usually tossed out by critics when referring to nature writing. Well, while I sit here carving out my quietly subversive prose, the bulldozers down the street at Stone's bluff are loudly subverting the soil. Hollowing out the Cape just as the beetles hollow out our beams.

But I'm not telling the full story (which in this case is a crime since what this essay is really about is the frustration of not telling the full story). When we choose to do a thing we in effect choose not to do many other things. The same with genre. As I complain about my previous genre's restrictions, I find myself bristling at my present constraints (those of the curmudgeonly personal essayist). Yes, Cape Cod can sometimes seem as desolate as Siberia, and yes, the sound of hammers banging is never far off, and yes, there have been plenty of times when, sitting in my cold room listening to the beetles *tcckk, tcckk, tcckk*-ing I longed for an escape from this drear peninsula. But something else has also happened. After my crack-up in early fall, I actually began to settle in. As the year sprawled on, moving slowly, ambling like no year I'd known before, I, despite myself, began to remember some not-unpleasant things about Cape Cod. Like October. A month when the tourists finally packed up and cleared out for good. A month when the full moon rose over the pink-blue pastel of the harbor sunset and the blue-grey juniper berries shone with chalky iridescence at dusk, and when masses of speckle-bellied starlings filled the trees (and the air with their squeaky-wheeled sounds). A month when the ocean vacillated between the foreboding slate grey of November and a summery, almost tropical blue (while occasionally hinting at its darker winter shades). Most of all, a month of color, a month when the entire neck caught fire in a hundred shades of red.

And though this is not what I intended to write about, these memories lead to other memories of the fall (a time that's becoming more romantic with each retrospective second). Like the first husky wisps of woodsmoke rising from my neighbor's chimneys, or the time I saw the seals playing tag between the offshore rocks or the haze of wood dust in the sunlight as I stacked the logs against the side of the house, fortifying us for winter, or the time I kayaked into the marsh and, sliding in through the channels, low and quiet, caught the great blue heron off guard and watched it walk across the spartina with its funky seventies TV pimp strut, head bobbing forward and back . . .

But there, you see. I'm going off again. Like heroin or nicotine, the nature habit's hard to break. I could, without much prodding, turn this essay into a paean to the beauty of the past year on Cape Cod, on how the year has been a deepening, a wedging into the physical world, a slowing down. If that was my story, then I would, of necessity, edit out certain details (like any mention of those sustained periods when I was sure that the beetles were sending messages to me through the phone lines). It wouldn't be so much lying to exclude these, as much as it would be a genre choice. The sort of choice we make semiconsciously almost any time we open our mouths.

And maybe what I'm sick of isn't the birds and trees and beach or even writing about the birds and trees and beach. Maybe what I'm really sick of is making the same choice over and over again. Of being one thing. Of constraint. Maybe I'm rebelling against my too-safe self. Rebelling against the formulaic in me, the way we squirm uneasily at a too-pat Hollywood movie.

But I'm the one calling the shots, after all, so why keep calling the same shot? Much has been written about the modern tendency toward specialization, and I won't add another long-winded celebration of the amateur. But it is true that from a young age Americans are taught that there's nothing like success, and that the way to *really* succeed is to do one thing well. Having spent a half dozen years out West, I can say this is particularly true of New Englanders. We proudly celebrate our uptightness. Our heroes as a rule are monomaniacally devoted—Larry Bird, John Irving, Ahab—and whether these heroes focus on basketball, novels, or whales, they are praised for directing their energy toward one thing without wasting time on diversions. But as the good Captain illustrates, this isn't always the surest road to mental health. In my case, focusing on one thing (even a thing as seemingly benign as nature-writing) was an invitation to those beetles to crawl into my skull.

It is now the middle of February on Cape Cod, a time that I dreaded during the melancholy of late November. The odd thing is that I really am settling in, really starting to enjoy it here. Winter insists on its own pace, dispensing with ambition, and when I do write I turn to whatever takes my fancy. Specialists may bring home more bacon in our society, but the impulse to variety is healthy, even thrilling. The pursuit of only one thing eventually grinds down to a grumbling feeling of work and obligation.

In that spirit, I have been undergoing a sects change operation, switching genres rather than gender. To support myself, I work for half the week as a substitute teacher and when I go into school, the real teachers always greet me with the same question. Wondering which of their peers I'm subbing for, they ask, "Who are you today?" I like the question and have written it down and taped it over my computer. Each day I strive to be a different who. If I feel like writing a haiku about the chickadees at the feeder, that's okay, but if I feel like creating a story about lying naked in a lawn chair, drunk, and blasting the chickadees with a scattergun, that's okay, too. These days I write as I please. To use a simile that would be scorned by my fellow nature writers, it's like watching TV with your thumb on the remote, a hundred channels at your disposal (and, honestly, how long do you ever really rest on the nature shows?—one good chase and kill by the lion and, click, it's off to *Baywatch*). Or to turn to a simile the nature-writing gestapo might like better, the health of the individual, as well as the ecosystem, is in diversity.

"A change is as good as a rest," said Churchill, and I do feel rested these days, jumping from genre to genre. Letting different voices fight it out inside me, I'm ignited by the spark of variety. Tabernash, our adopted stray cat, is never more cuddly than right after he's killed something. The thing that the confirmed specialist neglects is the incredible stores of energy that remain in other parts of us once one part is depleted. Though heretical, it could be suggested that variety isn't only more fun, it's more efficient.

I have already mentioned Ed Abbey (note to New Yorkers: not Edward *Albee*), and it is thanks in part to his consistent irreverence that I've always been a big fan. One thing a nature essay isn't supposed to be is funny. Or sexual. In this regard, I remain an admirer of Abbey, who insisted on constantly broadening the nature corral. Abbey fought against the nature label long before I did, lamenting, "I am not a naturalist" and complaining that what others called nature books were really volumes of personal history. He has been a kind of patron saint for my own efforts to break free. In his introduction to *Abbey's Road*, he complained that critics are always calling some nature writer or other the "Thoreau" of this or that place. He wrote of nature writing that it "should be a broader and happier field" and that, "Like vacuum cleaner salesmen, we scramble for exclusive territory on this oversold, swarming, shrivelling planet." It's only gotten worse in the years since Abbey's death: As the world grows more crowded, our fiefdoms shrink. Ten years ago, Cape Cod had only two living Thoreaus: Robert Finch and John Hay. Now there are a dozen more of us, scrambling and clawing for the remaining turf, happy to be called the Thoreau of East Harwich or the Thoreau of Dennisport. No less than the developers we revile, we try to make a living off the land and scenery, and so it's necessary to subdivide and develop new areas. And it's not only our plots of land that are smaller. Step right up and observe that freakish character—The Incredible Shrinking Nature Writer. If you drew us to scale and made Thoreau a giant, and placed Leopold and Carson at about his shoulder, you could keep drawing us smaller and smaller until you sketched in me and my crop of peers at insect size. It may be, as some suggest, that our time marks a renaissance of nature writing. But it's a renaissance of ants.

Fear has always led to the taming of diversity and wildness, and, in writing, as in so many other professions in this increasingly crowded and competitive world, fear breeds specialization. With more and more of us competing for the same food source, it's wise to stick to one genre and to the specific rules of that genre. It makes you identifiable. Marketable. Commodifiable. After all, we don't want to buy Lemon Pledge once and find out it works—"Boy, this stuff can really clean!"—only to buy it again and discover it has transformed itself into an underarm deodorant. That wouldn't be convenient. Or neat. And neatness counts, now more than ever.

So maybe it's neatness I'm really sick of. A born slob, I admire writers who jump from genre to genre, break-out artists not content to stay in one pasture for long. But I better watch myself: The genre border guards never rest. When I first moved back East, the Cape Cod Museum of Natural History refused to keep my book in stock or let me speak there, apparently fearing both fart jokes and activism. "We really only carry *nature* books," the manager of the bookstore told me, to which I replied, for once, that mine was a nature book, it even said so on the back cover. "It's really more of a personal narrative, isn't it?" the manager asked in a scolding voice. Particularly damning, it seems, is the fact that some reviewers used the word "funny" to describe the book. You don't want to do anything as drastic or volatile as mixing humor with nature; that wouldn't be proper, wouldn't be safe. When I speak to someone else about giving a talk, she tells me that, "We only deal with nature here and we don't want anything political," as if, in this day and age, the two could possibly be peeled apart.

For my part, I'll take writing that spills sloppily over genre walls, always expanding its borders. We all pay lip service to Whitman and his famous "contradictions," but it's not all that common to see writers contradicting themselves on the page. "My moods hate each other," wrote Emerson. Amen. I love to see Thoreau overcome by an urge to strangle a woodchuck or Abbey take a break from celebrating the stark beauty of the desert to throw a rock at a rabbit or Annie Dillard admitting she wrote of the beauties of nature while locked in her windowless, cinder-block study. I admire Rick Bass, for instance, when he interrupts an essay to practically grab readers by the collar and insist that they write their congressman to save his beloved Yaak Valley, and I also admire him for the way his "nature writing" has permeated his fiction. Another writer I admire, Reg Saner, has warned me not to make the natural world a stage for merely personal drama, and these are wise words. He points out that Emerson's little book got this whole mess started. "The trouble with *Nature*," Reg said, "is that there's very little actual nature in it. No rocks or trees or birds." But I *like* Emerson's self-contradictory title. And I want nature to occasionally act as a stage, as long as it's not only and always that. For instance, I want novels—where personal drama is imperative—set deeply in nature. After all, to write about humans is naturally to write about the things that matter in their world: weather, wind, plants, trees, animals, and water.

But today I want to make a plea not for wilderness, but for wildness. For freedom. For sloppiness. For the exhilaration of breaking down the Berlin Wall of genre.

A plea for amateurism, variety, danger, spontaneity, and honesty in a world growing increasingly professional, specialized, safe, pre-packaged, partitioned, and phony.

As novels are set more and more often in lands walled by style and concrete, it has been up to today's nonfiction writers to usurp the themes that have concerned us since the great romantics, reminding us that writing isn't some impotent, inert thing unrelated to actual life, and that stories don't all have to end with some subtle New Yorker flicker of hair that subtly signals something few of us get. On the other hand, there's no reason these larger concerns can't be re-invested in fiction, no reason other than prevailing fashion. We have all seen the damage done by the contemporary mania for partitioning. If nature writing is to prove worthy of a new, more noble name, it must become less genteel and it must expand considerably. It's time to take down the NO TRESPASSING signs. Time for a radical cross-pollination of genres. Why not let farce occasionally bully its way into the nature essay? Or tragedy? Or sex? How about painting and words combined to simulate immersion in the natural world? How about some retrograde essayist who suddenly breaks into verse like the old timers? How about some African American nature writers? (There are currently more black players in the NHL than in the Nature Writing League.) How about somebody other than Abbey who will admit to drinking in nature? (As if most of us don't tote booze as well as binoculars into the backcountry.) And how about a nature writer who actually seems to have a job? (Almost all seem to be men of leisure, often white guys from Harvard.)

Of course, genres help critics box things (and not incidentally allow us to write), but breaking through genres can be as exhilarating and dangerous as waves crashing over a sea wall. And that's where the action is today, when writing spills and splashes over genre barriers. Not just the fictional techniques in today's creative nonfiction—which is exciting in itself—but letting the material go where it will, even if it's "bad" and misbehaves and trespasses in Old Man McGinty's fictional backyard (and makes our fictional parents mad). Thorny, uncategorizable writing. Of course, this is nothing new. Revealing myself as an Emersonian recidivist, I say let the pages fit the man.

After all, though it gives critics and marketers fits, it's where things get most fuzzy that they're most interesting. There are always those ready to wield the word "autobiographical" like a club, to claim the current interest in memoir signals the end of civilization, but the overlapping of fiction and nonfiction is ultimately freeing. "Consider Philip Roth's *The Facts*—which isn't the facts at all . . ." wrote Wallace Stegner. "*The Facts* is as surely a novel posing as an autobiography as *Zuckerman Unbound* is an autobiography masquerading as a novel." Or as the writer Luis Urrea said: "I tell the truth in my novels and make things up in my non-fiction." Genre confusion, like gender confusion, is disconcerting, but it's overall a happy development, a sign of play and freedom. As Stegner says, it doesn't matter if it's autobiography. It matters if it's art.

But it's time to reel myself in.

I'm willing to write manifestos, but I'd prefer having others act them out. For all my declarations of freedom, I, too, am constrained. If genre were an invisible dog fence, I would already have been jolted by several zaps, and would have retreated meekly. So here comes the traditional twist and summary that marks the end of a personal essay. Of course I'm not sick of nature at all. Just sick of being boxed in, and of the genre itself being boxed too narrowly. In fact, having declared myself done with nature, I suddenly feel the itch of the contrary. Hell, after three days of sitting in the attic typing this too-personal essay while listening to an endless loop of the Butthole Surfer's second-to-last album (*Independent Worm Saloon*), I'm ready to get down to the beach and commune with some semipalmated plovers. Maybe even to write about them.

Lost in Eden: In Search of the Tree of Life

Derek Green

Mohammed called to tell me a friend of his knew someone who knew how to get to the Tree of Life. I'd arrived in Bahrain, the tiny island state in the Persian Gulf, earlier that week on business, and since, I'd been asking around about the Tree. The closest thing to a helpful answer I'd gotten so far was from the Filipino bartender in the Diplomat Hotel's Skylight Lounge. "It not too dangerous to find, but somehow very difficult," he told me. "I think you rather visit a nightclub."

Now my luck appeared to be on the mend. Mohammed's friend, a native Bahraini raised in the capital city of Manama, was getting directions to the Tree even as we spoke, and admitted that he himself wouldn't mind "having a look at the thing."

"How is it," I asked, "that this friend of yours hasn't seen the Tree of Life if he grew up here?"

"Haven't you ever heard," Mohammed replied, "of those people who live in New York and have never seen the Statue of Liberty?"

I supposed I had.

"We'll meet you in the lobby in ten minutes," he said.

I had first read of the Tree of Life a few years earlier. In the middle of the desert, the story went, stood an old, old tree surrounded by nothing but vast stretches of sand. Various writers had made controversial claims pinpointing the historical location of the Garden of Eden in Bahrain; the theories differed widely, but almost all of them made mention of the lonely old tree. Even my trusty *Lonely Planet Travel Guide* was in on the act, calling the Tree of Life the "centerpiece of the 'Bahrain-was-the-Garden-of-Eden' theory," adding that, to this day, the tree's age and source of water remained mysteries.

At home in Michigan, during the weeks leading up to the trip, I'd become something of a leisure authority on all this Garden of Eden speculation. (Okay, I'd gone on-line a few times to read articles about ancient Sumer and visit some university archaeological websites.) Here was my opportunity to see for myself whether these theories—far-fetched as they seemed—actually made sense. And anyway, I figured, when you're from Detroit and you get a chance to see Eden first hand, you go.

When I arrived in the hotel lobby, Mohammed was watching the coffeeman work. A small, ancient man in traditional Sunni clothing, he sat brewing coffee that smelled vaguely of cardamom and earth over glowing coals near the entrance to the lobby's Lebanese restaurant. Mohammed was a trim young man, born in Yemen, educated in Great Britain, and now living in Dubai. He was my principal contact in the Gulf, and over the last few years we had become friends.

He walked with me to the modern revolving doors. "So this Tree of Life you're so eager to see," he said, "I guess it turns out to be, like, superhard to find."

"That," I said, "is what everyone keeps telling me."

Outside waited a Jeep Cherokee. "This is Saeed," Mohammed said. The Jeep's owner wore khaki slacks, a shirt and tie, and a wide smile. I shook his hand Western-style from the back seat as Mohammed climbed in front. "You do not mind, I hope," Saeed said—he'd obviously been practicing the sentence for my benefit—"that I am having some errands to do in the city before we go to discover the Tree of Life."

I thanked him profusely and assured him I'd be happy to accompany him. At worst, I figured, we'd be seeing a pretty cool tree. At best—who knew?

We turned away from the coast on Sheikh Hamad Causeway and headed past the diplomatic sector, with its glass business towers and modern traffic signs. Saeed pointed out the building where he worked as an IT computer specialist for a bank. He and Mohammed bantered back and forth in Arabic.

In the Babylonian Epic of Gilgamesh, Bahrain is called Dilmun. Gilgamesh journeys to Dilmun in search of—get this—the Tree of Life. When he arrives, he meets a suspiciously Noah-like character who tells the story of a great flood. Though I had read the Gilgamesh in college, till now my own experience of Dilmun had been limited to meetings at the Diplomat. As we passed through the Bab Al Bahrain—the entryway into the city built by the British in 1945—that changed. The streets grew narrower, the buildings shorter. Oddly shaped alleys and irregular street corners served as informal gathering places and the old streets teemed with men and women in traditional garb. It wasn't hard to imagine the place as it must have looked 5,000 years ago, when Dilmun was the burning center of the universe and Eden not such a distant memory.

In the souk—the traditional market-place—the old and new collided in weird ways. A man in traditional clothing, seated on a stool over a pile of smoking incense, was selling Persian kilims from a canvas tent; across the street a brightly lit KFC restaurant did brisk late-afternoon business. The roads were barely the width of a car, and we crept along looking for a spot to squeeze through. We stopped for a snack of rolled shawarma and again to buy some CDs at a music shop. Our last errand was to pick up Saeed's son from soccer practice.

The boy climbed into the car in his soccer jersey, a little taken aback by all the strangers. "Say hello in English," his father said with clipped affection.

"This man has come from America." The boy turned bashfully to watch the scenery through the window. After dropping his son off at their apartment, Saeed grinned at me in the rearview mirror. "And so now we go to see your old tree that stands alone in paradise."

We left the city and drove south into the desert. The scant vegetation we had seen in town—kept alive by expensive irrigation or plain hard work—gave way now to stretches of gravelly, salt-flat wasteland. I asked the name of the road we were on, thinking of recording once and for all the directions to the elusive Tree of Life, but got only a laugh from Saeed. "Forget names," he said. "A few years ago there were not even roads here."

The farther from the city, the farther back in time we went. On either side of us grew rocky mounds of earth that looked like giant sand moguls or the humped backs of whales. I watched the shapes roll by for a while before it occurred to me that I was seeing Bahrain's famous burial mounds, dating to the second century B.C. The mounds caught the slanting sunlight, throwing gothic patterns of light and shadow. It would have been a pleasantly mythic flourish, I thought, had the Tree of Life obliged by presenting itself at the end of this vast city of the dead. Instead, we came upon a ranch where a few lazy camels and their herders lounged beside a chain-link fence, and then, of all things, a golf resort. Tall parasols dotted the sandy course like umbrellas on a beach; late-afternoon golfers toted patches of artificial turf from which to tee their shots.

The road looped through several turns, following a series of massive pipes that sprawled like tentacles from Bahrain's central refinery. At the edge of a stony outcropping—the highest point in Bahrain, Saeed told us—we stopped to gaze over the barren land. White refiner's fire lit the pile of steel and massive pipe works that made up the island's main petroleum processing plant, giving it the look of a small burning city. Behind it in the distance shimmered the capital, Manama, from where we had come. With no sign of the Tree, not to mention Eden, I was beginning to wonder whether our day trip to the Tree of Life might be turning into its own Gilgamesh-like epic.

"It's an amazing sight," Mohammed said. He turned to his friend. "Of course, you're lost, aren't you?"

"Well . . . " Saeed said. He frowned and rubbed his neck. "I am not lost. I am just not sure where I am."

Even on this high spot, pipes had been laid to bear up the underground river of oil.

"Imagine," I said, "laying down these pipelines in the sun."

Mohammed gazed out silently and shook his head.

"They've been here as long as I can remember," Saeed said. In this part of the world, mention oil and soon enough you're talking about politics. As the road veered away from the pipe fields, Mohammed turned in his seat to look at me. "And what do you think of your new president in the United States—Mr. Bush?" he asked.

I told him the verdict, as they say, was still out. "We're still barely sure he was actually elected," I said. "It was a strange fall."

I turned the heat onto Mohammed by asking what people in this region of the world thought. Saeed answered. "There is a lot of concern," he said. "No one knows, for instance, how the new administration will look on the problem of Palestine and Israel. And then there is the old feud between the Bush family and the Iraqi rulers."

It was not hard, here in the desert—separated from southern Iraq by a stretch of sea not much wider than the distance from Ann Arbor to Chicago—to imagine these disagreements as feuds between ruling families in separate lands. "In a way," Mohammed said, "the details don't matter. What is worrisome is that Bush and his family come from the American oil industry. There are many who believe that any hostility in the region benefits the administration and its friends. They can say, 'See, there go the Arabs, fighting each other again. So now we have to drill for oil in Alaska.' For them, whatever happens in our world, it seems they win."

A silence threatened to engulf the cab of the jeep. But then Saeed lit up with a smile. "Do you see?" he asked. "There, on the side of the road?" He pointed. A solitary brown road sign announced simply, in two languages, Tree of Life. A white arrow pointed ahead. "You see," Saeed said. "I told you I knew where I was going."

There were two more signs before a final one directed us off the paved road and onto a hard gravel track. We passed a scrap yard and a goatherd with his flock. Then, at end of the road, we made out the shape, sure enough, of a tree. The tree itself wasn't so remarkable—it looked like a tall acacia or maybe a mesquite tree, with a thick, gnarly trunk and a flat, tiered canopy of dusty leaves. As the guidebook had said, the surprising fact was the thing's existence here in the middle of the otherwise barren landscape. No desert weed or hardy spinifex. No American-style theme park with the Tree of Life Lounge and bathrooms marked "Adams" and "Eves." Just this tree. We stopped and regarded the lonely scene from the Jeep.

"Is this it?" I asked.

"It must be," Mohammed said. "It's the only tree I see."

"It looks quite old," Saeed observed.

We piled out and stood beside the Tree. Maybe it was just anticipation or the way the sun fell aslant on the dusty leaves. But there was something unsettling about this place and its lonely inhabitant, this single tree, which had managed somehow to struggle on, alive, in the middle of so much nothingness. A pair of black desert birds glided on updrafts far overhead.

Was this the Garden of Eden? Could there once have been a paradise here of which only this tree remained, a lone witness for the ages? If the Tree of Life held the answers to such secrets, it wasn't bothering to reveal them to us that day. We got back into the Jeep, Saeed took another turn around for a last look, and we headed back down the stony trail. A cloud of dust rose and obscured the tree behind us. We passed the goats, who watched with studied indifference, as we turned back onto the road beyond the dusty junk yard.

Snow

John Haines

To one who lives in the snow and watches it day by day, it is a book to be read. The pages turn as the wind blows; the characters shift and the images formed by their combinations change in meaning, but the language remains the same. It is a shadow language, spoken by things that have gone by and will come again. The same text has been written there for thousands of years, though I was not here, and will not be here in winters to come, to read it. These seemingly random ways, these paths, these beds, these footprints, these hard, round pellets in the snow: they all have meaning. Dark things may be written there, news of other lives, their sorties and excursions, their terrors and deaths. The tiny feet of a shrew or a vole make a brief, erratic pattern across the snow, and here is a hole down which the animal goes. And now the track of an ermine comes this way, swift and searching, and he too goes down that white shadow of a hole.

A wolverine, and the loping, toed-in track I followed uphill for two miles one spring morning, until it finally dropped away into another watershed and I gave up following it. I wanted to see where he would go and what he would do. But he just went on, certain of where he was going, and nothing came of it for me to see but that sure and steady track in the snow crust, and the sunlight strong in my eyes.

Snow blows across the highway before me as I walk—little, wavering trails of it swept along like a people dispersed. The snow people—where are they going? Some great danger must pursue them. They hurry and fall; the wind gives them a push, they get up and go on again.

I was walking home from Redmond Creek one morning late in January. On a divide between two watersheds I came upon the scene of a battle between a moose and three wolves. The story was written plainly in the snow at my feet. The wolves had come in from the west, following an old trail from the Salcha River, and had found the moose feeding in an open stretch of the overgrown road I was walking.

The sign was fresh, it must have happened the night before. The snow was torn up, with chunks of frozen moss and broken sticks scattered about; here and there, swatches of moose hair. A confusion of tracks in the trampled snow—the splayed, stabbing feet of the moose, the big, furred pads and spread toenails of the wolves.

I walked on, watching the snow. The moose was large and alone, almost certainly a bull. In one place he backed himself into a low, brush-hung bank to protect his rear. The wolves moved away from him—those moose feet are dangerous. The moose turned, ran on for fifty yards, and the fight began again. It became a running, broken fight that went on for nearly half a mile in the changing, rutted terrain, the red morning light coming across the hills from the sun low in the south. A pattern shifting and uncertain; the wolves relenting, running out into the brush in a wide circle, and closing again: another patch of moose hair in the trodden snow.

I felt that I knew those wolves. I had seen their tracks several times before during that winter, and once they had taken a marten from one of my traps. I believed them to be a female and two nearly grown pups. If I was right, she may have been teaching them how to hunt, and all that turmoil in the snow may have been the serious play of things that must kill to live. But I saw no blood sign that morning, and the moose seemed to have gotten the better of the fight. At the end of it he plunged away in thick alder brush. I saw his tracks, moving more slowly now, as he climbed through a low saddle, going north into the shallow, unbroken snow. The three wolves trotted east toward Banner Creek.

What might have been silence, an unwritten page, an absence, spoke to me as clearly as if I had been there to see it. I have imagined a man who might live as the coldest scholar on earth, who followed each clue in the snow, writing a book as he went. It would be the history of snow, the book of winter. A thousand-year text to be read by a people hunting these hills in a distant time. Who was here, and who was gone? What were their names? What did they kill and eat? Whom did they leave behind?

The Bats

Linda Hogan

The first time I was fortunate enough to catch a glimpse of mating bats was in the darkest corner of a zoo. I was held spellbound, seeing the fluid movement of the bats as they climbed each other softly and closed their wings together. They were an ink black world hanging from a rafter. The graceful angles of their dark wings opened and jutted out like an elbow or knee poking through a thin, dark sheet. A moment later it was a black, silky shawl pulled tight around them. Their turning was beautiful, a soundless motion of wind blowing great dark dunes into new configurations.

A few years later, in May, I was walking in a Minneapolis city park. The weather had been warm and humid. For days it had smelled of spring, but the morning grew into a sudden cold snap, the way Minnesota springs are struck to misery by a line of cold that travels in across the long, gray plains. The grass was crisp. It cracked beneath my feet. Chilled to the bone, and starting home, I noticed what looked like a brown piece of fur lying among the frosted blades of new grass. I walked toward it and saw the twiglike legs of a bat, wings folded like a black umbrella whose inner wires had been broken by a windstorm.

The bat was small and brown. It had the soft, furred body of a mouse with two lines of tiny black nipples exposed on the stomach. At first I thought it was dead, but as I reached toward it, it turned its dark, furrowed face to me and bared its sharp teeth. A fierce little mammal, it looked surprisingly like an angry human being. I jumped back. I would have pulled back even without the lightning fast memory of tales about rabid bats that tangle in a woman's hair.

In this park, I'd seen young boys shoot birds and turtles. Despite the bat's menacing face, my first thought was to protect it. Its fangs were still bared, warning me off. When I touched it lightly with a stick, it clamped down like it would never let go. I changed my mind; I decided it was the children who needed protection. Still, I didn't want to leave it lying alone and vulnerable in the wide spiny forest of grass blades that had turned sharp and brittle in the cold.

Rummaging through the trash can I found a lidded box and headed back toward the bat when I came across another bat. This bat, too, was lying brown and inert on the grass. That's when it occurred to me that the recent warm spell had been broken open by the cold and the bats, shocked back into hibernation, had stopped dead in flight, rendered inactive by the quick drop in temperature.

I placed both bats inside the box and carried them home. Now and then the weight would shift and there was the sound of scratching and clawing. I wondered if the warmth from my hands was enough heat to touch them back to life.

At home, I opened the box. The two bats were mating. They were joined together, their broken, umbrella wings partly open, then moving, slumping, and opening again. These are the most beautiful turnings, the way these bodies curve and glide together, fold and open. It's elegant beyond compare, more beautiful than eels circling each other in the dark waters.

I put them in a warm corner outside, nestled safe in dry leaves and straw. I looked at them several times a day. Their fur, in the springtime, was misted with dewy rain. They mated for three days in the moldering leaves and fertile earth, moving together in that liquid way, then apart, like reflections on a mirror, a four-chambered black heart beating inside the closed tissue of wings. Between their long, starry finger bones were dark webbings of flesh, wings for sailing jagged across the evening sky. The black wing membranes were etched like the open palm of a human hand, stretched open, offering up a fortune for the reading. As I watched, the male stretched out, opened his small hand-like claws to scratch his stomach, closed them again, and hid the future from my eyes.

By the fourth day, the male had become thin and exhausted. On that day he died and the female flew away with the new life inside her body.

For months after that, the local boys who terrorized the backyards of neighbors would not come near where I lived. I'd shown one the skeleton of the male and told them there were others. I could hear them talking in the alley late at night, saying, "Don't go in there. She has bats in her yard." So they'd smoke their cigarettes in a neighbor's yard while the neighbor watched them like a hawk from her kitchen window. My house escaped being vandalized.

My family lived in Germany once when I was a child. One day, exploring a forest with a friend, we came across a cave that went back into the earth. The dark air coming from inside the cave was cool, musty, and smelled damp as spring, but the entryway itself was dark and foreboding, the entrance to a world we didn't know. Gathering our courage, we returned the next day with flashlights and stolen matches. It was late afternoon, almost dusk, when we arrived back at the cave. We had no more than just sneaked inside and held up the light when suddenly there was a roaring tumult of sound. Bats began to fly. We ran outside to twilight just as the sky above us turned gray with a fast-moving cloud of their ragged wings, flying up, down, whipping air, the whole sky seething. Afraid, we ran off toward the safety of our homes, half-screaming, half-laughing through the path in the forest. Not even our skirts catching on the brambles slowed us down.

Later, when we mentioned the cave of bats, we were told that the cave itself had been an ammunition depot during World War II, and that bat guano was once used in place of gunpowder. During the war, in fact, the American military had experimented with bats carrying bombs. It was thought that they could be used to fly over enemy lines carrying explosives that would destroy the enemy. Unfortunately, one of them flew into the attic of the general's house and the bomb exploded. Another blew up a colonel's car. They realized that they could not control the direction a bat would fly and gave up on their strategy of using life to destroy life.

Recently I visited a cave outside of San Antonio with writer and friend Naomi Nye. It was only a small mouth of earth, but once inside it, the sanctuaries stretched out for long distances, a labyrinth of passageways. No bats have inhabited that cave since people began to intrude, but it was still full of guano. Some of it had been taken out in the 1940s to be used as gunpowder. Aside from that, all this time later, the perfect climate inside the cave preserved the guano in its original form, with thick gray layers, as fresh and moist as when the bats had lived there.

Bats hear their way through the world. They hear the sounds that exist at the edges of our lives. Leaping through blue twilight they cry out a thin language, then listen for its echo to return. It is a dusky world of songs a pitch above our own. For them, the world throws back a language, the empty space rising between hills speaks an open secret then lets the bats pass through, here or there, in the dark air. Everything answers, the corner of a house, the shaking leaves on a wind-blown tree, the solid voice of bricks. A fence post talks back. An insect is located. A wall sings out its presence. There are currents of air loud as ocean waves, a music of trees, stones, charred stovepipes. Even our noisy silences speak out in a dark dimension of sound that is undetected by our limited hearing in the loud, vibrant land in which we live.

Once, Tennessee writer Jo Carson stuck her hearing aid in my ear and said, "Listen to this." I could hear her speak, listening through the device. I could hear the sound of air, even the noise of cloth moving against our skin, and a place in the sky. All of it drowned out the voices of conversation. It was how a bat must hear the world, I thought, a world alive in its whispering songs, the currents of air loud as waves of an ocean, a place rich with the music of trees and stones.

It is no wonder that bats have been a key element in the medicine bundles of some southern tribes. Bats are people from the land of souls, land where moon dwells. They are listeners to our woes, hearers of changes in earth, predictors of earthquake and storm. They live with the goddess of night in the lusty mouth of earth.

Some of the older bundles, mistakenly opened by non-Indians, were found to contain the bones of a bat, wrapped carefully in brain-tanned rawhide. The skeletons were intact and had been found naturally rather than killed or trapped by people, which would have rendered them neutral; they would have withdrawn their assistance from people. Many Indian people must have waited years, searching caves and floors and the ground beneath trees where insects cluster, in order to find a small bony skull, spine, and the long finger bones of the folded wings. If a bat skeleton were found with meat still on it, it was placed beside an anthill, and the ants would pick the bones clean.

I believe it is the world-place bats occupy that allows them to be of help to people, not just because they live inside the passageways between earth and sunlight, but because they live in double worlds of many kinds. They are two animals merged into one, a milk-producing rodent that bears live young, and a flying bird. They are creatures of the dusk, which is the time between times, people of the threshold, dwelling at the open mouth of inner earth like guardians at the womb of creation.

The bat people are said to live in the first circle of holiness. Thus, they are intermediaries between our world and the next. Hearing the chants of life all around them, they are listeners who pass on the language and songs of many things to human beings who need wisdom, healing, and guidance through our lives, we who forget where we stand in the world. Bats know the world is constantly singing, know the world inside the turning and twisting of caves, places behind and beneath our own. As they scuttle across cave ceilings, they leave behind their scratch marks on the ceiling like an ancient alphabet written by diviners who traveled through and then were gone from the thirteen-month world of light and dark.

And what curing dwells at the center of this world of sounds above our own? Maybe it's as if earth's pole to the sky lives in a weightless cave, poking through a skin of dark and night and sleep.

At night, I see them out of the corner of my eye, like motes of dust, as secret as the way a neighbor hits a wife, a ghost cat slinks into a basement, or the world is eaten through by rust down to the very heart of nothing. What an enormous world. No wonder it holds our fears and desires. It is all so much larger than we are.

I see them through human eyes that turn around a vision, eyes that see the world upside down before memory rights it. I don't hear the high-pitched language of their living, don't know if they have sorrow or if they tell stories longer than a rainstorm's journey, but I see them. How can we get there from here, I wonder, to the center of the world, to the place where the universe carries down the song of night to our human lives. How can we listen or see to find our way by feel to the heart of every yes or no? How do we learn to trust ourselves enough to hear the chanting of earth? To know what's alive or absent around us, and penetrate the void behind our eyes, the old, slow pulse of things, until a wild flying wakes up in us, a new mercy climbs out and takes wing in the sky?

Moonmilk

Barbara Hurd

Each image changes, fuses with its contrary,
disengages itself, forms another image, and in
the end returns to the starting point.
—Octavio Paz

You're not supposed to touch moonmilk. It's fragile and has taken years to grow to this large mass oozing down the wall of an Oregon cave in the Siskiyou mountains. It looks like cream cheese, like an opaque-white, cave-dwelling jellyfish. What makes it so different from other formations, from the cave itself, is its softness. Rock looms everywhere else, stone, hardened calcite, boulders, and here's this gooey stuff you could shape with your hands, mound up and smooth, then place under your head like a pillow.

I'm inside a cave carved out of a gigantic block of marble. I'm walking along marble passageways, marble under my feet, above my head, marble chunks I step over, marble rooms I enter and leave. This isn't polished, of course; it's marble in its natural form, grayish white with a sugary texture that I can almost imagine cut into blocks and stacked into buildings, or sliced into small disks, coasters set beneath glasses of lemonade, images that vanish immediately when my elbow brushes against a jutting chunk. The ceiling hovers and the walls press, small clusters of gray-white chambers and crawlspaces where patches of moonmilk leak through the cracks.

You can't find moonmilk in eastern United States caves. Something about the temperatures, volume of seepage waters, and humidity have to combine in just the right way to allow its growth, a convergence that evidently doesn't happen in the East. But it's present in caves in the Italian Alps, in Australia, and in some western caves such as this one in Oregon. I've seen white inside a cave, of course, in calcite flowstones and stalagmites, in cave pearls and soda straws. But not this soft white, this shapeless mush of unknown origins. The ancient theory: When the moon's rays passed through rock and emerged into a cave, the rays took on substance, changed from light rays to white mass. Moonmilk, people believed, was embodied moonbeams. I like imagining why the rock of the moon would reflect sunlight while the rock of the cave would transform moonlight, what would make one a mirror and the other a shape-shifter.

Perhaps the difference has something to do with the cave as cocoon. In a cave or cocoon, you can't forget you've gone *inside* something the outside can't easily enter. You're cut off from the upper world, ensconced in the unlavished elsewhere, isolated, sealed away. You're protected from weather and hidden from predators; hidden, too, from mirrors and from others who can remind you who you are. Just the conditions conducive to change.

I think of the monarch caterpillar hanging upside down in its cocoon for fourteen days, safeguarded from marauders, the sun, rain. Inside its silky case, it doesn't have to think about hunger, a mate, where to find shelter. Protected, held, insulated, it does what it went inside to do. It changes; it rearranges itself, becomes something else.

And of a pearl, how inside the dark nook of an oyster shell it grows, layer after layer, thousands of layers of concentric spheres of calcite crystals known as aragonite, the same white mineral that leaks into caves and grows underground into flowerlike formations. The pearl grows undisturbed, a luster crystallized around a wound inside the darkness of the shell.

And of a black bear inside the dark cranny of her den, sleeping in hibernation while her own cubs emerge, wriggle to the nearest teat, settle in for weeks of sucking. They grow in the dark, even with their mother half-oblivious, while the cave shelters them from cold and others' hungers.

Pockets, sacs, recesses of protection and privacy. Pouches, pods, cocoons, chambers; think, even, of Clark Kent and his phone booth.

Vaults and crypts. What does the body's ultimate transformation require? That we minimize distractions so that our attention not be diverted from the monumental task at hand? Dark bedrooms, quiet hospice centers. Or that we orchestrate things so our minds stay stimulated, alive as long as possible? Rooms full of visitors, walls busy with photographs. Things lose substance, take on substance, change substance, and they often do so in enclosed environments that foster such change—the dark alcoves, the rooms so often small and sealed off like a hermetic chamber: cloisters and caves.

This cave began two hundred million years ago. There was no Pacific Ocean then, no Cascade Mountains, no rivers, nothing we could call a continent. There were rocks, a planet made of rocks. They lay in massive shields that shifted and ground, sometimes rose and fell. Two hundred twenty million years ago, in what we now call the Pacific Northwest, two massive rock formations began to angle toward each other, a stone creeping that probably took thousands of years of closer and closer until they finally sideswiped each other, the colliding edges buckling and folding, ripping open a massive depression into which water trickled and collected and deepened until the Pacific Ocean began to fill and small shelled creatures—mollusks, snails, scallops—began to evolve and die and drop to the bottom. The tiny bodies piled up and collapsed beneath the weight of the water, a whole layer of calcite-laden mud that hardened into limestone.

Thousands of years later the slow sideswiping turned more direct; the ocean basin rock—limestone—collided head-on with the continent. Rock melted, creating a massive molten mass that collided again with the limestone. And here's the most interesting change: When the molten rock got close to the limestone, the heat cooked it. Baked it. Turned it to marble that then rose and twisted and eroded, small cracks widening, leaving a labyrinth of down-sloping passages and small rooms.

That's what this cave is—one of the few marble caves in the country—small chambers of baked limestone that was once the compacted shells of sea creatures who once swam in an ocean that no longer exists. I think of the Taj Mahal, the marble monument to mourning that Shah Jahan built after his beloved died. I've stood inside that edifice, felt the way only such exquisite emptiness, such utter motionlessness on the banks of the River Yumuna, could ease the Shah's decades of grief. Its balm has something to do with the marble and light, how beauty can almost transform grief into stillness, make it possible for us to live with what's lost.

The guides in Agra like to place a flashlight against the marble of the Taj Mahal, show tourists the way the stone becomes translucent, how it seems to glow from inside. The first time I saw that white glow, I thought of deep-sea divers, the way the light from their headlamps is soft, diffused by darkness. But there in the Taj Mahal, marble all around me, the tour guide shining his light through one section and then another, the light gets diffused by whiteness, everywhere around me a white ocean with tiny lamps, the struggle of Shah Jahan to lighten his grief, to lift it into domes and minarets in a way that I can't do, can't find any corollary to marble, white oceans, any antidote for the thickening sadness around me.

The rock in this cave is too thick to transmit any light except, as people used to think, for moonlight. Moonmilk is actually a cave deposit of calcite crystals and polycrystalline chains that accreted thousands of years ago in a process not unlike the making of most other cave formations. Moonmilk, however, has a high water content and some other ingredient that makes it oozy, and it's this ooziness that has mystified scientists for many years. Something organic? Someone touched the moonmilk inside an Australian cave eight years ago, left a handprint a centimeter deep, a handprint that has now disappeared, prompting speculation that the moonmilk had actually grown over the print, that moonmilk is, in fact, organic, alive. On the cave wall in front of me, it looks now like an albino blob escaping from a hidden crack in the stone.

It's easy to imagine creatures lurking or crashing around in here. In many mythologies, the cave is the passage connecting Hades and the daily aboveground life. Literature and mythology are full of beings—Zeus, Hermes, even Jesus—brought into or taken from the world through a cave, bodies forming and dissolving in these subterranean rough marbled places. Here in this passage named Paradise Lost, stalagmites rise out of the marble floor and stalactites hang from marble ceilings. I peer into recessed alcoves, back behind half-walls, into the pocked up-above. Everywhere, small protrusions, hands, fingers, dismembered body parts. In the Ghost Room, more stubs, nubbins—relics, all of them, of larger formations that have been broken off or dissolved by acids, reminding me that it's often in caves that shamans of many cultures work their magic, singing over sickness and the future, changing their own shapes and the shapes of what floats in and out of their vision.

No ghosts, no monsters, no shamans here at all, of course. Knowing this doesn't stop me from remembering the time I watched a man in a cave change into a werewolf. It was my earliest memory of terror. I was much too young—maybe five or six—for such a movie. My mother had no idea what the show was about, that her twins shouldn't be sitting on either side of her watching the close-ups of a man's face as he turned into something else, his lips getting thicker, hair sprouting from his cheeks, his forehead, his flesh disappearing under a sudden mane of facial hair. It seemed like it took hours. I couldn't look away. Days later, at home in front of the bathroom mirror, I studied my own face, wondered if it could happen to anyone and what the first sign would be.

I think of Jonah.

Moving on down the passage, I leave the moonmilk and ghost images and enter a long, skinny room called the Whale's Belly. The stone seems to arch over and around; I'm walking down its throat and into its belly. I'm in a chamber that's inside a chamber. The rock looks rippled and then ribbed, grayish-white marble that's become bone and then gut. I imagine Jonah inside, the live chamber he rocked in for three days and nights in the darkness, weeds wrapped around his head as the whale dove and swam and rolled in the ocean. Whatever had made him flee from the task God had given him—fear? stubbornness?—he had three days to think about it, three nights to consider his death. Maybe sometimes it takes being locked in solitude, held away, isolated, in order to shift from defiance to gratitude. Or vice versa.

Or despair to resolve. My father was a POW in World War II. When I was thirteen, I wanted to know everything about his twenty-two months in Stalag Luft 3. I wanted descriptions of the camp, of the men, the way the guards treated them, what they ate for breakfast. My father was reluctant to talk about such details. "It was a long time ago," he'd tell me. I turned to books, especially to one called *Kriegie*. I made my father a character in the book so I could watch him move around the camp, thin, perhaps afraid, standing in lines for hours, forced to clean latrines and sleep on hard bunks. I imagined him miserable, a young man wrenched from his bride and having to endure cattle cars and meager rations.

Years later I realized what I'd wanted to know was how he'd gone from being that man to the man I knew—mostly cheerful, a big planner of projects, the president of the neighborhood civic association, a solid citizen, active member of the church—and whether that thin, imprisoned man was still inside him as he mowed the lawn and straightened his bow tie before work. Whether the postwar world, the demands of job and family had layered over his past like secretions over the irritant in an oyster or whether in the quiet of some too-long night, the long-buried past still pressed outward, sent him sailing alone on the Chesapeake with wartime despair, fragility, the patriotic rage not quite below the surface. "A lifetime ago," he'd remind me.

And I think of Kenny, one of my best friends, a practical, upbeat man who loves his wife and nuzzles his horses. Thirty years ago, as a sniper in Vietnam, he'd gotten hundreds of men in his rifle sights and pulled the trigger. I've spent countless hours with this man as each of us married others, raised our children, divorced, married others, countless hours over wine and Scotch and bowls of groundnut stew. I don't know that man in the jungle and I don't know how he went from one to the other. "A different me," he tells me, "from a different life, now over." Sometimes I watch him chopping wood, bending iron over the fire, and I try to see that other man inside him, the one I'm sure is still in there. And in my dad. Maybe in Jonah too, long after he'd gone on to years of praising God. No doubt inside us all are those other selves that we've silenced, perhaps for good reasons, or outgrown, or maybe partially transformed.

I think of pouches and eggs and of helmets, those cranium cradles, rounded shells of protection, how Hermes won't roam the underworld without one. On his head, it becomes one of the ultimate shape-shifters: It makes him invisible. In this altered shape he can travel back and forth between the worlds above and below. Underneath the helmet, the familiar winged feet, curly hair, and caduceus fade away, vanish, as he goes about delivering his messages, retrieving Persephone from the underworld, escorting Eurydice back to it. Hermes knows what happens in those regions, how to don a helmet and become something else, what orchestration of silence and invisibility it takes to get a message to the proper recipient.

I don't like helmets, don't like the way my hair gets smashed inside one, how my head feels a little wobbly with its weight. But I'd never go into a wild cave without one. Too many loose rocks, jutting walls, sharp corners, too many chances to split your skull open. It's the most crucial protection in a cave. If a cap in the underworld made Hermes invisible, a helmet in a cave seems merely to disguise the wearer; without telltale hair color or style, I have a hard time recognizing people underground. But like Hermes, too, a helmet allows the caver to squeeze into places no human should go. With your skull well protected, you feel freer to twist your head sideways, suck your chest in, contort your torso, squirm feet-first around a bend, become a shape less recognizably yours. I've been in wild caves with serene people who panicked, with aboveground bumblers who traversed a breakdown with the grace of Baryshnikov. Things happen to people down there. They become, on occasion, more or less than they were.

Or other than. A cave's cocoon-ness and its characters remind me we're probably all more loosely constructed than we can admit, that our selves are more truly, as Dr. Jekyll says, "trembling immateriality, the mist-like transience, of this seemingly so solid body in which we walk attired." Maybe it was that fear I felt the first time in a cave ten years ago when it seemed a Mack truck was bearing down on me, and I felt less firm than I'd thought, flimsy even, in the low-ceilinged chambers of ancient shape-shifting lore. I don't believe in literal cave monsters or vehicles barreling through tight passages and could not understand, could only feel, a sudden crowding. And now I wonder if that fear was some deeply embedded realization that I was crawling in a place that had, for many thousands of years, been the site of ancient shape-shifting. And maybe I was afraid of the transformation myself, not physical—not me into bats, vampires, bears, shamans, werewolves, Hyde—but me into other me's, the shifting of my own pasts and other selves, what's not quite disappeared inside, what lingers unseen, almost unheard. Perhaps I felt the embryonic flutter inside of another presence, and another, several, a whole congregation of fetal heartbeats beginning to stir, a myriad of other selves inside me awakened from deep slumber and beginning to stretch inside my body. "This human being is a guest house," Persian poet Rumi sings; "Every morning a new arrival." What I remember in that cave isn't song but fear and how heavy on my head my helmet seemed and how quickly, after I'd scrambled out of the entrance in a panic, I'd taken it off and dropped it. It rocked for a few seconds on the ground, rocked like a dark blue, broken-open, just-emptied eggshell.

This might be, then, the real sense of shape-shifting: not that anyone's face or body is permanently rearranged, but that here in the place where others can't see us, what's been hidden inside us might appear. The psyche might be reshuffled. Other, long-buried parts of ourselves might emerge. My father dropped bombs in the war, carried out secret missions, built cradles for his daughters' dolls, taught his son to sail. Kenny wiped out a hundred men, makes jewelry for his wife, loves to rest his cheek against a horse's muzzle.

A friend tells me a story about a man's transformation inside a cave. A brilliant, well-respected brain surgeon, the man stuttered so severely he could blurt out only a sentence or two before his tongue seized up, before his mouth locked into a series of misfired beginnings he couldn't speak his way out of. He'd practically given up talking and relied, instead, on writing notes to friends, colleagues, and patients. A friend who loved caving took him to a cave in France, a wild cave that they entered on their bellies, hunching themselves forward by haunches and elbows until they reached a deep subterranean room decorated with hundreds of stalactites hanging down, not quite touching the hundreds of stalagmites reaching up, none of the formations joined to form a solid column. It was a room full of one thing almost connecting to the other, and the surgeon gasped and blurted out, "It's so beautiful!" and then four or five more praises and then realized that for the first time in years he wasn't stuttering at all, a realization that launched him into hours and hours of fluency. Who knows what he said? The friend who told me the story didn't know and it didn't matter. What mattered was the cave and how, somehow, in its vault of incomplete columns, the man's syllables connected in one graceful sentence after another. When it was time to go, they retraced their steps and belly-crawls and reemerged into the sunshine where the stutter, though reduced, resumed. The man repeated the experience again and again, squirmed into the cave the way others might check into rehab, took his cure underground among the disconnected stones.

Inside this Oregon cave, moonmilk oozes down another marble wall. There are no reflective surfaces in these passages, not even enough pooled water to look into. The cave is full of fossils, is, itself, carved out of the graveyard of ancient shells that became limestone and then marble, which Shah Jahan used to transform his grief into beauty. I want to remember this, how the belowground world might give rise to change—shape, emotion, psyche. I can't see much of anything in the dim light; anything, anyone, is possible. Mother Teresa once said she knew she had a little bit of a Hitler inside her. And I, most likely, a bit of a Hyde.

Moonlight to moonmilk, human to ghost, vampire to bat—prime cave-dweller which, the Kanarese people of India say, is itself the product of a failed transformation. They believe that bats were once birds that wanted badly to be changed into humans. In their bat form, they entered the temple chamber to pray for such a change, and the gods, in their perversity, decided to grant them a little of what they wished for and changed them from bird to mammal. They substituted a snub nose for a beak, moved their eyes to the front of their faces, gave them a pair of breast nipples for suckling their young, removed the feathers and gave them hair instead, and finally put some teeth in their mouths. I'd like to have witnessed the story-making, seen how the Kanarese studied birds and bats and imagined bird eyes migrating to the front, feathers losing their silk, becoming whiskery. I'd like to have been there when mystery turned into story, when the unknown took on a different shape. But, no, the gods evidently decided, no witnessing by humans, and no substituting hands for wings and no upright posture. And for comedic effect: big ears. What emerged from the temple was a creature halfway between bird and beast, so ashamed of its appearance it fled to the caves and emerges only at night.

There are bats in this cave, Townsend's big-eared bats and Pallid bats, some of which live record-long lives here, up to twenty-six years. But no vampire bats, which, it turns out, don't suck blood at all. They lap it up, like a dog at its water dish. A small bite on the skin of a cow, a pig, sometimes horses or birds, and the bat settles down at the edge of the wound and leans over, its small tongue flicking the blood into its mouth, its presence a barely noticeable flutter on the neck.

Here in this Oregon cave, I'm glad today for the lights, room to walk upright, more moonmilk on the wall. In spite of the taboo against touching, I touch it. It's soft; it yields; I can press my finger into it. Its name comes from the German word *mannlimilch*, meaning "little earth-man"; gnomes, in other words, who supposedly delivered the white mush from the netherworlds and left it in caves for humans to use. Which they did. Whether people believed moonmilk was reflected moonlight transformed into substance or a gift from the gnomes of the underworld, they believed in its curative powers and used to spread it, like cream cheese, on livestock wounds. Unlike magic, it cured infections, speeded healing, acted as a balm for wounds.

Scientists suspect now that the stuff is home to a certain microbe, *Macromonas bipunctata*, the same type of bacteria used in modern antibiotics like Neosporin. But the mythologies haunt: this cave, this chamber of shapeshifting, of image disengaging, reforming, harbors a mysterious substance, maybe a gnome-gift or reflected moonlight that's taken on form. And whatever its origin, here's what it does: It closes the wound.

We Are Greyhound

Robert Isenberg

We are the people waiting. Our spines ache and we're hungry. We are the slouching folks perched like crows on our luggage. The TV, affixed to the ceiling, is playing a John Wayne movie for us. Our tickets are folded with masses of sales receipts and gum wrappers in our pockets. The bathroom stinks of dry urine, and the stalls are markered with gang signs. We stare at the gate number until our vision blurs and our eyelids droop and an acid taste wells up in our throats.

We are Greyhound.

We drink too much Mountain Dew, to keep from falling asleep. We eat Cheetos and freeze-dried fish sandwiches to keep our stomachs from rumbling. We drag trays across the counters of low-lit cafeterias, and the fat woman in the splattered apron counts our change too slowly. The air smells like burnt crust, and the tables are dotted with ketchup and crumbs, balled-up napkins and old newspapers.

We all glance at each other. Is there no one we can trust? The sleeping man, doubled over his ripped trash bags full of clothes, his beard flecked with gristle? The girl with a pantomime's eyeshadow, her neck clasped by an angry boyfriend with a shaved head and an enormous fake-diamond-studded cross dangling from his pencil-neck? We give each other space; we buffer our pissing with an empty urinal; we'd sooner lean against a wall than wedge between two strangers on a wire bench. We're afraid of lice. A sick man's coughing makes us flinch. The toilet bowls are plugged, and the dried urine on the seats makes us fear hepatitis. The floors are smeared with dirty footprints. The fluorescent lights cast everything in yellow. Every surface sticks like gaff tape.

We are Greyhound—shuttled into parking lots, shuffled into concrete shelters, shrieked at, told again and again to *wait ten minutes*. We hand our licenses to the sleepy agent, and she types our information into an old computer with two-inch press-on nails. The keyboard is covered in a hygienic plastic sheet. The woman prints out our ticket and slaps it on the counter and calls out, "Can I help who's next?" She never says *hello* or *have a nice trip*. There's an understanding between us—we are cattle, she's the cowhand.

In Los Angeles, the signs tell us not to bring knives, guns, or bombs into the station. A security guard stretches open our bags and investigates our things like a bored gynecologist. He smiles and lets us through the turnstile. We can't blame him: outside the station, men sprawl on the South Central sidewalks like casualties of war, but they're alive and breathing, eyes closed against the white desert sun. A bloated rat lies belly-up on the concrete, its dead tongue hanging out.

A groggy young man turns to us and says, "I just got out of jail. Where am I?"

"Los Angeles."

"Really?"

"Yeah."

The man stumbles away, toward the chain-link fence that barricades the station from the city. Can't be too careful around here. They pay attention to colors; here, they take blue and red seriously. Greyhound is where people slip facelessly away. This is the parolee's revolving door. Beaten wives escape from these platforms, waiting in line with deadbeat dads and drug dealers on the run. We are lost, carried in a tide of fumes and midnight snack stops.

In Albany, our station is a makeshift homeless shelter, surrounded by acres and acres of parking lot. The horizon is circumscribed with elevated highway. No two skyscrapers look the same, but they are all far away. Empty squad cars are parked outside. Every pair of eyes is bloodshot. When the door opens, the wind slithers inside, carrying flecks of snow, and the chill reminds us that we will one day die.

In Rutland, a man offers us whiskey from a flask. He asks to use our cell phone. He's old and skinny and mumbles to himself. He asks us for a ride to his friend's house. The man collapses on his side and sleeps for a few minutes, saying, "I'm gonna get some shut-eye." But then he's up again, and he says: "In nineteen-seventy-eight, I was arrested for trying to smuggle ninety-five tons of marijuana into the United States."

He says: "I'd been in Colombia and made some friends in the cartels. They were offering serious money. I would've gotten away with it, too, because we were in international waters. But then NASA had a splashdown right next to our ship, and the Coast Guard showed up and wondered who the hell we were. Turned out I was the only one who could speak English, so everybody assumed I was the skipper. So they threw me in jail for two years. But I wouldn't talk, 'cause I knew the Colombians would kill my family, so after two years they just sorta let me go."

He says: "After that, I got tired of working, so I found a sugar mama in Florida who took care of me. I spend half the year in Florida, half the year in Vermont. But now that bitch has got a vagina the size of half a watermelon, so I'm done with her. Fuck her. I don't need her."

The Greyhound stop in Middlebury is just a gas station with an empty parking lot. The store is closed. When the doors open, we leap out of the bus and start running. We run through the bitter air and slide on the ice and wonder if the man has a gun.

"Wait!" the man screams after us. "I thought you were my fucking *friends!*"

We are Greyhound, and we have rules. We will never cut in line, but we never leave it either. First come, first served. Nothing is guaranteed. In Greensboro, the bus is already packed when it arrives; riders are standing in the center-aisle, and we are forty people standing like assholes in a parking lot, realizing that we aren't going anywhere, because there's no way to board. The bus driver shakes his head at our sweat stains, our desperate eyes, and just shouts, "No room, y'all! Should be another bus in three hours!"

Our friend drives us forty minutes, to the next bus station, near Duke University. There's already a line of men wearing straw fedoras and reading newspapers. In front of them, there's a line of luggage. If you're willing to leave your luggage unattended on the dirty-ass floor of a Greyhound station, then you deserve to keep your place in line, no matter where you wander. That's the code we live by. Because if your cell phone gets stolen, or somebody roots through your side-pockets, that's your problem. Greyhound is risky business. Slurp more cold coffee. Stay awake, people.

In Richmond, the bodies clump around the nylon gates. Bodies are strewn on the floor. The apocalypse will look like this—atrophied muscles wrapped in track pants and hooded sweatshirts, the sneering rage of five hundred dead souls, sharing with nameless strangers a musty hangar. The PA crackles, but the accented words are washed out with static; people respond with fearful eyes, exclaiming: "What gate? Is that us? Do we gotta go? Would somebody fucking explain what's going on?"

We step outside, but the flatland is covered in asphalt and drenched in hot rain. The land is only a graveyard of warehouses. Trucks flash past, and somebody in a sports car laughs out his window while flicking a cigarette into the grass. The trash cans are overflowing; the welcome mat is littered with crushed cups, dented plastic bottles, butts, gum, ticket envelopes.

In Washington, D.C., a quarter-mile from the pristine white Capitol, men with gnarled beards pace in front of doorways; their toes peek through their torn shoes. Every single one asks where we're going, then for money, then for a cigarette. They ask without enthusiasm; the questions are mantras. If they work, great. If not, whatever.

We are too tired to fear them. There's a sharp pain behind our kidneys. Our throats are dried out and we can barely talk. The mucus in our nostrils has solidified. When it's dark, we miss the daylight, and everything is bathed in an orange glow. When the sun rises, it pierces our eyes like arrows, and we squint away our blindness.

We're not fond of each other, but we've made progress. Until 1960, we were segregated, and riders who crossed color lines were sentenced to hard labor, or they were lynched on the spot by salivating mobs. The Freedom Riders were still testing segregation laws in the mid-1960s, risking life and liberty to sit in the front rows of a Greyhound bus. The Klan sprayed buses with gasoline and set their frames afire. Today we're sitting silently together—black, white, Latino, Asian, Indian—and we think nothing of it. People were shot, raped, burned alive, beaten with bicycle chains so that we could sit silently in the same place, hopelessly behind schedule, together.

We're not just Greyhound—we're a slice of America. We're the underbelly; we are where the sun don't shine. They bury us in the basement of Penn Station, where our throngs are invisible to Times Square traffic. We spread out in downtown Winston-Salem, where nobody but a crack-dealer would hang out for fun, and none of the payphones seem to work. We arrive at gravel lots, converted houses, oversized trailers; the land that Greyhound surveys is scorched and brutal. Our walls are scratched and our frameworks rusty. The air smells of chemicals; the stagnant water is navy-gray. This is America's cesspool, and we are America's excretion.

We arrive on Fremont Street, where a bony black woman in extra-high-heels is screaming to the sky: *"Somebody stole my motherfucking money! I was gonna go home! I gotta see my baby! Somebody stole it! They stole my motherfucking money!"* She falls to the curb and weeps; when a security guard helps her, she buries her face in his badge and tie, and he whispers, "It's all right, baby, it's all right." And this is the only human sympathy we've ever seen in our hundreds of hours in Greyhound stations and buses. We marvel at it, until a man in snakeskin boots steps out of the Fremont Street station and takes one look at them and snarls, "Welcome to Vegas!"

We toss back beer, swallow pills, lean our heads against the windows and try to sleep. A fat redneck in Burlington offers us a hit on his bowl. "It's not illegal 'til ya put pot in it," he says. "And even if it's illegal after that, who fuckin' cares?"

We watch the old Vietnamese woman with her papyrus skin, blinking at signs she can't read. She asks: "Montana? This is the line for Montana?"

And when security asks to see inside her suitcase, she pulls it away, anxious and confused. They try to grab her case, but she pulls back, and the tug-of-war game only ends when the suitcase splits open and her clothes tumble out, and her voice cracks as she screams. More guards appear, grappling her arms and pulling her away from the bus. Her legs buckle beneath her, but nobody raises a finger to stop it. We watch as she's dragged away, her suitcase carried separately, round the station's corner. *"Montaaaaaaana!"* she screams, shrieking and begging, but the guards only throw her on the sidewalk.

The bus pulls onto the street, and the driver spits, to us, to no one: "What was I supposed to do? Huh? What was I supposed to do?"

We are Greyhound. We are snake tattoos and Walmart gym bags and Payless shoes. We are three-dollar mini-bags of Combos and too much mascara. We are borrowed books of matches beneath the Smoking Section sign. We are double-cheeseburgers from the dollar menu and pried-open eyes at five in the morning. We are blunt cigars with plastic tips and a swig of moonshine from a Pepsi bottle from a bearded man in a parking lot. We are the curious Hispanic child, riding alone, stroking his smooth mullet as he stares at the Nevada desert. We watch the blade of light shoot out of the Luxor hotel and into the violet sky. New York drifts past us as a million gridded lights. We are every phase of moon, washed out by cloud cover, a fingernail between buildings, a white-hot silver dollar blasting over the Rockies.

We are hours behind schedule. We are blanketed in sweatshirts. We all hate the bus driver, who talks in a bored voice over the intercom, who threatens to pull over and kick off riders who don't obey the rules. "I *will* pull this bus over," he says. "I had to leave a guy at a rest-stop just the other day." We resent the driver because he sits behind a plastic shield. We resent every bomb-threat we've ever heard. Some of us carry knives. Some of us jerk off in the bathroom. Someone is opening a bag of potato chips, and the crunching of the bag is driving us insane because we're trying to take a fucking *nap*. Someone is reading a romance novel, because those gray pages are close as she'll ever get to love.

We tell stories. A woman sits down in Morgantown, and she's attractive and sad. "What a fucking day," she says. "I have to get all the way to Florida. I'm gonna be on this bus 'til Thursday. Thirty-five hours. Can you believe that shit? My Mom was like, You should fly, you should fly. Well, guess what, Mom: I ain't flying nowhere with no money, okay? Waiting for settlement money is, like— shoot me in the fucking face, you know? Like, that guy owes me so much. . . ."

She says: "You wanna know why? You wanna know why he owes me so much? Get this: So my husband, my *ex*-husband, he was a cop, right? And we're all married, and we're all happy. And I'm, like, his trophy housewife, keeping things neat in our happy little house. Outdoor wedding. Talking about kids. All that crap. And then—one day, out of nowhere, this SWAT team comes barreling through the door. They break the windows. They knock down the door.

They're like, *Get on the ground*. And I'm like: You are so *fucked*. My husband's a state trooper, and he's gonna hand you your asses. And what do I find out? *He's* the reason we're getting raided. My state trooper husband is dealing *heroin* out of his *squad car*. To *high school kids*. Like, Hello, Jerry Springer! We're white trash now! Waddup, Ohio?"

We don't know what to say, so we ask what she does.

"What do I do?" she says. "Uh—I'm a nurse. A registered nurse. At this nursing home. Like with all the old, geriatric people. Bathing old people. That kind of thing. It sucks."

She says: "And I'm a, uh—dancer. Like, you know. Like pole-dancing. Erotic dancing. At a club. So that's what I do."

We sit in silence for awhile, and she says: "What sucks is, I don't even have to work. I've got this sugar daddy. This guy. Down in Florida. He pays for everything. Pays for my condo, on the beach. Pays for dinner, my car. All I gotta do is fuck him."

We sit in silence for a few more miles, and she says: "I hate him. He's kinda classy, but kinda gross. And old. Like fifty-four, maybe? It's really all about the money. That's all he is, is money. He owns like a million properties in Ft. Lauderdale, like all these condos and developments and shit—something like fifteen percent of Ft. Lauderdale, all the property, the residential property, like anything you can live on, he owns that. And that's all he'll talk about—day in, day out, just money this, real estate that. Like, what a life.

"And then my roommate—I don't even need a roommate, but I'm just trying to be nice, 'cause her boyfriend was beating her up. But, like, when I see how many rails that girl blows, I'm thinking maybe she was asking for it, you know? And I've done plenty of coke in my time. But, like, when you're doing it all the time?"

We are this woman. We are there when she says, "Hey, can I lean on you? Is that okay?" Our shirt is there to collect her tears, because nowhere is really home, and we strangers are as good to her as anybody has ever been. We are floating between cities the way plague ships once floated between continents, reviled by every port of call. We are America's failure, gathered together and boxed away in the musty attics of dying cities. We are poison pumped through the bloodstream of America's highways. We are bad decisions and messy divorces and foreclosed houses. We are the weird friend crashing on your couch. We haven't showered for awhile. We are lonely.

We are stopping. The lights switch on. This woman sniffs and stands up, rocky on her heels. She clops toward the door, dragging her roller-bag behind her. The door opens, and she steps out, and we never see each other again.

Because we are Greyhound, and we don't stay in touch.

Critter Control

Lori Jakiela

My mother was in the driveway in her robe and running shoes. Her hair was in pin curls.

She wore pantyhose under her robe and, as far as I could tell, nothing else.

It was noon. It was Spring. I'd gone to work and left her alone for a few hours. And now the sun was shining, the birds were singing, and my mother had a shovel. She was holding it over her head.

"Jesus Mary and Joseph!" she screamed. "Bitch and bastard."

She pumped the shovel up and down. She stomped her feet. She looked like people on the news, right before they burn a mop dressed like a president.

"Mom," I said, "what the hell are you doing? Would you please tell me what you're doing?

She pointed. Her chest heaved.

"Snake," she said between breaths. "A goddamn snake."

The snake was frantic. Part of its tail was yellow and squashed flat. This made it stick to the driveway. I'd never seen a snake limp before, and it was sad the way it tried to squiggle and jerk itself free. I hate snakes, but I felt sorry for this one, right until it worked up momentum, unglued its tail, and headed for me.

Then I did what any responsible adult caregiver of an aging, unwell, and possibly deranged parent would do. I screamed, darted back toward the garage, and hid behind my mother.

"It's okay," she said. "I've got it."

I made my voice calm. I said, "Let's go inside. Now."

From where I crouched behind my mother's right shoulder, I tried to evaluate things. The snake was small. My mother was worked up. The shovel was heavy. Killing snakes was not on her doctor's Heart Safe Approved Activities list. It would, judging from the way my own heart was going at it, rank right up there with roller coasters, haunted houses, and Tantric sex. I should have grabbed the shovel and gone after the snake myself, but instead I tried to talk her down.

"Let it go," I said. "It's just a little garter snake."

"Garter snake my ass," my mother said. She didn't look at me. She eyeballed the snake. "That," she said. "Is a copperhead."

Years ago, when I was around six, my mother had taken me blackberry picking. We'd run into a copperhead. It was wrapped around the base of a blackberry bush. We lived near thick woods and there would often be a black rat snake the size of a sewer pipe or a ribbony garter snake slithering around somewhere in the neighborhood. But I'd never seen a copperhead before. The head was large, almost heart-shaped, and penny-colored. The rest of the snake was brown and spotted. It seemed huge, as most things from childhood do. It seemed thick as my father's arm.

Back then, my mother was calm and certain. She eased my hand out of the bush and held a finger to her lips. We stepped back.

"If you don't bother it, it won't bother you," she said.

But now, things were different. The world seemed a much more dangerous place.

"Let it go?" my mother was saying. "Let it go and the next thing you know it's in the house. You want to wake up with that thing in bed with you?"

Ever since my mother had gotten sick and I'd moved back in to take care of her, I'd been sleeping in my childhood bed. I knew there was little chance of the snake ending up there, but the thought was enough. I'd already been having bad dreams where people and animals stopped by for visits. Specifically, there was my dead grandmother, who sat on the edge of my bed and told me I needed to get up, scrub the bathtub, and get her a bowl of cornflakes. There were spiders the size of softballs that showed up whenever I felt stressed or ate pepperoni. And there was my dog, who'd been dead for over a dozen years and who was buried in the back yard. In my dreams, she'd curl up at my feet, the way she'd always done, and try to gnaw my socks off.

All the lumps in the bed were exactly where I'd worn them, though my body was bigger now and didn't fit as neatly as it used to. It seemed strange to wake up in my old room. Every morning, when my mother would snap open the shade and sing the same good morning song that made me want to smother myself as a kid, I felt transported. I could have been 12. I could have been 34. Neither would have surprised me.

It didn't help that little had changed since I'd left for college in 1982. There was the same raspberry shag carpeting, the same pink afghan, the same dresser with the same cracked mirror. There was even my old doorknocker on the door. It was a plastic Woody Woodpecker.

"Good Morning to You," my mother sang every morning at 8 a.m. and let Woody rip.

The tune was Happy Birthday. Her voice was a little weak, but persistent. It didn't help that she'd always been tone deaf and no one, not even my father, the singer, had ever told her. The whole effect was like waking up to Edith Bunker a cappella.

My mother followed the good morning song with an interpretation of reveille, complete with air bugle. Then she'd snap the shade and yank the covers off my bed. She did this for the first 18 years of my life. She did it now.

"You've never been a morning person," she said. "Don't sleep your life away."

Most nights, I stayed awake and listened to her snore in the next room. Most nights, I had trouble sleeping. The house was in the suburbs, but wilderness was everywhere. Which meant snakes, of course, but other things, too.

"I wish I had a gun," my mother would say when she looked out of her bedroom window to find deer in her vegetable garden. She'd make an imaginary gun, thumb and forefinger. She'd pull the trigger and say *pow*.

There were squirrels and groundhogs and moles and rabbits. There were hawks and field mice, real woodpeckers and bats. And there were raccoons.

One night, not long after my mother had come home from the hospital, there was a sound outside my window. It was furious and feral, a growl, then a snarl, then another and another. Then a crash of metal and breaking glass. It was terrifying, much worse than the sirens and car alarms and human snarling I'd grown accustomed to in New York.

The next morning, there was trash all over the backyard. Broken bottles glittered on the neighbor's porch.

"Raccoons. Those bastards," my mother said. "I'm calling Critter Control. Get me the magnet off the fridge."

"You're calling what?" I said.

"Just get me the goddamn magnet," she said.

On the fridge was a magnet shaped like a van. Cartoon critters poked their heads out of the van's windows. A raccoon was driving. The magnet said *Critter Control: Protecting People, Property, and Wildlife Since 1983.*

The phone number was 1-800-CRITTER.

Even before my father died, my mother had become a regular at Critter Control. The company's experts relocate problem animals. They set traps to help unhappy homeowners catch everything from rattlesnakes to pigeons. When the critter in question gets caught in a trap, Critter Control comes back and relocates it somewhere wild and safe and far far away. At least that's what the ads say.

"I am not putting up with this crap," my mother said. "Go through my garbage and make a mess in my yard? We'll just see about that."

The Critter Control guy who came when we called was nice. He was professional. He dressed like a postal worker. He had very large teeth.

"Don't you worry, ma'am," he told my mother. "We always get 'em." When he smiled, his mouth looked like a trap. "We get 'em," he said. "One way or another."

He handed my mother a pamphlet that cited Critter Control's latest offerings. On the back panel was a list of Fun Animal Facts.

Did you know . . . Fleas have changed history. As carriers of the bubonic plague, fleas killed one-third of the population of Europe in the 14th Century.

Did you know . . . Mosquitoes are the deadliest animal on earth.

"You have a great day now, ma'am," the Critter Control guy said. "And don't worry. Everything will be under control in a few days. Call us when you get a full trap."

My mother giggled and glowed like a schoolgirl.

Raccoons are smart. Although exclusion was the best method for dealing with raccoons, the new Critter Control pamphlet said, they'd also recommend shooting them. "Shooting is very effective, particularly if trained hounds are used to tree the raccoons," the pamphlet said. "Local regulations may apply."

"I wish I had a gun," my mother said.

It took weeks for the raccoons to stumble into the traps. By the time they did, I'd almost forgotten about them. I'd been forgetting a lot of things, mostly what my life was like before I'd become this 30-something woman who slept in a room with a Donald Duck nightlight and whose mother tried to regulate her bedtime.

"Are you going to stay up all night reading?" my mother would say.

"Are you going to burn that light all night long? Electricity's expensive."

"What's so important in that book that you can't put it down?"

"You're going to ruin your eyes if you don't stop it already."

I remembered the picture the doctor had shown me, my mother's heart, how sick she was underneath it all. But the new medicines seemed to be working. She didn't seem sick. Sure, she walked a little more slowly and didn't do stairs, and sometimes, when I caught her sitting alone with a cup of tea, she looked far off and sad and vulnerable. Most of the time, though, she seemed very much herself—tough, invincible, the same woman who'd had Last Rites five times and lived to joke about it.

"I'm a cat, Father," she'd said to the little eight-ball priest the last time. "You can throw me off a building and I'll land on all fours."

That was my mother. Now she was back. She was angry. And this time, she didn't have my father to focus on.

"I haven't had a second of peace since I married her," my father used to say. "She'll nag me straight to the grave. She'll nag me straight to hell."

My mother loved my father, and he loved her, but they fought. According to my mother, my father ate too much or too little. His clothes were a mess. He breathed heavy, chewed with his mouth open, and snored.

"He just doesn't know any better," my mother would say. "His mother never taught him and now he's my problem."

Now that my father wasn't around, my mother became my problem and I became hers.

"Are you going to stay in that bathtub all night?" she'd say as she pounded on the bathroom door.

"Why don't you eat meat loaf?" she'd say. "You're probably anemic, you're so pale. You think you're too good for meat loaf?"

"Your hair looks so much better longer," she'd say when I'd get a haircut.

And, no matter what I had on, there was the everyday classic: "You're wearing *that?*"

"She's making me crazy," I told my friend Gina on the phone. "I know she's sick. But she's really made a comeback."

"I'll be right over," Gina said.

Gina had been working a lot. She'd been traveling between Pittsburgh and a ratty hotel room in Columbus, Ohio. Her own mother had been acting up. She had demands. Gina could either get married or move home.

"Cut the charades already," Gina's mother Estelle told her. "Your life, your *life*. What life? What's so special about this life of yours anyway? I need you here. What kind of daughter turns her back on her mother?"

The last thing Gina needed was to hear me whine.

"You're a good woman," I told her.

"I'm a saint," she said.

When Gina showed up, she brought bags of seafood. She'd stopped by Wholey's, the seafood market in Pittsburgh's Strip District. Wholey's is one of the few places in Pittsburgh where you can order a live fish from a tank and watch while a butcher whacks it over the head with a mallet, then skins it fresh. It seems awful and cruel and people line up to watch. Wholey's slogan is "Where the fish is so fresh some of it's still swimming."

"Hiya, Bert," Gina said to my mother and smiled. Whenever Gina smiled, she looked like a kid trying to hide a wad of gum under her tongue. "Thought I'd come over and cook you a decent meal."

"What's that?" my mother said, pointing at the bags. "Don't tell me you brought fish. You're going to stink up my whole house with that."

"Oh come on, Bert," Gina said, still smiling. "We've got crab legs, shrimp, a little lemon sole. It's all good."

"My whole house is going to stink like fish. It's going to smell like the greasy spoon," my mother said. "And you expect me to be happy."

"Relax," Gina said.

"Relax, she says," my mother said. "In my own house." She turned around, walked back to her bedroom, and closed the door.

"See. This is what I'm talking about," I told Gina. "What am I supposed to do?"

"We'll start with dinner," Gina said, "then go from there."

It was all, of course, about control.

My mother, seafood or no seafood, didn't want Gina and me puttering around in her kitchen. She didn't want raccoons rummaging through her garbage. She didn't want someone burning her lights all night long or holing up in her bathtub. She wanted order. She wanted to be in charge. She wanted what I wanted, what Gina wanted. My mother wanted her life.

Back in the driveway, she was standing with her legs apart, the shovel held high. She looked completely in and out of control all at once.

"That's no copperhead," I said. The snake was gimping along now, headed for the road that separated our house from the woods. "It's just a garter . . . ."

And then my mother sprinted forward. She whacked the snake again. The shovel clanged against the asphalt, and the snake spun, coiled, and tried to strike. It had the kind of confidence that was backed up by venom.

"I told you, I told you!" my mother was screaming.

She jumped back and brought the shovel down again, this time square on the snake's lispy skull. My mother had never looked stronger or more determined in her life.

"Not in my house," she said as she pounded the snake flat. "Not in my house."

The Ugly Tourist

Jamaica Kincaid

If you go to Antigua as a tourist, this is what you will see. If you come by aeroplane, you will land at the V. C. Bird International Airport. Vere Cornwall (V. C.) Bird is the Prime Minister of Antigua. You may be the sort of tourist who would wonder why a Prime Minister would want an airport named after him—why not a school, why not a hospital, why not some great public monument? You are a tourist and you have not yet seen a school in Antigua, you have not yet seen the hospital in Antigua, you have not yet seen a public monument in Antigua. As your plane descends to land, you might say, What a beautiful island Antigua is—more beautiful than any of the other islands you have seen, and they were very beautiful, in their way, but they were much too green, much too lush with vegetation, which indicated to you, the tourist, that they got quite a bit of rainfall, and rain is the very thing that you, just now, do not want, for you are thinking of the hard and cold and dark and long days you spent working in North America (or, worse, Europe), earning some money so that you could stay in this place (Antigua) where the sun always shines and where the climate is deliciously hot and dry for the four to ten days you are going to be staying there; and since you are on your holiday, since you are a tourist, the thought of what it might be like for someone who had to live day in, day out in a place that suffers constantly from drought, and so has to watch carefully every drop of fresh water used (while at the same time surrounded by a sea and an ocean—the Caribbean Sea on one side, the Atlantic Ocean on the other), must never cross your mind.

You disembark from your plane. You go through customs. Since you are a tourist, a North American or European—to be frank, white—and not an Antiguan black returning to Antigua from Europe or North America with cardboard boxes of much needed cheap clothes and food for relatives, you move through customs swiftly, you move through customs with ease. Your bags are not searched. You emerge from customs into the hot, clean air: immediately you feel cleansed, immediately you feel blessed (which is to say special); you feel free. You see a man, a taxi driver; you ask him to take you to your destination; he quotes you a price. You immediately think that the price is in the local currency, for you are a tourist and you are familiar with these things (rates of exchange) and you feel even more free, for things seem so cheap, but then your driver ends by saying, "In U.S. currency." You may say, "Hmmmm, do you have a formal sheet that lists official prices and destinations?" Your driver obeys the law and shows you the sheet, and he apologises for the incredible mistake he has made in quoting you a price off the top of his head which is so vastly different (favouring him) from the one listed. You are driven to your hotel by this taxi driver in his taxi, a brand-new Japanese-made vehicle. The road on which you are travelling is a very bad road, very much in need of repair. You are feeling wonderful, so you say, "Oh, what a marvellous change these bad roads are from the splendid highways I am used to in North America." (Or worse, Europe.) Your driver is reckless; he is a dangerous man who drives in the middle of the road when he thinks no other cars are coming in the opposite direction, passes other cars on blind curves that run uphill, drives at sixty miles an hour on narrow, curving roads when the road sign, a rusting, beat-up thing left over from colonial days, says 40 MPH. This might frighten you (you are on your holiday; you are a tourist); this might excite you (you are on your holiday; you are a tourist), though if you are from New York and take taxis you are used to this style of driving: most of the taxi drivers in New York are from places in the world like this. You are looking out the window (because you want to get your money's worth); you notice that all the cars you see are brand-new, or almost brand-new; and that they are all Japanese made. There are no American cars in Antigua—no new ones, at any rate; none that were manufactured in the last ten years. You continue to look at the cars and you say to yourself, Why, they look brand-new, but they have an awful sound, like an old car—a very old, dilapidated car. How to account for that? Well, possibly it's because they use leaded gasoline in these brand-new cars whose engines were built to use non-leaded gasoline, but you mustn't ask the person driving the car if this is so, because he or she has never heard of unleaded gasoline. You look closely at the car; you see that it's a model of a Japanese car that you might hesitate to buy; it's a model that's very expensive; it's a model that's quite impractical for a person who has to work as hard as you do and who watches every penny you earn so that you can afford this holiday you are on. How do they afford such a car? And do they live in a luxurious house to match such a car? Well, no. You will be surprised, then, to see that most likely the person driving this brand-new car filled with the wrong gas lives in a house that, in comparison, is far beneath the status of the car; and if you were to ask why you would be told that the banks are encouraged by the government to make loans available for cars, but loans for houses not so easily available; and if you ask again why, you will be told that the two main car dealerships in Antigua are owned in part or outright by ministers in government. Oh, but you are on holiday and the sight of these brand-new cars driven by people who may or may not have really passed their driving test (there was once a scandal about driving licences for sale) would not really stir up these thoughts in you. You pass a building sitting in a sea of dust and you think, It's some latrines for people just passing by, but when you look again you see the building has written on it PIGOTT'S SCHOOL. You pass the hospital, the Holberton Hospital, and how wrong you are not to think about this, for though you are a tourist on your holiday, what if your heart should miss a few beats? What if a blood vessel in your neck should break? What if one of those people driving those brand-new cars filled with the wrong gas fails to pass safely while going uphill on a curve and you are in the car going in the opposite direction? Will you be comforted to know that the hospital is staffed with doctors that no actual Antiguan trusts; that Antiguans always say about the doctors, "I don't want them near me"; that Antiguans refer to them not as doctors but as "the three men" (there are three of them); that when the Minister of Health himself doesn't feel well he takes the first plane to New York to see a real doctor; that if anyone of the ministers in government needs medical care he flies to New York to get it?

It's a good thing that you brought your own books with you, for you couldn't just go to the library and borrow some. Antigua used to have a splendid library, but in The Earthquake (everyone talks about it that way—The Earthquake; we Antiguans, for I am one, have a great sense of things, and the more meaningful the thing, the more meaningless we make it) the library building was damaged. This was in 1974, and soon after that a sign was placed on the front of the building saying, THIS BUILDING WAS DAMAGED IN THE EARTHQUAKE OF 1974. REPAIRS ARE PENDING. The sign hangs there, and hangs there more than a decade later, with its unfulfilled promise of repair, and you might see this as a sort of quaintness on the part of these islanders, these people descended from slaves—what a strange, unusual perception of time they have. REPAIRS ARE PENDING, and here it is many years later, but perhaps in a world that is twelve miles long and nine miles wide (the size of Antigua) twelve years and twelve minutes and twelve days are all the same. The library is one of those splendid old buildings from colonial times, and the sign telling of the repairs is a splendid old sign from colonial times. Not very long after The Earthquake Antigua got its independence from Britain, making Antigua a state in its own right, and Antiguans are so proud of this that each year, to mark the day, they go to church and thank God, a British God, for this. But you should not think of the confusion that must lie in all that and you must not think of the damaged library. You have brought your own books with you, and among them is one of those new books about economic history, one of those books explaining how the West (meaning Europe and North America after its conquest and settlement by Europeans) got rich: the West got rich not from the free (free—in this case meaning got-for-nothing) and then undervalued labour, for generations, of the people like me you see walking around you in Antigua but from the ingenuity of small shopkeepers in Sheffield and Yorkshire and Lancashire, or wherever; and what a great part the invention of the wristwatch played in it, for there was nothing noble-minded men could not do when they discovered they could slap time on their wrists just like that (isn't that the last straw; for not only did we have to suffer the unspeakableness of slavery, but the satisfaction to be had from "We made you bastards rich" is taken away, too), and so you needn't let that slightly funny feeling you have from time to time about exploitation, oppression, domination develop into full-fledged unease, discomfort; you could ruin your holiday. They are not responsible for what you have; you owe them nothing; in fact, you did them a big favour, and you can provide one hundred examples. For here you are now, passing by Government House. And here you are now, passing by the Prime Minister's Office and the Parliament Building, and overlooking these, with a splendid view of St. John's Harbour, the American Embassy. If it were not for you, they would not have Government House, and Prime Minister's Office, and Parliament Building and embassy of powerful country. Now you are passing a mansion, an extraordinary house painted the colour of old cow dung, with more aerials and antennas attached to it than you will see even at the American Embassy. The people who live in this house are a merchant family who came to Antigua from the Middle East less than twenty years ago. When this family first came to Antigua, they sold dry goods door to door from suitcases they carried on their backs. Now they own a lot of Antigua; they regularly lend money to the government, they build enormous (for Antigua), ugly (for Antigua), concrete buildings in Antigua's capital, St. John's, which the government then rents for huge sums of money; a member of their family is the Antiguan Ambassador to Syria; Antiguans hate them. Not far from this mansion is another mansion, the home of a drug smuggler. Everybody knows he's a drug smuggler, and if just as you were driving by he stepped out of his door your driver might point him out to you as the notorious person that he is, for this drug smuggler is so rich people say he buys cars in tens—ten of this one, ten of that one—and that he bought a house (another mansion) near Five Islands, contents included, with cash he carried in a suitcase: three hundred and fifty thousand American dollars, and, to the surprise of the seller of the house, lots of American dollars were left over. Overlooking the drug smuggler's mansion is yet another mansion, and leading up to it is the best paved road in all of Antigua—even better than the road that was paved for the Queen's visit in 1985 (when the Queen came, all the roads that she would travel on were paved anew, so that the Queen might have been left with the impression that riding in a car in Antigua was a pleasant experience). In this mansion lives a woman sophisticated people in Antigua call Evita. She is a notorious woman. She's young and beautiful and the girlfriend of somebody very high up in the government. Evita is notorious because her relationship with this high government official has made her the owner of boutiques and property and given her a say in cabinet meetings, and all sorts of other privileges such a relationship would bring a beautiful young woman.

Oh, but by now you are tired of all this looking, and you want to reach your destination—your hotel, your room. You long to refresh yourself; you long to eat some nice lobster, some nice local food. You take a bath, you brush your teeth. You get dressed again; as you get dressed, you look out the window. That water—have you ever seen anything like it? Far out, to the horizon, the colour of the water is navy-blue; nearer, the water is the colour of the North American sky. From there to the shore, the water is pale, silvery, clear, so clear that you can see its pinkish-white sand bottom. Oh, what beauty! Oh, what beauty! You have never seen anything like this. You are so excited. You breathe shallow. You breathe deep. You see a beautiful boy skimming the water, godlike, on a Windsurfer. You see an incredibly unattractive, fat, pastrylike-fleshed woman enjoying a walk on the beautiful sand, with a man, an incredibly unattractive, fat, pastrylike-fleshed man; you see the pleasure they're taking in their surroundings. Still standing, looking out the window, you see yourself lying on the beach, enjoying the amazing sun (a sun so powerful and yet so beautiful, the way it is always overhead as if on permanent guard, ready to stamp out any cloud that dares to darken and so empty rain on you and ruin your holiday; a sun that is your personal friend). You see yourself taking a walk on that beach, you see yourself meeting new people (only they are new in a very limited way, for they are people just like you). You see yourself eating some delicious, locally grown food. You see yourself, you see yourself . . . You must not wonder what exactly happened to the contents of your lavatory when you flushed it. You must not wonder where your bathwater went when you pulled out the stopper. You must not wonder what happened when you brushed your teeth. Oh, it might all end up in the water you are thinking of taking a swim in; the contents of your lavatory might, just might, graze gently against your ankle as you wade carefree in the water, for you see, in Antigua, there is no proper sewage-disposal system. But the Caribbean Sea is very big and the Atlantic Ocean is even bigger; it would amaze even you to know the number of black slaves this ocean has swallowed up. When you sit down to eat your delicious meal, it's better that you don't know that most of what you are eating came off a plane from Miami. And before it got on a plane in Miami, who knows where it came from? A good guess is that it came from a place like Antigua first, where it was grown dirt-cheap, went to Miami, and came back. There is a world of something in this, but I can't go into it right now.

The thing you have always suspected about yourself the minute you become a tourist is true: A tourist is an ugly human being. You are not an ugly person all the time; you are not an ugly person ordinarily; you are not an ugly person day to day. From day to day, you are a nice person. From day to day, all the people who are supposed to love you on the whole do. From day to day, as you walk down a busy street in the large and modern and prosperous city in which you work and live, dismayed, puzzled (a cliché, but only a cliché can explain you) at how alone you feel in this crowd, how awful it is to go unnoticed, how awful it is to go unloved, even as you are surrounded by more people than you could possibly get to know in a lifetime that lasted for millennia, and then out of the corner of your eye you see someone looking at you and absolute pleasure is written all over that person's face, and then you realise that you are not as revolting a presence as you think you are (for that look just told you so). And so, ordinarily, you are a nice person, an attractive person, a person capable of drawing to yourself the affection of other people (people just like you), a person at home in your own skin (sort of; I mean, in a way; I mean, your dismay and puzzlement are natural to you, because people like you just seem to be like that, and so many of the things people like you find admirable about yourselves—the things you think about, the things you think really define you—seem rooted in these feelings): a person at home in your own house (and all its nice house things), with its nice back yard (and its nice back-yard things), at home on your street, your church, in community activities, your job, at home with your family, your relatives, your friends—you are a whole person. But one day, when you are sitting somewhere, alone in that crowd, and that awful feeling of displacedness comes over you, and really, as an ordinary person you are not well equipped to look too far inward and set yourself aright, because being ordinary is already so taxing, and being ordinary takes all you have out of you, and though the words "I must get away" do not actually pass across your lips, you make a leap from being that nice blob just sitting like a boob in your amniotic sac of the modern experience to being a person visiting heaps of death and ruin and feeling alive and inspired at the sight of it; to being a person lying on some faraway beach, your stilled body stinking and glistening in the sand, looking like something first forgotten, then remembered, then not important enough to go back for; to being a person marvelling at the harmony (ordinarily, what you would say is the backwardness) and the union these other people (and they are other people) have with nature. And you look at the things they can do with a piece of ordinary cloth, the things they fashion out of cheap, vulgarly colored (to you) twine, the way they squat down over a hole they have made in the ground, the hole itself is something to marvel at, and since you are being an ugly person this ugly but joyful thought will swell inside you: their ancestors were not clever in the way yours were and not ruthless in the way yours were, for then would it not be you who would be in harmony with nature and backwards in that charming way? An ugly thing, that is what you are when you become a tourist, an ugly, empty thing, a stupid thing, a piece of rubbish pausing here and there to gaze at this and taste that, and it will never occur to you that the people who inhabit the place in which you have just paused cannot stand you, that behind their closed doors they laugh at your strangeness (you do not look the way they look); the physical sight of you does not please them;

you have bad manners (it is their custom to eat their food with their hands; you try eating their way, you look silly; you try eating the way you always eat, you look silly); they do not like the way you speak (you have an accent); they collapse helpless from laughter, mimicking the way they imagine you must look as you carry out some everyday bodily function. They do not like you. *They do not like me!* That thought never actually occurs to you. Still, you feel a little uneasy. Still, you feel a little foolish. Still, you feel a little out of place. But the banality of your own life is very real to you; it drove you to this extreme, spending your days and your nights in the company of people who despise you, people you do not like really, people you would not want to have as your actual neighbour. And so you must devote yourself to puzzling out how much of what you are told is really, really true (Is ground-up bottle glass in peanut sauce really a delicacy around here, or will it do just what you think ground-up bottle glass will do? Is this rare, multicoloured, snout-mouthed fish really an aphrodisiac, or will it cause you to fall asleep permanently?). Oh, the hard work all of this is, and is it any wonder, then, that on your return home you feel the need of a long rest, so that you can recover from your life as a tourist?

That the native does not like the tourist is not hard to explain. For every native of every place is a potential tourist, and every tourist is a native of somewhere. Every native everywhere lives a life of overwhelming and crushing banality and boredom and desperation and depression, and every deed, good and bad, is an attempt to forget this. Every native would like to find a way out, every native would like a rest, every native would like a tour. But some natives—most natives in the world—cannot go anywhere. They are too poor. They are too poor to go anywhere. They are too poor to escape the reality of their lives; and they are too poor to live properly in the place where they live, which is the very place you, the tourist, want to go—so when the natives see you, the tourist, they envy you, they envy your ability to leave your own banality and boredom, they envy your ability to turn their own banality and boredom into a source of pleasure for yourself.

Wounds and Words

Elizabeth Kirschner

I've lived most of my life, particularly my writing life, in what I call the open wound.

Most of us walk through the world wounded, but I would argue that for the writer, wounds are wombs where poems, stories, and essays are born. Sometimes I see my soul, literally, as a damaged web, and my job is to transform that web into a cocoon. The work incubates in these cocoons, sometimes for years, even decades, till suddenly a wing appears. That wing is the word whose forward motion is to migrate. Poems, stories, essays, then, as winged migrations. Some migrations are exhilarating, others so exhausting the wings feel leaden, and the labor is all about survival for both the writer and the word.

Wound as womb I want to say, wound as womb wherein the ache pulses. Putting one's finger on that pulse creates the work's rhythm and cadence, its musicality. I was first trained as a singer, so the study of music preceded the study of writing. I sang all the time, but when I encountered poetry for the first time some thirty-five years ago, I knew that all I wanted to do was sing on the page. My wounds, then, are also musical. A scar can't sing, for it is two lips closed. But a wound can, as it has both voice and a story to tell.

In the end, that's the gift wounds bring us—a story set to song. If I ignore my mortal woundedness, I risk ignoring my humanity. Imagine the wound as sacred. Imagine the wound as schooling us. For me, that's where the pull of writing is, and if I can manage living in the open wound, I can also believe in healing.

Presence of Another

Amanda Leskovac

I'm all by myself being taken somewhere by two strange men. It's a plot ripped straight from a horror movie. The nurses in the ICU had said I was going to rehabilitation, but since I've only heard rehab synonymous with addicts, I have no idea what to expect. The huge collar around my neck prevents me from seeing much beyond the EMT, so I've got nowhere else to focus my fear. I try again.

"You can call me Mandi. My friends call me Mandi." I watch him trace the careful lines of his goatee with his thumb and index finger. "What's yours?"

He finally turns his head and looks at me. "Henry. My friends call me Henry." We both smile. "And Tyler's driving." He careens his neck up toward the front. "Say hi to Mandi, Tyler."

I feel safer, somehow, knowing their names.

"All right, Mandi," Henry says, pulling out a folder and shuffling through pages. "I need to make sure we've got the right information before we drop you off at the rehab center. That okay with you?" His smile dents his full, round face.

"I suppose. But make it quick. I've got dinner plans."

His laugh booms throughout the small, metal space, then his face turns quickly serious. "So, you just turned 21 six weeks ago?" I nod as much as my collar allows. "You were in a car accident?" I nod again. "Were you driving?"

"No."

"Were they drinking?"

"I don't remember much." And while it's true that a couple fuzzy details remain after leaving the bar, I'm not ready to come completely clean.

"Man." He rubs his forehead. "I got a lot of buddies who do that shit."

Even without complete disclosure, I have officially become one of those *who do that shit.*

1-2-3 lifts me from the ambulance gurney onto freshly-made linen. I imagine 500-count, Egyptian cotton.

"I'm Gail, and I'll be your head nurse," says the woman who orchestrated my transfer onto the bed. She grabs my hand and holds on tightly. She's got quite a grip for such a petite woman. "Your mom called and said your family would be here soon. I told them not to worry because we'd be with you all morning. You need anything right now?"

I shake my head, but don't let go of her hand. I need a lot of things, but for now, her touch will do just fine.

"Looks like you're exhausted. Shut your eyes for a bit. I need to round up some help to get you settled." She leans over and fixes the oxygen tubing that's in my nose, tightens up the straps around my neck holding my trach in place. I wince and take a deep breath in. She smells like vanilla, clean. I drift off to sleep.

My eyelids pop open, and a piercing pain shoots down the right side of my neck, followed by a heavy ache that reverberates through every synapse of my body. It's the same cycle every time I wake up, even from ten-minute naps. I can't understand the science, have never been good with science, but still.

How can I be paralyzed and still hurt this badly?

How can I feel so shitty when I can't even feel?

It's as if my body recognizes that it's lost the war, as the pain has gotten worse instead of better. Pain is its way of proving a treaty has been signed, and there is no bargaining I can do to turn it around, as I'm obviously powerless. Once my spinal cord had been severed, there was only so much the doctors could do—metal plates, screws. My body says *too little, too late.*

"Knock-knock." Gail and another nurse barrel around the corner into my room. By the time the last consonant in *knock* is enunciated, they have already planted themselves in front of me. I'm starting to understand that a revolving door comes standard with paralysis.

"We need to weigh you." Gail pulls down the metal bed rail and introduces me to Marcia. I look up at her briefly, but . . . Did she just say *weigh*?

They push a big metal contraption next to my bed. "We just need to roll you and get this tarp under you," Marcia says. "Then we'll attach it to the frame and jack you up to get your weight. Okay, honey?"

Jack me up? I suddenly feel like a '57 Chevy.

And while Marcia technically asked my permission, there's only one right answer. Seconds later, they roll me from left to right until I'm smack dab in the middle of the tarp. It wraps around me like a cocoon. If only this would transform me into a beautiful butterfly.

Gail begins pumping a huge silver arm, and I realize why Marcia used the verb *jack.* I slowly ascend into the air, and the tarp gets tighter and tighter until I can't move my arms or see either of the nurses. Finally, Gail stops when I'm completely off the bed. I rock back and forth and feel, quite literally, like a whale being transported from the ocean to a boat. Another plus for my ego.

After a minute or so, Marcia releases a button, eases me back down and begins to unwrap me. Gail scribbles into a binder about the width of an encyclopedia; it reads "Leskovac, Amanda" across the front. I'm suddenly paranoid, wonder what she's writing, wonder what's already been written. My life has been condensed. Whatever came before the accident doesn't matter. This new book is only concerned in the *after.*

The diary I had when I was little—trimmed in red, a teddy bear with a bow around its neck adorning the cover, full of accounts of my first cartwheel, my first kiss, my fears about the future—was completely under my control. I hid it underneath my mattress and every night, willed osmosis to make my words reality. But I'm not in charge of this new book, these new details. Only people who know me by "Amanda—21-year-old quadriplegic" can record the facts. Only they hold the key.

"Well . . . ?" I've been avoiding full-length mirrors for a while, have made it an art form, even speed past windows if I catch a reflection of myself. This has been especially true in the past year when college became a late-night eating fest. Truth is, it had been more like a beer and marijuana fest, but food naturally took a close third—the domino effect.

Gail looks up from my chart. "Scale says 190 pounds."

"A hundred and what?" Perhaps the paralysis has affected my hearing.

"Ninety." She repeats it slowly and loudly. "One hundred and ninety."

My head feels fuzzy. Not only am I paralyzed, but I'm paralyzed and extremely fat. I look down at my body, but can't see it because of the collar. I imagine, estimating the length of my legs, the width of my hips. I long to tuck my feet up under my butt, lean this way, stretch that way, drape my arm across my stomach, pose my body in the way I'd practiced through high school and college—accentuate the positive, contort the negative.

I take a deep breath and feel my lungs strain against the mucus weighing them down, trying to suffocate me. My left lung has collapsed four times already; though each time, the doctors had to tell me it happened, that I was only getting 50% of my usual oxygen intake. I may have noticed sore ribs or difficulty breathing, but my idea of "collapsing" is way more dramatic: a hotel gets blown up in Vegas, its frame *collapses* under the weight; a severe pain shoots down an old man's left arm, he *collapses* from a heart attack. I need proof—smoke and rubble, a huge POW of some kind. I can't quite figure how all of this happens *inside* me, but I'm the last to know.

After the second collapse, they performed a tracheotomy. People can only go so long with the ventilator getting ripped in and out through their mouths, so they take a more direct approach. They cut an incision in my windpipe and inserted a tube into the opening to access my lungs. I've been vent-free for five days, but they're leaving the trach in for who knows how long *just in case*. Mucus builds up, and since I broke my neck, the muscles in my diaphragm are partially paralyzed. And I'm up against some powerful snot.

I try to muffle the wheeze by clearing my throat, but Gail's ears perk up.

"You need to cough, honey? I'll help you get it up." She grabs my hand and squeezes.

"What do you mean, *help me*?" I'm wary. In the hospital, their idea of "help" was to stick a catheter through my trach hole and suction out the phlegm until I was gagging and out of breath.

"It's an assisted cough." She winks. "Trust me."

She climbs up on my bed and looms over me. "Whenever you're ready, I'll follow your lead." She places her hands in the space right below my rib cage and straightens her arms.

When *I'm* ready.

I inhale and taste the artificial oxygen they've got pumping through my nose, like I'm getting Sweet 'n Low, and everyone else is breathing pure sugar air. On the exhale, Gail plunges all of her 100 pounds into me and pushes upward. Once, twice, three times—breathe in, breathe out. Each exhale, each push against my diaphragm induces a retched gag and leaves me straining for air. The phlegm gurgles and rises up into my throat. When I've audibly hit my gag apex, Gail leans back and steps off my bed. We're both panting.

"That sounded productive." Marcia hands me a wad of tissues, and I spit out a giant mouthful of snot. It's beautifully disgusting.

"What color is it?" Gail flips my chart open, pen in hand.

"Huh?" I wipe off my mouth and search for a garbage can. "What color is what?"

"Your mucus. Open up the tissue and let me see it. I need to record the color and thickness." She pulls on a pair of gloves.

I hold onto the corner of the tissue and pass it over. I've never offered such a vile piece of myself to anyone. She opens it, shakes her head and looks disappointed. I'm confused. What did she expect?

She scribbles in my chart. "Green is not good. It's a sign of infection—especially if it's green and thick like yours. I was hoping for yellow. It's still not great, but it's better. White is the best. Looks like we have a long way to go."

What's next—the texture and consistency of my earwax? Gail closes my chart after recording another unsatisfactory mark—my weight and now my mucus. My body will be sent to the principal's office soon.

Gail and Marcia show up an hour later and tell me it's time for my shower. A woman I haven't met before stands beside them holding towels.

"This is Karen," Gail says.

I wave and attempt a smile, pull the flimsy cotton hospital gown tighter around me. I've been bathing myself since I was five. Mom says I adopted my "I do it" mantra and insisted on dressing myself, pouring my cereal, and brushing my teeth. Sixteen years later, I'm joined in the shower by three almost complete strangers. I've discovered that paralysis leaves no room for pride.

"Won't it feel good to wash that hospital off you?" Karen's voice comes out soft, like she's coddling a small child.

I nod and touch my head. My fingers instantly tangle in a clump of hair. It's matted and coarse. I'm well on my way to sporting dreadlocks—well on my way to being Quadriplegic Marley. Small scabs border my hairline and rise up sporadically throughout my scalp. Evidence. I don't remember the actual accident, but the blood and dirt in my hair connect me to it, make me part of the story—perhaps the *whole* story.

Marcia ducks out for a minute and comes back rolling in a big, white chair.

"What's that? It looks like it's made of plastic."

"A shower chair." Marcia situates it flush up against my bed and puts the brakes on. "Don't worry. We've had patients a lot bigger than you, and it held them just fine."

I pause. *Bigger than me?* I want to believe she just intended to reassure me. But my 190-pound translation tells me that she thinks I'm a cow; whatever the shower chair is made of will still hold me—the other patients had been buffalos. I want to tell them to forget it. I want to lay my dirty, paralyzed body down and tell them to leave. But I've got no say. My body is moving, and I'm nothing more than a passenger.

Gail slowly swings my legs off the bed then scoots my hips over, so I'm sitting on the edge of the bed. The other girls spot me from behind, make sure I can feel their hands on my back. My balance is off, partly because of the big collar around my neck, but mostly because I've lost the muscles to keep myself up without help.

She tells me she's going to do a quad lift. I figure any lift would be a quad lift since they are lifting me and I'm a quad. But I've only technically been one for two weeks, so I'm not hip to all the "quad lingo" yet. As much as I usually like to be well-informed, like to know what people are saying—especially when it pertains to me—I don't ask what it means. I want to remain as ignorant as long as I possibly can.

She pins my legs between her knees, then leans in and hugs me hard, wraps both arms around me and pulls me forward.

"Ready?" My chin is smashed against her shoulder. I nod, but it's just a formality.

"One, two . . . " We rock back and forth together until "three" lifts me up in the air. I hold my breath, shut my eyes. I'm at least five inches taller than Gail and almost double her weight. I'm positive we'll both hit the floor, almost wish it, so I can stay in bed. But Gail's an expert, has performed the same steps on patients before me, possibly even bigger than me. When my backside lands on the chair, Gail untangles her arms from mine and steps back.

"You comfortable?"

I stare at her. *Is she kidding?*

My ass has made contact only with the front of the seat, and my left cheek hangs off to the side. Plus, the oxygen tubing has been yanked out of my nose and hangs across my face. I'm slouched, twisted and irritated. Comfortable isn't exactly the word I'd use.

Once they get me situated, Gail pushes the shower chair while Marcia pulls the oxygen tank and Karen opens the door. The water is already running, and the room is filled with steam. It isn't until I see the enormous-sized bathroom that I understand how a wheelchair, an oxygen tank and three nurses are going to fit into a shower. It's split in half, with a toilet and sink on one side and a roll-in shower on the other. The floor of the shower is flush with the rest of the bathroom, and a vinyl curtain is the only thing separating it. I foresee a flood.

We stop in the entranceway. All three women crouch down, take their shoes and socks off, then cuff the bottom of their pants. Now I'm convinced this is going to be messy, and I wonder why they're willing to go through such trouble for someone who made such a stupid mistake. They stand up and wait for my go, but I say nothing, don't know if I'm ready for this, don't even know what *this* is. I try to detach myself, become "Amanda, the quadriplegic," need to let go of *before* and dive into the *after*.

When I nod, Marcia unties the gown from around my neck and slips it off my arms. The room is filled with steam, but goose bumps instantly creep over my skin. I keep my head down, unable to look at them. Even when I've been intimate with my boyfriends, I've never allowed them to see me so candidly. Now, not only am I aware I'm 190 pounds, I must factor in the paralysis. It makes feeling impossible, but it's got to *look* like something. The worst possible image surfaces.

I look up at the girls for confirmation, try to locate my reflection in their eyes. But they're not helping. Instead, their faces are soft, their eyes locked on mine. My image shatters between us. I'm ashamed of the pieces that they don't even see.

Gail moves the hand-held shower hose so that it shoots into the wall then rolls me into the shower. Once I'm in with my oxygen tank beside me, they put the brakes on. I'm forced to wonder exactly what happened that night, how my body had been ejected and the three other girls remained in their seats— what exactly happened to land me in an enormous wheelchair-accessible shower with three strange women.

Gail tells me to tilt my head back and, holding the shower nozzle nearby, she wets my hair. Hot water streams across my face and down my back. I sputter as water goes up my nose and finds my open mouth. Suddenly I'm back in beginner's swimming lessons, unaware that I should shut my mouth and hold my breath when water comes at my face. Gail brings my head back up straight.

"Sorry, honey. You okay?"

I'm just about to tell her I am when a tiny trickle of water sneaks down my neck, seeps into my trach hole and takes my breath away. I think the obvious counter-action is to inhale and try to get it back, but that only exacerbates the gag.

Gail points the water toward the floor and thumps me on the back while Marcia takes a towel and blots around my trach site. I work through the cough and breathe like Gail taught me, but I feel my head becoming light and ears beginning to ring. Showering has become another dangerous activity: give me cleanliness or give me death.

Gail wipes my cheeks and eyes with a washcloth. When she hits my right eye, I jump, surprised at the pain.

"I'm trying to be as gentle as I can, but you've got some pretty nasty cuts. I just want to make sure they're cleaned out." I flinch again as she moves to my forehead and wipes off the cuts there and in my hairline. I haven't looked at my face in over two weeks, but I imagine the cuts and bruises, want Gail to polish them, keep them bright pink. They tell me I've broken my neck, but I can't see that, can't see for myself why I've become what I've become. The marks on my face are something I can hold onto, evidence that my body was hurled out of a moving vehicle. For a brief second, I feel like a bad-ass.

"Tell me if it's too hot." She pours water on my head; only a couple streams spill down my face and neck. The water is hot, *way* too hot. I can feel every pore of my scalp open up. Unlike most of my body, my scalp pulses, whispers, *I'm alive.*

"It's perfect," I tell her.

She lathers my hair, digs her fingers in and scrubs, nails prodding, massaging. To fix my neck, the surgeons had to shave a portion of my hair. The shaved part itches with new hair growth, and Gail's nails are my salvation.

As she finishes, Karen lathers a couple washcloths and begins cleaning my body—first my arms and underarms, then my chest and belly. She drops the first washcloth to the floor, and then uses the other for my feet, calves, thighs and between my legs. She apologizes and "excuses" herself before each touch. I never thought something could be so intimate without being sexual. Nor did I think I could sit in a wheelchair, fat and nude without crying.

But in this moment, none of that matters. I'm less embarrassed about what they're doing and what I look like than I am about what caused this. Humbled, I want to apologize for being here, for needing them to take care of me. I want to tell them that I'm a good kid, that it was a stupid mistake, that *I wasn't even planning to go out that night.*

I didn't so much as pick up a bar of soap, but I'm exhausted. The girls plop me down onto the bed, and I'm instantly engulfed in the smell of bleach. I wonder how many other patients have laid on these sheets. Wonder how many other fat, paralyzed women have gotten showered by near-strangers beforehand. I'd like to think I'm special, that I'm the first. I begin to close my eyes when a small, older man wearing an un-ironed seersucker suit walks around the corner. The little guy does a beeline toward me and grabs my hand. His are soft and small, and before he ever says a word, I like him.

"Hello, Amanda. I'm Dr. Brenes." I'm jarred when I hear his accent. He sounds like a French man speaking Russian. He doesn't hit all his syllables, and his words flow into one another, like he's singing. *Amanda* feels safe coming out of his mouth.

He keeps ahold of my hand. "How are you?"

It is a simple question, but I've got a few answers.

Physically: *My neck is killing me, I've got this strange pain shooting down my arms into my hands and there seems to be no end to the amount of snot I've got in my lungs.*

Mentally: *My family still isn't here, they just weighed me like a Mack truck, and I still don't know exactly how I ended up here.*

But I settle with "could be better . . . could be worse."

"Okay, Amanda. You will sit up, and I will assess you." Usually, I resist all types of movement. I've just sat through a thirty-minute shower and my neck is throbbing. I want to scream: *I can't. It hurts too badly. I am paralyzed!*

And even though all my arguments are potentially true, I can't seem to look Dr. Brenes in the eyes and resist. I feel like if I don't sit up, I'll be letting him down personally. I've only known him a minute, but for whatever reason, I know I can't do that.

With Gail helping from the left and Dr. Brenes on the right, I pull my body forward to the sitting position. My stomach lurches, my neck screams, but I pull forward.

"Okay, Amanda," he grabs my right hand and holds my wrist in place. "I want you to try to squeeze as hard as you can." I follow his instructions, tell my fingers to make a fist, urge my long fingers to wrap around his short ones.

My brain demands *squeeze.* My fingers start shaking, but ignore the request, defiantly remain straight. Then my thumb gives me the ultimate *fuck you* by remaining curled inward and drooped. I feel betrayed and embarrassed.

Dr. Brenes doesn't look especially surprised, mumbles a set of numbers to Gail and moves quickly to my left hand. "Okay. Now you do it again."

He says "again" like I had done it the first time. I send the same message to my left and watch as all five fingers curl obediently. The pinky and ring finger clutch tightly around his hand while the other three aren't far behind. It isn't a perfect fist, but it isn't bad. I'm proud.

"Okay." Dr. Brenes releases my hand. "Good."

He says *good*, but his facial expression only says *all right*. I feel like I've failed, and what's worse is that I know I've done my best. I'm not used to getting an "all right" score when I put in a 100% effort. I could accept a "C" when I hadn't really studied, drank a few beers the night before the test and only gotten two hours of sleep. This kind of *all right* is new to me.

Dr. Brenes moves to my legs, and I feel doomed. He wraps a tape measure around each one of my thighs, then takes a marker and draws a line when it has reached its circumference. I'm suddenly some kind of cutting-edge art project gone terribly wrong.

"Okay, now try to push your legs into the bed." He stares intently at my legs. I know I can't do what he wants. When I'd done the same thing for the doctors in the hospital, they'd nod at each other, and then hustle out of the room, none of them looking me in the face. I felt such shame. I don't want to show anyone else, don't want to talk about it anymore. But he is waiting, isn't giving me a choice.

I close my eyes and attempt to locate my leg muscles inside my body. I dig my hands into the mattress, think *push* and send the message down through my body for my legs to intercept. I utilize every ounce of energy I have, tighten every muscle that can be tightened. A tingling runs through my body; had I ever felt a tingle before?

"Okay, now relax."

I let out a breath I didn't know I was holding, open my eyes and wait. His face is blank, and I don't dare ask. I can't bear hearing the confirmation. I had known, of course, but it is within the trying that makes it real. Paralyzed.

He continues instructing me to *try to push them left, right, push your feet up, your toes down.* After awhile, I'm not sure what I'm trying to move anymore. I just know that I'm failing.

Suddenly, my body tenses up, and without any direction from me, my legs bend and pull toward me. Before I know it, I'm on my side in the fetal position. I look up at Dr. Brenes, scared at how my body has just manipulated itself. Scared that I had no say in it. Up until now, my body has remained pretty motionless; I have been lying on my back or propped up on my side for about two weeks. Because I can't feel it, I have barely even noticed its presence. Now I'm curled up in a ball without even a small warning.

"Your spasms are kicking in." He smiles and grabs my hand. I'm not used to a doctor talking to me so directly. "Don't worry. They're natural."

Later, someone will explain the muscle spasms as my body's way of "talking to me," of letting me know it's still there. But right now, if it's not going to allow me control, I'd rather it just shut up.

When the assessment is over, everyone leaves my room; I want the bed to open up like a tiny portal into another time and suck me in. I look down at the outline underneath the blanket, the legs that I used to own. They stare back at me, unflinching. I reach my hand out, place it on the right lump and close my eyes. I curl my fingers in, let my nails sink into the blanket, into flesh, will my body to feel it. The response is less than nothing. It is nothing wrapped in emptiness, a present I don't want to open.

My Drawer

Phillip Lopate

I am looking through the top drawer of my bedroom dresser this morning—
something I almost never do. I have a reticence about examining these articles,
which I don't quite understand; it's as though the Puritan side of me said it was
a waste of time, if not faintly indecent. Since I have moved my socks to another
drawer there is even less reason to visit these redundant objects. Six months
go by without my doing any more than feeling around blindly for a cuff link.
My top drawer is a *way station* in which I keep the miscellanea that I cannot
bear to throw away just yet, but that I fully intend to, the moment things get
out of hand. So far the drawer can take it. It is too early for triage. But this
morning I have an urge to make an inventory of the drawer, in a last attempt to
understand the symbolic underpinnings of my character.

In it I find a pair of 3-D movie glasses. A silver whistle. A combination lock
in good repair but whose combination has long been lost. A strip of extra cuff
material for the legs of my white linen suit—should I ever grow an inch or two
I can sew it on. One plastic and one aluminum shoehorn. A button that says
BOYCOTT LETTUCE. Keys to old houses and offices. My last pair of glasses
before the prescription changed—who can throw out a pair of eyeglasses?
Two nail clippers. Cuff links. A pair of rusty unusable children's scissors. A
windproof lighter I won at an amusement park; too bad I don't smoke. Oh, and
lots more, much more. But before I go on, shouldn't I try to approach this mess
more systematically—to categorize, to make generalizations?

One category that suggests itself is gifts I have no particular affection for,
but am too superstitious to chuck out. (If you throw away a gift, something
terrible will happen: the wastebasket will explode, or you'll never get another.)
They include this pair of cloth finger puppets that I suppose were meant to give
me endless hours of delight while sitting on my bed pretending to be Punch
and Judy with myself. Because I work with children, people keep bringing me
juvenile toys—magic sets, mazes with ball bearings, paddle-balls—confusing
the profession with the profession's clients. Over the years I have been given a
whole collection of oddities that do not really amuse me or match my sense of
perversity. Nothing is trickier than bringing someone a novelty gift, since each
person's definition of cute or campy is such a private affair.

Now we come to my "jewelry." Most of these items wandered into my possession toward the middle of the sixties, during those few seconds in American
history when it was considered progressive for men to wear medallions and

layers of necklaces. In my top drawer I find an imitation-elephant-tusk necklace, a multicolored string of Amerindian beads, and a hodgepodge of what I can only call spiritual amulets—tangled-up chains and rings that are supposed to contain special powers or that symbolize the third eye. Usually these ornaments were given to me with the explanation that most men the donor knew would be too uptight to wear jewelry like this in public, but that I was free enough to be at peace with my feminine side. Little did they know. Each and every one has landed in my top drawer, enough for me to open my own jewelry stall at a street fair.

Other mementos of hipper days include a large brown-velvet King's Road bow tie, a pack of moldering Bambu cigarette papers, and both DUMP LBJ and IMPEACH NIXON buttons. I find it hard to throw away political buttons—as hard as it was in those days actually to wear them. There is also a badge from a conference, with the words "Hi! I'm—" and my name on it. Toward the back of the drawer are my war medals: my high-school American history award, with its pea green / navy blue / red tricolor; my yellow-and-white-ribboned English award; the silver badge from the Fire Department for best fire-prevention essay. Glory days! They do cheer me up when I see them, though they are as useless now as the keys that no longer fit my door.

The keys belong to the category of things I kept to be *on the safe side.* For instance, an official bank card for cashing checks, no good to me now since I no longer go to that bank, but what if it were to fall into the wrong hands? I find also a wristwatch case with midnight-blue lining that seemed too pretty to part with, and that would make an excellent box for safety pins or—whatever. Oh, and a suede-looking drawstring purse that once held a bottle of over-priced shampoo (I seem particularly susceptible to these packages for luxury items). I realize I'm fooling myself when I say I will someday find a use for these containers. How can I when I ignore them for months at a time, and forget that they're there? They live a hidden life in the back street of my consciousness. Perhaps the drawer's purpose is to house objects that arouse only half-digested desires never fantasized all the way through. That is why I must not look into it too often. These are secret fantasies even I am not supposed to understand.

Even more than desire, these objects seem to have the power of arousing guilt; that is, they have fixed me with the hypnotizing promise not to throw them away. I find myself protecting them with an uneasy conscience, like someone whom I caused to be crippled and who now has the upper hand. I suppose if I were to examine the derivations of each of these keepsakes, many would call up some road not taken, some rejection of possibility. Or perhaps they are secretly connected to each other by surrealist logic, like the objects in a Joseph Cornell box, and if I were to lay them out on top of the dresser I could put together the story of my subconscious mind.

When I consider my peculiar, fitful relation to the drawer as a whole, I have to think back to the original top drawer: the one in my parents' house when I was seven and eight years old. There was nothing I liked better than to sneak into their bedroom when everyone else was out of the house, and to approach their large, dark mahogany dresser, with its altar top composed of the round reversible mirror, the wedding photograph, the stray hair-curlers, and the Chinese black-lacquered music box where my mother kept her Woolworth jewelry. Then, taking my time, I would pull open the three-sectioned top drawer by its brass handles. What was so fascinating about rifling through their drawer? I used to find nothing very unusual: some objects of obscure masculine power, like my father's leather traveling case, a shaving brush, a pair of suspenders, a wallet with photos of us, the children. Then I would go over to my mother's side of the drawer, and visit her bloomers and her gypsy scarves. I would pick up each item and smell the perfume: Arabia! Then back to my father's side, for some clues into his stolid, remote, Stakhanovite personality. In the middle section was no-man's-land, with elastic bands, garters, pipe cleaners. Once, it seems to me, I found a deck of pornographic playing cards. Am I imagining this? Isn't this rather what I kept looking for and not finding? I know I came across the rumored box of prophylactics, which my older brother had assured me would be there. Yet these balloons did not thrill me much, or as much as they might have if I had only been seeking "dirty things." I was searching for, not clarification, but a mystery, the mystery of masculine and feminine. Certainly I was looking for the tools of sexuality that held together the household, but this went further than mere rude instruments; it included everything that made my mother so different from my father, and that still enabled them to share the same life, as they shared this drawer. The drawer recorded without explanation the ordinariness of this miracle that had given birth to me.

And now I live alone—Oedipal child that I am. The contradictions of my top drawer stem from my own idiosyncrasies and not from any uneasy cohabitation of two creatures of the opposite sex. To pry through their things, I see now, was a kind of premasturbation. Where better to indulge than in the bedroom of one's parents? Even now I must be affected by that old taboo against self-abuse—in going through drawers, at least—which explains why I go through my own top drawer with embarrassed haste.

My drawer has its secrets as well. To honor the old prying and bring it down to earth, so to speak, I keep a box of prophylactics. Also, toward the back, I am ashamed to admit, are a few of those ads handed to me in the street for massage parlors: "Beautiful Girls—Complete Privacy—One Price. . . . Tahitia—Gives You Just What You Expect!" and an awful color photo of two women in a bubble bath with a grinning curly-headed man. These are also kept just in case, to be on the safe side. Here is a squashed-up tube of diaphragm cream, with just enough in it for one more go. Kay must have left it behind, as she did this frayed pair of panties. Do you know we almost moved in together, before we broke up for the very last time? And finally, the most forbidden object of all: the five-and-ten I.D. heart with Kay's name on it. Since I have forbidden myself to brood about her anymore, I must open and shut the drawer very quickly to skip seeing it, and inevitably I do catch sight of that heart-shaped button, the sort that high-school sweethearts wear. She gave it to me in our first year, and thinking I didn't love her enough, she accused me of being ashamed to wear it in front of my friends. She was right, of course—I have always been wary about advertising my heart on my sleeve, whether political or amorous. Kay was right, too, that in the beginning I did not love her enough. And now that I do, and she loves me not, I faithfully continue to wear her pin, in my top drawer. It has the place of honor in that reliquary, in my museum of useless and obsolete things that stand ready to testify at any moment to all that is never lost.

Trends of Nature

BK Loren

A friend of mine says coyotes are passé. He says they've gone the way of the whale. "The whale," he says, "was the first one to make a big splash." He laughs when he says this.

"What was it before whales?" I ask.

"Happy faces. I think it went: happy faces, whales, coyotes. But that nature stuff—it's all passé now."

"Oh?"

"Yeah. Now, it's angels."

We were in a desert canyon, and it was the dead of summer, so no one pitched a tent. We, six of us, or so, slept along the banks of a river, most of us lying on top of our sleeping bags. It's one of the simplest, most exhilarating things to do: sleep under the naked sky without a tent, without a sleeping bag, without clothes, if possible. You can feel the stars on your skin. It jump starts something wild in you, like sticking your finger into a live socket and connecting up with nature. After all, you breathe differently out here. Certain things slow down (your heart rate; the noise in your head), while other things speed up (your awareness; your ability to laugh).

So maybe it was because of how good it feels when there's nothing between you and the sky, but when my eyes peeled open that morning, everything seemed like a hallucination. My friends were sleeping on shore, as they should have been, and the sun was rising, as it does. But there was no separation between earth and sky. What I mean is this: The world felt like an organism, and I was a cell moving through the riparian veins of some single, living creature too huge to name. Over there were my friends, buddies on the molecular level, I assumed.

The sky was the color of the inside of a vein: red clouds on the eastern horizon bleeding into white, moving like liquid. The sun pulsed like a huge heart, and everything moved slowly, like lava.

That's when I saw them. In that light, they looked like ghosts. Their legs were longer, skinnier than I'd imagined. The crisp outlines of their scrawny bodies blurred in my sight. There were three of them. Coyotes. Their gait was silent, as if they were not even touching the earth. I might not have believed they existed, except I could see them breathing. I could hear their breath, a certain rhythm almost like panting, but less desperate, more quiet.

It takes awhile for the brain to file information straight from nature. You don't expect it. No matter how many times you go out into the woods, you don't expect to see wild animals this close to you. At first, they loped. Then they crouched and lowered their heads, sniffing toward my sleeping friends. *I should warn everyone*, I thought. One coyote wouldn't have posed too much of a threat, but three might have come up with a way to slow human population growth in their canyon. But I was not recognizing this sight as "reality." I felt as if my dreams had seeped out of my brain and their images were pouring into my waking life: *This* was an illusion.

I remained motionless. And the light of the morning changed from soft reds to a brilliant dome of blue burned through by a hot dime of white sun.

The coyotes vanished as the day began. It was as if they knew I was on the verge of believing they were real, so they teased my tenuous grasp of reality, and disappeared. Suddenly, one coyote stopped and looked up. They all stood at attention for a second, then ran. The way they ran made me certain I'd been hallucinating because I couldn't track them. There was nothing tricky about it. They didn't take some wild and hidden path. They just vanished. I can't tell you where they went. If they had gone up the sides of the canyon, as I thought, why wasn't I able to see them as they loped away? It was as if they entered the walls of the canyon, the way the dead baseball players in *Field of Dreams* entered the cornfields—except, better. A lot better.

Eventually, my friends woke up and, while it was great to be outdoors, there was nothing dreamlike about the day. We ate breakfast the way river runners eat breakfast: eggs, milk, coffee, hash browns, pancakes, French toast, syrup, orange juice, tortilla chips, salsa, beans, etc. We didn't scrimp. We celebrated and indulged. After all, this was nature. This was home. It would be weeks before we saw the inside of an office building or a shopping mall.

Everyone is allowed to be in any mood they want in a place like this, and I was quiet that morning. I couldn't shake the image of the coyotes, but for some reason, I didn't want to tell my friends about them. I still felt like some particulate matter floating inside a monstrous creature. I don't know why the coyotes affected me this way; they just did. I kept repeating the word "lope" to myself. My tongue leaned from the "l" into the "oohh" then fell softly onto the "pah" of the "p." *Lope.* It sounded like coyotes to me, the way their thin legs moved, the way their paws stopped with a *pah* on the soft earth. *Lope. Lope.*

That's how I paddled my kayak that morning. My shoulder was loose and relaxed. My paddle tilled the water softly. The river was calm, class two all day. And I was a coyote. Or, more accurately, I was a human with the arrogance to believe that for a few hours before noon on that day, I moved with some sort of animal grace. Truth was, I couldn't get their beauty out of my mind. They moved like every perfection I'd ever strived to attain. Yet they were anything but perfect. They just were.

Like anything wild.

After the river trip ended and I returned home to Taos, a pack of coyotes began trotting by my home at twilight. My windowsill was level with the ground, no screen attached, so the coyotes would stick their heads inside, sniff curiously, then continue into the night. My roommate would squirt them with water to scare them away, but I enjoyed their visits. When I was alone in the house, I just greeted them and wished them a prosperous hunt.

When I landed a job in northern California, I bid the pack and their new spring pups farewell and moved on.

I entered another time zone upon my arrival on the west coast. I'd picked Santa Cruz because I'd heard it was a "laid back town." When I lived in Taos, businesses, even banks, closed on whim. If you wanted the day off, you didn't call in sick; you called up your fellow employees and you all took a few days off. Customers would return another day. The weather, an ephemeral thing, was beautiful. That took precedence.

This wasn't the way in California. It turns out, "laid back," referred to a style of dress, not a way of life. Coffee was essential to survival. Putting in fifty hours a week, I was a slacker.

Add this to the commute. I couldn't afford a place "close in," so I drove forty miles to work each morning, along with thousands of other ants. The colony gathered just after dawn, and by seven, we were head-to-butt in line, gassing our cars and SUVs into the Silicon Valley where we'd spend the day in smaller colonies working fast and hard, talking faster and harder, before returning home via the same, frantic route to enjoy whatever thin slice of evening remained.

A month of this, and I was spent. I decided to start my commute before dawn to avoid traffic. I didn't drive fast. I sauntered. I pondered the redwoods ensconced in ocean mist making the forest look two dimensional—black and white, shadowed. When the sun poured over the hills and the fog lifted, the whole place turned to a labyrinth of red spires draped with green.

But at least once a week I overslept, skipped breakfast, slammed down coffee, jockeyed my way over the hill, and sprinted to my eight o'clock class, tests and essays flying from my briefcase, and my students already in their seats awaiting my presence. My wimpish ability to adopt a California pace set my circadian rhythms to twitching like chiggers beneath my skin. I was living in a blur of a world that passed by so fast I couldn't wrap my fingers around anything certain, and I'd grown addicted to the adrenalin rush that accompanied this pace. My car was an extension of myself, and I never thought twice about it until my car and I, speeding over "America's Most Dangerous Highway," killed a coyote.

She was the first coyote I'd seen in California. And in the split second when I first saw her, I remembered the ghostlike grace of the pack I'd seen by the river. Though I'd seen scores of other animals in the wild, coyotes always seemed to me as if they'd risen straight out of the earth, like phantoms. But this one was not an apparition, not a hallucination. My eyes connected with hers, and there was no time to move my foot from gas pedal to brake. She emerged from behind the concrete highway divider, looked through my windshield, lost, sniffing toward me, and my car barreled into her.

Still alive, she tumbled over the hood and into the steady stream of traffic behind me. Several other cars struck her before she landed on the shoulder of the highway. I watched this through my rearview mirror as I tried to change lanes and cut my way to the side of the road. Traffic never slowed.

Sometimes when I tell this story, I talk about how I immediately parked my car and walked to the coyote's side. I explain the fear I felt as I approached a wounded animal, something I'd been told was dangerous. I tell the story of how her eyes turned toward me, how I could hear her breath, fast and shallow, like small wings.

I say, "I wondered if she was smelling me the way animals smell, the way they take in information through air, if she could smell her own death on me as I stood there, watching her die."

But the gap between the story I tell and what actually happened is equal to the gap between who I wanted to be and who I'd become.

I did stop. The next morning.

Night haunted me. All the possibilities of what I would have seen and felt if I'd watched her die and known I had killed her played like a film in my head. But the thing that got to me most was that the reason I was feeling anything at all was pure ego. This was the coyote *I* killed. *I* was on my way to work. *I* didn't stop. *I* could have stopped. I made myself sick.

What about the scores of coyotes—and other animals—I'd seen strewn along roadsides before? Why did it take my direct participation in a death to push me to the point of change? Why, in that moment, did I decide to move closer to my work and start riding a bicycle everywhere? Why didn't the years of carnage I'd seen have any real effect on me?

For weeks afterward, I felt caught. Not caught doing something wrong, but caught doing something I had not chosen to do. Peer pressure: simple as that. When I saw the spark of brown eyes framed by clumps of blondish-gray fur, the ears cocked like a quizzical pup's, the graceful stride, the familiar lope, it was like retrieving a huge part of myself. For a split second, I remembered who I was. And then I saw myself driving fast, cutting people off, flipping that middle finger proudly, as if the marks of good character were summed up in a fast car, quick driving reflexes, and making a forty-minute drive in under thirty. So when the coyote emerged, I couldn't stop. I killed her.

The next morning I left before dawn. I drove slowly. When I reached the coyote's body, I stopped. I wish I could say I was overcome with guilt, or anger, or fear. Any emotion would have been good. But I wasn't overcome with anything. For the first time in my life I felt what it meant to be numb. It began in the marrow of my bones and radiated outward. It wasn't that I felt nothing. I felt everything at once and everything became a wall of emptiness that separated me from who I'd planned to be.

It took awhile to find a place to live closer to work. Until then, I watched the coyote's body decompose as I drove over the hill every morning. First it stiffened, then bloated. Then parasites and scavengers devoured her muscles, and her blond-gray fur was blown away by wind.

When I run along the paved trails carved through City Open Space, I think of the Nacirema, a primitive tribe who sought to alter their world to an extreme. No natural place was sacred until it was transformed. Trees were okay, as long as they didn't grow in their native setting. Where there was desert, the Nacirema brought in water and created lakes and models of oceans. In time, they say, the Nacirema would have sought to alter the stars and sun. They worshipped unnatural light.

So I figure the Nacirema must have paved these Open Space trails, and I'm grateful for the little bit of nature they allow in my city. They're wonderful for a quick jog. Mornings, I sprint past the tennis courts, picnic tables and barbecues, then I turn eastward and travel alongside a water canal that I pretend is a natural river. Here, I've seen cormorants, kestrels, a variety of hawks and thrushes. The place brims with life.

Recently, however, the houses along this stretch have begun breeding at an unreasonable rate. The oversized embryos develop each time I see them. First, there are the pine poles flagged with red surveyor's tape, a housing developer's announcement of estrus. Once these are up, you know the land will be fucked. Next, the wooden skeletons form, followed by the foil-covered, fatty layer of insulation. Then the hammers begin palpitating, echoing an off-beat rhythm through the empty air.

Sometimes, to avoid watching this unrestrained propagation, I look only at my feet as I run. I concentrate on my breathing. I put on blinders.

That's how I was running that afternoon. There was no reason to look up. But for some reason, I did. I looked up in that way you do when you know you're about to run into something—a pole, another person, a wild animal.

I gasped, and that banal utterance, "Oh my god," slipped through my lips. By now, I was familiar with every curve and outline of a coyote. But I didn't expect to find one here, and I don't think he expected to find himself here, either. It was a young male. He stood about five feet in front of me, right in the middle of the path. I didn't know what to do. I just stared. The coyote just stared. Then he shifted his gaze from one side to the other.

My eyes followed his. To the north, those houses were breeding like humans. To the south, the City was installing a golf course.

I know a wild animal is wild and anything suggesting otherwise is a fairytale. When the gates of Eden finally swung open, the animals made a firm decision. They fled, never again to befriend the creature responsible for destroying paradise. But what I saw in that animal's eyes was not wildness, or at least, not as we've come to know it. I took a step toward the coyote. He didn't move, but shifted his eyes again. Then he looked back at me and tilted his head. One of us had to move, and I think he wanted it to be him. But he didn't know where to go.

I'm reading all of this into the languageless space between me and the coyote, of course. But what else can explain that he compromised with me? As I passed, he sidestepped just enough to let me by. He never snarled, or even lowered his head. My heart pounded—with exhilaration? Fear? I don't know.

I ran backwards for awhile so I could watch what he would do next. He stayed in that spot for as long as I watched. Then my path rounded a bend.

When I returned a few minutes later, he was gone. Crusty snow blanketed a nearby ravine, and I saw his tracks, but not where they led. I didn't want to see where they led. I wanted him to live out his life there. I hoped no one would ever find him. I hoped his small space would remain wild.

Recently the "proliferation" of coyotes in our area has made headlines. Coyotes have been sighted on bicycle trails and walking paths. They've become a problem.

Yesterday morning from my kitchen window I watched a pack return from their hunt. They ran across the field in a cloud of dust, then dropped behind the berm near the horse stables. The horses raised their heads and scattered for a moment, the contrails of their breath rising in the morning air. Then they went back to grazing.

When I first moved to this neighborhood, I spoke to a woman who said she was feeding coyotes in her backyard. I suggested this might not be a good idea.

"But they have puppies," she said. Her husband was the man who told me coyotes are "passé."

"We see coyotes so often now, they're really overexposed," he said. "The hot trend today is angels."

I took his statement to mean that the popular trend of nature as commodity has descended; the thing today is angels—beautiful, ethereal beings who grant quick miracles. They hover above the earth, are not born of soil, and come from a place more "heavenly" than ours.

I try to conjure the image of an angel and a place more beautiful than earth. But I see them again, the ghostlike outlines of those graceful coyotes loping by the river where I lay perfectly naked beneath the round sky before dawn.

Villa Augusta

Jo McDougall

It's 1942. Having survived the second grade, I arrive for my annual summer visit with my paternal grandparents, Augusta and Peter Joseph Garot. Grandfather has left his Arkansas Delta rice farm to my father and retired to a life of fishing and landscaping. Villa Augusta, their cottage on Lake Hamilton near Hot Springs, Arkansas, smells of mold, the lake, and tobacco.

Named for my grandmother, the villa presents, at nine hundred square feet, a decided contrast to my parents' rambling farm house. Grandmother consigns the glassed-in sleeping porch to me, pushing an anemic cot into position directly under a window. "The better," she offers, "to catch the moon." In a stingy closet, wire hangers natter as I hang up my clothes. Homesickness flickers in my stomach, quick as a minnow. I step out onto the portico to make sure the lake is still there.

"Come on, Jo Hamel," Grandfather says, as I perch on the sofa to buckle my sandals. He uses my middle name, knowing I'm not fond of it. On the second day of my visit, we're departing for the morning's first, solemn chore: feeding the goldfish that live in the midst of Villa Augusta's gardens. To make his steeply-sloping property navigable, Grandfather created gardens on four levels leading from house to lake. He designed and sculpted in concrete the curving terrace walls and finial urns that mark each set of connecting steps. The goldfish reside on the second terrace.

The sun settles on my shoulders like a sleeping cat as Granddad and I, fish food in hand, head down the garden steps to the expectant fish. They wait in a small pool featuring a fountain with four sculptured frogs, one for each point of the compass. Granddad designed the pool; when he turns a hidden handle at the base of it, water gushes as if by sorcery out of the frogs' mouths. A lizard rattles through the grass.

I measure the fish food according to Granddaddy's instructions. A motorboat, all power and speed, fades in the distance. Far from the hurtling business of the farm, I'm standing in almost unnerving serenity. Grandfather, once the bustling overseer of pumping plants, harrows, plows, and threshing machines, imparts to this moment an even, patient gloss, quiet as the stubbing out of a cigarette.

In one of Mother's art books, a print depicts a peasant woman sowing grain in a field. I try to imitate her gesture, casting the fish food evenly upon the water. The goldfish, seeing my outstretched hand, rise up like warriors. Granddad keeps a close eye, commenting if I mete out too much or too little. "Gotta be fair to all the fish," he says, smiling. "We can't have any of them mad at us."

A blend of order and unregimented time marks these lakeside days. Granddad keeps the fish food always in the same cabinet on the same shelf, never has to search for a lost sweater, religiously keeps the car keys on a hook in the kitchen. Unlike my parents' household where clutter runs amok, holding eyeglasses and socks hostage for weeks, Villa Augusta hums through the days unruffled.

Later in the afternoon, I'll spend time strolling Granddad's terraces, practicing tap dance routines, imagining myself Ginger Rogers. All, of course, is not paradise on this rocky terrain. At seven, I'm not inured to the appearance of the native scorpion and tarantula. If such a creature presents, I'll run pell-mell up every flight of steps, howling for Grandmother.

Some one hundred miles away from Granddad's enchanted terraces, in the flatlands, under the overheated, white-misted sky of the Delta, my father stalks through one of his fields, cursing the drought, the shriveled soybeans. Sweat drenches his khaki shirt; it clings to his back like an overgrown barnacle. "It doesn't look good," he says to my mother at supper. "Don't buy anything you don't have to." He lifts a slice of ham onto his plate. "When's Jo coming home from Hot Springs?"

"In a few days." Mother folds and refolds her napkin. The wall clock, always off by forty minutes, ticks stubbornly on its misguided way. "She's going to need new school clothes."

"No." My father slams down his fork. "Not until it rains. If it ever rains."

Rain, too much or not enough; drought, splitting open the dirt of the fields; grasshoppers and blackbirds, stripping like plague the maturing grain—these are my father's enemies. He pushes back from the table, announcing to my mother that he's lost his appetite.

If it rains within the week, Dad will return to his normal, generous self. I will have new clothes to enter the third grade, and my father will admire them. If not, I'll hear my parents arguing into the night. It never occurs to either of them, evidently, to pursue another way of making a living. They are beholden to the generous sunsets of this unencumbered landscape, to the smells of water irrigating a dry field, to the color of rice at harvest, like burnt butter. They are beholden to the dirt.

Thirteen Ways of Looking at the Weather

Debra Marquart

The blackbird whirled in the autumn winds.
It was a small part of the pantomime.
   —Wallace Stevens, "Thirteen Ways of Looking at a Blackbird"

1.

Footage of a tornado this spring morning on The Weather Channel. Tuberous as a taproot, it dips, retracts, stretches thin, then holds, taut as a sprung coil. Dark topsoil rises in spinning wisps as the funnel makes contact with the ground, widens, then moves like a vacuum across flat, unfortunate Kansas.

On the far horizon, the nub of a white clapboard farmhouse—neat crop of outbuildings, small stand of trees—disappears under the swath, the funnel getting darker, spewing up broken boards, strips of paper, sheetrock, metal. The caption on the bottom of the TV screen reads like a poem:
                 Danger Remains on the Plains.

2.

We didn't run to the basement like the weathermen say you should. No bracing in bathtubs or solid doorways for us. This was North Dakota, 1975—the time before Doppler, too deep in the country to hear sirens. Instead, we ran outside, into the swirl of wind, as country people do, to get a closer look at the weather.

In the wind-spun circle of our yard, between the house, the garage, and the barn—the well-worn path and turnaround spot where no grass grew—we shielded our eyes and watched the dark sky move above us. Our hair rose and fell in the wind. Our clothes lifted and whipped around our bodies.

Then in one split second, the wind fell to nothing. The air hung around us, humid, time-stopped. We stood there waiting, in eerie, suspended quiet. And I remember Father pointing his bony finger straight up, directing our attention to where the sky had shifted to a violet gray.

We were in the calm center of something developing.

Overhead we could make out two strata of shifting clouds. One layer, low and dark, moved in a clockwise direction; and the other layer, light and touched on the edges by the sun, spun high and counterclockwise.

It was a true miracle of nature's coordination, I remember thinking at the time. It was like that playground trick I could never master—spinning my right hand on my belly in one direction, and my left hand on the top of my head in another direction, all the while standing on one foot and whistling a familiar tune.

3.

When I tell my fiction class I'm writing an essay about Midwestern weather, they break into spontaneous chatter. They are so brimming full of meteorological curiosities, anecdotes, and spare knowledge about weather, I cannot start class.

They turn to each other and gesticulate, they gab, then they begin to shout weather stories at me, three at a time—the great flood and where they were, the big blizzard and who got stuck, the time they sat on top of a roof and watched bathtubs float by, the time they hunkered in the basement under a mattress and heard the tornado roar overhead.

Wait, wait, wait, I say. I can't include all these stories. I'm from North Dakota, the land of weather extremes. I have a head full of my own weather stories. I have to tell about the big blizzards of my own youth! The winter of '66—the way the snowfall was so deep, it covered up whole houses. People just chipped archway tunnels out of the snow drifts in order to get out of their front doors.

I have to tell about the time a few years ago in Fargo when four people died of exposure stranded in a car on 18th Street, only two blocks away from the NDSU campus. The passengers stayed with the car through the night and into the next day as you're always told to do: *Never leave the safety of your car.*

The streets were so socked in with snow, the drifts so high, they must not have realized they were still in the middle of the city. The workers found the car full of frozen people when they began to clear the streets. People talked about it for weeks. What a shame. If only they'd gotten out and walked, they would have been to someone's house in minutes.

4.

I have to tell about that spring afternoon in northern Iowa, 1995, on the way home from Minneapolis, when I drove unsuspectingly into high winds and threatening clouds, and how I parked on the side of I-35 in my Eagle Summit, listening to the National Weather Service interrupt NPR with that *EH, EH, EH* sound, then the electronic voice coming on (as if all living, breathing people had been destroyed and only this machine was left to warn us).

And the voice was saying, in patched together snippets of pre-recorded phonemes, that the National Weather Service has issued a tornado warning for Franklin, Butler, and Cerro Gordo counties, and I remember thinking that I, personally, would have preferred a few names of cities, since I didn't yet know the counties in Iowa, and neither, I suspected, did the dozens of cars and semis lined up and down the road around me with license plates from Michigan, Oregon, New York, Pennsylvania, California and other far-flung (and soon-to-be farther-flung) places.

I knew for certain you must never park under the overpasses, as it is your instinct to do, thinking they are shelters, when really they are wind-blown death traps that the tornadoes like to suck themselves under and smash things into.

And I remember wondering as my little car rocked side to side on its wheels, if I would know the exact moment when it was time to abandon the car, to throw myself into the ditch, face down in the grass, and dig my fingers into the clots of dirt.

Would I feel my car begin to lift? I imagined my burgundy wagon rising and spinning intact in the clouds, just as Dorothy's house had done in *The Wizard of Oz*, then being set down unharmed in some strange faraway land.

And in those long minutes on the side of I-35, as the rain blurred the windshield beyond seeing, I calculated that the car would roll to the east—the wind blowing in a northeasterly direction as tornadoes typically do—and so I moved into the passenger seat to avoid having the car roll over me when I bailed out, and I waited like that with my hand on the door latch.

5.

Confession: I never look out the window to check the weather. If I want to know what the day will be like, I turn on The Weather Channel.

Confession: I have one of those cell phones with Doppler radar and a satellite view of the weather. I often check it to see what's happening around me, weatherwise, even when nothing much is happening, weatherwise.

Confession: I like to watch *Storm Stories*. I'm fascinated by inclement weather and surprise storms. I enjoy anomalous weather patterns, as long as they don't involve me.

6.

In stories by Ernest Hemingway, the weather exerts a climate control over the plot, often pacing and foreshadowing calamitous events or unspoken secrets lurking inside the characters. When it finally hails or snows, or rains or blows, everything comes out—people crash and burn; they lose limbs; tempers flare; husbands confess infidelities; character flaws are finally revealed. Everything that was contained in the climate of the story from the first sentence comes out, but only the weather knows how the story will unfold.

7.

Sometimes I think the weather is trying to tell me something, but I'm missing the necessary equipment to decode the message, like when you accidentally dial a fax number and all you hear is that jangled buzzing on the other end of the line. To you, it sounds like noise, but you know it makes all kinds of sense to another fax machine.

I want to know what the lightning was trying to tell me that humid July night in southern Minnesota, 1981, driving home from the Kandiyohi County Fair gig with my band—the last of four one-nighters in a row spread across three states.

The road crew stayed behind with the bus to pack the equipment. The rest of the band climbed into the van for the long drive home. Usually, our bass player drove, or our keyboard player. After that, the guitar players would pitch in and take the wheel. But this night everyone in the band was too tired to drive, so I took over at two a.m.

I remember feeling responsible for lives that night as I drove. I could see them in the rear view mirror, all those trusting bodies sleeping in sprawls in the back of the van—heads resting on crumpled-up jean jackets, long legs thrown over armrests—and me in the front with only the sibilance of the radio and the column of headlights spreading before me on the dark road.

What causes me to remember that night so vividly, even now, is not what happened the next morning—the phone that rang too early. It would be the first in a succession of early-morning or late-night phone calls, strung out over the next few months, all of which began with the words, "I've got some bad news," then continuing with details of bus rollovers, drug busts, truck fires, lost equipment, embezzling agents, lawsuits.

But what causes me to remember that night so vividly is the storm that threatened, the lightning that came in constant flashes, illuminating the entire circle of the sky, one fragment at a time. And the variation! Soft puffs of heat lightning all around and large flashes that popped off. Explosions on the horizon, the tentacles of lightning that spread like arcing wires across the length of the sky, and the deadly bolts that cracked open the darkness high above and drove a line straight to the ground somewhere in the unforeseeable distance.

For that night, the storm was all around—before me, behind me, flashing on every horizon—but it remained elsewhere. It was where I was not. And no matter how long or hard I drove, I could not reach it. It was the last unbroken night of my life.

8.

Weather stories, by nature, are subjective, full of nebulous and atmospheric detail, which is hard to capture in words—the piercing cold, your wet shoes, the pelting rain, the gales that shook the windows, the slush under the tires, that free glide of wheels on black ice when your steering wheel becomes useless.

Sometimes weather stories get long in the telling. They're like that made-for-TV docu-drama that your coworker wants to summarize for you during the coffee break the next morning, or the strange dream your lover or mother or sister suddenly remembers and wants to recount over breakfast.

You know the story will include confusing shifts in time, scene, and action, and that you'll have to listen along carefully and ask questions in the right places. You know you'll never really get the feeling.

You know it will probably end with "to make a long story short" or "I guess you had to be there." You almost hate for them to start.

9.

Weather theory: No conversation feels complete in the Midwest unless it includes some discussion, however cursory, of the weather.

Weather case-in-point: The movie, *Fargo*, begins with a long image of a lonely Minnesota highway which quickly dissolves into a white, snow-filled landscape. The movie is set in winter, which is unusual. Maybe snow is too hard to capture, or too expensive to recreate, or too uncomfortable to film in. Maybe film crews and actors don't like to stand around in the cold. For whatever reason, fewer and fewer American films feature winter landscapes.

So, the image of a snow-covered field is unusual to see in a film, but it is not unusual to see in the Midwest where it's ubiquitous. In *Fargo*, a car finally appears on the road, emerging through the snowfall like a mirage. As it gets closer, we see that the car is towing a trailer with another car mounted on it. And so, the story begins.

The action of the movie turns on high crimes driven by the worst of human nature—kidnapping, embezzlement, grisly murders, one famously featuring a wood chipper. Police investigations ensue.

In one scene, Officer Olson, a small-town deputy, follows up a lead called in by a local citizen, Mr. Mohra. When Officer Olson arrives, Mr. Mohra is clearing his driveway.

Mr. Mohra leans on his shovel and gets to the point, passing along the information he has overheard—there's a funny lookin' guy out at Ecklund and Swedlin's, where he tends bar, was asking about where he can find a prostitute and bragging about how the last guy who said he was a jerk turned up dead.

"I understand." Officer Olson nods his head. "It's probably nothing," he says, when in fact it will prove to be their biggest lead. He turns to go.

"Looks like she's gonna turn cold tonight," Olson shouts back as he walks toward his car.

"Oh, yah, got a front coming in," Mohra answers.

"Yah, you got that right."

Weather Postscript: A fun thing to do in Fargo—the real Fargo, not the movie—is to drive around town with a four-wheel drive during snow storms and rescue people. It's an austere landscape; you have to make your own fun.

On the coldest, snowiest nights, I've gone out in warm boots and good mittens with friends and found dozens of people to push and shovel out of snow banks. In the middle of a rescue, if you discover that a driver doesn't know how to use his transmission to rock his car out of a snow rut, you feel embarrassed for him, like he's missing some basic skill for survival. You assume he's not from around here.

10.

The meteorologist for the NPR station in the university town where I teach is obsessed with the weather phenomenon, *El Niño*. To a lesser degree, he's also unnaturally interested in *La Niña*, *El Niño*'s little sister. He's like the guy who keeps bringing the conversation around to the subject of his Corvette, or who only wants to talk about the stock market or the New England Patriots. Only, for him, it's All-*El-Niño*-All-the-Time.

He can segue to the subject of *El Niño* from any topic under discussion—corn futures, hog reports, poetry readings, shipping logs for Lake Superior, the pharmaceutical industry, the long-running success of the musical, *Cats*. His weatherman voice is deep and comforting, like someone you'd like to hear reading you a bedtime story. And when he speaks of *El Niño*, there is something close to love in his voice.

But the months and years between *El Niños* must get long for him. I hear deep sighs after a forecast for another sunny day and whimsy in his warning about another thunderstorm. Garden-variety weather. He waits for the day when he can flex his *El Niño* muscles and explain again, in a way we can never hope to understand, the mysteries of the Southern Oscillation Index.

In the meantime, he contents himself with side notes and digressions, small tidbits inserted after a report on the New York fashion industry about the current meteorological indicators—how they point (or do not point) to *El Niño*'s imminent return.

El Niño Footnote: In 1998, during an especially active *El Niño* season, a retired naval pilot from Nipomo, California named Al Nino began to get irate phone calls from people accusing him of being responsible for the climatic changes. One man blamed him for the torrential rains and begged him to please stop them. A farmer accused him of causing his strawberry crop to fail. The BBC reports that another man called alleging that Al Nino had caused his daughter to lose her virginity, although it was never made clear what the weather might have had to do with that.

11.

My husband and I used to take long walks in the neighborhood after dinner. We said it was for the exercise. Really, it was just to get the bowels moving. We were eating too much and talking too little.

On these walks, we could chat about flowerbeds and trimmed lawns without fear of anything important coming up. We often passed by other couples from the neighborhood out for their nightly walk. Perhaps they too had stagnant intestines and stuck tongues. We'd smile and say hello. Sometimes we'd stop and comment on the pleasantness of the weather.

One night, my husband and I ventured too far, and at our farthest point from home, the weather suddenly changed. The air grew heavy as syrup. The clouds went from white to black.

We turned for home, breathing hard, sweating as if climbing uphill. A mist started to fall, the wind picked up. We broke into a run. Then lightning began to flash all around us. There was no thunderclap to follow; it was all soft, diffused light. Still it scared us. We ran home like this, holding hands, heat lightning flashing around us every few seconds, as if we were being photographed by the paparazzi.

By the time we got home to our stoop the storm had broken fully. We ran up the front steps, laughing hard and drenched clean through.

12.

Every summer, after another tornado hit some farm in my hometown, my father would pile us into the Chevy, and we'd drive out to survey the damage. On the way, up and down the gravel road, we'd pass other families in their cars doing the same thing.

The tornado always seemed mysterious to us—judgmental, malevolent. Why had it taken the new house, but left the old barn; why had it smashed the shiny Mustang to bits, but left alone the rusted Ford; why had it leveled every last building, separated every board from every nail, but left unscathed the small shrine to the Virgin Mary in the front yard.

That afternoon in 1975, after our family stood in our yard and watched the funnel form above the farm, we grabbed each other and ran inside to escape the wind. Minutes later when the storm passed, we could see that the tornado had touched down one mile north of us on the Harrison farm. The buildings were mostly gone. Even then, the Harrisons were trapped inside the collapsed walls of their house with a young baby.

But when I think about this story, I realize that something is wrong with my memory of the day. Everyone in my family is present in the scene—my parents, my three older sisters, my brother—but, by 1975, we kids would have all moved away from home.

When I question my older sister, she reminds me that the tornado hit the day of Grandpa Geist's funeral. We had just come home from the cemetery, so that's why we were all at the farm together. And when she tells me this, I remember something I read years ago about ferocious storms, about how they sometimes coincide with the death of large-souled people, as if the atmosphere cannot handle this new element that has been loosed into its presence and must disperse it in torrents of wind and rain back into the world.

13.

In a 1924 brochure, created by the Northern Pacific Railroad and distributed widely in the eastern United States to lure farmers to new territories in the Midwest, the reader is encouraged to "Come to North Dakota!" The first page of the brochure features a line drawing of the North American continent. The caption above the drawing proclaims, "North Dakota: the Center of the North American Hemisphere."

In the drawing, lines coming from four directions of the continent all end in arrows pointing at North Dakota, which is shaded darker so that it appears to hover large above all the lesser states. The first line coming from the west coast reads, "not too dry." The second line coming from the east coast reads, "not too wet." The third line, coming from the Gulf Coast reads, "not too hot." And the fourth line originating in the Arctic Circle, reads, "not too cold."

The text at the bottom of the page explains that "extremes of temperature to which the state is subject are not unpleasant due to low humidity. Hot, muggy days are very rare in summer and long twilight periods and nights are always cool. . . . The winters are cold, but it is the dry, crisp, clear cold that is more healthful and more pleasant for man and beast than the winter weather of regions of so-called moderate climates." The infamous dry heat and dry cold. Were there ever more useful weather euphemisms?

Lewis and Clark, in journal entries describing the Corps of Discovery's encampment in what is now North Dakota near the Mandan villages during the winter of 1804–05, note the temperature regularly: January 7, 1805: Minus 20 degrees; January 9: 21 degrees below zero; January 10: 40 degrees below zero.

72° below the freesing point, Clark writes.

The journal entries are full of references to the cold, to frostbitten limbs, frozen toes. The Mitutanka, the village of Mandans closest to the Corp's encampment, appear often checking on the expedition. Sometimes they answer Lewis and Clark's questions about what they know about the territories lying west. They visit the fort, accompany the expedition hunters to find food. One wonders how differently the history of western expansion might have unfolded if the Mandans had neglected to check on Lewis and Clark, if they had feigned ignorance when asked to provide a "Scetch of the Countrey as far as the high mountains."

But the Mandans did not leave Lewis and Clark to freeze or flounder. Maybe they could not? For an unspoken code exists in cold landscapes—silent watchfulness for acts of stupidity by the uninitiated, followed by begrudging helpfulness once the forces of weather have outstripped arrogance.

And so we are here in cold places. And so I have my own stories of twenty-below zero nights that I tried to drive through in North Dakota—whether through stupidity or desperation.

Once, a little drunk in the 1980s, two a.m., after the amorous advances of my married boss during a company Christmas party, I stormed off in my Plymouth Fury. I took the long frozen artery of Main Street through Fargo to be safer, navigating by peering through the two-inch porthole I'd chipped out of my icy windshield.

All along Main Street as I drove, I could make out the shapes of abandoned cars—makes, far more expensive, and models, far newer than mine—all of them frosted-over, as if powdered with sugar, parked at odd angles just where they'd stalled or been pushed at odder angles onto the side of the road. It looked like Mars or the Moon to me then, some alien, inhospitable landscape.

Nothing you've heard about twenty-below zero cold is an exaggeration. Any attempt at description is a reduction in terms, a failure of language. Spit does freeze before it hits the ground. So does piss. Any part in your car that's weak will break. Your pipes will freeze and burst. Those nights, I would set my alarm clock for every two hours, so that I could go outside and start my Plymouth Fury to warm it up. Otherwise, it would have been a solid block of unstartable ice by morning.

But the Fury never failed me; it never left me on the side of the road. Not even that twenty-below night, coming home from my husband's grandmother's funeral in South Dakota. Almost midnight, thirty miles from Fargo, our gas line began to freeze. We lurched and stalled on the side of I-94.

I got out and lifted the hood of the Plymouth to prime the carburetor, unscrewing the butterfly nut, lifting off the lid of the air cleaner, and propping the flap of the carburetor open with a ballpoint pen, then pouring the liquid Heet straight down into the engine's gullet.

My husband sat behind the wheel, grinding the ignition and gunning the gas, until the Fury roared to life. Then I'd hop in and we'd proceed another three or four miles down the freeway until the car choked and we'd have to repeat the process again. We made it home that way, those last thirty miles, in three-mile increments.

By now, I've forgotten the precise feeling of cold, and I can't recall why I was the one who got out and worked under the hood while my husband stayed warm behind the wheel. It was my car; I suppose I understood its workings, and I was always better with machines.

But how to capture in words the feeling of the air that night—crisp and rarefied; clear, still skies; unadulterated winter; capital-C cold, like the sound of one thin violin note stinging through the air.

I'm certain we were worried as we struggled with the Fury, and I suppose we were on the brink of extinction. But what I remember most is that we were not alone out there. Each time I got out of the car, I heard the sounds of other people stranded along the road—hoods and car doors slamming in the distance; people talking and calling to each other in the cold night; and laughter, I swear, somewhere out there it sounded like a party was going on.

Each time I jumped back in the car and we lurched forward, I didn't even try to tell my husband what I'd heard out there. Some things about weather are too hard to explain, and some things are even harder to believe. Sometimes when weather gets that bad, all that's left for you to do is put your head down and laugh right into the teeth of it.

Killing Laughter

Kathryn Miles

The hunters arrived in the full light of day. With their dogs and radio transmitters, their phalanx of trucks, the geometry of their movements, they seemed a military operation. All afternoon five of them—each in his own vehicle—drove the ten-mile area that circumscribes a square parcel of woods, coasting between their 90-degree turns with radio telemetry and guns brandished. Inside the wooded parameter an unknown number of dogs brayed, their collective shout announcing the pack's changing position as they ran this way and that. Meanwhile, the hunters continued their circuit, driving up one road and down the next, following their own tracks as they kept radio tabs on the moving pack of dogs.

In a landscape made austere by a lingering winter, the movement of these hunters was easy to mark: the colorful trucks of American make, tinted in patriotic shades and winter rust; the sounds of engines deliberately made loud and tough. Still, it would take a while before my dog, Ari, and I noticed them.

Our property—a small, ten-acre plot—occupies this same area. And on this particular Sunday afternoon, we were hunting too: following tracks of deer and fox and snowshoe hares, trying to recreate their movements and the conversations they might have had along the way. Six months of compressed snow made our mission easy, buoying us up above the tangled vegetation, providing a record of every foot that had passed by. Cataloguing these travels was our stated goal for the afternoon. We were looking for signs of life, hoping we could spy on an existence other than our own. We found both in good supply, though hardly what we intended.

The sound of my feet on compacted snow masked the truck noise for the first lap or two. By the third or fourth, I noticed with interest the flicker of their procession through the trees. By the seventh or eighth, we left the woods and stationed ourselves along the road, marking this parade as it passed. After a couple more of these transects, I finally summoned the courage to stop one of the trucks and ask what this business was about. I knew, of course. But I wanted to hear the explanation nevertheless.

Inside the truck was a man I would call elderly except that doing so would raise ire and rancor on the part of Maine's wizened residents. Seventy-five years old or so, he wore the traditional hunting clothes of our region: red and black checked wool coat; dark green work pants; fluorescent orange cap. His thick hands were bare: broad, calloused fingers grafted onto a Ford steering wheel. His face, inscribed by years of combating an unforgiving climate, was held in the familiar posture known here as Yankee Reserve: laconic, suspicious, but nevertheless polite and ready to help if the need arises.

Whether or not it seemed strange that a woman, who he had already passed several times, now raised her arm to hail his truck, he did not say. But he did stop and allow me to lean into his passenger side window, which, like the driver's side, was rolled down despite the chill. And, to his credit, his demeanor did not change when I asked, with more gumption than was probably appropriate, what he was after.

"Coyote," he replied. "But don't worry. We'll get 'em."

My eyes narrowed. I wanted to take issue with his assumption that I was okay—even enthusiastic—about this project. That I, too, saw it a worthwhile way to spend a day. That killing something posing neither a threat nor a meal was right. That expanding definitions of fair chase to include vehicles and radio-collared dogs and who knows what else was somehow anything other than shooting fish in a barrel.

I didn't say any of that, though.

I am an outsider in this place—what the locals call a "flatlander" or someone who is "from away." Having lived here for eight years, I am barely even recordable as an occupant. After fifty years of continued civic contribution, I may someday be considered a resident. However, I will always be an alien, not having come from generations of people born and raised in this landscape. I have internalized this outsider position. I don't have to. I understand, though, that doing otherwise is not only an act of hubris, but also one of absolute futility. I can state my allegiance and sense of connection to this place until my lungs are empty. It's not going to change my status. And frankly, I'm a little intimidated by that.

I have never been someone who holds her tongue. But I've learned to do just that here, in a place where values are deeply held and, more often than not, admirably defendable. This is a community where necessity makes people frugal, resourceful, and independent. Sustainable. These are all attributes I value. And because I admire these things but have not succeeded in wholly integrating them into my own life, I often surprise myself by deferring to a local culture that has—even when I don't always agree with it.

So, although I wanted to take issue with the coyote hunter, I instead nodded and stepped away from his truck. And I did so without doing what I really wanted, which was to ask him why.

Maybe that's because I didn't believe I'd get a real answer. What I wanted was not an easy response about the thrill of the chase or the need to manage animal populations or because the state allows it, but the more complicated one about how and why we take a life.

There are, after all, many reasons to kill: revenge, self-defense, personal gain, adventure, a desire for trophies. When it comes to violence against our own species, criminologists divide a killer's motivations into four categories: defensiveness born out of a perceived threat to our own safety; frustration arising from a victim's refusal to do what we want; fear that the victim is evil; or a combination of the latter two motivations. What's important here, says Richard Rhodes in *Why They Kill*, is that those people who take another life nearly always see themselves as justified in doing so. The rest of society may content ourselves by believing that murderers are necessarily insane or deranged, but that doesn't square with what happens inside the mind of a killer, who sees his or her act as in keeping with a moral and practical framework. That person's system of beliefs probably is not the same as ours. It may not even be comprehensible to us. But the system is almost always defendable and categorical to the killers themselves. If only for a split second, they considered the act, squared it with their moral system, and continued. Killing makes sense.

There are obvious differences between murder and hunting. And yet, those who study hunters have found similar categories of motivation behind the act itself. The most notable voice on the subject is Stephen Kellert, who published a small article entitled "Attitudes and Characteristics of Hunters and Anti-hunters" in 1978. Although only ten pages long, Kellert's essay has remained the definitive work on the subject, cited often by people on both sides of the hunting debate. Like Rhodes, Kellert divides his subjects into several distinct groups, based upon the impetus for their actions. When it comes to animals, he says people kill for three basic reasons: as a way of acquiring meat, as a sport, and as a way of appreciating the natural cycle of life. This third category, which is arguably the most nebulous, is also the smallest, comprising less than 20% of the total population. The remaining hunters are nearly equally divided between meat or "utilitarian" hunters on the one hand, and sport or "dominionistic" hunters on the other.

Regardless of these motivations, the act of hunting becomes an increasingly controversial one each year, as we move farther and farther away from securing our own food. And as we make this shift, we lose sight of the fact that, for millennia, hunting has been an activity that allows for our survival as a species. In fact, our evolutionary predecessors—Neanderthals, and even their ancestor, the 600,000-year old *Homo heidelbergensis*, hunted animals of all sizes. Anthropologists suspect that these prehistoric groups began claiming prey as an act of self-preservation. They killed those animals that threatened them; they ate or wore those that seemed like they might prove beneficial.

And so, from the start, to be human has been to hunt. Even the word itself is one of the oldest we have; its roots so deep and old that etymologists have a hard time locating its source on the tree of wizened Teutonic language. What they do know is that, in its earliest form, the word simply meant to seize or capture. To kill.

As cultures evolved and became more rooted in agrarian food production, the reasons for hunting began to diversify. The activity continued to provide meat for communities, but it also began functioning as training for war. Just as a wild animal might pose a threat, so too might other groups of humans. And so, if one could kill an animal, then why not a human? And why not use the same methodologies? Many of antiquity's greatest warriors were, not surprisingly, great hunters: Samson, Orion, Hercules, Gilgamesh, even the Egyptian god Horus. They learned their skills for killing enemies by hunting animals.

In that regard, it can be hard to distinguish the two pursuits. And I sometimes wonder if we'd be better off if we stopped trying so hard. Certainly we'd all benefit from confronting the violence and ethical implications inherent in both. But maybe I've just been enculturated to believe so.

Like many Americans, I come from a place where death—in any of its permutations—is hidden. We place sheets over traffic victims the moment they are pronounced deceased. We call exterminators to remove dead animals from our homes so that we don't have to. We purchase meat hermetically sealed and made anemic by scientifically engineered pillows that collect blood and fluid. In this version of America, the sight of a human and gun in plain view almost always connotes an immediate threat to the other humans nearby. It's an aberration, a breakdown of law and order. We respond to that person as an immediate threat: one of our kind, now strangely transmogrified into angry predator. Someone who has turned values inside out, exposing something monstrous and profane.

That's not true in rural America. At least, not usually. Here, death is a part of life: creatures deemed nuisances are summarily exterminated; old farm animals are routinely shot; wildlife is hunted and trapped and eaten and worn. For several months out of the year, people walk down our roads, rifle or shotgun in hand, tipping their hats politely or inquiring how your day is going. Gas stations and convenience store parking lots are filled with recently killed deer and moose waiting to be tagged or to have a tooth extracted by state biologists for their research. Once taken from these lots, their disemboweled carcasses hang from trees and basketball hoops in front yards, the inner workings of muscle and sinew exposed to all who pass by.

I arrived in this world not only a foreigner to the culture of hunters, but one who practiced strict and self-righteous vegetarianism. My food came from supermarket shelves and backyard gardens. My dog and I walked the same roads as these men and their hounds. We all were paying attention to the landscape and its inhabitants. But the similarities ended there. My dog has never worked a day in her life. I have never faced an animal, pulled a trigger, and watched it fall. The idea of causing this death, of then taking a knife and opening up the still warm animal, tugging out entrails and organs, horrified me. I hated those moments when I, too, would need to pull into the parking lot of a general store, where the hunters seemed to stand so blithely and unaffectedly by their kill.

In time, I have learned to make sense of this scene. I've even made a kind of fragile peace. And, while it can sometimes feel a struggle, I have taught myself to eat the meat of some of the animals that share this place with me. When confronted with the coyote hunters that day, however, I came to an important realization: I have not so much made peace with the act of hunting as I have the act of sustainable food acquisition. I would much prefer that people eat steak that comes from the wilderness around them than from a feedlot somewhere in the heart of Middle America. I'm more than comfortable with anyone who shoots an animal and so feeds a family. What I haven't come to terms with is the idea that someone might kill an animal for other reasons.

I know, of course, that these other motivations exist. Ari and I have found multiple animal carcasses in the woods around our house. Some have been bound and dragged behind all-terrain vehicles. One was, somewhat mysteriously, wrapped in an old piece of carpet. All had been shot. Most were canid. Not long ago, Ari happened upon a decayed coyote carcass and the bullet that killed it. She took the skull in her mouth and brought it back to our house. I don't know what it meant to her. A trophy? A totem? A memorial? She wanted to bring it inside. We compromised and left it on the front porch, nestled between other treasures gleaned on our walks: a rusting jug, blue glass bottles, cattails and quartz. There it has remained, its empty eye sockets appraising us each time we pass by.

Meanwhile we continue to study it, along with its living relatives. We know these animals. Not like kin, but at least as well as most of our human neighbors. We see their scat change in composition throughout the year, marking a shift in diet from late season fruit to carrion to, in the depths of winter, fur and hide and bone and anything else they can find. Mountain biking in the summer, I sometimes come upon their pups, wrestling in a clearing or splashing in puddles. It's hard not to feel affection for this blend of tenacity and play.

And really, there's an awful lot about *Canis latrans* we ought to like. They're monogamous. Both parents, and sometimes even older siblings, help to raise pups, and they're incredibly protective of these kids. They maintain bonds with extended family members and often provide gifts of food or other means of support. They are skilled home decorators, adept at renovating dens abandoned by woodchucks and other animals. They're social and even gregarious verbal communicators. They have a penchant for melon and grains. They do well in just about any landscape. And not only do they appear nonplussed by our presence, they seem to enjoy it—the manmade passageways and hiding spots, the food sources and, in a few cases, the camaraderie of our domesticated dogs. And, like us, coyotes are just about everywhere.

In the U.S., they occupy every state except for Hawaii. But that doesn't make them welcome occupants. In fact, each of these forty-nine states have robust hunting seasons: unlike other commonly hunted animals like the white-tailed deer, coyotes may be killed year-round in many places. The majority of states also allow for night hunting, as well as the use of bait, traps, dogs, and electronic equipment. Few states have limits to the numbers of coyotes a hunter can get; some, like New York, do not even require them to report a kill.

Our species' penchant for hunting these animals can get extreme. As I write this essay, a coyote hunting tournament is underway here in Maine. Over the next month, participants are encouraged to kill as many of the wild dogs as they possibly can. Prizes will be awarded for the biggest and most coyotes bagged. The lame-duck democratic governor of this very independent state recently spoke out against the hunt, calling it inhumane. Although tournament organizers agreed when he asked them to remove advertisements from radio stations and other media outlets, blogging hunters were incensed. They called his reaction an example of liberal extremism and an attack on their way of life. Many other state residents agreed, which made me wonder if this is why the governor waited until his eighth and final year in office to take a public stand on this annual event.

At issue for the objecting hunters is what they perceive to be the ecological damage caused by *Canis latrans*. They insist coyotes don't belong here—that the survival of the white-tailed deer in our region depends upon the canid's extermination. It's a motivation that doesn't quite fit into the hunting categories proscribed by Kellert. In some ways, it gets closest to one of the ideas advanced by Richard Rhodes—that people kill because their target is bad or a perceived threat to safety. In this case, though, the motivation is a complicated chain of associations: the hunters see the coyotes as a threat, not to themselves, but to the safety of the deer population and, as a result, the hunters' ability—and desire—to hunt the ungulates.

However, science does not support this claim. Currently, North America boasts the largest deer population since the start of European settlement. And given a choice, coyotes would much prefer to eat something less formidable. A mesopredator, *Canis latrans* is too small to hunt animals like deer efficiently. They must resort to dogged pursuit and a series of injuring strikes, rather than the near-instant kills caused by animals like the grizzly bear, cougar, or even the wolf. Dogged pursuit takes a lot of work and, like many of us, coyotes would rather eat whatever is most convenient, even if someone else killed it. If that kind of meat is not available, they'll hunt whatever they deem the easiest to catch. That, sometimes, can include fawns or chickens or other targets we may not approve of. More often, it includes rodents or injured birds. The ecological effect of this diet, say biologists, is of no more consequence than any other omnivore in the food chain.

Why, then, do states allow for—and even promote—the hunting of these animals? One significant reason is financial. There is a lot of money to be gained through the issuing of hunting permits, along with the added profits of gear and food and lodging. The organizers of the coyote tournament underway here (who also happen to be the Chamber of Commerce for the economically-depressed host town) admit the tournament is not so much an exercise in animal husbandry as it is economic opportunism.

The fact is, a lot of people really, really like hunting coyotes. Articles and brochures luring hunters to the woods emphasize the coyote's cleverness and cunning—that it takes an equal amount of both on the part of the hunter if he or she is going to bag this wild dog. They talk about the added thrill of pursuing a predator. As one person put it, "you are hunting the hunter, and trying to beat him at his own game." In that regard, it's kind of the ultimate sport.

And remember, that's why approximately 40% of all hunters hunt. To many, it's what the very word denotes. And just like the activity itself, this motivation is nothing new. By the time we regularly recorded language use, the word "hunt" brought with it a persistent connotation of chase and pursuit. Some of the great early chroniclers of language use—Ælfric, Julian of Norwich, Chaucer, Shakespeare, Spenser—used the word to mean the excitement of a quest. By the time we arrived at our modern vernacular, the word had also come to mean eager exertion and sport.

Sport, of course, is about recreation and personal bests. It's about taxing one's mind and body through strategy and fitness and sometimes adventure. It's about play. When these associations are added to hunting, the act almost necessarily changes. The aim becomes far less about what happens after the kill, and instead, emphasizes the actual moment of death. According to Kellert, this category of hunters is more interested in mastering or controlling animals than they are meeting them on their own terms. The interaction is a contest. A competition. But not one in which both parties agree to the rules. Kellert also explains that, of all hunters, those who do so for sport tend to have the least amount of knowledge about their prey and environment.

That's always been a particular problem for coyotes, who carry with them the added weight of our collective mythologies. And they are rarely the hero in these tales. Their very name—*Canis latrans*—means "dog that barks," though that is often changed to "laughing dog" in common vernaculars. And why not? In many mythologies, coyote plays the part of trickster. He is the wily foil to the Road Runner; he points out our own foibles; he is brash, nosy, hypersexual.

As a rule, mythological tricksters do not like boundaries. That's also true where the biological coyote is concerned. In *The Mammals of North America*, E. Raymond Hall and Keith R. Kelson identify nineteen subspecies of *Canis latrans*. Most of these animals are hybrids. Based on DNA samples, scientists theorize that the eastern coyote who roams my woods (*Canis latrans var*), is actually the result of generations of interbreeding between western coyotes and the gray wolf. Most of these biologists agree that *Canis latrans var* is not native to the eastern United States. But when the species appeared is something of a debate. Some contend its arrival is a recent one—that reports of coyotes in this region didn't really begin until sometime in the last century. However, Pennsylvania state biologists say they have fossils dating the appearance of the eastern coyote to the Pleistocene period. If that's true, they've been around here for a million years. Even if it's not, they've been here for close to a hundred. Is that enough time to be considered a natural part of the landscape? To belong?

As far as many locals are concerned, the answer is a decided *no*. But ecologists are more tentative—even conflicted—in their assessment. There is no consensus about when an organism loses its hybrid status and becomes a species. Or when it ceases to be considered a foreigner in a landscape. What they do agree upon, however, is twofold: the movement of species from one habitat to another has occurred for as long as there have been species, and any attempt we make to draw boundaries around these habitats or ranges is both artificial and arbitrary.

Scientists have also arrived at clever ways of talking about such movements. They call animals not originally from a location *nonnative* or *exotic*. Those that cause harm to the environment are considered *invasive*, whereas those that become a part of the biome are deemed *naturalized*. These last two categories are human-based and determined by the degree to which we perceive a species as damaging or becoming engrained within a cultural landscape.

It's hard not to draw associations between this theory and human relations. Even the words used to describe nonnative species and their habitats—colonies, immigration, community, alien, native—are ones used to describe our own conditions within a place. And as someone well aware of her own nonnative status, I have a particular interest in how others like me are faring. Which may be why the activities of these hunters so rankled me. And why I found excuses to walk that same dirt road for the rest of the afternoon, wishing I had the courage to obstruct their activities. Since I didn't, I instead played something between voyeur and magistrate: recording their progress, judging their motives.

It was approaching dusk when Ari and I watched one of the hunters drag the dead coyote from the woods and drop it on a snow bank. About my age, he wore oversized camouflage pants and a sweatshirt emblazoned with a NASCAR driver I did not recognize. His face was ruddy with exertion, and he breathed heavily from the weight of his efforts. Meanwhile, his two dogs—German shorthairs—sat obediently a few steps away, still wearing their radio collars and looking at the coyote with interest. Their trophy was about 40 pounds or so, with thick tawny fur and red tipped ears. It had been shot through the chest—a clean kill.

From the start, I knew this moment would be the inevitable conclusion to the hunters' efforts. So I wasn't surprised when I met this scene. I was, of course, saddened by the sight of this dead animal, which lay bleeding on the snow and bore what I thought was an uncanny resemblance to my dog. But what I felt more than anything at that moment was a collective awkwardness. The hunter and I stood there—he with his working dogs, me and my dilettante canine companion—casting our eyes from the coyote to one another and back again. Our otherness could not have been more apparent. And there was an edge to our silent interaction, as if we were both daring the other to make a misstep, to question our right to be there; as if we were wondering if we even spoke the same language. Soon after, the other hunters joined our ranks. One made a halfhearted joke about Bugs Bunny cartoons; another speculated to no one in particular about the coyote's weight. The wild dog's mass didn't really matter. It was an average coyote, unremarkable in every way, save for the fact that it now lay before us. And no one quite seemed to know what to do about that. We studied our boots, the trees, anything other than the carcass that lay before us.

I left their group before they decided what to do with the animal: I didn't want to watch as it was tossed into the back of a truck or worse. On the way home, I stopped by the home of the neighbors who own the property on which the coyote was killed. A middle-aged Finnish couple, they are filled with warmth and humor. I have come to depend upon the gifts of cardamom bread they bring at Christmastime; the sound of the husband on his snowmobile, whooping for joy as he grooms the woods for cross-country skiing. If I were to open the chest freezer in their garage, I would find a year's supply of moose and venison. I like that about them. And it made me wonder if they could help me to make sense of what was happening further down the road.

Cami and her golden retriever Miko answered the door when I knocked. I told her I had seen the hunters—that they had been on my land, and I wondered if they had permission to be on theirs.

"Coyotes always have permission to be on our property," she said, visibly upset. "Coyote hunters do not."

Aside from her fondness for the wild dogs, I think what angered Cami the most is that the hunters were transgressive. Here in the east, most land is posted, meaning no one may hunt upon it without the owner's permission. Often, that permission is readily granted. But it needs to be sought. For some, this is a vestige of colonial invasions and the idea that autonomy is established through control. For most, it's a matter of safety—the need to know when and who and how many armed people are occupying the same space as you. Our area may look like wilderness, but tucked behind those acres of wooded landscape is something not entirely unlike suburbia with kids and parents and dogs playing outside. People want to feel secure. And so we create these artificial boundaries by tacking waxed signs to trees and telephone poles, assuming that they alone will create an uncrossable fence. These hunters violated that barrier, and that upset my neighbor.

Herein lies the greatest irony of the day: this disdain for transgression is precisely what Cami and I had in common with the hunters. We did not like that they had stepped across our property boundaries. We assumed they had breached an ethical one in killing for sport. Meanwhile (and I am of course speculating here) they probably thought the same of us. We who bought these parcels of a dozen or so acres, who knew them mostly as places to loaf, who turned our noses at the idea that hunting could be considered recreation. In doing so, we were stepping across some cultural expectations as well.

And then there was the transgression of *Canis latrans* to consider. Cami and I disliked the ambiguity surrounding the status of this animal. We wanted it to be considered a welcome resident in our landscape, endowed with the same consideration as any other species. The hunters disliked the ambiguity as well; they just arrived at a different way to alleviate it. We all, it seemed, wanted something that approached absolutism. And in the death of the coyote that day, we learned that such certainty can be hard to come by.

That doesn't usually sit well with our species. Whether it concerns ideas of ownership and relationships or ethics and morality, we like discrete categories. And once we've assigned something to a place, we generally like it to remain there. Domestic dogs are bosom friends; coyotes are eradicable vermin. Maine residents are either from here or away. An action is either right or wrong. Most of the time, we insist things remain in these categories. Sometimes, we force things to fit into them. We get angry when they leak out. And we tell ourselves that that's okay; that it's right to be steely serious about our need for things to stay put.

But maybe there's another, better response. Maybe we ought to invite in the transgressive, if only for a while. Maybe we ought to just laugh.

In *The Book of Laughter and Forgetting,* Milan Kundera argues that doing so creates an equilibrium between the otherwise tidy categories of good and evil:

> Things deprived suddenly of their putative meaning, the place assigned to them in the ostensible order of things, makes us laugh. Initially, therefore, laughter . . . has a certain malice to it (things have turned out differently from the way they tried to seem), but a certain beneficent relief as well (things are looser than they seemed, we have greater latitude in living with them, their gravity does not oppress us).

According to Kundera, laughter frees us from the limits imposed by boundaries and categories. It also demands we recognize that a lot about our life is absurd. When we laugh, we acknowledge that absurdity: we recognize we probably can't change it; and yet we refused to be encumbered by it. And so, like Sisyphus, we watch our boulder again tumble down its mountain. And instead of saying this is good or bad; right or wrong; foreign or familiar, we just say it is. And that it doesn't have to make sense, so long as we embrace it. And then we pitch back our heads and guffaw.

That's a good thing. After all, there's much about our existence that is absurd. Even with our big brains and confidence in our superior rationality, we are still very much a part of the animal kingdom. And it's a kingdom in which creatures kill. We fight against our moral imperative and animal nature all the time: the incisors and digestive track that tell us to consume; the cerebellum that tells us to protect. Probably some version of this struggle is what leads people like the coyote hunters to pursue their prey. Certainly it dictates a lot in my own life.

It was rationality that led me to vegetarianism fifteen years ago. That same sense of reason also compelled me to begin eating meat again this year. This recent decision feels right to me, both physically and morally. The carbon footprint for eating local meat is considerably less than industrial agriculture's tofu and veggie burgers. And for whatever reason, my body seems to do better with animal protein. And so, if pressed, I could probably make a sound argument on behalf of these choices and justifications. I even think I could make an argument about why killing any animal for sport is wrong.

But the rationality of my decision ends there. When I did decide to begin eating meat again, I chose lamb. Partly because I happened to be sitting in a London pub and it seemed a fitting choice (or at least one that—unlike blood pudding—did not seem too great a culinary stretch). Mostly, though, I chose sheep as my first meal based on a loose and indefensible hierarchy of animal value: tuna are becoming increasingly rare; cows somehow seem sympathetic; pigs are said to be smart. Sheep, I told myself, are more of an empty vessel. When I discovered that they also taste great, it was all over. In a single moment, I became some kind of Dionysian figure, gnawing on bones and all but licking my plate in ecstasy.

I like my new diet. But I don't yet know how far I'm willing to go in its name. I see the potential for dangerous hypocrisy in eating meat without procuring it. And so next year, I will go on my first deer hunt. Will I pull a trigger? Hard to say. But I do know that I will deliberately put myself in a place where I am forced to watch an animal die. Every moment of the hunt will be incredibly uncomfortable for me. So much so that I don't know if I'll be able to eat meat afterward. But, perhaps for the first time, I will at least know something of my neighbors and the spoke they occupy on the wheel of ecological life. For that moment, at last, I will step within the circle that describes the way they live their lives. Perhaps I will come to understand a little bit about the role violence and death play within all our identities—that we are all complicit in bringing it about. Lest I take too seriously this quest, I will also be reminded of the teasing wild dog. The trickster. And I will hope that he is watching from a hidden spot nearby, laughing at my folly.

Season of the Body

Brenda Miller

How good it's been to slide back
the heart's hood awhile, how fortunate
there's a heart and a covering for it,
and that whatever is still warm
has a chance.
   —Stephen Dunn

I.

October 1, the first day of hunting season in Wyoming, and I wear a fluorescent orange cap wherever I go, smug in the knowledge that my human heart this month makes me more sacred than a deer's running flanks. The deer graze close to the road, jerk their heads up to stare and freeze for the few moments it would take, if I had a gun, to set them clearly in my sights. Only then do they run, noiselessly sailing over sage and alfalfa, their white tails giving them away. A pickup full of shotguns passes. The orange cap bobs on my head, says *I am human, I am human*, and it's a relief, somehow, to have it all so clear today, the demarcations so sharp: who is edible and who is not.

But the next day I'll forget my orange cap. I'll stand at the edge of the field, my animal heart beating and beating. For some reason I'm wearing wild turkey feathers in my breast pocket and so I rustle when I move, a hunted thing. I'm wearing pants the color of sagebrush, a shirt the brown of new leather. I know I'm asking for it. I feel myself in their sights, appraised for the tone of my skin, the structure of my bones.

I'll make it out alive. We'll eat roast pheasant for dinner. The meat, when I tear it with my teeth, tastes faintly of sage, tastes of what they fed on, these iridescent birds in the underbrush. I nibble the meat from the bone, grind it between my molars, swallow. I keep eating and eating, can't stop, can't put a halt to my hunger, not so much for the meat but for the afterthought of sage, for what seasons the meat as it grows. I sit back at the table, my fingernails bright with grease, and wonder what I'll taste like when they finally get me. Will I have a bouquet of chocolate, the faintest waft of cinnamon? The sour-sweet tang of French bread and butter? I once saw twelve antelope strung up in my landlord's garage. He took a slice from each of them, grilled the meat so we could taste each one, find the bad ones in the batch, the ones that stank of fear.

Think of roasted garlic, Kalamata olives, Asiago cheese. Think of green chilies, poblanos, the snap of red pepper. Think of how your pores open during sex. Think of yourself drunk on good champagne, or the glass of Chardonnay like a bell on your tongue. Think of these odors wafting through you as an aftertaste, the taste that comes after you're gone.

II.

Once, in the summer of 1982, we shot a deer by the banks of the Big River. We shot him because he refused to move, refused to make it easy on all of us and migrate downriver to another garden, one with more roses than ours, or perhaps a garden with the sweet flowers of marijuana to make him mellow, let him roll around in the grass and forget about jumping fences. This was California after all, Mendocino county, and the gardens there were potent, hidden, cash crops with buds pungent as sex, sticky and warm. But the deer, a puritan, liked our roses better and Seth tracked him upstream, found the hole in the fence, fixed it, but still the deer wiggled in and ate the buds, nibbled the blossoms off the newborn squash. If this kept up, we'd have no food, no beauty that year.

So Seth borrowed a gun, who knows what kind, and tracked the deer again, saw him against the fence, too complacent to run, sated with the sugar of roses. His hunger made us angry, though it was common hunger, instinctual. Seth shot him clean through the chest. He told me how the deer buckled, fell to its knees as if in a last-ditch effort at apology.

Seth ate the heart that night. Maybe it was the liver, but I prefer to remember it as the heart, slices of it sautéed in butter and garlic, a bit of thyme. He ate it as a kind of restitution. He'd read that when Native American hunters killed a bear, they ate the heart right out of its chest, still beating. It went well with a bit of French bread, a salad of wild greens. At night I heard rustling in the garden and expected to see Seth on all fours among the roses, nibbling the folded petals, stepping delicately among the thorns.

But more often than not it was the raccoons, their eyes blinking at the open window, their human hands guilty on the compost.

III.

If you go to an acupuncturist complaining of heart trouble, he might turn your forearm pale-side up, trace the pericardial meridian with his fingertips. He'll start at your wrist and glide his finger across the dip of your elbow, the declination of a shoulder. "The pericardium," he tells you, "is the organ from which the feeling of happiness comes." He knows that what protects the heart brings the most pleasure. Not the heart itself, which is too meaty, too practical for love, beating and beating inside the sac. Cells of heart muscle cultured in a dish will beat on their own, thoughtlessly, ferocious, even with no body to sustain.

Close your eyes and your body has no bounds. Or it is all sheath, all skin, holding what balks at being contained. Trace the meridian all the way to the breastbone, return the way that you came: a brush of the shoulder, a swoon of the elbow, a question mark on the wrist. Wait for the needle, patiently, the way you might wait for a kiss.

Or pretend you're in another kind of doctor's office, one where they enter the body and take away a vial of blood. Feel your arm in the same position: open, flat against the steel table, so pale it's gone luminous. Blood runs close to the surface here, that's why it hurts so much and feels so good when they hand you the clean cotton ball and you press it to the wound and bend.

IV.

Admit it. What we want is to get at the heart: not the metaphorical heart, not the heart that is symmetrical and good-natured and red. We want to lay a finger on the unthinking muscle, the beating core of the body. Writing for *The New York Times Magazine*, Charles Siebert describes holding a transplanted heart in his hand. "I was expecting to feel a kind of gelatinous warble," he writes, "but got instead these hot, firm, repeated blows against my palm, the force resonating up my arm. I can feel them still." It's a language that exists before the tongue; feel your own tongue rising to drink it.

After Rhea gave birth to Sean, she ate a bit of the placenta. The meat of it looked like heart muscle to me, glossy, bright. I touched it in the special ceramic bowl; it felt like the living flesh of someone's abdomen. Rhea sautéed it in butter and onions. I watched her. She took tiny bites, chewing carefully. *This is my body*, I thought I heard her say. *Eat of it and be healed.*

V.

When they gutted their first chicken, Rhea told me, she saw the eggs, all the eggs the chicken would lay in her life, spiraled inside a sac: the largest egg at the lip, then decreasing in size until they clustered as a mass of microbes in the core. The shells, she said, were opalescent as pearls. All of them intact and edible, for someone with fingers and lips delicate enough to touch them without breaking.

She tells me this, describes the egg spiral with her hands, while we're camped in Kodachrome Basin in southern Utah. In the cooler we have "farm fresh" eggs bought from a Mormon family in Cannonville, brown and enormous, waiting to be soft-boiled in the morning, their shells rough like sandpaper against my fingertips. We bought them from two boys playing in their yard. We stopped at Bryce Valley Supply where the lights were off and the salsa jars sat dusty on the shelf. We thought *soft-boiled eggs with salsa and toast* in the morning, and already the meal existed, already we longed for the yolk of eggs melting on the bread, wanted the night to be done with so we could eat.

The campground has been taken over by a convocation of teen-aged girls. They are lovely and exasperating, whinnying to each other on the way to and from the bathroom. They stand a long time disapproving of themselves in the bathroom mirrors, their eyes narrow, their thin hands fluttering about their faces, touching one invisible blemish and then another. Their thighs are smooth and brown and hairless—no scars, no bites, no veins. They wait in line for the shower; they twirl bits of hair around their index fingers. They spread their makeup kits along the narrow counter; some have many compartments holding creams, lotions, and pots of dusty pigment.

I think of their eggs, inside them already, in a spiral, weightless as bubbles.

The girls have chaperones. They stand outside the bathroom, forever waiting for the girls to be done, but they will never be done, they will continue their ablutions forever in the damp, fogged mirrors. Rhea and I have no chaperone except for "Big Stony," a mammoth, penis-shaped rock above campsite #17. The girls, I think, take no notice of it, their vision narrowed down to the path between campsite and bathroom, but we joke about the rock's anatomical correctness: the rounded arrowhead of the tip, the two testicles anchoring the phallus to the mesa. When night falls the penis looms above us, pointing toward the stars. It demands sacrifice and worship, the silhouette like a God of Sensual Longing, a God who wants and wants without surcease.

That night I dream of something that wakes me crying "No!" I look outside the tent, and Big Stony towers in the moonlight, unmoved, unchanged. The girls do not sleep but spiral through the campground in their chaperones' cars, desperate for a mirror.

In the morning I wake and soft-boil the eggs, time them for exactly three minutes, while the chukars come out of hiding. They are partridges from Asia, with crowned heads, a low coo, brought to this desert for decoration. They strut in the damp morning dirt, clucking for bits of lettuce, the discarded rinds of fruit.

When the eggs are done I crack the shells and scoop out their soft hearts with a spoon.

VI.

My hunger knows no bounds. Yours, too, my dear, I see it beating in your gums. My what big teeth you have, bigger than a newborn's heart, which is only one inch wide, weighs under an ounce. How easy it would be to swallow such a heart if you could get to it.

The infant I care for, Emma, knows the world through her mouth, holds my lips with her fingers, touches my dangerous teeth. I touch her heart with my fingertip when she sleeps, to make sure she's still alive. When she wakes, she pries open my mouth, looks fearlessly into the abyss of my hunger, tries to put her whole head into that yawning expanse. *I could eat you up,* I growl to her, and she laughs.

VII.

When I was a small child of seven or eight I watched my mother make chopped liver. She made it every year for Hanukkah, and I remember her gutting the chicken with her bare hands. I saw her at the kitchen counter, saw her right hand hold down the carcass, her left hand enter that dark cavern. I thought how convenient for the entrails to emerge so nicely packaged and bound with string. At that age I had no clear idea of the arrangement of my own viscera (I still don't—looking at a diagram in the *Encyclopedia Britannica* I'm shocked to discover my liver so enormous, bigger than my heart and so near it, way up in the top strata of my rib cage). This package both humbled and horrified me. She pulled out the neck, the gizzards, the heart. She pulled out the cubes of liver, added extra ones from a plastic tub in the fridge, fried them in chicken fat with onions, chopped them with a cleaver and mixed them with boiled eggs, mayonnaise, a little salt, a little pepper. She set the bowl out on the counter next to a platter of thickly sliced *challah,* a bread the color of yolk.

We ate it quickly, scooping up big gobs of chopped liver with torn hunks of bread, mumbling our pleasure through full mouths. Yet whenever any of us felt rejected, underappreciated, we raised our voices and exclaimed: *"So what am I, chopped liver?"* as if chopped liver were something negligible. I heard my grandfather shout it to my grandmother in their bedroom in Brooklyn. I heard my father laugh it to my mother in the kitchen in Los Angeles. I repeated it on my way to school, my feet kicking the leaves on the sidewalk. *What am I, chopped liver? What am I?* The mere mention of chopped liver set my mouth watering, and then, in this transfiguring chant, I *became* the dish, a conflation that made me dizzy with words, with hunger, my body a sudden and accidental source of satiation.

VIII.

It's not just the animal body I want, the mathematics of sex, the coupling: I want another heart, an extra one, a contrabassoon to echo my everyday pulse. It's not my imagination. I hear it there, beating inside me. My bones pop and creak in their sockets.

IX.

Hunger does not belong to the belly. Even those with stomachs removed still feel hunger loose within their bodies, pangs in the abdomen, the tongue. Scientists, despite prodding the various centers of the brain, do not know where hunger lives, have yet to discover precisely hunger's location. It is not a finger on the inner lining of the heart. It is not a tooth grating on the esophagus.

But they know this hunger starts in utero. In the womb, we drink what our mother's bodies create. We drink the fluid in which we float, regulating the amnion in perfect equilibrium. In utero, breathing, drinking, eating: all the same, an orgy of consumption. And even as a fetus we know the bitter from the sweet, and we choose the one with sugar in it. Sometimes the amniotic fluid goes bitter, the fetus will refuse to drink, and the solution, unregulated, swells in the uterus, creating a fatal condition. Both mother and child will die.

So do not fault me for my sweet tooth; it's what we use to survive. Do not complain if you find me among the rosebushes, nibbling the amber petals. Do not fault me for my thirst, my hunger, my desire to absorb every delectable thing. *This is my body*, a voice nudges you in the dark. *Drink of it and be healed.*

X.

And when you finally eat me, when your hunger can no longer be contained, start with my arm. Mouth the little curves that lead to the pericardium. Turn my wrist to trace the subcutaneous secrets of my heart. Be a phlebotomist: extract this double evidence of life and desire. Find the Auricle, Ventricle, Vein. The Arch of Aorta, Superior Vena Cava, beating behind their glossy shield. Probe for the fluid of the womb, sip it, I swear it will be sweet.

XI.

Yes, love, here are my bones. Gnaw them until they gleam.

Ander Monson

. . . . I HAVE BEEN THINKING ABOUT SNOW . . . .
. . . . and the way
to get inside it, like through the entrance of an ice maze during winter carnival,
Michigan Technological University's yearly festival of snow, where the Greeks
and other student organizations build ice sculptures sometimes fifty feet deep
and high out of carefully packed snow . . . .
. . . . This was one of my pleasures as a child—
winding through the tunnels they would carve, carving our own in the
snowbanks that would sometimes rise above ten feet high around the yard . . .
. . . . Partially this is because I have gone so long without it,
living in Alabama . . . .
. . . . People in Alabama are mystified and terrified by it .
The forecasts are big news if they can predict even the possibility, the one-in-
twenty chance of it gathering around dust particles in the clouds and
descending indirectly to the earth. James Spann, meteorologist on ABC 33/40,
a Birmingham station, is very excited to predict that we might receive some
precipitation. This is a great moment for him. You can see it in the lines around
his mouth as they crease and bend. There are lines around the block at the li-
quor store. Runs on canned goods and milk at Bruno's, the local "gourmet"

grocery store chain, which is run by the same company as the less-uppity and apparently duller Food World. We have not received much yet this winter but there is much talk . . . . The University of Alabama cancelled classes two years ago on just the threat of snow. All my students trudged home, fearing and expectant. Though none came . . . . When I was in New York over Christmas 2002, there were only rinds around the curbs. I thought about peeling some away and bringing it home to Alabama in a Ziploc bag. There is the problem of melting, however. Would the snow be the same when I came home. Would I have to keep it on ice or frozen in order to keep it snow? Or could I let it melt then freeze it once home. Would it then be snow, or would it just be dirty New York ice . . . . I asked my father to send some snow from my home in Houghton, Michigan, about as far north as you can go in Michigan's Upper Peninsula. We get 250+ inches a year there. I thought he could send me some on ice in Ziploc bags, freeze-packed and FedExed . . . . They haven't had much yet this year. Every email I get from him contains an update on how much is on the ground, how much they are expecting, how many inches fell but melted, how many feet have accumulated, how much he cleared—or rather, moved, since in Upper Michigan you don't shovel or clear snow: you only move it—with one of his three snowblowers which are all now in the shop. Which leaves him to clear it out by hand. Which used to be my job and my brother's job. Which we did not enjoy but which we did of course. That's what the sons do in the winter . . . . My grandmother—approaching 90—refuses to let my father clear her walkway . . . . She is not technically my grandmother but is my step-grandmother. If that makes sense. She usually clears her own snow but sometimes she cannot and so my father does it secretly. Sometimes when she realizes this she gets angry but it is a risk that he likes to take . . . .

.. *1829* Virginia Lit. Museum *16 Dec. 418 Blizzard, a violent blow.* [OED] . . . . . .

. . . . *1881* N. Y. Nation *184 The hard weather has called into use a word which promises to become a national Americanism, namely 'blizzard'. It designates a storm (of snow and wind) which men cannot resist away from shelter.* [OED] . . . .

. . . . Think blizzard, think flurry in terms of boxing. A rain of blows. Many meteorological terms make that particular transition. Think fist as force .Think the body as a matter of nature . . . . . .

. . . I saw flakes today. Some minor evidence of potential weather. You do see frost starring everything on the ground . . . .

. . . Of course the weather matters to the growers a great deal, whether Midwestern or in the South. One reason why everyone in Michigan talks about it all the time . . . .

. . . . Frost—even a dip in the temperature— can be catastrophic to the orange-growing industry, especially in Florida. Where they admittedly do not get much snow . . . .

. . . . Where my brother lives for the time being, not missing snow . . . .

. . . . How can you not miss the snow, when you've lived most of your life in the half-year winters of Upper (far north of the area that residents call "Northern") Michigan? . . . .

. . . . "The upper level pattern over North America is dominated by a huge vortex over eastern Canada and a large ridge just off the Pacific Coast. The jetstream splits around the Pacific ridge, with the subtropical jet racing across the southern half of the country. The subtropical flow is bringing a good bit of moisture in at high levels, resulting in a beautiful pattern of high clouds across Alabama."* —ABC 33/40, Birmingham, Alabama, 02/09/03 . . . .

. . . . It is very difficult for professional meteorologists to predict the weather with any accuracy more than four or five days in advance . . . .

. . . .
. . . . Although how hard could it be I think . . . .
. . . .
. . . . Admittedly, everything is com-
plicated, is beautiful and intricate, infinitely recursive, when seen closely . . . .
. . . .
. . . .
. . . .
. . . .
. . . . A string of tornadoes came through Tuscaloosa and Western Ala-
bama in November 2001 and November 2002, doing huge amounts of damage.
They decimated a just-about-to-open grocery store next to a local community
college entirely but did not touch the college buildings. The tornado system in
2001 was followed by weeks of freezing temperatures, with over 30,000 Ala-
bama residents without power for days . . . .
. . . .
. . . . Which men cannot resist away from shelter . . .
. . . .
. . . .
. . . .
. . . . Culture is the opposite of weather. Is a hedge against
it. Is a fight beneath it. Is a losing fight a boxing match a match struck in hard
wind and extinguished immediately . . . .
. . . .
. . . .
. . . . Consider the threat of mass
extinction at the hands of one of the trillion comets or midsize and up aster-
oids that we will not see until they hurtle right into us, raise a hundred square
kilometers of the ocean, fog us over, kill us off . . . .
. . . .
. . . .
. . . . Is snow a lack or a mass. The white suggests the lack, but
such weight! I used to demand that my brother cover me over with snow until
it weighed enough that I could not move. My head would pop out of the patted-
down bank like a Whack-a-Mole. My brother would begin to pelt me with
snowballs. That weight would feel so good above me. Watch my body lose its
heat. Watch this body lose its heat to the weight of nature packed hard above
this body. He'd pretend to run away and leave me there. When I got cold enough
that I couldn't any longer tell the difference between outside and in, I'd blink
my eyes three times, which meant unbury me, let me back up into your world
. . . .
. . . .

. . . The body keeps the temperature right around 98.6. Mine was closer to 99. 1 most days. The doctors always told me that it was normal. I am sure it is. How come my brother's was always low—98.3 or so. If the body can't tolerate much of a dip in temperature—so like orange trees in Florida—why is there a difference from one body to another? . . . .
. . . .
. . . . I have been thinking about snow, or its lack. Would I really want to live away from it for so long. Away from the reasonable possibility of it. Away from the expectation of its mounting force. Away from all that white along the eyes. Away from sunburn on bright days when the sun reflects off the gleaming snow—the only way of course we can see the gleaming snow is the sun—and on the skin. And who thinks to wear sunscreen in middle January? . . . .
. . . .
. . . .
. . . . Artificial snow machines. Generating the necessary inches for the lodges at Ski Brule to operate, to keep the tourists coming in, to keep the ski lifts running and the tourists coming down the mountain, moving side to side, leaving their horde of zigzag slalom tracks . . . .
. . . .
. . . .
. . . . Artificial snow is real snow. It is made in the same way that true snow is. Except that it's gunned from nozzles at 350 to 400 psi, breaking the water into very tiny particles that are easier to freeze. Highly compressed air is gunned from nozzles into the atomized water, which causes the water to freeze as the air expands. A fan sucks the new snow out and fires it on the slopes and on the tracks . . . .
. . . .
. . . . There's no such thing as cold . . . .
. . . . in physics . . . .
. . . . . Just the lack of heat, of molecular motion . . . .
. . . .
. . . . It takes a lot of water to make snow. It takes a lot of electricity to make snow . . . .
. . . .
. . . . 53,712,000 pounds of water per day equals one foot of snow on a two lane road that is 10 miles long . . . . . .
. . . .
. . . .
. . . .

. . . . Artificial snow was first introduced and used for skiing on Mt. Greylock in Massachusetts. Artificial snow was invented in 1946 . . . .
. . . .
. . . .
. . . . And why an artificial snow?
. . . .
. . . . Aside from the economic necessity for ski runs and slopes, to extend the skiing season, to compensate for the whim of nature whose patterns we simply cannot yet predict far out with any accuracy . . . .
. . . .
. . . .
. . . .
. . . .
. . . .
. . . . A flurry is—one definition—*the death-throes of a dying whale* [OED]
. . . .
. . . . so think Melville, think obsession, think big and white and gone
. . . .
. . . .
. . . .
. . . .

. . . . and I am gone, and I am thinking about never coming back to the snow country for any appreciable length of time . . . .
. . . .
. . . .
. . . .
. . . .
. . . .
. . . .
. . . .
. . . . I am thinking about snow and structure . . . .
. . Is there an order to it / pattern in it / evidence of God or atom force . . . .
. . . . William A. Bentley photographed snowflakes on slides for years . .
. . . . He found regularities, symmetries . . . .
. . . . The photographs are stunning, lovely . .
. . . .
. . . . Some claimed he'd faked them . . . .
. . . . found an order . . . . .

. . . .

. . . . where there logically was none . . . .

. . . . that they were *too perfect* and couldn't exist in nature

. . . .

. . . .

. . . .

. . . .

. . . . I am thinking of the tracks my boots make in the snow, irrevocable except by act of God or weather or a movement of the heart. Or intentional disruption with a pine branch. Still there would be a mark . . . .

. . . .

. . . . some indication of obfuscation . . . .

. . . .

. . . .

. . . . The snow they had in New York barely qualified. It was the last gasp of a storm left for days on the streets. Getting black and dirty. If I brought it home, it would melt into water, sand, and cigarette ash. Refreeze it to turn it to an awful Popsicle . . . .

. . . .

. . . .

. . . .

. . . . . Several years ago in my home town in Michigan, two men robbed a bank in the heart of January on a snowmobile. The police followed the tracks back to their cabin and arrested them. They only got $22,000. It's hard to carry much more in bills, though the movies would like you to believe the opposite

. . . .

. . . .

. . . . I am thinking of snow and crime, of snow and drunkenness. Number of churches. Number of bars. Number of county jails. The ratio between . . . .

. . . .

. . . .

. . . .

. . . . Number of times I have gone through the ice in my dreams . .

. . . .

. . . . Number of snowmobiles sold as opposed to cars in the Northern half of Michigan . . . .

. . . .

. . . .

. . . . Number of tickets given to snowmobiles . . . .

. . . .

. . . Most snowmobiles can go 60 miles an hour on open, well-packed snow . . .

. . . .

. . . .

. . . . A fast-moving snowmobile can move over open water for miles

. . . .

. . . . they even have summer water snowmobile races . . . .

. . . .

. . . . a kid I knew from high school, not someone I particularly liked .

. . . . (in fact I disliked him inasmuch as one can in high school . .

. . . . given one's own predilection for asininity) . . . .

. . . . is now a semi-professional racer . . . .

. . . . of both snowmobiles and JetSkis . . . . . .

. . . .

. . . . —what does this mean, I ask myself— . . . .

. . . .

. . . .

. . . . Number of dollars brought in by snowmobile tourism . . . .

. . . . Number of deaths brought in by snowmobile tourism . . . . . .

. . . .

. . . .

. . . . *1883* Let. *in* Advance *1 Mar., Driving snow, with very blizzardly tendencies. 1888 San Francisco News Let. (Farmer), I should like to have seen the Colonel's face when he got that very cold blizzardy letter. 1892 GUNTER Miss Dividends I.vi.67 Then he suddenly ejaculates 'Well I'm blizzarded!' 1946* Chicago Daily News *5 Mar. 8/4 [It] would ruin the disposition of the throngs... especially on blizzardy nights* [OED] . . . .

. . . .

. . . .

. . . .

. . . . fig. *1820 J. Q. ADAMS* Mem. *2 June (1875) V. 137 His flurries of temper pass off as quickly as they rise* [OED] . . . .

. . . .

. . . .

. . . . the storm as a function of temper . . . .

. . . . the temper of the weatherman or my father . . . .

. . . .

. . . . When my father used to drink, we would be afraid of his temper .

. . . .

. . . .

. . . . (not afraid of physical violence exactly . . . .

. . . . and this is no different than fear of any father . .

. . . . but of something else, maybe of his shadow . . . .

. . . . of isolation, disapproval, one of many sorts of weather patterns)

. . . .
. . . . and even seven states away I find that I still am,
much to my wife's annoyance . . . .
. . . .
. . . . although it (my fear and my wife's annoyance) . . . .
. . . . is mostly Midwestern, contained, implicit— . . . .
. . . .
. . . . like nukes on television, all duck and cover, all threat
. . . . and imminence, all interiority, potential energy on the edge
. . . . of translation into kinetic . . . .
. . . .
. . . . We are all afraid in one way or another . . . .
. . . . of our parents and their judgments . . . .
. . . . of their wrath, interest in us, or lack thereof . .
. . . .
. . . .
. . . . . . And now we are separated by a time zone, over a thousand miles, a
couple hundred page breaks, a political party, a generation, and the threat of
weather or its end . . . .
. . . .
. . . . When my wife and I drive
up North for winter (she is from Minnesota, where they know cold), we rarely
make it to my home in Michigan without being blizzarded in and staying nights
in inexpensive hotels in places like Louisville, Kentucky, where they can't handle snow, but where they get it often enough to be a problem . . . .
. . . .
. . . .
. . . . Even crossing the state line from
Wisconsin into Upper Michigan, the snow is immediately a foot higher, the
roads not so well graded, the public radio more lonely & depressing, the nights
a power of 10 darker . . . .
. . . .
. . . . . . whether this is through some obscure intent or sheer weird chance . . . .
. . . .
. . . .
. . . . In a blizzard, we pulled
over to the side of the road and listened to the story of the whaleship *Essex* and
its travails, on which *Moby-Dick* was based . . . .
. . . .
. . . . Gruesome stuff to say the least . . . .
. . . .
. . this weather, this text, this consciousness, this spacing out across the page
. . . .

Such

.... isolation ....

....
....
....
....
....
....
.... Such ....
....
....
....
....
....
.... staggering weight—that can collapse a barn,
hundreds of roofs yearly, particularly those that have an insufficient grade:
someone has to push off all the snow and that someone is the father unless the
father designates it to the sons ....
....
....
.... More weight than all the miles of atmosphere above us ...
....
... More than all the minor matters of the heart that seem so large and gauzy .
....
....
.... But it's a good weight, one I have grown to love ....
....
....
....
.... So we are not just separated by distance but by act
of God or threat of act of God ....
....
.... or by the threat of God himself ....
....
.... Is this by choice or is it accident ....
....
....
.... There are a lot of accidents ....
....
....
....
.... b. Chiefly U. S. A sharp and sudden shower; a sudden
rush (of birds) [OED] ....
....
....

. . . .
. . . . *Which men cannot resist away from shelter* . . . . .
. . . .
. . . .
. . . .
. . . . *1698 FRYER* Acc. E. India & P.
128 marg., *Flurries from the Hills carry Men and Oxen down the Precipice.*
1726-7 SWIFT Gulliver *I.i.22 The boat was overset by a sudden flurry from the*
north. 1831 SCOTT Jrnl. *18 Nov., Wind...dies away in the morning, and blows*
in flurries rather contrary. 1890 Pall Mall G. *3 Dec. 1/3 You may watch 'catspaws'*
and 'flurries' on their rapid way. [OED] . . . .
. . . .
. . . .
. . . .
. . . .
. . . .
. . . .
. . . . How rapidly do relationships decline? .
. . . .
. . . .
. . . .
. . . . How much space does it
take around you to drive you to the bar when you've told yourself . . . .
. . . .
. . . . over . . . .
. . . .
. . . . and over . . . .
. . . . that you wouldn't go again under any circumstances . .
. . . .
. . . . Churches are perhaps first a house the house
of God a roof a sanctuary, apex, narthex, model homes for the improvement of
our souls, arms stretched out above us, shelter, shelter, a form of shelter . . . .
. . . .
. . . .
. . . . My parents stopped taking me to church when I stole
the merit badges from the Boy Scout trove kept in a closet by the kitchen . . . . .
. . . .
. . . . I felt that I deserved them for so many winters, so
much weight borne under snow, so many skills demonstrated: fire building,
vandalism, plagiarism, compromise-brokering, dodging bottles and bottle
rockets, anger management, living through the oblong story of depression,
weather and wilderness survival . . . .

. . . . *Flurry, 1.* trans. *To bewilder or confuse as by haste or noise; to agitate, 'put out'* [OED] . . . . I have been thinking about snowdrifts and the feeling of falling in them again, losing whatever heat keeps the meat of the body alive and twitching . . . . I have been thinking about loss . . . . How each winter is the story of a burial . . . . gradual . . . . (and each spring another revelation) . . . . a compilation . . . . a complication . . . . until we are up to our necks . . . . in North . . . . in enough . . . . in what we feel . . . . what we contain . . . . in what we are contained . . . . in what we barely understand . . . .

Son of Mr. Green Jeans: An Essay on Fatherhood, Alphabetically Arranged

Dinty W. Moore

Allen, Tim

Best known as the father on ABC's *Home Improvement* (1991–99), the popular comedian was born Timothy Allen Dick on June 13, 1953. When Allen was eleven years old, his father, Gerald Dick, was killed by a drunk driver while driving home from a University of Colorado football game.

Bees

"A man, after impregnating the woman, could drop dead," critic Camille Paglia suggested to Tim Allen in a 1995 *Esquire* interview. "That is how peripheral he is to the whole thing."

"I'm a drone," Allen responded. "Like those bees."

"You are a drone," Paglia agreed. "That's exactly right."

Carp

After the female Japanese Carp gives birth to hundreds of tiny babies, the father carp remains nearby. When he senses approaching danger, he sucks the helpless babies into his mouth, and holds them there until the coast is clear.

Divorce

University of Arizona psychologist Sanford Braver tells the story of a woman who felt threatened by her husband's close bond with their young son. The husband had a flexible work schedule but the wife did not, so the boy spent the bulk of his time with the father. The mother became so jealous of the tight father-son relationship that she filed for divorce, and successfully fought for sole custody. The result was that instead of being in the care of his father while the mother worked, the boy was now left in daycare.

Emperor Penguins

Once a male emperor penguin has completed mating, he remains by the female's side for the next month to determine if the act has been successful. When he sees a single greenish-white egg emerge from his mate's egg pouch, he begins to sing. Scientists have characterized his song as "ecstatic."

Father Knows Best

In 1949, Robert Young began *Father Knows Best* as a radio show. Young played Jim Anderson, an average father in an average family. The show later moved to television, where it was a major hit, but Young's successful life was troubled by alcohol and depression.

In January 1991, at age 83, Young attempted suicide by running a hose from his car's exhaust pipe to the interior of the vehicle. The attempt failed because the battery was dead and the car wouldn't start.

Green Genes

In Dublin, Ireland, a team of geneticists is conducting a study to determine the origins of the Irish people. By analyzing segments of DNA from residents across different parts of the Irish countryside, then comparing this DNA with corresponding DNA segments from people elsewhere in Europe, the investigators hope to determine the derivation of Ireland's true forefathers.

Hugh Beaumont

The actor who portrayed the benevolent father on the popular TV show *Leave It to Beaver* was a Methodist minister. Tony Dow, who played older brother Wally, reports that Beaumont actually hated kids. "Hugh wanted out of the show after the second season," Dow told the *Toronto Sun*. "He thought he should be doing films and things."

Inheritance

My own Irish forefather was a newspaperman, owned a nightclub, ran for mayor, and smuggled rum in a speedboat during Prohibition. He smoked, drank, ate nothing but red meat, and died of a heart attack in 1938.

His one son, my father, was a teenager when my grandfather died. I never learned more than the barest details about my grandfather from my father, despite my persistent questions. Other relatives tell me that the relationship had been strained.

My father was a skinny, asthmatic, and eager-to-please little boy, not the tough guy his father had wanted. My dad lost his mother at age three, and later developed a severe stuttering problem, perhaps as a result of his father's disapproval. My father's adult vocabulary was outstanding, due to his need for alternate words when faltering over hard consonants like B or D.

The stuttering grew worse over the years, with one exception: after downing a few whiskeys, my father could sing like an angel. His Irish tenor became legend in local taverns, and by the time I entered the scene my father was spending every evening visiting the bars. Most nights he would stumble back drunk around midnight; some nights he was so drunk he would stumble through a neighbor's back door, thinking he was home.

As a boy, I coped with the family's embarrassment by staying glued to the television—shows like *Father Knows Best* and *Leave It to Beaver* were my favorites. I desperately wanted someone like Hugh Beaumont to be my father, or maybe Robert Young.

Hugh Brannum, though, would have been my first choice. Brannum played Mr. Green Jeans on *Captain Kangaroo*, and I remember him as being kind, funny, and extremely reliable.

Jaws

My other hobby, besides television, was an aquarium. I loved watching the tropical fish give birth. Unfortunately, guppy fathers, if not moved to a separate tank, will sometimes come along and eat their young.

Kitten

Kitten, the youngest daughter on *Father Knows Best*, was played by Lauren Chapin.

Lauren Chapin

Chapin's father molested her and her mother was a severe alcoholic. After *Father Knows Best* ended in 1960, Chapin's life came apart. At age 16, she married an auto mechanic. At age 18, she became addicted to heroin and began working as a prostitute.

Male Breadwinners

Wolf fathers spend the daylight hours away from the home—hunting—but return every evening. The wolf cubs, five or six to a litter, rush out of the den when they hear their father approaching and fling themselves at their dad, leaping up to his face. The father backs up a few feet and disgorges food for them, in small, separate piles.

Natural Selection

When my wife Renita confessed to me her ambition to have children, the very first words out of my mouth were, "You must be crazy." Convinced that she had just proposed the worst imaginable idea, I stood from my chair, looked straight ahead, then marched out of the room.

Ozzie

Oswald Nelson, at 13, was the youngest person ever to become an Eagle Scout. Oswald went on to become Ozzie Nelson, the father in *Ozzie and Harriet*. Though the show aired years before the advent of reality television, Harriet was Ozzie's real wife, Ricky and David were his real sons, and eventually Ricky and David's wives were played by their actual spouses. The current requirements for Eagle Scout make it impossible for anyone to ever beat Ozzie's record.

Penguins, Again

The female emperor penguin "catches the egg with her wings before it touches the ice," Jeffrey Moussaieff Masson writes in his book *The Emperor's Embrace*. She then places it on her feet, to keep it from contact with the frozen ground.

At this point, both penguins will sing in unison, staring at the egg. Eventually, the male penguin will use his beak to lift the egg onto the surface of his own feet, where it remains until hatching.

Not only does the male penguin endure the inconvenience of walking around with an egg balanced on his feet for months, but he also will not eat for the duration.

Quiz

1. What is Camille Paglia's view on the need for fathers?
2. Why did Hugh Beaumont hate kids?
3. Who played Mr. Green Jeans on *Captain Kangaroo*?
4. Who would you rather have as your father: Hugh Beaumont, Hugh Brannum, a wolf, or an emperor penguin?

Religion

In 1979, Lauren Chapin, the troubled actress who played Kitty, had a religious conversion. She credits her belief in Jesus with saving her life. After his television career ended, Methodist Minister Hugh Beaumont became a Christmas tree farmer.

Sputnik

On October 4, 1957, *Leave It to Beaver* first aired. On that same day, the Soviet Union launched Sputnik I, the world's first artificial satellite. Sputnik I was about the size of a basketball, took roughly 98 minutes to orbit the Earth, and is credited with starting the US-Soviet space race.

Later, long after *Leave It to Beaver* ended its network run, a rumor that Jerry Mathers, the actor who played Beaver, had died at the hands of the communists in Vietnam, persisted for years. The rumor was false.

Toilets

Leave It to Beaver was the first television program to show a toilet.

Use of Drugs

The National Center on Addiction and Substance Abuse at Columbia University claims that the presence of a supportive father is irreplaceable in helping children stay drug-free.

Lauren Chapin may be a prime example here, as would Tim Allen, who was arrested for dealing drugs in 1978 and spent two years in prison.

The author of this essay, though he avoided his father's drinking problems, battled his own drug habit as a young man. Happily, he was never jailed.

Vasectomies
I had a vasectomy in 1994.

Ward's Father
In an episode titled "Beaver's Freckles," the Beaver says that Ward had "a hittin' father," but little else is ever revealed about Ward's fictional family. Despite Wally's constant warning—"Boy, Beav, when Dad finds out, he's gonna clobber ya!"—Ward does not follow his own father's example, and never hits his sons on the show. This is an excellent example of xenogenesis.

Xenogenesis
(*zen' u*-jen' *u*-*sis*), n. *Biol.* 1. heterogenesis 2. the supposed generation of offspring completely and permanently different from the parent.

Believing in xenogenesis—though at the time I couldn't define it, spell it, or pronounce it—I changed my mind about having children about four years after my wife's first suggestion of the idea. Luckily, this was five years before my vasectomy.

Y-Chromosomes
The Y-chromosome of the father determines a child's gender, and is unique, because its genetic code remains relatively unchanged as it passes from father to son. The DNA in other chromosomes, however, is more likely to get mixed between generations, in a process called recombination. What this means, apparently, is that boys have a higher likelihood of inheriting their ancestral traits.

My Y-chromosomes were looking the other way, so my only child is a daughter. So far Maria has inherited many of what people say are the Moore family's better traits—humor, a facility with words, a stubborn determination. It is yet to be seen what she will do with the many negative ones.

Zappa
Similar to the "Beaver died in Vietnam" rumor of the 1960s and '70s, during the late 1990s, Internet chatrooms and discussion lists repeatedly recycled the news that the actor who played Mr. Green Jeans was the father of musician Frank Zappa. But in fact, Hugh Brannum had only one son, and he was neither Frank Zappa nor this author.

Sometimes, though, he still wonders what it might have been like.

Grammar Lessons: The Subjunctive Mood

Michele Morano

Think of it this way: learning to use the subjunctive mood is like learning to drive a stick shift. It's like falling in love with a car that isn't new or sporty but has a tilt steering wheel and a price you can afford. It's like being so in love with the possibilities, with the places you might go and the experiences you might have, that you pick up your new used car without quite knowing how to drive it, sputtering and stalling and rolling backward at every light. Then you drive the car each day for months, until the stalling stops and you figure out how to downshift, until you can hear the engine's registers and move through them with grace. And later, after you've gained control over the driving and lost control over so much else, you sell the car and most of your possessions and move yourself to Spain, to a place where language and circumstance will help you understand the subjunctive.

Remember that the subjunctive is a mood, not a tense. Verb tenses tell *when* something happens; moods tell *how true.* It's easy to skim over moods in a new language, to translate the words and think you've understood, which is why your first months in Spain will lack nuance. But eventually, after enough conversations have passed, enough hours of talking with your students at the University of Oviedo and your housemate, Lola, and the friends you make when you wander the streets looking like a foreigner, you'll discover that you need the subjunctive in order to finish a question, or an answer, or a thought you couldn't have had without it.

In language, as in life, moods are complicated, but at least in language there are only two. The indicative mood is for knowledge, facts, absolutes, for describing what's real or definite. You'd use the indicative to say, for example:

I was in love.
Or, *The man I loved tried to kill himself.*
Or, *I moved to Spain because the man I loved, the man who tried to kill himself, was driving me insane.*

The indicative helps you tell what happened or is happening or will happen in the future (when you believe you know for sure what the future will bring).

The subjunctive mood, on the other hand, is uncertain. It helps you tell what could have been or might be or what you want but may not get. You'd use the subjunctive to say:

I thought he'd improve without me.
Or, *I left so that he'd begin to take care of himself.*

Or later, after your perspective has been altered, by time and distance and a couple of *cervezas* in a brightly lit bar, you might say:

I deserted him (indicative).
I left him alone with his crazy self for a year (indicative).
Because I hoped (after which begins the subjunctive) *that being apart might allow us to come together again.*

English is losing the subjunctive mood. It lingers in some constructions ("If he *were* dead . . . ," for example), but it's no longer pervasive. That's the beauty and also the danger of English—that the definite and the might-be often look so much alike. And it's the reason why, during a period in your life when everything feels hypothetical, Spain will be a very seductive place to live.

In Spanish, verbs change to accommodate the subjunctive in every tense, and the rules, which are many and varied, have exceptions. In the beginning you may feel defeated by this, even hopeless and angry sometimes. But eventually, in spite of your frustration with trying to explain, you'll know in the part of your mind that holds your stories, the part where grammar is felt before it's understood, that the uses of the subjunctive matter.

1. With Ojalá

Ojalá means "I hope" or, more literally, "that Allah is willing." It's one of the many words left over from the Moorish occupation of Spain, one that's followed by the subjunctive mood because, of course, you never know for sure what Allah has in mind.

During the first months in Spain, you'll use the word by itself, a kind of dangling wish. "It's supposed to rain," Lola will say, and you'll respond, "*Ojalá.*" You'll know you're confusing her, leaving her to figure out whether you want the rain or not, but sometimes the mistakes are too hard to bear. "That Allah is willing it wouldn't have raining," you might accidentally say. And besides, so early into this year of living freely, you're not quite sure what to hope for.

Each time you say *ojalá*, it will feel like a prayer, the *ja* and *la* like breaths, like faith woven right into the language. It will remind you of La Mezquita, the enormous, graceful mosque in Córdoba. Of being eighteen years old and visiting Spain for the first time, how you stood in the courtyard filled with orange trees, trying to admire the building before you. You had a fever then, a summer virus you hadn't yet recognized because it was so hot outside. Too hot to lift a hand to fan your face. Too hot to wonder why your head throbbed and the world spun slowly around you.

Inside, the darkness felt like cool water covering your eyes, such contrast, such relief. And then the pillars began to emerge, rows and rows of pillars supporting red-and-white brick arches, a massive stone ceiling balanced above them like a thought. You swam behind the guide, not even trying to understand his words but soothed by the vastness, by the shadows. Each time you felt dizzy you looked up toward the arches, the floating stone. Toward something that felt, you realized uncomfortably, like God. Or Allah. Or whatever force inspired people to defy gravity this way.

Ten years later, after you've moved to Oviedo, the man you left behind in New York will come to visit. You'll travel south with him, returning to La Mezquita on a January afternoon when the air is mild and the orange trees wave tiny green fruit. He'll carry the guidebook, checking it periodically to get the history straight, while you try to reconcile the place before you with the place in your memory, comparing the shadows of this low sun with the light of another season.

You'll be here because you want this man to see La Mezquita. You want him to feel the mystery of a darkness that amazes and consoles, that makes you feel the presence in empty spaces of something you can't explain. Approaching the shadow of the door, you'll each untie the sweaters from around your waists, slipping your arms into them and then into each other's. He will squint and you will hold your breath. *Ojalá*, you'll think, glimpsing in the shadows the subjunctive mood at work.

2. After Words of Suasion and Negation

In Oviedo, you'll become a swimmer. Can you imagine? Two or three times a week you'll pack a bag and walk for thirty-five minutes to the university pool, where you'll place clothes and contact lenses in a locker, then sink into a crowded lane. The pool is a mass of blurry heads and arms, some of which know what they're doing and most of which, like you, are flailing. You keep bumping into people as you make your way from one end of the pool to the other, but no one gets upset, and you reason that any form of motion equals exercise.

Then one day a miracle happens. You notice the guy in the next lane swimming like a pro, his long arms cutting ahead as he glides, rhythmically, stroke-stroke-breath. You see and hear and feel the rhythm, and before long you're following him, stroking when he strokes, breathing when he breathes. He keeps getting away, swimming three laps to your every one, so you wait at the edge of the pool for him to come back, then follow again, practicing. At the end of an hour, you realize that this man you don't know, a man you wouldn't recognize clothed, has taught you to swim. To breathe. To use the water instead of fighting against it. For this alone, you'll later say, it was worth moving to Spain.

Stroke-stroke-breath becomes the rhythm of your days, the rhythm of your life in Oviedo. All through the fall months, missing him the way you'd miss a limb, your muscles strain to create distance. Shallow end to deep end and back, you're swimming away. From memories of abrupt mood shifts. From the way a question, a comment, a person walking past a restaurant window could transform him into a hunched-over man wearing anger like a shawl. From the echo of your own voice trying to be patient and calm, saying, "Listen to me. I want you to call the doctor." In English you said "listen" and "call," and they were the same words you'd use to relate a fact instead of make a plea. But in Spanish, in the language that fills your mind as you swim continually away, the moment you try to persuade someone, or dissuade, you enter the realm of the subjunctive. The verb ends differently so there can be no mistake: requesting is not at all the same as getting.

3. With Si or Como Si

Si means "if." Como si means "as if." A clause that begins with si or como si is followed by the subjunctive when the meaning is hypothetical or contrary to fact. For example:

If I'd known he would harm himself, I wouldn't have left him alone.

But here we have to think about whether the if-clause really is contrary to fact. Two days before, you'd asked him what he felt like doing that night and he'd responded, "I feel like jumping off the Mid-Hudson Bridge." He'd looked serious when he said it, and even so you'd replied, "Really? Would you like me to drive you there?" *As if* it were a joke.

If you had known he was serious, that he was thinking of taking his life, would you have replied with such sarcasm? In retrospect it seems impossible not to have known—the classic signs were there. For weeks he'd been sad, self-pitying. He'd been sleeping too much, getting up to teach his freshman composition class in the morning, then going home some days and staying in bed until evening. His sense of humor had waned. He'd begun asking the people around him to cheer him up, make him feel better, please.

And yet he'd been funny. Ironic, self-deprecating, hyperbolic. So no one's saying you should have known, just that maybe you felt a hint of threat in his statement about the river. And maybe that angered you because it meant you were failing to be enough for him. Maybe you were tired, too, in need of cheering up yourself because suddenly your perfect guy had turned inside out. Or maybe that realization came later, after you'd had the time and space to develop theories.

The truth is, only you know what you know. And what you know takes the indicative, remember?

For example: You knew he was hurting himself. The moment you saw the note on his office door, in the campus building where you were supposed to meet him on a Sunday afternoon, you knew. The note said, "I'm not feeling well. I'm going home. I guess I'll see you tomorrow." He didn't use your name.

You tried calling him several times but there was no answer, so you drove to the apartment he shared with another graduate student. The front door was unlocked, but his bedroom door wouldn't budge. You knocked steadily but not too loud, because his housemate's bedroom door was also closed and you assumed he was inside taking a nap. *If* you'd known that his housemate was not actually home, you would have broken down the door. That scenario is hypothetical, so it takes the subjunctive—even though you're quite sure.

The human mind can reason its way around anything. On the drive to your own apartment, you told yourself, He's angry with me. That's why the door was locked, why he wouldn't answer the phone. You thought, If he weren't so close to his family, I'd really be worried. If today weren't Mother's Day. If he didn't talk so affectionately about his parents. About his brother and sisters. About our future. If, if, if.

When the phone rang and there was silence on the other end, you began to shout, "What have you done?"

In Spain, late at night over *chupitos* of bourbon or brandy, you and Lola will trade stories. Early on you won't understand a lot of what she says, and she'll understand what you say but not what you mean. You won't know how to say what you mean in Spanish; sometimes you won't even know how to say it in English. But as time goes on, the stories you tell will become more complicated. More subtle. More grammatically daring. You'll begin to feel more at ease in the unreal.

For example: *If* you hadn't gone straight home from his apartment. *If* you hadn't answered the phone. *If* you hadn't jumped back into your car to drive nine miles in record time, hoping the whole way to be stopped by the police. *If* you hadn't met him on the porch where he had staggered in blood-soaked clothes. *If* you hadn't rushed upstairs for a towel and discovered a flooded bedroom floor, the blood separating into water and rust-colored clumps. *If* you hadn't been available for this emergency.

As the months pass in Spain, you'll begin to risk the *then.* His housemate would have come home and found him the way you found him: deep gashes in his arm, but the wounds clotting enough to keep him alive, enough to narrowly avoid a transfusion. His housemate would have called the paramedics, ridden to the hospital in the ambulance, notified his parents from the emergency room and greeted them after their three-hour drive. His housemate would have done all the things you did, and he would have cleaned the mess by himself instead of with your help, the two of you borrowing a neighbor's wet-dry vac and working diligently until you—or he—or both of you—burst into hysterical laughter. Later this housemate would have moved to a new apartment, just as he has done, and would probably be no worse off than he is right now.

You, on the other hand, would have felt ashamed, guilty, remiss for not being available in a time of crisis. But you wouldn't have found yourself leaning over a stretcher in the emergency room, a promise slipping from your mouth before you could think it through: "I won't leave you. Don't worry, I won't leave you." *As if* it were true.

4. After Impersonal Expressions
Such as *it is possible, it is a shame, it is absurd.*

"*It's possible* that I'm making things worse in some ways," you told the counselor you saw on Thursday afternoons. He'd been out of the hospital for a few months by then and had a habit of missing his therapy appointments, to which you could only respond by signing up for your own.

She asked how you were making things worse, and you explained that when you told him you needed to be alone for a night and he showed up anyway at 11:00, pleading to stay over, you couldn't turn him away. She said, "*It's a shame* he won't honor your request," and you pressed your fingernails into the flesh of your palm to keep your eyes from filling. She asked why you didn't want him to stay over, and you said that sometimes you just wanted to sleep, without waking up when he went to the bathroom and listening to make sure he came back to bed instead of taking all the Tylenol in the medicine cabinet. Or sticking his head in the gas oven. Or diving from the balcony onto the hillside three stories below. There is nothing, you told her, nothing I haven't thought of.

She said, "Do you think he's manipulating you?" and you answered in the mood of certainty, "Yes. Absolutely." Then you asked, "*Isn't it absurd* that I let him manipulate me?" and what you wanted, of course, was some reassurance that it wasn't absurd. That you were a normal person, reacting in a normal way, to a crazy situation.

Instead she said, "Let's talk about why you let him. Let's talk about what's in this for you."

5. After Verbs of Doubt or Emotion
You didn't think he was much of a prospect at first. Because he seemed arrogant. Because in the initial meetings for new instructors, he talked as if he were doing it the right way and the rest of you were pushovers. Because he looked at you with one eye squinted, as if he couldn't quite decide.

You liked that he was funny, a little theatrical and a great fan of supermarkets. At 10:00, after evening classes ended, he'd say, "Are you going home?"

Sometimes you'd offer to drop him off at his place. Sometimes you'd agree to go out for a beer. And sometimes you'd say, "Yeah, but I have to go to the store first," and his eyes would light up. In the supermarket he'd push the cart and you'd pick items off the shelf. Maybe you'd turn around and there would be a whole rack of frozen ribs in your cart, or after you put them back, three boxes of Lucky Charms. Maybe he'd be holding a package of pfeffernusse and telling a story about his German grandmother. Maybe it would take two hours to run your errand because he was courting you in ShopRite.

You doubted that you'd sleep with him a second time. After the first time, you both lay very still for a while, flat on your backs, not touching. He seemed to be asleep. You watched the digital clock hit two-thirty a.m. and thought about finding your turtleneck and sweater and wool socks, lacing up your boots and heading out into the snow. And then out of the blue he rolled toward you, pulled the blanket up around your shoulders, and said, "Is there anything I can get you? A cup of tea? A sandwich?"

You were thrilled at the breaks in his depression, breaks that felt like new beginnings, every time. Days, sometimes even weeks, when he seemed more like himself than ever before. Friends would ask how he was doing, and he'd offer a genuine smile. "Much better," he'd say, putting his arm around you, "She's pulling me through the death-wish phase." Everyone would laugh with relief, and at those moments you'd feel luckier than ever before, because of the contrast.

Do you see the pattern?

6. To Express Good Wishes

Que tengas muy buen viaje, Lola will say, kissing each of your cheeks before leaving you off at the bus station. *May you have a good trip.* A hope, a wish, a prayer of sorts, even without the *ojalá*.

The bus ride from Oviedo to Madrid is nearly six hours, so you have a lot of time for imagining. It's two days after Christmas, and you know he spent the holiday at his parents' house, that he's there right now, maybe eating breakfast, maybe packing. Tonight his father will drive him to Kennedy Airport, and tomorrow morning, very early, you'll meet him at Barajas in Madrid. You try to envision what he'll look like, the expression on his face when he sees you, but you're having trouble recalling what it's like to be in his presence.

You try not to hope too much, although now, four months into your life in Spain, you want to move toward, instead of away. Toward long drives on winding, mountain roads, toward the cathedral of Toledo, the mosque at Córdoba, the Alhambra in Granada. Toward romantic dinners along the Mediterranean. Toward a new place from which to view the increasingly distant past. You want this trip to create a separation, in your mind and in his, between your first relationship and your real relationship, the one that will be so wonderful, so stable, you'll never leave him again.

Once you've reached Madrid and found the *pensión* where you've reserved a room, you'll get the innkeeper to help you make an international call. His father will say, "My God, he can't sit still today," and then there will be his voice, asking how your bus ride was, where you are, how far from the airport. You'll say, "I'll see you in the morning." He'll reply, "In seventeen hours."

The next morning, the taxi driver is chatty. He wants to know why you're going to the airport without luggage, and your voice is happy and excited when you explain. He asks whether this boyfriend writes you letters, and you smile and nod at the reflection in the rearview mirror. "Many letters?" he continues, "Do you enjoy receiving the letters?" In Spain you're always having odd conversations with strangers, so you hesitate only a moment, wondering why he cares, and then you say, "Yes. Very much." He nods emphatically. "*Muy bien.*" At the terminal he drops you off with a broad smile. "*Que lo pases bien con tu novio,*" he says. *Have a good time with your boyfriend.* In his words you hear the requisite subjunctive mood.

7. In Adverbial Clauses Denoting Purpose, Provision, Exception
How different to walk down the street in Madrid, Toledo, Córdoba, to notice an elaborate fountain or a tiny car parked half on the sidewalk, and comment aloud. You've loved being alone in Spain and now, even more, you love being paired.

On the fifth day you reach Granada, find lodging in someone's home. Down the hallway you can hear the family watching TV, cooking, preparing to celebrate New Year's Eve.

In the afternoon you climb the long, slow hill leading to the Alhambra and spend hours touring the complex. You marvel at the elaborate irrigation system, the indoor baths with running water, the stunning mosaic tiles and views of the Sierra Nevada. Here is the room where Boabdil signed the city's surrender to Ferdinand and Isabella; here is where Washington Irving lived while writing *Tales of the Alhambra*. Occasionally you separate, as he inspects a mural and you follow a hallway into a lush courtyard, each of your imaginations working to restore this place to its original splendor. When you come together again, every time, there's a thrill.

He looks rested, relaxed, strolling through the gardens with his hands tucked into the front pockets of his pants. When you enter the Patio of the Lions—the famous courtyard where a circle of marble lions project water into a reflecting pool—he turns to you, wide-eyed, his face as open as a boy's.

"Isn't it pretty?" you keep asking, feeling shy because what you mean is: "Are you glad to be here?"

"*So* pretty," he responds, taking hold of your arm, touching his lips to your hair.

The day is perfect, you think. The trip is perfect. You allow yourself a moment of triumph: I left him *so that* he would get better without me, and he did. I worked hard and saved money and invited him on this trip *in case* there's still hope for us. And there is.

Unless. In language, as in experience, we have purpose, provision, exception. None of which necessarily matches reality, and all of which take the subjunctive.

On the long walk back down the hill toward your room, he turns quiet. You find yourself talking more than usual, trying to fill the empty space with cheerful commentary, but it doesn't help. The shape of his face begins to change until there it is again, that landscape of furrows and crags. The jaw thrusts slightly, lips pucker, eyebrows arch as if to say, "I don't care. About anything."

Back in the room, you ask him what's wrong, plead with him to tell you. You can talk about anything, you assure him, anything at all. And yet you're stunned when his brooding turns accusatory. He says it isn't fair. You don't understand how difficult it is to be him. Your life is easy, so easy that even moving to a new country, taking up a new language, is effortless. While every day is a struggle for him. Don't you see that? Every day is a struggle.

He lowers the window shade and gets into bed, his back turned toward you.

What to do? You want to go back outside into the mild air and sunshine, walk until you remember what it feels like to be completely alone. But you're afraid to leave him. For the duration of his ninety-minute nap, you sit paralyzed. Everything feels unreal, the darkened room, the squeals of children in another part of the house, the burning sensation in your stomach. You tremble, first with sadness and fear, then with anger. Part of you wants to wake him, tell him to collect his things, then drive him back to the airport in Madrid. You want to send him home again, away from your new country, the place where you live unencumbered—but with a good deal of effort, thank you. The other part of you wants to wail, to beat your fists against the wall and howl, *Give him back to me.*

Remember: purpose, provision, exception. The subjunctive runs parallel to reality.

8. After Certain Indications of Time, If the Action Has Not Occurred

While is a subjunctive state of mind. So are *until, as soon as, before,* and *after.* By now you understand why, right? Because until something *has happened,* you can't be sure.

In Tarifa, the wind blows and blows. You learn this even before arriving, as you drive down route 15 past Gibraltar. You're heading toward the southernmost point in Spain, toward warm sea breezes and a small town off the beaten path. You drive confidently, shifting quickly through the gears to keep pace with the traffic around you. He reclines in the passenger's seat, one foot propped against the dashboard, reading from *The Real Guide* open against his thigh. "Spreading out beyond its Moorish walls, Tarifa is known in Spain for its abnormally high suicide rate—a result of the unremitting winds that blow across the town and its environs."

You say, "Tell me you're joking." He says, "How's that for luck?" Three days before, you'd stood in Granada's crowded city square at midnight, each eating a grape for every stroke of the New Year. If you eat all twelve grapes in time, tradition says, you'll have plenty of luck in the coming year. It sounds wonderful—such an easy way to secure good fortune—until you start eating and time gets ahead, so far ahead that no matter how fast you chew and swallow, midnight sounds with three grapes left.

In Tarifa, you come down with the flu. It hits hard and fast—one minute you're strolling through a whitewashed coastal town, and the next you're huddled in bed in a stupor. He goes to the pharmacy and, with a handful of Spanish words and many gestures, procures the right medicine. You sleep all day, through the midday meal, through the time of siesta, past sundown and into the evening. When you wake the room is fuzzy and you're alone, with a vague memory of him rubbing your back, saying something about a movie.

Carefully you rise and make your way to the bathroom—holding onto the bed, the doorway, the sink—then stand on your toes and look out the window into the blackness. By day there's a thin line of blue mountains across the strait, and you imagine catching the ferry at dawn and watching that sliver of Morocco rise up from the shadows to become a whole continent. You imagine standing on the other side and looking back toward the tip of Spain, this tiny town where the winds blow and blow. That's how easy it is to keep traveling once you start, putting distance between the various parts of your life, imagining yourself over and over again into entirely new places.

Chilly and sweating, you make your way back to bed, your stomach fluttering nervously. You think back to Granada, how he'd woken from a nap on that dark afternoon and apologized. "I don't know what got into me today," he'd said, "This hasn't been happening." You believe it's true, it hasn't been happening. But you don't know *how true.*

You think: He's fine now. There's no need to worry. He's been fine for days, happy and calm. I'm overreacting. But overreaction is a slippery slope. With the wind howling continuously outside, the room feels small and isolated. You don't know that he's happy and calm right now, do you? You don't know how he is today at all, because you've slept and slept and barely talked to him.

You think: If the movie started on time—but movies never start on time in Spain, so you add, subtract, try to play it safe, and determine that by ten forty-five your fretting will be justified. At eleven you'll get dressed and go looking, and if you can't find him, what will you do? Wait until midnight for extra measure? And then call the police? And tell them what, that he isn't back yet and you're afraid because you're sick and he's alone and the wind here blows and blows, enough to make people crazy, the book says, make them suicidal? This is the *when*, the *while*, the *until*. The *before* and *after*. The real and the unreal in precarious balance. This is what you moved to Spain to escape from, and here it is again, following you.

The next time you wake, the room seems brighter, more familiar. You sit up and squint against the light. His cheeks are flushed, hair mussed from the wind. His eyes are clear as a morning sky. "Hi sweetie," he says, putting a hand on your forehead. "You still have a fever. How do you feel?" He smells a little musty, like the inside of a community theater where not many people go on a Sunday night in early January. He says, "The movie was hilarious." You ask whether he understood it and he shrugs. Then he acts out a scene using random Spanish words as a voice over, and you laugh and cough until he flops down on his stomach beside you.

Here it comes again, the contrast between what was, just a little while ago, and what is now. After all this time and all these miles, you're both here, in a Spanish town with a view of Africa. You feel amazed, dizzy, as if swimming outside yourself. You're talking with him, but you're also watching yourself talk with him. And then you're sleeping and watching yourself sleep, dreaming and thinking about the dreams. Throughout the night you move back and forth, here and there, between what is and what might be, tossed by language and possibility and the constantly shifting wind.

9. In Certain Independent Clauses
There's something extraordinary—isn't there?—about learning to speak Spanish as an adult, about coming to see grammar as a set of guidelines not just for saying what you mean but for understanding the way you live. There's something extraordinary about thinking in a language that insists on marking the limited power of desire.

For example: At Barajas Airport in Madrid, you walk him to the boarding gate. He turns to face you, hands on your arms, eyes green as the sea. He says, "Only a few more months and we'll be together for good. Right sweetie?" He watches your face, waiting for a response, but you know this isn't a decision, something you can say yes to. So you smile, eyes burning, and give a slight nod. What you mean is, *I hope so*. What you think is, *Ojalá*. And what you know is this: The subjunctive is the mood of mystery. Of luck. Of faith interwoven with doubt. It's a held breath, a hand reaching out, carefully touching wood. It's humility, deference, the opposite of hubris. And it's going to take a long time to master.

But at least the final rule of usage is simple, self-contained, one you can commit to memory: Certain independent clauses exist only in the subjunctive mood, lacing optimism with resignation, hope with heartache. *Be that as it may*, for example. Or the phrase one says at parting, eyes closed as if in prayer, *May all go well with you.*

Thank You in Arabic

Naomi Shihab Nye

Shortly after my mother discovered my brother had been pitching his Vitamin C tablets behind the stove for years, we left the country. Her sharp alert, "Now the truth be known!" startled us at the breakfast table as she poked in the dim crevice with the nozzle of her vacuum. We could hear the pills go click, click, up through the long tube.

My brother, an obedient child, a bright-eyed, dark-skinned charmer who scored high on all his tests and trilled a boy's sweet soprano, stared down at his oatmeal. Four years younger than I, he was also the youngest and smallest in his class. Somehow he maintained an intelligence and dignity more notable than that of his older, larger companions, and the pills episode, really, was a pleasant surprise to me.

Companions in mischief are not to be underestimated, especially when everything else in your life is about to change.

We sold everything we had and left the country. The move had been brewing for months. We took a few suitcases each. My mother cried when the piano went. I wished we could have saved it. My brother and I had sung so many classics over its keyboard—"Look for the Silver Lining" and "Angels We Have Heard on High"—that it would have been nice to return to a year later, when we came straggling back. I sold my life-size doll and my toy sewing machine. I begged my mother to save her red stove for me, so I could have it when I grew up—no one else we knew had a red stove. So my mother asked some friends to save it for me in their barn.

Our parents had closed their imported-gifts stores, and our father had dropped out of ministerial school. He had attended the Unity School of Christianity for a few years, but decided not to become a minister after all. We were relieved, having felt like impostors the whole time he was enrolled. He wasn't even a Christian, to begin with, but a gently non-practicing Muslim. He didn't do anything like fasting or getting down on his knees five times a day. Our mother had given up the stern glare of her Lutheran ancestors, raising my brother and me in the Vedanta Society of St. Louis. When anyone asked what we were, I said, "Hindu." We had a Swami, and sandalwood incense. It was over our heads, but we liked it and didn't feel very attracted to the idea of churches and collection baskets and chatty parish good-will.

Now and then, just to keep things balanced, we attended the Unity Sunday School. My teacher said I was lucky my father came from the same place Jesus came from. It was a passport to notoriety. She invited me to bring artifacts for Show and Tell. I wrapped a red and white *keffiyah* around my friend Jimmy's curly blond head while the girls in lacy socks giggled behind their hands. I told about my father coming to America from Palestine on the boat and throwing his old country clothes overboard before docking at Ellis Island. I felt relieved he'd kept a few things, like the *keffiyah* and its black braided band. Secretly it made me mad to have lost the blue pants from Jericho with the wide cuffs he told us about.

I enjoyed standing in front of the group talking about my father's homeland. Stories felt like elastic bands that could stretch and stretch. Big fans purred inside their metal shells. I held up a string of olive wood camels. I didn't tell our teacher about the Vedanta Society. We were growing up ecumenical, though I wouldn't know that word till a long time later in college. One night I heard my father say to my mother in the next room, "Do you think they'll be confused when they grow up?" and knew he was talking about us. My mother, bless her, knew we wouldn't be. She said, "At least we're giving them a choice." I didn't know then that more clearly than all the stories of Jesus, I'd remember the way our Hindu swami said a single word three times, "Shanti, shanti, shanti"—peace, peace, peace.

Our father was an excellent speaker—he stood behind pulpits and podiums easily, delivering gracious lectures on "The Holy Land" and "The Palestinian Question." He was much in demand during the Christmas season. I think that's how he had fallen into the ministerial swoon. While he spoke, my brother and I hovered toward the backs of the auditoriums, eyeing the tables of canapés and tiny tarts, slipping a few into our mouths or pockets.

What next? Our lives were entering a new chapter, but I didn't know its title yet.

We had never met our Palestinian grandmother, Sitti Khadra, or seen Jerusalem, where our father had grown up, or followed the rocky, narrow alleyways of the Via Dolorosa, or eaten an olive in its own neighborhood. Our mother hadn't either. The Arabic customs we knew had been filtered through the fine net of folktales. We did not speak Arabic, though the lilt of the language was familiar to us—our father's endearments, his musical blessings before meals—but that language had never lived in our mouths.

And that's where we were going, to Jerusalem. We shipped our car, a wide golden Impala the exact color of a cigarette filter, over on a boat. We would meet up with it later.

The first plane flight of my whole life was the night flight out of New York City across the ocean. I was fourteen years old. Every glittering light in every skyscraper looked like a period at the end of the sentence. Good-bye, our lives.

We stopped in Portugal for a few weeks. We were making a gradual transition. We stopped in Spain and Italy and Egypt, where the pyramids shocked me by sitting right on the edge of the giant city of Cairo, not way out in the desert as I had imagined them. While we waited for our baggage to clear customs, I stared at six tall African men in brilliantly patterned dashikis negotiating with an Egyptian customs agent and realized I did not even know how to say "Thank you" in Arabic. How was this possible? The most elemental and important of human phrases in my father's own tongue had evaded me till now. I tugged on his sleeve, but he was busy with visas and passports. "Daddy," I said. "Daddy, I have to know. Daddy, tell me. Daddy, why didn't we ever *learn*?" An African man adjusted his turban. Always thereafter, the word *shookrun*, so simple, with a little roll in the middle, would conjure up the vast African baggage, the brown boxes looped and looped in African twine.

We stayed one or two nights at the old Shepherd's Hotel downtown, but couldn't sleep because of the heat and honking traffic beneath our windows. So our father moved us to the famous Mena House Hotel next to the pyramids. We rode camels for the first time, and our mother received a dozen blood-red roses at her hotel room from a rug vendor who apparently liked her pale brown ponytail. The belly dancer at the hotel restaurant twined a gauzy pink scarf around my brother's astonished ten-year-old head as he tapped his knee in time to her music. She bobbled her giant cleavage under his nose, huge bosoms prickled by sequins and sweat.

Back in our rooms, we laughed until we fell asleep. Later that night, my brother and I both awakened burning with fever and deeply nauseated, though nobody ever threw up. We were so sick that a doctor hung a Quarantine sign in Arabic and English on our hotel room door the next day. Did he know something we didn't know? I kept waiting to hear that we had malaria or typhoid, but no dramatic disease was ever mentioned. We lay in bed for a week. The aged doctor tripped over my suitcase every time he entered to take our temperatures. We smothered our laughter. "Shookrun," I would say. But as soon as he left, to my brother, "I feel bad. How do you feel?"

"I feel really, really bad."

"I think I'm dying."

"I think I'm already dead."

At night we heard the sound and lights show from the pyramids drifting across the desert air to our windows. We felt our lives stretching out across thousands of miles. The Pharaohs stomped noisily through my head and churning belly. We had eaten spaghetti in the restaurant. I would not be able to eat spaghetti again for years.

Finally, finally, we appeared in the restaurant again, thin and weakly smiling, and ordered the famous Mena House *shorraba*, lentil soup, as my brother nervously scanned the room for the belly dancer. Maybe she wouldn't recognize him now.

In those days Jerusalem, which was then a divided city, had an operating airport on the Jordanian side. My brother and I remember flying in upside down, or in a plane dramatically tipped, but it may have been the effect of our medicine. The land reminded us of a dropped canvas, graceful brown hillocks and green patches. Small and provincial, the airport had just two runways, and the first thing I observed as we climbed down slowly from the stuffy plane was all my underwear strewn across one of them. There were my flowered cotton briefs and my pink panties and my slightly embarrassing raggedy ones and my extra training bra, alive and visible in the breeze. Somehow my suitcase had popped open in the hold and dropped its contents the minute the men pried open the cargo door. So the first thing I did on the home soil of my father was recollect my underwear, down on my knees, the posture of prayer over that ancient holy land.

Our relatives came to see us at a hotel. Our grandmother was very short. She wore a long, thickly embroidered Palestinian dress, had a musical, high-pitched voice and a low, guttural laugh. She kept touching our heads and faces as if she couldn't believe we were there. I had not yet fallen in love with her. Sometimes you don't fall in love with people immediately, even if they're your own grandmother. Everyone seemed to think we were all too thin.

We moved into a second-story flat in a stone house eight miles north of the city, among fields and white stones and wandering sheep. My brother was enrolled in the Friends Girls School and I was enrolled in the Friends Boys School in the town of Ramallah a few miles farther north—it seemed a little confused. But the Girls School offered grades one through eight in English and high school continued at the Boys School. Most local girls went to Arabic-speaking schools after eighth grade.

I was a freshman, one of seven girl students among two hundred boys, which would cause me problems later. I was called in from the schoolyard at lunchtime, to the office of our counselor who wore shoes so pointed and tight her feet bulged out pinkly on top.

"You will not be talking to them anymore," she said. She rapped on the desk with a pencil for emphasis.

"To whom?"

"All the boy students at this institution. It is inappropriate behavior. From now on, you will only speak with the girls."

"But there are only six other girls! And I only like one of them!" My friend was Anna, from Italy, whose father ran a small factory that made matches. I'd visited it once with her. It felt risky to walk the aisles among a million filled matchboxes. Later we visited the factory that made olive oil soaps and stacked them in giant pyramids to dry.

"No, thank you," I said. "It's ridiculous to say that girls should only talk to girls. Did I say anything bad to a boy? Did anyone say anything bad to me? They're my friends. They're like my brothers. I won't do it, that's all."

The counselor conferred with the headmaster and they called a taxi. I was sent home with a note requesting that I transfer to a different school. The charge: insolence. My mother, startled to see me home early and on my own, stared out the window when I told her.

My brother came home from his school as usual, full of whistling and notebooks. "Did anyone tell you not to talk to girls?" I asked him. He looked at me as if I'd gone goofy. He was too young to know the troubles of the world. He couldn't even imagine them.

"You know what I've been thinking about?" he said. "A piece of cake. That puffy white layered cake with icing like they have at birthday parties in the United States. Wouldn't that taste good right now?" Our mother said she was thinking about mayonnaise. You couldn't get it in Jerusalem. She'd tried to make it and it didn't work. I felt too gloomy to talk about food.

My brother said, "Let's go let Abu Miriam's chickens out." That's what we always did when we felt sad. We let our fussy landlord's red and white chickens loose to flap around the yard happily, puffing their wings. Even when Abu Miriam shouted and waggled his cane and his wife waved a dishtowel, we knew the chickens were thanking us.

My father went with me to St. Tarkmanchatz Armenian School, a solemnly ancient stone school tucked deep into the Armenian Quarter of the Old City of Jerusalem. It was another world in there. He had already called them on the telephone and tried to enroll me, though they didn't want to. Their school was for Armenian students only, kindergarten through twelfth grade. Classes were taught in three languages, Armenian, Arabic and English, which was why I needed to go there. Although most Arab students at other schools were learning English, I needed a school where classes were actually taught in English—otherwise I would have been staring out the windows triple the usual amount.

The head priest wore a long robe and a tall cone-shaped hat. He said, "Excuse me, please, but your daughter, she is not an Armenian, even a small amount?"

"Not at all," said my father. "But in case you didn't know, there is a stipulation in the educational code books of this city that says no student may be rejected solely on the basis of ethnic background, and if you don't accept, we will alert the proper authorities."

They took me. But the principal wasn't happy about it. The students, however, seemed glad to have a new face to look at. Everyone's name ended in –*ian*, the beautiful, musical Armenian ending—Boghossian, Minassian, Kevorkian, Rostomian. My new classmates started calling me Shihabian. We wore uniforms, navy blue pleated skirts for the girls, white shirts, and navy sweaters. I waited during the lessons for the English to come around, as if it were a channel on television. While my friends were on the other channels, I scribbled poems in the margins of my pages, read library books, and wrote a lot of letters filled with exclamation points. All the other students knew three languages with three entirely different alphabets. How could they carry so much in their heads? I felt humbled by my ignorance. Again and again and again. One day I felt so frustrated in our physics class—still another language—that I pitched my book out the open window. The professor made me go collect it. All the pages had let loose at the seams and were flapping into gutters along with the white wrappers of sandwiches.

Every week the girls had a hands-and-fingernails check. We had to keep our nails clean and trim, and couldn't wear any rings. Some of my new friends would invite me home for lunch with them, since we had an hour-and-a-half break and I lived too far to go to my own house.

Their houses were a thousand years old, clustered beehive fashion behind ancient walls, stacked and curled and tilting and dark, filled with pictures of unsmiling relatives and small white cloths dangling crocheted edges. We ate spinach pies and white cheese. We dipped our bread in olive oil, as the Arabs did. We ate small sesame cakes, our mouths full of crumbles. They taught me to say, "I love you" in Armenian, which sounded like *yes-kay-see-goo-see-rem*. I felt I had left my old life entirely.

Every afternoon I went down to the basement of the school where the kindergarten class was having an Arabic lesson. Their desks were pint-sized, their full white smocks tied around their necks. I stuffed my fourteen-year-old self in beside them. They had rosy cheeks and shy smiles. They must have thought I was a very slow learner.

More than any of the lessons, I remember the way the teacher rapped the backs of their hands with his ruler when they made a mistake. Their little faces puffed up with quiet tears. This pained me so terribly I forgot all my words. When it was my turn to go to the blackboard and write in Arabic, my hand shook. The kindergarten students whispered hints to me from the front row, but I couldn't understand them. We learned horribly useless phrases: "Please hand me the bellows for my fire." I wanted words simple as tools, simple as *food* and *yesterday* and *dreams*. The teacher never rapped my hand, especially after I wrote a letter to the city newspaper, which my father edited, protesting such harsh treatment of young learners. I wished I had known how to talk to those little ones, but they were just beginning their English studies and didn't speak much yet. They were at the same place in their English that I was in my Arabic.

From the high windows of St. Tarkmanchatz, we could look out over the Old City, the roofs and flapping laundry and television antennas, the pilgrims and churches and mosques, the olive wood prayer beads and fragrant *falafel* lunch stands, the intricate interweaving of cultures and prayers and songs and holidays. We saw the barbed wire separating Jordan from Israel then, the bleak, uninhabited strip of no-man's land reminding me how little education saved us after all. People who had differing ideas still came to blows, imagining fighting could solve things. Staring out over the quiet roofs of afternoon, it seemed so foolish to me. I asked my friends what they thought about it and they shrugged.

"It doesn't matter what we think about it. It just keeps happening. It happened in Armenia too, you know. Really, really bad in Armenia. And who talks about it in the world news now? It happens everywhere. It happens in *your* country one by one, yes? Murders and guns. What can we do?"

Sometimes after school, my brother and I walked up the road that led past the crowded refugee camp of Palestinians who owned even less than our modest relatives did in the village. The kids were stacking stones in empty tin cans and shaking them. We waved our hands and they covered their mouths and laughed. We wore our beat-up American tennis shoes and our old sweatshirts and talked about everything we wanted to do and everywhere else we wished we could go.

"I want to go back to Egypt," my brother said. "I sort of feel like I missed it. Spending all that time in bed instead of exploring—what a waste."

"I want to go to Greece," I said. "I want to play a violin in a symphony orchestra in Austria." We made up things. I wanted to go back to the United States most of all. Suddenly I felt like a patriotic citizen. One of my friends, Sylvie Markarian, had just been shipped off to Damascus, Syria, to marry a man who was fifty years old, a widower. Sylvie was exactly my age—we had turned fifteen two days apart. She had never met her future husband before. "Tell your parents no thank you," I urged her. I thought this was the most revolting thing I had ever heard of. "Tell them you *refuse.*"

Sylvie's eyes were liquid, swirling brown. I could not see clear to the bottom of them.

"You don't understand," she told me. "In United States you say no. We don't say no. We have to follow someone's wishes. This is the wish of my father. Me, I am scared. I never slept away from my mother before. But I have no choice. I am going because they tell me to go." She was sobbing, sobbing on my shoulder. And I was stroking her long, soft hair. After that, I carried two fists inside, one for Sylvie and one for me.

Most weekends my family went to the village to sit with the relatives. We sat and sat and sat. We sat in big rooms and little rooms, in circles, on chairs or on woven mats or brightly-covered mattresses piled on the floor. People came in and out to greet my family. Sometimes even donkeys and chickens came in and out. We were like movie stars or dignitaries. They never seemed to get tired of us.

My father translated the more interesting tidbits of conversation, the funny stories my grandmother told. She talked about angels and food and money and people and politics and gossip and old memories from my father's childhood, before he emigrated away from her. She wanted to make sure we were going to stick around forever, which made me feel very nervous. We ate from mountains of rice and eggplant on silver trays—they gave us plates of our own since it was not our custom to eat from the same plate as other people. We ripped the giant wheels of bread into triangles. Shepherds passed through town with their flocks of sheep and goats, their long canes and cloaks, straight out of the Bible. My brother and I trailed them to the edge of the village, past the lentil fields and to the green meadows studded with stones, while the shepherds pretended we weren't there. I think they liked to be alone, unnoticed. The sheep had differently colored dyed bottoms, so shepherds could tell their flocks apart.

During these long, slow, smoke-stained weekends—the men still smoked cigarettes a lot in those days, and the old *taboon*, my family's mounded bread-oven, puffed billowy clouds outside the door—my crying jags began. I cried without any warning, even in the middle of a meal. My crying was usually noiseless but dramatically wet—streams of tears pouring down my cheeks, onto my collar or the back of my hand.

Everything grew quiet.

Someone always asked in Arabic, "What is wrong? Are you sick? Do you wish to lie down?"

My father made valiant excuses in the beginning. "She's overtired," he said. "She has a headache. She is missing her friend who moved to Syria. She is feeling homesick."

My brother stared at me as if I had just landed from Planet X.

Worst was our drive to school every morning, when our car came over the rise in the highway and all Jerusalem lay sprawled before us in its golden, stony splendor pockmarked with olive trees and automobiles. Even the air above the city had a thick, religious texture, as if it were a shining brocade filled with broody incense. I cried hardest then. All those hours tied up in school lay just ahead. My father pulled over and talked to me. He sighed. He kept his hands on the steering wheel even when the car was stopped and said, "Someday, I promise you, you will look back on this period in your life and have no idea what made you so unhappy here."

"I want to go home." It became my anthem. "This place depresses me. It weighs too much. I hate all these old stones that everybody keeps kissing. I'm sick of pilgrims. They act so pious and pure. And I hate the way people stare at me here." Already I'd been involved in two street skirmishes with boys who stared too hard and long, clucking with their tongues. I'd socked one in the jaw and he socked me back. I hit the other one straight in the face with my purse.

"You could be happy here if you tried harder," my father said. "Don't compare it to the United States all the time. Don't pretend the United States is perfect. And look at your brother—he's not having any problems!"

"My brother is eleven years old."

I had crossed the boundary from uncomplicated childhood where happiness was a good ball and a horde of candy-coated Jordan almonds.

One problem was that I had fallen in love with four different boys who all played in the same band. Two of them were even twins. I never quite described it to my parents, but I wrote reams and reams of notes about it on loose-leaf paper that I kept under my sweaters in my closet.

Such new energy made me feel reckless. I gave things away. I gave away my necklace and a whole box of shortbread cookies that my mother had been saving. I gave my extra shoes away to the gypsies. One night when the gypsies camped in a field down the road from our house, I thought about their mounds of white goat cheese lined up on skins in front of their tents, and the wild *oud* music they played deep into the black belly of the night, and I wanted to go sit around their fire. Maybe they could use some shoes.

I packed a sack of old loafers that I rarely wore and walked with my family down the road. The gypsy mothers stared into my shoes curiously. They took them into their tents. Maybe they would use them as vases or drawers. We sat with small glasses of hot, sweet tea until a girl bellowed from deep in her throat, threw back her head, and began dancing. A long bow thrummed across the strings. The girl circled the fire, tapping and clicking, trilling a long musical wail from deep in her throat. My brother looked nervous. He was remembering the belly dancer in Egypt, and her scarf. I felt invisible. I was pretending to be a gypsy. My father stared at me. Didn't I recognize the exquisite oddity of my own life when I sat right in the middle of it? Didn't I feel lucky to be here? Well, yes I did. But sometimes it was hard to be lucky.

When we left Jerusalem, we left quickly. Left our beds in our rooms and our car in the driveway. Left in a plane, not sure where we were going. The rumbles of fighting with Israel had been growing louder and louder. In the barbed-wire no-man's land visible from the windows of our house, guns cracked loudly in the middle of the night. We lived right near the edge. My father heard disturbing rumors at the newspaper that would soon grow into the infamous Six-Day War of 1967. We were in England by then, drinking tea from thin china cups and scanning the newspapers. Bombs were blowing up Jerusalem. We worried about the village. We worried about my grandmother's dreams, which had been getting worse and worse, she'd told us. We worried about the house we'd left, and the chickens, and the children at the refugee camp. But there was nothing we could do except keep talking about it all.

My parents didn't want to go back to Missouri because they'd already said good-bye to everyone there. They thought we might try a different part of the country. They weighed the virtues of various states. Texas was big and warm. After a chilly year crowded around the small gas heaters we used in Jerusalem, a warm place sounded appealing. In roomy Texas, my parents bought the first house they looked at. My father walked into the city newspaper and said, "Any jobs open around here?"

I burst out crying when I entered a grocery store—so many different kinds of bread.

A letter on thin blue airmail paper reached me months later, written by my classmate, the bass player in my favorite Jerusalem band. "Since you left," he said, "your empty desk reminds me of a snake ready to strike. I am afraid to look at it. I hope you are having a better time than we are."

Of course I was, and I wasn't. *Home* had grown different forever. *Home* had doubled. Back *home* again in my own country, it seemed impossible to forget the place we had just left: the piercing call of the *muezzin* from the mosque at prayer time, the dusky green tint of the olive groves, the sharp, cold air that smelled as deep and old as my grandmother's white sheets flapping from the line on her roof. What story hadn't she finished?

Our father used to tell us that when he was little, the sky over Jerusalem crackled with meteors and shooting stars almost every night. They streaked and flashed, igniting the dark. Some had long golden tails. For a few seconds, you could see their whole swooping trails lit up. Our father and his brothers slept on the roof to watch the sky. "There were so many of them, we didn't even call out every time we saw one."

During our year in Jerusalem, my brother and I kept our eyes cast upwards whenever we were outside at night, but the stars were different since our father was a boy. Now the sky seemed too orderly, stuck in place. The stars had learned where they belonged. Only the people on the ground kept changing.

Against Nature

Joyce Carol Oates

> *We soon get through with Nature. She excites an expectation which she cannot satisfy.*
> —Thoreau, *Journal*, 1854

> *Sir, if a man has experienced the inexpressible, he is under no obligation to attempt to express it.*
> —Samuel Johnson

The writer's resistance to Nature.

It has no sense of humor: in its beauty, as in its ugliness, or its neutrality, there is no laughter.

It lacks a moral purpose.

It lacks a satiric dimension, registers no irony.

Its pleasures lack resonance, being accidental; its horrors, even when premeditated, are equally perfunctory, "red in tooth and claw" et cetera.

It lacks a symbolic subtext—excepting that provided by man.

It has no (verbal) language.

It has no interest in ours.

It inspires a painfully limited set of responses in "nature-writers" —REVERENCE, AWE, PIETY, MYSTICAL ONENESS.

It eludes us even as it prepares to swallow us up, books and all.

I was lying on my back in the dirt-gravel of the towpath beside the Delaware-Raritan Canal, Titusville, New Jersey, staring up at the sky and trying, with no success, to overcome a sudden attack of tachycardia that had come upon me out of nowhere—such attacks are always "out of nowhere," that's their charm—and all around me Nature thrummed with life, the air smelling of moisture and sunlight, the canal reflecting the sky, red-winged blackbirds testing their spring calls—the usual. I'd become the jar in Tennessee, a fictitious center, or parenthesis, aware beyond my erratic heartbeat of the numberless heartbeats of the earth, its pulsing pumping life, sheer life, incalculable. Struck down in the midst of motion—I'd been jogging a minute before—I was "out of time" like a fallen, stunned boxer, privileged (in an abstract manner of speaking) to be an involuntary witness to the random, wayward, nameless motion on all sides of me.

Paroxysmal tachycardia is rarely fatal, but if the heartbeat accelerates to 250-270 beats a minute you're in trouble. The average attack is about 100-

150 beats and mine seemed so far to be about average; the trick now was to prevent it from getting worse. Brainy people try brainy strategies, such as thinking calming thoughts, pseudo-mystic thoughts, *If I die now it's a good death*, that sort of thing, *if I die this is a good place and a good time*, the idea is to deceive the frenzied heartbeat that, really, you don't care: you hadn't any other plans for the afternoon. The important thing with tachycardia is to prevent panic! you must prevent panic! otherwise you'll have to be taken by ambulance to the closest emergency room, which is not so very nice a way to spend the afternoon, really. So I contemplated the blue sky overhead. The earth beneath my head. Nature surrounding me on all sides, I couldn't quite see it but I could hear it, smell it, sense it—there is something *there*, no mistake about it. Completely oblivious to the predicament of the individual but that's only "natural" after all, one hardly expects otherwise.

When you discover yourself lying on the ground, limp and unresisting, head in the dirt, and helpless, the earth seems to shift forward as a presence; hard, emphatic, not mere surface but a genuine force—there is no other word for it but *presence*. To keep in motion is to keep in time and to be stopped, stilled, is to be abruptly out of time, in another time-dimension perhaps, an alien one, where human language has no resonance. Nothing to be said about it expresses it, nothing touches it, it's an absolute against which nothing human can be measured. ...Moving through space and time by way of your own volition you inhabit an interior consciousness, a hallucinatory consciousness, it might be said, so long as breath, heartbeat, the body's autonomy hold; when motion is stopped you are jarred out of it. The interior is invaded by the exterior. The outside wants to come in, and only the self's fragile membrane prevents it.

The fly buzzing at Emily's death.

Still, the earth *is* your place. A tidy grave-site measured to your size. Or, from another angle of vision, one vast democratic grave.

Let's contemplate the sky. Forget the crazy hammering heartbeat, don't listen to it, don't start counting, remember that there is a clever way of breathing that conserves oxygen as if you're lying below the surface of a body of water breathing through a very thin straw but you can breathe through it if you're careful, if you don't panic, one breath and then another and then another, isn't that the story of all lives? careers? Just a matter of breathing. Of course it is. But contemplate the sky, it's there to be contemplated. A mild shock to see it so blank, blue, a thin airy ghostly blue, no clouds to disguise its emptiness. You are beginning to feel not only weightless but near-bodiless, lying on the earth like a scrap of paper about to be blown off. Two dimensions and you'd imagined you were three! And there's the sky rolling away forever, into infinity—if "infinity" can be "rolled into"—and the forlorn truth is, that's where you're going too. And the lovely blue isn't even blue, is it? isn't even there, is it? a mere optical illusion, isn't it? no matter what art has urged you to believe.

Early Nature memories. Which it's best not to suppress.

... Wading, as a small child, in Tonawanda Creek near our house, and afterward trying to tear off, in a frenzy of terror and revulsion, the sticky fat black bloodsuckers that had attached themselves to my feet, particularly between my toes.

... Coming upon a friend's dog in a drainage ditch, dead for several days, evidently the poor creature had been shot by a hunter and left to die, bleeding to death, and we're stupefied with grief and horror but can't resist sliding down to where he's lying on his belly, and we can't resist squatting over him, turning the body over...

... The raccoon, mad with rabies, frothing at the mouth and tearing at his own belly with his teeth, so that his intestines spilled out onto the ground ... a sight I seem to remember though in fact I did not see. I've been told I did not see.

Consequently, my chronic uneasiness with Nature-mysticism; Nature-adoration; Nature-as-(moral)-instruction-for-mankind. My doubt that one can, with philosophical validity, address "Nature" as a single coherent noun, anything other than a Platonic, hence discredited, isness. My resistance to "Nature-writing" as a genre, except when it is brilliantly fictionalized in the service of a writer's individual vision—Thoreau's books and *Journal*, of course—but also, less known in this country, the miniaturist prose-poems of Colette (*Flowers and Fruit*) and Ponge (*Taking the Side of Things*)—in which case it becomes yet another, and ingenious, form of storytelling. The subject is there only by the grace of the author's language.

Nature has no instructions for mankind except that our poor beleaguered humanist-democratic way of life, our fantasies of the individual's high worth, our sense that the weak, no less than the strong, have a right to survive, are absurd.

In any case, where *is* Nature? one might (skeptically) inquire. Who has looked upon her/its face and survived?

But isn't this all exaggeration, in the spirit of rhetorical contentiousness? Surely Nature is, for you, as for most reasonably intelligent people, a "perennial" source of beauty, comfort, peace, escape from the delirium of civilized life; a respite from the ego's ever-frantic strategies of self-promotion, as a way of insuring (at least in fantasy) some small measure of immortality? Surely Nature, as it is understood in the usual slapdash way, as human, if not dilettante, *experience* (hiking in a national park, jogging on the beach at dawn, even tending, with the usual comical frustrations, a suburban garden), is wonderfully consoling; a place where, when you go there, it has to take you in?—a palimpsest of sorts you choose to read, layer by layer, always with care, always cautiously, in proportion to your psychological strength?

Nature: as in Thoreau's upbeat Transcendentalist mode ("The indescribable innocence and beneficence of Nature,—such health, such cheer, they afford forever! and such sympathy have they ever with our race, that all Nature would be affected . . . if any man should ever for a just cause grieve"), and not in Thoreau's grim mode ("Nature is hard to be overcome but she must be overcome").

Another way of saying, not *Nature-in-itself* but *Nature-as-experience.*

The former, Nature-in-itself, is, to allude slantwise to Melville, a blankness ten times blank; the latter is what we commonly, or perhaps always, mean when we speak of Nature as a noun, a single entity—something of *ours.* Most of the time it's just an activity, a sort of hobby, a weekend, a few days, perhaps a few hours, staring out the window at the mind-dazzling autumn foliage of, say, Northern Michigan, being rendered speechless—temporarily—at the sight of Mt. Shasta, the Grand Canyon, Ansel Adams's West. Or Nature writ small, contained in the back yard. Nature filtered through our optical nerves, our "senses," our fiercely romantic expectations. Nature that pleases us because it mirrors our souls, or gives the comforting illusion of doing so. As in our first mother's awakening to the self's fatal beauty—

> I thither went
> With unexperienc't thought, and laid me down
> On the green bank, to look into the clear
> Smooth Lake, that to me seem'd another Sky.
> As I bent down to look, just opposite,
> A Shape within the watr'y gleam appear'd
> Bending to look on me, I started back,
> It started back, but pleas'd I soon return'd,
> Pleas'd it return'd as soon with answering looks
> Of sympathy and love; there I had fixt
> Mine eyes till now, and pin'd with vain desire.

—in these surpassingly beautiful lines from Book IV of Milton's *Paradise Lost.*

Nature as the self's (flattering) mirror, but not ever, no, never, Nature-in-itself.

Nature is mouths, or maybe a single mouth. Why glamorize it, romanticize it, well yes but we must, we're writers, poets, mystics (of a sort) aren't we, precisely what else are we to do but glamorize and romanticize and generally exaggerate the significance of anything we focus the white heat of our "creativity" upon...? And why not Nature, since it's there, common property, mute, can't talk back, allows us the possibility of transcending the human condition for a while, writing prettily of mountain ranges, white-tailed deer, the purple crocuses outside this very window, the thrumming dazzling "life-force" we imagine we all support. Why not.

Nature *is* more than a mouth—it's a dazzling variety of mouths. And it pleases the senses, in any case, as the physicists' chill universe of numbers certainly does not.

Oscar Wilde, on our subject: "Nature is no great mother who has borne us. She is our creation. It is in our brain that she quickens to life. Things are because we see them, and what we see, and how we see it, depends on the Arts that have influenced us. To look at a thing is very different from seeing a thing.... At present, people see fogs, not because there are fogs, but because poets and painters have taught them the mysterious loveliness of such effects. There may have been fogs for centuries in London. I dare say there were. But no one saw them. They did not exist until Art had invented them.... Yesterday evening Mrs. Arundel insisted on my going to the window and looking at the glorious sky, as she called it. And so I had to look at it.... And what was it? It was simply a very second-rate Turner, a Turner of a bad period, with all the painter's worst faults exaggerated and over-emphasized."

(If we were to put it to Oscar Wilde that he exaggerates, his reply might well be: "Exaggeration? I don't know the meaning of the word.")

Walden, that most artfully composed of prose fictions, concludes, in the rhapsodic chapter "Spring," with Henry David Thoreau's contemplation of death, decay, and regeneration as it is suggested to him, or to his protagonist, by the spectacle of vultures feeding off carrion. There is a dead horse close by his cabin and the stench of its decomposition, in certain winds, is daunting. Yet: ". . . the assurance it gave me of the strong appetite and inviolable health of Nature was my compensation. I love to see that Nature is so rife with life that myriads can be afforded to be sacrificed and suffered to prey upon one another; that tender organizations can be so serenely squashed out of existence like pulp,—tadpoles which herons gobble up, and tortoises and toads run over in the road; and that sometimes it has rained flesh and blood! ...The impression made on a wise man is that of universal innocence."

Come off it, Henry David. You've grieved these many years for your elder brother John, who died a ghastly death of lockjaw; you've never wholly recovered from the experience of watching him die. And you know, or must know, that you're fated too to die young of consumption. . . . But this doctrinaire Transcendentalist passage ends *Walden* on just the right note. It's as impersonal, as coolly detached, as the Oversoul itself: a "wise man" filters his emotions through his brain.

Or through his prose.

Nietzsche: "We all pretend to ourselves that we are more simpleminded than we are; that is how we get a rest from our fellow men."

> Once out of nature I shall never take
> My bodily form from any natural thing,
> But such a form as Grecian goldsmiths make
> Of hammered gold and gold enamelling
> To keep a drowsy Emperor awake;
> Or set upon a golden bough to sing
> To lords and ladies of Byzantium
> Of what is past, or passing, or to come.
> —*William Butler Yeats*, "Sailing to Byzantium"

Yet even the golden bird is a "bodily form taken from (a) natural thing." No, it's impossible to escape!

The writer's resistance to Nature.
Wallace Stevens: "In the presence of extraordinary actuality, consciousness takes the place of imagination."

Once, years ago, in 1972 to be precise, when I seemed to have been another person, related to the person I am now as one is related, tangentially, sometimes embarrassingly, to cousins not seen for decades,—once, when we were living in London, and I was very sick, I had a mystical vision. That is, I "had" a "mystical vision"—the heart sinks: such pretension—or something resembling one. A fever-dream, let's call it. It impressed me enormously and impresses me still, though I've long since lost the capacity to see it with my mind's eye, or even, I suppose, to believe in it. There is a statute of limitations on "mystical visions" as on romantic love.

I was very sick, and I imagined my life as a thread, a thread of breath, or heartbeat, or pulse, or light, yes it was light, radiant light, I was burning with fever and I ascended to that plane of serenity that might be mistaken for (or *is*, in fact) Nirvana, where I had a waking dream of uncanny lucidity—

My body is a tall column of light and heat.

My body is not "I" but "it."

My body is not one but many.

My body, which "I" inhabit, is inhabited as well by other creatures, unknown to me, imperceptible—the smallest of them mere sparks of light.

My body, which I perceive as substance, is in fact an organization of infinitely complex, overlapping, imbricated structures, radiant light their manifestation, the "body" a tall column of light and blood-heat, a temporary agreement among atoms, like a high-rise building with numberless rooms, corridors, corners, elevator shafts, windows. . . . In this fantastical structure the "I" is deluded as to its sovereignty, let alone its autonomy in the (outside) world; the most astonishing secret is that the "I" doesn't exist!—but it behaves as if it does, as if it were one and not many.

In any case, without the "I" the tall column of light and heat would die, and the microscopic life-particles would die with it . . . will die with it. The "I," which doesn't exist, is everything.

But Dr. Johnson is right, the inexpressible need not be expressed.

And what resistance, finally? There is none.

This morning, an invasion of tiny black ants. One by one they appear, out of nowhere—that's their charm too!—moving single file across the white Parsons table where I am sitting, trying without much success to write a poem. A poem of only three or four lines is what I want, something short, tight, mean, I want it to hurt like a white-hot wire up the nostrils, small and compact and turned in upon itself with the density of a hunk of rock from the planet Jupiter. . . .

But here come the black ants; harbingers, you might say, of spring. One by one by one they appear on the dazzling white table and one by one I kill them with a forefinger, my deft right forefinger, mashing each against the surface of the table and then dropping it into a wastebasket at my side. Idle labor, mesmerizing, effortless, and I'm curious as to how long I can do it, sit here in the brilliant March sunshine killing ants with my right forefinger, how long I, and the ants, can keep it up.

After a while I realize that I can do it a long time. And that I've written my poem.

Normal Lives: Israel, Spring 2003

Alicia Ostriker

What is it like to visit Israel in a time of crisis? It is always a time of crisis in Israel. We are in the middle of the "Second Intifada," the Palestinian uprising that began in September 2000 after the failure of the Oslo accords, after the assassination of Prime Minister Begin, after the withdrawal of Israel from Lebanon, after the failed talks at Camp David, after hard-liner Ariel Sharon visited the Temple Mount—the third-holiest site in Islam—accompanied by hundreds of Israeli riot police, to emphasize Israeli sovereignty over the area. After, after. . . .

But I am at Bar Ilan University in a suburb of Tel Aviv for a conference on "Creative Writing in a Jewish Context." We are celebrating the first anniversary of the first Creative Writing Program in Israel, and it is a smashing success. All the sessions were crowded, the question periods lively. The guards at every entrance at first disconcerted the Americans among us, but soon became routine. We dressed up for our poetry reading in the elegant former home of the great poet Chaim Bialik, where the American consulate provided us with wine and strawberries under the hot night sky. After the conference I stay with poetry friends in Tel Aviv and Jerusalem. We eat and drink, we look at each other's poems. So it is a lot like home, my Jewish counterparts are living normal lives, or almost normal ones. A suicide bombing occurs in one neighborhood, and the shops shift to another. Everyone knows people who have been killed in bombings. No longer do these men and women shop at the supermarket. They do not show up at work. One doesn't see them any more at parties. An old friend cannot get over mourning her son. Neighbors get sick. Israelis live in small worlds, those worlds are made of wide sticky webs, and the webs are full of holes.

I have dinner with the novelist and playwright Michal Govrin and her two daughters on a quiet street in Jerusalem. Uphill a bit is a small overgrown park with a tomb from the time of the Maccabees. Salad, hummus, two kinds of quiche, on their back balcony, trees waving below. It is the close of the Sabbath, so Michal and her daughters say the havdalah prayers, and the sky darkens above us. Michal's older daughter describes her friend. Not that much of a friend, really more an acquaintance who lived in the same dorm at Hebrew University. Michal's daughter is doing her alternative service teaching retarded children in a day-care. She avoided the army by saying she was religious. She called last summer to confirm a date to meet this girl in Haifa, and learned the girl was paralyzed from the chest down after being wounded by the bomb at the Hebrew University cafeteria. The papers print the names only of the dead, not the wounded. Michal's daughter thought it her duty to visit this girl, in her special university room with round-the-clock care, diapers and so on, though visiting her was depressing. The girl was cynical about life before the incident, so imagine how she feels now. As Michal's daughter tells this story, I find myself responding silently, as probably many hearers of this and other such stories do. I would want to die if that happened to me, I think.

After we leave Michal's daughter at the university, we take a long nocturnal drive through Arab sections of the city, and keep circling. At the Haas Promenade, which is the Jerusalem equivalent of the Piazzale Michelangelo in Florence, we stop to look out over the view, in a high wind that sends us quickly back to the car. Michal teaches theatre directing, and describes her relationship over the years with an Arab student who has become a director. Open, closed, open, as Amichai says. No, not open but partway open, after Michal wrote an essay describing its closure. The rejection by her ex-student who would not introduce her to colleagues at a conference. We talk about her recent essay that describes the tragic dimensions of the conflict, and the long history behind the idea of sacrifice and martyrdom. For the Palestinians, to be a suicide bomber is to be a martyr. Young men make videos of themselves saying farewell to their families and friends the day before they will have explosives strapped to their bodies and head for a Jewish shopping district or a bus station. Afterward, they will be celebrated. Posters of their dead faces will adorn walls, schools, restaurants. What is it, I wonder, that makes people eager to be martyrs? I propose that the other face of martyrdom is triumphalism; the belief that your side is pure and righteous and will ultimately conquer everything. Don't the Jewish Israelis likewise feel pure and righteous? Michal thinks maybe so. And don't Americans feel the same way? Isn't this what got us into Iraq? Isn't it what lets us use phrases like "the evil empire?"

Everybody I meet is warm, alive, friendly to me, with the exception of some grumpy taxi drivers. I spend a morning reading Linda Zisquit's new poems and talking about her mother's death and my mother's death. Both of us struggled with our mothers, now we struggle over missing them. The show in Linda's art gallery right now is by a woman who has done portraits of a range of ordinary people in a style that is at first glance flat, but grows on me, deeper than I thought. Arab women in their headscarves, hands folded in their laps, middle-aged faces without makeup gazing out of the picture frame. These women are mothers, though they look so different from my mother, Linda's mother.

I do not go anyplace dangerous, though Linda, her husband Donald, and I walk up through parts of the Old City for a dinner with one of the organizers of the conference, as Jews stream down stone lanes going home from services.

The dinner is on the top floor of a house that long ago belonged to an Arab family. From its balcony you can see the beautiful gold Dome of the Rock, an image familiar all over the world because it adorns so many travel posters of Israel. Is it ironic that the Dome is a Muslim shrine? Nobody appears to think so. Nobody, though everyone here is decent and kind, seems disturbed about having appropriated an Arab's home. Of course, it was all so long ago.

Next day Donald and his 16-year-old son are watching TV. A soccer team from Nazareth has just won a crucial game and vaulted from the bottom to the top of its league. The players have ripped their shirts off and are dancing with joy, hugging, kissing, circle dancing, belly-dancing, waving to the crowd in the stands to cheer. The coach (who is Druze) has ripped his own shirt from his hairy barrel chest and climbs atop a fence, dancing there. A reporter asks him how he feels about his team, which is partly Jews, partly Arabs, one Nigerian. "I beat them all!" he roars. "I beat Sharon! I beat Arafat! I show them we love each other!" The joy goes on for a half hour before I stop watching. On Saturday night Linda and Donald host a pinyon ha-ben party, a redemption of the first-born son, for friends of theirs. Their house and garden overflow with a couple of hundred guests, largely the extended family of the Sephardi inlaws, and huge piles of food. I talk to a woman who has been teaching at Bar Ilan but before that was a literary agent for Joyce Carol Oates and is also a women's boxing champion. Her husband is black and extremely handsome; her baby is the color of honey.

My Israeli friends are writers and intellectuals, all basically part of the liberal left, more or less. They are part of the majority that wants peace, and would be happy to trade land for it, if they thought they could really get peace. Of course they know the whole idea is a gamble but they would do it. Is there any equivalent, among Palestinian writers and intellectuals, of the public denunciations of the Occupation? Polls claim a majority of Palestinians likewise wants a two-nation solution. Are there visible, audible Palestinians urging an end to dreams of vengeance and a beginning to normal life alongside Israel? Why not, why not? Or do they exist and cannot be heard?

Of course most Israeli Jews including my friends cannot see, either literally or metaphorically, the suffering of the Palestinians. This is understandable. They cannot see that the death rate of Palestinians during the intifada is three times that of Jews. I mean they can see it as a statistic but not feel it as a reality, or they feel it but have to suppress it or life would become intolerable. Americans ought to understand that. Most people have no wish to cause the suffering of others. And if they do cause it, they don't want to be conscious that they do. In the case of the Israeli occupation, not only death but humiliation is inflicted; the former is sporadic, the latter constant. Bulldozed houses, ancient olive groves razed. Movement radically inhibited so that one's home is prison. At every point of official interface, a burning pain as if a lit cigarette were jabbed in one's arm. Whose arm? Does the cigarette feel pain? Yes, but a different kind, and one that can scarcely be spoken of. Palestinian pain is right on the surface, though most Jews cannot see it. Still, the joke goes round, "It all started when he hit me back." The joke suggests that denial is only skin deep.

The woman who cleans Karen Alkalay-Gut's apartment was going crazy because the government was not issuing updated gasmasks to the Israeli Arab community before the War on Iraq. Karen made sure her cleaning woman got a proper gasmask. Karen is editing, with an Arab student, an anthology of Jewish and Palestinian poetry. Numerous small Israeli-Arab relationships and groups exist. Instances like these are candles in a tunnel, but the tunnel is still very dark. The reason you see everyone carrying a cell phone, Karen explains in her dark laughing voice that is a compound of the Yiddish she was born to, the English she grew up with, and the Hebrew she lives, is that you want to be able to contact your family immediately when there is an incident.

The more I grow aware of the details of Israeli fear, the more I wonder about the Palestinian fear and anguish that the bubble of my privilege protects me from knowing. Would I have to square Israeli pain to arrive at Palestinian pain? Cube it? Factor past into present? I am in the dark. I am in the darkness of ignorance.

The physical light on the other hand is magnificent. In Tel Aviv it bounces off the Mediterranean. Tel Aviv reminds me of the New York City I grew up in, in the forties and fifties. Plenty of garbage in the streets. Buildings of plain concrete as ubiquitous as the housing project brick and prosperous stone of New York. Rich and poor neighborhoods. Big billboards. Twin towers shaped like a triangle and a circle dominating the downtown landscape, their facades a grid, quite attractive. The promenade along the beach one of the best civic spaces I have ever seen, Israel's answer to Brighton Beach. Cats. Hundreds of thousands of cats roaming the streets. People feed them the way we feed pigeons, especially now when the public dumpsters have been made inaccessible to them. Karen says that with the dumpsters closed and the cats being fed by pitying people, the cats have gotten plumper and less aggressive. But they have been multiplying like wild, so the city is sending teams out with cages to catch them so they can be sterilized. One morning out walking Karen's dog we see one such team. A young man and woman. The young woman, carrying a plastic sack of cat food, looks shy and embarrassed.

Tel Aviv at night, a street of several bars and clubs, each with its tough guard out front. Karen's son owns a café and a bar and is about to open a more upscale bar next door—it's being remodeled and we walk through the plastered and papered rooms. Karen's son still looks like a rock musician, not a businessman, I am happy to say. He says business is a little slow right now because there haven't been any incidents lately so people are not so feverishly bent on making merry as after an incident, when they are all worrying about dying tomorrow, but he is as cheerful as if he had Ecclesiastes whispering to him, "Rejoice, O young man, in thy youth."

The light in Jerusalem is high and very bright, made brighter by reflecting white stone, though everywhere made slightly hazy by sand. It is a unique light, Michal says.

Jerusalem is so beautiful it hurts the bones. It breaks the heart. But the eye is gratified. You go up to Jerusalem from Tel Aviv. It takes a bit less than an hour. The car speeds and winds. Sand and stone and desert vegetation gradually yield to developments. Peculiar word, "development." It implies a natural process, and in a sense the planning and building of these roads and massive housing tracts, their faces flat and pale, is completely natural. "There is no art but nature makes that art," says Perdita in Shakespeare's "The Winter's Tale," the lost girl on her way to being found and becoming a princess. For better and worse, the will to build is hard-wired in our species. You drive over crests until finally you see the Old City, dominated by two structures, David's Citadel in rosy white stone and the Dome of the Rock in gold. Looking at these shapes you are looking at thousands of years crystallized into a moment. The back of the mind reads this text. Reads it instantly. We know so much more than we know. Like a frame around a picture, a high thick wall surrounds the Old City. Or the wall is a door to another world. Or it is attempting to hide and protect the city within. But for ages the city has been sculpting itself outside those walls, spreading over ridge after ridge. Jerusalem stone, rosy and shining. The only stone, Amichai says in a poem, that knows how to weep. Leaving some tracts weedy, sandy, wild and waste. They too are part of the beauty of the city. As are its cascades of flowers.

Jerusalem is a woman, a bride, a desired one. Poem after poem uses this metaphor. Then there is Babylon her enemy, on whom revenge must be taken, her children's heads dashed against the wall in punishment for what she did to us, as it says in the 137th Psalm. Sidra's talk at the conference claimed that the metaphor has been taken all too literally: Jerusalem is a virgin, a bleeding wife, or a whore, or an aguna, a deserted wife, in any case waiting for a redeemer to avenge her sullied honor. Sidra quotes Judah Halevi, the 12th century poet of romantic love of the ruined Jerusalem, her hills and her mountain clefts which he longs to caress: "Jerusalem, won't you ask after your captives," he writes from Andalusia . . . "I'd soar on eagle wings if only to mix my tears with your dust. I will kiss and cherish your stones, your earth sweeter to my lips than honey." Halevi died before reaching Palestine, according to legend. Or perhaps just afterward. The desire for ecstatic union with Eretz Israel, the land of Israel, is it a desire for death? Must it always be vengeful and toxic? Must it always crave possession? Another option has been available all along, Sidra says, from the Song of Songs, where a woman is a city (not the reverse), and there is intimacy but no possession, on down to another Yehudah. Yehudah Amichai, who writes not of exalted love *of* the city, but normal love *in* the city. Ordinary human love, which is comic, not tragic. "Turn over now . . . See the bold supports / of the loins, columns of legs / and hellenistic curlicues / of hair above the genitals. The gothic arch that rises / toward the heart . . . If she stoops, she'll be perfect arabesque . . . "

A little before I left, I had a brief discussion with Donald. He is a family lawyer, charming, endearing, easygoing, with a great smile, and religious. He loves to look things up in Talmud. This gives him an intensity he would not otherwise have. He gives off a sort of blue-white aura. The daughter of a friend of theirs is marrying a German, a goy, a non-Jew. I mention the marriage of my Hasidic brother-in-law in Toronto to a Russian émigré woman, and the wedding of my nephew to a Muslim girl he met at work in New York. Because this girl's father was from a very good family, he said if his daughter married my nephew, he would kill himself. So my nephew converted to Islam, the wedding was in Casablanca and lasted two days, and the marriage has turned him from a kid into a mensch. My brother-in-law, who was always a mensch, is now, in addition, happy. The women are rather alike, a blonde one and a dark one, both large, warm, maternal, straightforward, both exiles. To me, the marriages are mirror images of each other, and I delight in both. Donald, smiling, points out that as a Jew he disapproves of mixed marriages. I, in an equally friendly way, say that of course I approve of them, I like to see things mixing, I'm not a friend of purity.

I wish I had said that *as a Jew* I approve of mixing. Some of my best friends are mixed! One of my sons-in-law is a convert to Judaism, one is a Celtic infidel, both my daughters are happy. Ever since we left Egypt with a mixed multitude, I approve of this. Ever since we were told to love the stranger. What is a stranger? Sometimes when people love each other, they marry and have children. Every so often a small stretch of the wall between ourselves and the others crumbles. I approve of mixing ever since Ruth married Boas. A Moabite and a man of Judah, the tribe founded, incidentally, on the children had by Tamar after she pretended to be a whore and seduced him: the forbidden wed to the forbidden, in the course of time producing King David. And David ultimately fathering the anticipated Messiah. The complete man and the complete superman are to be born from those forbidden loins. I approve of mixing ever since we Jews spread over the globe, carrying our strange beliefs and morals with us with what Blake calls a "firm conviction." Spreading them, as it were, around. Maybe this is what we were chosen for? The actual meaning of being a light to the nations?

A legend says that Abraham, our first patriarch, was sent to live in a far country because he was to teach the nations the truth of the One God. At home in Ur, he was like a jar of precious oil with a stopper in it.

I would like to ask a marriage counselor: What saves marriages? Our media is full of divorce, but it does not give us any information about mending. Relationships are all seen as throwaway, like tissues. The trouble is that you can't, short of genocide, throw away a whole people. Or, rather, you can—there are numerous examples of tribes dying of despair—but if a remnant survives, it is a pebble in the shoe or a thorn in the flesh. It would be better to take the wall down than to keep stabbing at each other through it. But nobody yet knows how.

In the *Trib* this morning, a quotation from David Grossman's new and despairing book, *Death as a Way of Life*: "Noise . . . gunshots and shouts, incendiary words and mournful laments, and explosions and demonstrations, and heaps of clichés and special broadcasts from the scenes of terrorist attacks, and calls for revenge . . . And within that whirlwind, in the eye of the storm, there is silence. It can't be heard; it is felt, in every cell of the body. A silence such as one feels in the brief moment between receiving bad news and comprehending it, between the blow and the pain. This is the empty place in which every person, Israeli or Palestinian, knows with piercing certainty all that he does not want to or does not dare to know."

I think this is close to my own vision of the meaning behind apparent meanings. There is also the joke. "It all started when he hit me back." Amichai's eroticism, Grossman's eloquence, and the joke: each is for me the voice of the true God within us.

The Idea of a Garden

Michael Pollan

The biggest news to come out of my town in many years was the tornado, or tornadoes, that careened through here on July 10, 1989, a Monday. Shooting down the Housatonic River Valley from the Berkshires, it veered east over Coltsfoot Mountain and then, after smudging the sky a weird gray green, proceeded to pinball madly from hillside to hillside for about fifteen minutes before wheeling back up into the sky. This was part of the same storm that ripped open the bark of my ash tree. But the damage was much, much worse on the other side of town. Like a gigantic, skidding pencil eraser, the twister neatly erased whole patches of woods and roughly smeared many other ones, where it wiped out just the tops of the trees. Overnight, large parts of town were rendered unrecognizable.

One place where the eraser came down squarely was in the Cathedral Pines, a famous forest of old-growth white pine trees close to the center of town. A kind of local shrine, this forty-two-acre forest was one of the oldest stands of white pine in New England, the trees untouched since about 1800. To see it was to have some idea how the New World forest must have looked to the first settlers, and in 1985 the federal government designated it a "national natural landmark." To enter Cathedral Pines on a hot summer day was like stepping out of the sun into a dim cathedral, the sunlight cooled and sweetened by the trillions of pine needles as it worked its way down to soft, sprung ground that had been unacquainted with blue sky for the better part of two centuries. The storm came through at about five in the evening, and it took only a few minutes of wind before pines more than one hundred fifty feet tall and as wide around as missiles lay jackstrawed on the ground like a fistful of pencils dropped from a great height. The wind was so thunderous that people in houses at the forest's edge did not know trees had fallen until they ventured outside after the storm had passed. The following morning, the sky now clear, was the first in more than a century to bring sunlight crashing down onto this particular patch of earth.

"It is a terrible mess," the first selectman told the newspapers; "a tragedy," said another Cornwall resident, voicing the deep sense of loss shared by many in town. But in the days that followed, the selectman and the rest of us learned that our responses, though understandable, were shortsighted, unscientific, and, worst of all, anthropocentric. "It may be a calamity to us," a state environmental official told a reporter from the *Hartford Courant*, but "to biology it is not a travesty. It is just a natural occurrence." The Nature Conservancy, which owns Cathedral Pines, issued a press release explaining that "Monday's storm was just another link in the continuous chain of events that is responsible for shaping and changing this forest."

It wasn't long before the rub of these two perspectives set off a controversy heated enough to find its way into the pages of *The New York Times*. The Nature Conservancy, in keeping with its mandate to maintain its lands in a "state of nature," indicated that it would leave Cathedral Pines alone, allowing the forest to take its "natural course," whatever that might be. To town officials and neighbors of the forest this was completely unacceptable. The downed trees, besides constituting an eyesore right at the edge of town, also posed a fire hazard. A few summers of drought, and the timber might go up in a blaze that would threaten several nearby homes and possibly even the town itself. Many people in Cornwall wanted Cathedral Pines cleared and replanted, so that at least the next generation might live to see some semblance of the old forest. A few others had the poor taste to point out the waste of more than a million board-feet of valuable timber, stupendous lengths of unblemished, knot-free pine.

The newspapers depicted it as a classic environmental battle, pitting the interests of man against nature, and in a way it was that. On one side were the environmental purists, who felt that *any* intervention by man in the disposition of this forest would be unnatural. "If you're going to clean it up," one purist declared in the local press, "you might as well put up condos." On the other side stood the putative interests of man, variously expressed in the vocabulary of safety (the fire hazard), economics (the wasted lumber), and aesthetics (the "terrible mess").

Everybody enjoys a good local fight, but I have to say I soon found the whole thing depressing. This was indeed a classic environmental battle, in that it seemed to exemplify just about everything that's wrong with the way we approach problems of this kind these days. Both sides began to caricature each other's positions: the selectman's "terrible mess" line earned him ridicule for his anthropocentrism in the letters page of *The New York Times*; he in turn charged a Yale scientist who argued for non-interference with "living in an ivory tower."

But as far apart as the two sides seemed to stand, they actually shared more common ground than they realized. Both started from the premise that man and nature were irreconcilably opposed, and that the victory of one necessarily entailed the loss of the other. Both sides, in other words, accepted the premises of what we might call the "wilderness ethic," which is based on the assumption that the relationship of man and nature resembles a zero-sum game. This idea, widely held and yet largely unexamined, has set the terms of most environmental battles in this country since the very first important one:

the fight over the building of the Hetch Hetchy Dam in 1907, which pitted John Muir against Gifford Pinchot, whom Muir used to call a "temple destroyer." Watching my little local debate unfold over the course of the summer, and grow progressively more shrill and sterile, I began to wonder if perhaps the wilderness ethic itself, for all that it has accomplished in this country over the past century, had now become part of the problem. I also began to wonder if it might be possible to formulate a different ethic to guide us in our dealings with nature, at least in some places some of the time, an ethic that would be based not on the idea of wilderness but on the idea of a garden.

Foresters who have examined sections of fallen trees in Cathedral Pines think that the oldest trees in the forest date from 1780 or so, which suggests that the site was probably logged by the first generation of settlers. The Cathedral Pines are not, then, "virgin growth." The rings of felled trees also reveal a significant growth spurt in 1840, which probably indicates that loggers removed hardwood trees in that year, leaving the pines to grow without competition. In 1883, the Calhouns, an old Cornwall family whose property borders the forest, bought the land to protect the trees from the threat of logging; in 1967 they deeded it to the Nature Conservancy, stipulating that it be maintained in its natural state. Since then, and up until the tornado made its paths impassable, the forest has been a popular place for hiking and Sunday outings. Over the years, more than a few Cornwall residents have come to the forest to be married.

Cathedral Pines is not in any meaningful sense a wilderness. The natural history of the forest intersects at many points with the social history of Cornwall. It is the product of early logging practices, which clear-cut the land once and then cut it again, this time selectively, a hundred years later. Other human factors almost certainly played a part in the forest's history; we can safely assume that any fires in the area were extinguished before they reached Cathedral Pines. (Though we don't ordinarily think of it in these terms, fire suppression is one of the more significant effects that the European has had on the American landscape.) Cathedral Pines, then, is in some part a man-made landscape, and it could reasonably be argued that to exclude man at this point in its history would constitute a break with its past.

But both parties to the dispute chose to disregard the actual history of Cathedral Pines, and instead to think of the forest as a wilderness in the commonly accepted sense of that term: a pristine place untouched by white men. Since the romantics, we've prized such places as refuges from the messiness of the human estate, vantages from which we might transcend the vagaries of that world and fix on what Thoreau called "higher laws." Certainly an afternoon in Cathedral Pines fostered such feelings, and its very name reflects the pantheism that lies behind them. Long before science coined the term *ecosystem* to describe it, we've had the sense that nature undisturbed displays a miraculous order and balance, something the human world can only dream about. When man leaves it alone, nature will tend toward a healthy and abiding state of equilibrium. Wilderness, the purest expression of this natural law, stands out beyond history.

These are powerful and in many ways wonderful ideas. The notion of wilderness is a kind of taboo in our culture, in many cases acting as a check on our inclination to dominate and spoil nature. It has inspired us to set aside such spectacular places as Yellowstone and Yosemite. But wilderness is also a profoundly alienating idea, for it drives a large wedge between man and nature. Set against the foil of nature's timeless cycles, human history appears linear and unpredictable, buffeted by time and chance as it drives blindly into the future. Natural history, by comparison, obeys fixed and legible laws, ones that make the "laws" of human history seem puny, second-rate things scarcely deserving of the label. We have little idea what the future holds for the town of Cornwall, but surely nature has a plan for Cathedral Pines; leave the forest alone and that plan—which science knows by the name of "forest succession"—will unfold inexorably, in strict accordance with natural law. A new climax forest will emerge as nature works to restore her equilibrium—or at least that's the idea.

The notion that nature has a plan for Cathedral Pines is a comforting one, and certainly it supplies a powerful argument for leaving the forest alone. Naturally I was curious to know what that plan was: what does nature do with an old pine forest blown down by a tornado? I consulted a few field guides and standard works of forest ecology hoping to find out.

According to the classical theory of forest succession, set out in the nineteenth century by, among others, Henry Thoreau, a pine forest that has been abruptly destroyed will usually be succeeded by hardwoods, typically oak. This is because squirrels commonly bury acorns in pine forests and neglect to retrieve many of them. The oaks sprout and, because shade doesn't greatly hinder young oaks, the seedlings frequently manage to survive beneath the dark canopy of a mature pine forest. Pine seedlings, on the other hand, require more sunlight than a mature pine forest admits; they won't sprout in shade. So by the time the pine forest comes down, the oak saplings will have had a head start in the race to dominate the new forest. Before any new pines have had a chance to sprout, the oaks will be well on their way to cornering the sunlight and inheriting the forest.

This is what I read, anyway, and I decided to ask around to confirm that Cathedral Pines was expected to behave as predicted. I spoke to a forest ecologist and an expert on the staff of the Nature Conservancy. They told me that the classical theory of pine-forest succession probably does describe the underlying tendency at work in Cathedral Pines. But it turns out that a lot can go, if not "wrong" exactly, then at least differently. For what if there are no oaks nearby? Squirrels will travel only so far in search of a hiding place for their acorns. Instead of oaks, there may be hickory nuts stashed all over Cathedral Pines. And then there's the composition of species planted by the forest's human neighbors to consider; one of these, possibly some exotic (that is, non-native), could conceivably race in and take over.

"It all depends," is the refrain I kept hearing as I tried to pin down nature's intentions for Cathedral Pines. Forest succession, it seems, is only a theory, a metaphor of our making, and almost as often as not nature makes a fool of it. The number of factors that will go into the determination of Cathedral Pines' future is almost beyond comprehension. Consider just this small sample of the things that could happen to alter irrevocably its future course:

A lightning storm—or a cigarette butt flicked from a passing car—ignites a fire next summer. Say it's a severe fire, hot enough to damage the fertility of the soil, thereby delaying recovery of the forest for decades. Or say it rains that night, making the fire a mild one, just hot enough to kill the oak saplings and allow the relatively fire-resistant pine seedlings to flourish without competition. A new pine forest after all? Perhaps. But what if the population of deer happens to soar the following year? Their browsing would wipe out the young pines and create an opening for spruce, the taste of which deer happen not to like.

Or say there is no fire. Without one, it could take hundreds of years for the downed pine trees to rot and return their nutrients to the soil. Trees grow poorly in the exhausted soil, but the seeds of brambles, which can lie dormant in the ground for fifty years, sprout and proliferate: we end up with a hundred years of brush. Or perhaps a breeze in, say, the summer of 1997 carries in seedpods from the Norway maple standing in a nearby front yard at the precise moment when conditions for their germination are perfect. Norway maple, you'll recall, is a European species, introduced here early in the nineteenth century and widely planted as a street tree. Should this exotic species happen to prevail, Cathedral Pines becomes one very odd-looking and awkwardly named wilderness area.

But the outcome could be much worse. Let's say the rains next spring are unusually heavy, washing all the topsoil away (the forest stood on a steep hillside). Only exotic weed species can survive now, and one of these happens to be Japanese honeysuckle, a nineteenth-century import of such rampant habit that it can choke out the growth of all trees indefinitely. We end up with no forest at all.

Nobody, in other words, can say what will happen in Cathedral Pines. And the reason is not that forest ecology is a young or imperfect science, but because *nature herself doesn't know what's going to happen here.* Nature has no grand design for this place. An incomprehensibly various and complex set of circumstances—some of human origin, but many not—will determine the future of Cathedral Pines. And whatever that future turns out to be, it would not unfold in precisely the same way twice. Nature may possess certain inherent tendencies, ones that theories such as forest succession can describe, but chance events can divert her course into an almost infinite number of different channels.

It's hard to square this fact with our strong sense that some kind of quasi-divine order inheres in nature's workings. But science lately has been finding that contingency plays nearly as big a role in natural history as it does in human history. Forest ecologists today will acknowledge that succession theories are little more than comforting narratives we impose on a surprisingly unpredictable process; even so called climax forests are sometimes superseded. (In many places in the northern United States today, mature stands of oak are inexplicably being invaded by maples—skunks at the climax garden party.) Many ecologists will now freely admit that even the concept of an ecosystem is only a metaphor, a human construct imposed upon a much more variable and precarious reality. An ecosystem may be a useful concept, but no ecologist has ever succeeded in isolating one in nature. Nor is the process of evolution as logical or inexorable as we have thought. The current thinking in paleontology holds that the evolution of any given species, our own included, is not the necessary product of any natural laws, but rather the outcome of a concatenation of chance events—of "just history" in the words of Stephen Jay Gould. Add or remove any single happenstance—the asteroid fails to wipe out the dinosaurs; a little chordate worm called *Pikaia* succumbs in the Burgess extinction—and humankind never arrives.

Across several disciplines, in fact, scientists are coming to the conclusion that more "just history" is at work in nature than had previously been thought. Yet our metaphors still picture nature as logical, stable, and ahistorical—more like a watch than, say, an organism or a stock exchange, to name two metaphors that may well be more apt. Chance and contingency, it turns out, are everywhere in nature; she has no fixed goals, no unalterable pathways into the future, no inflexible rules that she herself can't bend or break at will. She is more like us (or we are more like her) than we ever imagined.

To learn this, for me at least, changes everything. I take it to be profoundly good news, though I can easily imagine how it might trouble some people. For many of us, nature is a last bastion of certainty; wilderness, as something beyond the reach of history and accident, is one of the last in our fast-dwindling supply of metaphysical absolutes, those comforting transcendental values by which we have traditionally taken our measure and set our sights. To take away predictable, divinely ordered nature is to pull up one of our last remaining anchors. We are liable to float away on the trackless sea of our own subjectivity.

But the discovery that time and chance hold sway even in nature can also be liberating. Because contingency is an invitation to participate in history. Human choice is unnatural only if nature is deterministic; human change is unnatural only if she is changeless in our absence. If the future of Cathedral Pines is up for grabs, if its history will always be the product of myriad chance events, then why shouldn't we also claim our place among all those deciding factors? For aren't we also one of nature's contingencies? And if our cigarette butts and Norway maples and acid rain are going to shape the future of this place, then why not also our hopes and desires?

Nature will condone an almost infinite number of possible futures for Cathedral Pines. Some would be better than others. True, what we would regard as "better" is probably not what the beetles would prefer. But nature herself has no strong preference. That doesn't mean she will countenance any outcome; she's already ruled out many possible futures (tropical rain forest, desert, etc.) and, all things being equal, she'd probably lean toward the oak. But all things aren't equal (her idea) and she is evidently happy to let the free play of numerous big and little contingencies settle the matter. To exclude from these human desire would be, at least in this place at this time, arbitrary, perverse and, yes, unnatural.

Establishing that we should have a vote in the disposition of Cathedral Pines is much easier than figuring out how we should cast it. The discovery of contingency in nature would seem to fling open a Pandora's box. For if there's nothing fixed or inevitable about nature's course, what's to stop us from concluding that anything goes? It's a whole lot easier to assume that nature left to her own devices knows what's best for a place, to let ourselves be guided by the wilderness ethic.

And maybe that's what we should do. Just because the wilderness ethic is based on a picture of nature that is probably more mythical than real doesn't necessarily mean we have to discard it. In the same way that the Declaration of Independence begins with the useful fiction that "all men are created equal," we could simply stipulate that Cathedral Pines *is* wilderness, and proceed on that assumption. The test of the wilderness ethic is not how truthful it is, but how useful it is in doing what we want to do—in protecting and improving the environment.

So how good a guide is the wilderness ethic in this particular case? Certainly treating Cathedral Pines as a wilderness will keep us from building condos there. When you don't trust yourself to do the right thing, it helps to have an authority as wise and experienced as nature to decide matters for you. But what if nature decides on Japanese honeysuckle—three hundred years of wall-to-wall brush? We would then have a forest not only that we don't like, but that isn't even a wilderness, since it was man who brought Japanese honeysuckle to Cornwall. At this point in history, after humans have left their stamp on virtually every corner of the Earth, doing nothing is frequently a poor recipe for wilderness. In many cases it leads to a gradually deteriorating environment (as seems to be happening in Yellowstone), or to an environment shaped in large part by the acts and mistakes of previous human inhabitants.

If it's real wilderness we want in Cathedral Pines, and not merely an imagined innocence, we will have to restore it. This is the paradox faced by the Nature Conservancy and most other advocates of wilderness: at this point in history, creating a landscape that bears no marks of human intervention will require a certain amount of human intervention. At a minimum it would entail weeding the exotic species from Cathedral Pines, and that is something the Nature Conservancy's strict adherence to the wilderness ethic will not permit.

But what if the Conservancy was willing to intervene just enough to erase any evidence of man's presence? It would soon run up against some difficult questions for which its ethic leaves it ill-prepared. For what is the "real" state of nature in Cathedral Pines? Is it the way the forest looked before the settlers arrived? We could restore that condition by removing all traces of European man. Yet isn't that a rather Eurocentric (if not racist) notion of wilderness? We now know that the Indians were not the ecological eunuchs we once thought. They too left their mark on the land: fires set by Indians determined the composition of the New England forests and probably created that "wilderness" we call the Great Plains. For true untouched wilderness we have to go a lot further back than 1640 or 1492. And if we want to restore the landscape to its pre-Indian condition, then we're going to need a lot of heavy ice-making equipment (not to mention a few woolly mammoths) to make it look right.

But even that would be arbitrary. In fact there is no single moment in time that we can point to and say, *this* is the state of nature in Cathedral Pines. Just since the last ice age alone, that "state of nature" has undergone a thorough revolution every thousand years or so, as tree species forced south by the glaciers migrated back north (a process that is still going on), as the Indians arrived and set their fires, as the large mammals disappeared, as the climate fluctuated—as all the usual historical contingencies came on and off the stage. For several thousand years after the ice age, this part of Connecticut was a treeless tundra; is *that* the true state of nature in Cathedral Pines? The inescapable fact is that, if we want wilderness here, we will have to choose *which* wilderness we want—an idea that is inimical to the wilderness ethic. For wasn't the attraction of wilderness precisely the fact that it relieved us of having to make choices—wasn't nature going to decide, letting us off the hook of history and anthropocentrism?

No such luck, it seems. "Wilderness" is not nearly as straightforward or dependable a guide as we'd like to believe. If we do nothing, we may end up with an impoverished weed patch of our own (indirect) creation, which would hardly count as a victory for wilderness. And if we want to restore Cathedral Pines to some earlier condition, we're forced into making the kinds of inevitably anthropocentric choices and distinctions we turned to wilderness to escape. (Indeed, doing a decent job of wilderness restoration would take all the technology and scientific know-how humans can muster.) Either way, there appears to be no escape from history, not even in nature.

The reason that the wilderness ethic isn't very helpful in a place like Cathedral Pines is that it's an absolutist ethic: man or nature, it says, pick one. As soon as history or circumstance blurs that line, it gets us into trouble. There are times and places when man or nature is the right and necessary choice; back at Hetch Hetchy in 1907 that may well have been the case. But it seems to me that these days most of the environmental questions we face are more like the ambiguous ones posed by Cathedral Pines, and about these the wilderness ethic has less and less to say that is of much help.

The wilderness ethic doesn't tell us what to do when Yellowstone's ecosystem begins to deteriorate, as a result not of our interference but of our neglect. When a species threatens to overwhelm and ruin a habitat because history happened to kill off the predator that once kept its population in check, the ethic is mute. It is confounded, too, when the only hope for the survival of another species is the manipulation of its natural habitat by man. It has nothing to say in all those places where development is desirable or unavoidable except: Don't do it. When we're forced to choose between a hydroelectric power plant and a nuclear one, it refuses to help. That's because the wilderness ethic can't make distinctions between one kind of intervention in nature and another—between weeding Cathedral Pines and developing a theme park there. "You might as well put up condos" is its answer to any plan for human intervention in nature.

"All or nothing," says the wilderness ethic, and in fact we've ended up with a landscape in America that conforms to that injunction remarkably well. Thanks to exactly this kind of either/or thinking, Americans have done an admirable job of drawing lines around certain sacred areas (we did invent the wilderness area) and a terrible job of managing the rest of our land. The reason is not hard to find: the only environmental ethic we have has nothing useful to say about those areas outside the line. Once a landscape is no longer "virgin" it is typically written off as fallen, lost to nature, irredeemable. We hand it over to the jurisdiction of that other sacrosanct American ethic: laissez-faire economics. "You might as well put up condos." And so we do.

Indeed, the wilderness ethic and laissez-faire economics, antithetical as they might at first appear, are really mirror images of one another. Each proposes a quasi-divine force—Nature, the Market—that, left to its own devices, somehow knows what's best for a place. Nature and the market are both self-regulating, guided by an invisible hand. Worshippers of either share a deep, Puritan distrust of man, taking it on faith that human tinkering with the natural or economic order can only pervert it. Neither will acknowledge that their respective divinities can also err: that nature produces the AIDS virus as well as the rose, that the same markets that produce stupendous wealth can also crash. (Actually, worshippers of the market are a bit more realistic than worshippers of nature: they long ago stopped relying on the free market to supply us with such necessities as food and shelter. Though they don't like to talk about it much, they accept the need for society to "garden" the market.)

Essentially, we have divided our country in two, between the kingdom of wilderness, which rules about 8 percent of America's land, and the kingdom of the market, which rules the rest. Perhaps we should be grateful for secure borders. But what do those of us who care about nature do when we're on the market side, which is most of the time? How do we behave? What are our goals? We can't reasonably expect to change the borders, no matter how many power lines and dams Earth First! blows up. No, the wilderness ethic won't be of much help over here. Its politics are bound to be hopelessly romantic (consisting of impractical schemes to redraw the borders) or nihilistic. Faced with hard questions about how to confront global environmental problems such as the greenhouse effect or ozone depletion (problems that respect no borders), adherents of the wilderness ethic are apt to throw up their hands in despair and declare the "end of nature."

The only thing that's really in danger of ending is a romantic, pantheistic idea of nature that we invented in the first place, one whose passing might well turn out to be a blessing in disguise. Useful as it has been in helping us protect the sacred eight percent, it nevertheless has failed to prevent us from doing a great deal of damage to the remaining 92 percent. This old idea may have taught us how to worship nature, but it didn't tell us how to live with her. It told us more than we needed to know about virginity and rape, and almost nothing about marriage. The metaphor of divine nature can admit only two roles for man: as worshipper (the naturalist's role) or temple destroyer (the developer's). But that drama is all played out now. The temple's been destroyed—if it ever was a temple. Nature is dead, if by nature we mean something that stands apart from man and messy history. And now that it is, perhaps we can begin to write some new parts for ourselves, ones that will show us how to start out from here, not from some imagined state of innocence, and let us get down to the work at hand.

Thoreau and Muir and their descendants went to the wilderness and returned with the makings of America's first environmental ethic. Today it still stands, though somewhat strained and tattered. What if now, instead of to the wilderness, we were to look to the garden for the makings of a new ethic? One that would not necessarily supplant the earlier one, but might give us something useful to say in those cases when it is silent or unhelpful?

It will take better thinkers than me to flesh out what such an ethic might look like. But even my limited experience in the garden has persuaded me that the materials needed to construct it—the fresh metaphors about nature we need—may be found there. For the garden is a place with long experience of questions having to do with man in nature. Below are some provisional notes, based on my own experiences and the experiences of other gardeners I've met or read, on the kinds of answers the garden is apt to give.

1. An ethic based on the garden would give local answers. Unlike the wilderness idea, it would propose different solutions in different places and times. This strikes me as both a strength and a weakness. It's a weakness because a garden ethic will never speak as clearly or univocally as the wilderness ethic does. In a country as large and geographically various as this, it is probably inevitable that we will favor abstract landscape ideas—grids, lawns, monocultures, wildernesses—which can be applied across the board, even legislated nationally; such ideas have the power to simplify and unite. Yet isn't this power itself part of the problem? The health of a place generally suffers whenever we impose practices on it that are better suited to another place; a lawn in Virginia makes sense in a way that a lawn in Arizona does not.

So a garden ethic would begin with Alexander Pope's famous advice to landscape designers: "Consult the Genius of the Place in all." It's hard to imagine this slogan ever replacing Earth First!'s "No Compromise in Defense of Mother Earth" on American bumper stickers; nor should it, at least not everywhere. For Pope's dictum suggests that there are places whose "genius" will, if hearkened to, counsel "no compromise." Yet what is right for Yosemite is not necessarily right for Cathedral Pines.

2. The gardener starts out from here. By that I mean, he accepts contingency, his own and nature's. He doesn't spend a lot of time worrying about whether he has a god-given right to change nature. It's enough for him to know that, for some historical or biological reason, humankind finds itself living in places (six of the seven continents) where it must substantially alter the environment in order to survive. If we had remained on African savanna things might be different. And if I lived in zone six I could probably grow good tomatoes without the use of plastic. The gardener learns to play the hand he's been dealt.

3. A garden ethic would be frankly anthropocentric. As I began to understand when I planted my roses and my maple tree, we know nature only through the screen of our metaphors; to see her plain is probably impossible. (And not necessarily desirable, as George Eliot once suggested: "If we could hear the squirrel's heartbeat, the sound of the grass growing, we should die of

that roar." Without the editing of our perceptions, nature might prove unbearable.) Melville was describing all of nature when he described the whiteness of the whale, its "dumb blankness, full of meaning." Even wilderness, in both its satanic and benevolent incarnations, is an historical, man-made idea. Every one of our various metaphors for nature—"wilderness," "ecosystem," "Gaia," "resource," "wasteland"—is already a kind of garden, an indissoluble mixture of our culture and whatever it is that's really out there. "Garden" may sound like a hopelessly anthropocentric concept, but it's probably one we can't get past.

The gardener doesn't waste much time on metaphysics—on figuring out what a "truer" perspective on nature (such as biocentrism or geocentrism) might look like. That's probably because he's noticed that most of the very long or wide perspectives we've recently been asked to adopt (including the one advanced by the Nature Conservancy in Cathedral Pines) are indifferent to our well-being and survival as a species. On this point he agrees with Wendell Berry—that "it is not natural to be disloyal to one's own kind."

4. That said, though, the gardener's conception of his self-interest is broad and enlightened. Anthropocentric as he may be, he recognizes that he is dependent for his health and survival on many other forms of life, so he is careful to take their interests into account in whatever he does. He is in fact a wilderness advocate of a certain kind. It is when he respects and nurtures the wilderness of his soil and his plants that his garden seems to flourish most. Wildness, he has found, resides not only out there, but right here: in his soil, in his plants, even in himself. Overcultivation tends to repress this quality, which experience tells him is necessary to health in all three realms. But wildness is more a quality than a place, and though humans can't manufacture it, they can nourish and husband it. That is precisely what I'm doing when I make compost and return it to the soil; it is what we could be doing in Cathedral Pines (and not necessarily by leaving the place alone). The gardener cultivates wildness, but he does so carefully and respectfully, in full recognition of its mystery.

5. The gardener tends not to be romantic about nature. What could be more natural than the storms and droughts and plagues that ruin his garden? Cruelty, aggression, suffering—these, too, are nature's offspring (and not, as Rousseau tried to convince us, culture's). Nature is probably a poor place to look for values. She was indifferent to humankind's arrival, and she is indifferent to our survival.

It's only in the last century or so that we seem to have forgotten this. Our romance of nature is a comparatively recent idea, the product of the industrial age's novel conceit that nature could be conquered, and probably also of the fact that few of us work with nature directly anymore. But should current weather forecasts prove to be accurate (a rapid, permanent warming trend accompanied by severe storms), our current romance will look like a brief historical anomaly, a momentary lapse of judgment. Nature may once again turn dangerous and capricious and unconquerable. When this happens, we will quickly lose our crush on her.

Compared to the naturalist, the gardener never fell head over heels for nature. He's seen her ruin his plans too many times for that. The gardener has learned, perforce, to live with her ambiguities—that she is neither all good nor all bad, that she gives as well as takes away. Nature's apt to pull the rug out from under us at any time, to make a grim joke of our noblest intention. Perhaps this explains why garden writing tends to be comic, rather than lyrical or elegiac in the way that nature writing usually is: the gardener can never quite forget about the rug underfoot, the possibility of the offstage hook.

6. The gardener feels he has a legitimate quarrel with nature—with her weeds and storms and plagues, her rot and death. What's more, that quarrel has produced much of value, not only in his own time here (this garden, these fruits), but over the whole course of Western history. Civilization itself, as Freud and Frazer and many others have observed, is the product of that quarrel. But at the same time, the gardener appreciates that it would probably not be in his interest, or in nature's, to push his side of this argument too hard. Many points of contention that humankind thought it had won—DDT's victory over insects, say, or medicine's conquest of infectious disease—turned out to be Pyrrhic or illusory triumphs. Better to keep the quarrel going, the good gardener reasons, than to reach for outright victory, which is dangerous in the attempt and probably impossible anyway.

7. The gardener doesn't take it for granted that man's impact on nature will always be negative. Perhaps he's observed how his own garden has made this patch of land a better place, even by nature's own standards. His gardening has greatly increased the diversity and abundance of life in this place. Besides the many exotic species of plants he's introduced, the mammal, rodent, and insect populations have burgeoned, and his soil supports a much richer community of microbes than it did before.

Judged strictly by these standards, nature occasionally makes mistakes. The climax forest could certainly be considered one (a place where the number and variety of living things have declined to a crisis point) and evolution teems with others. At the same time, it should be acknowledged that man occasionally creates new ecosystems much richer than the ones they replaced, and not merely on the scale of a garden: think of the tall-grass prairies of the Midwest, England's hedgerow landscape, the countryside of the Ile de France, the patchwork of fields and forests in this part of New England. Most of us would be happy to call such places "nature," but that does not do them (or us) justice; they are really a kind of garden, a second nature.

The gardener doesn't feel that by virtue of the fact that he changes nature he is somehow outside of it. He looks around and sees that human hopes and desires are by now part and parcel of the landscape. The "environment" is not, and has never been, a neutral, fixed backdrop; it is in fact alive, changing all the time in response to innumerable contingencies, one of these being the presence within it of the gardener. And that presence is neither inherently good nor bad.

8. The gardener firmly believes it is possible to make distinctions between kinds and degrees of human intervention in nature. Isn't the difference between the Ile de France and Love Canal, or a pine forest and a condo development, proof enough that the choice isn't really between "all or nothing"? The gardener doesn't doubt that it is possible to discriminate; it is through experience in the garden that he develops this faculty.

Because of his experience, the gardener is not likely to conclude from the fact that some intervention in nature is unavoidable, therefore "anything goes." This is precisely where his skill and interest lie: in determining what does and does not go in a particular place. How much is too much? What suits this land? How can we get what we want here while nature goes about getting what she wants? He has no doubt that good answers to these questions can be found.

9. The good gardener commonly borrows his methods, if not his goals, from nature herself. For though nature doesn't seem to dictate in advance what we can do in a place—we are free, in the same way evolution is, to try something completely new—in the end she will let us know what does and does not work. She is above all a pragmatist, and so is the successful gardener.

By studying nature's ways and means, the gardener can find answers to the questions, What is apt to work? What avails here? This seems to hold true at many levels of specificity. In one particular patch of my vegetable garden—a low, damp area—I failed with every crop I planted until I stopped to consider what nature grew in a similar area nearby: briars. So I planted raspberries, which are of course a cultivated kind of briar, and they have flourished. A trivial case, but it shows how attentiveness to nature can help us to attune our desires with her ways.

The imitation of nature is of course the principle underlying organic gardening. Organic gardeners have learned to mimic nature's own methods of building fertility in the soil, controlling insect populations and disease, recycling nutrients. But the practices we call "organic" are not themselves "natural," any more than the bird call of a hunter is natural. They are more like man-made analogues of natural processes. But they seem to work. And they at least suggest a way to approach other problems—from a town's decision on what to do with a blown-down pine forest, to society's choice among novel new technologies. In each case, there will be some alternatives that align our needs and desires with nature's ways more closely than others.

It does seem that we do best in nature when we imitate her—when we learn to think like running water, or a carrot, an aphid, a pine forest, or a compost pile. That's probably because nature, after almost four billion years of trial-and-error experience, has wide knowledge of what works in life. Surely we're better off learning how to draw on her experience than trying to repeat it, if only because we don't have that kind of time.

10. If nature is one necessary source of instruction for a garden ethic, culture is the other. Civilization may be part of our problem with respect to nature, but there will be no solution without it. As Wendell Berry has pointed out, it is culture, and certainly not nature, that teaches us to observe and remember, to learn from our mistakes, to share our experiences, and perhaps most important of all, to restrain ourselves. Nature does not teach its creatures to control their appetites except by the harshest of lessons—epidemics, mass death, extinctions. Nothing would be more natural than for humankind to burden the environment to the extent that it was rendered unfit for human life. Nature in that event would not be the loser, nor would it disturb her laws in the least—operating as it has always done, natural selection would unceremoniously do us in. Should this fate be averted, it will only be because our culture—*our* laws and metaphors, our science and technology, our ongoing conversation about nature and man's place in it—pointed us in the direction of a different future. Nature will not do this for us.

The gardener in nature is that most artificial of creatures, a civilized human being: in control of his appetites, solicitous of nature, self-conscious and responsible, mindful of the past and the future, and at ease with the fundamental ambiguity of his predicament—which is that though he lives in nature, he is no longer strictly of nature. Further, he knows that neither his success nor his failure in this place is ordained. Nature is apparently indifferent to his fate, and this leaves him free—indeed, obliges him—to make his own way here as best he can.

What would an ethic based on these ideas—based on the idea of the garden— advise us to do in Cathedral Pines? I don't know enough about the ecology of the place to say with certainty, but I think I have some sense of how we might proceed under its dispensation. We would start out, of course, by consulting "the Genius of the Place." This would tell us, among other things, that Cathedral Pines is not a wilderness, and so probably should not be treated as one. It is a cultural as well as a natural landscape, and to exclude the wishes of the townspeople from our plans for the place would be false. To treat it now as wilderness is to impose an abstract and alien idea on it.

Consulting the genius of the place also means inquiring as to what nature will allow us to do here—what this "locale permits, and what [it] denies," as Virgil wrote in *The Georgics*. We know right off, for instance, that this plot of land can support a magnificent forest of white pines. Nature would not object if we decided to replant the pine forest. Indeed, this would be a perfectly reasonable, environmentally sound thing to do.

If we chose to go this route, we would be undertaking a fairly simple act of what is called "ecological restoration." This relatively new school of environmentalism has its roots in Aldo Leopold's pioneering efforts to re-create a tall-grass prairie on the grounds of the University of Wisconsin Arboretum in the 1930s. Leopold and his followers (who continue to maintain the restored prairie today) believed that it is not always enough to conserve the land—that sometimes it is desirable, and possible, for man to intervene in nature in order to improve it. Specifically, man should intervene to re-create damaged ecosystems: polluted rivers, clear-cut forests, vanished prairies, dead lakes. The restorationists also believe, and in this they remind me of the green thumb, that the best way to learn about nature's ways is by trying to imitate them. (In fact much of what we know about the role of fire in creating and sustaining prairies comes from their efforts.) But the most important contribution of the restorationists has been to set forth a positive, active role for man in nature—in their conception, as equal parts gardener and healer. It seems to me that the idea of ecological restoration is consistent with a garden ethic, and perhaps with the Hippocratic Oath as well.

From the work of the ecological restorationists, we now know that it is possible to skip and manipulate the stages of forest succession. They would probably advise us to burn the fallen timber—an act that, though not strictly speaking "natural," would serve as an effective analogue of the natural process by which a forest is regenerated. The fires we set would reinvigorate the soil (thereby enhancing *that* wilderness) and at the same time clear out the weed species, hardwood saplings, and brush. By doing all this, we will have imitated the conditions under which a white pine forest is born, and the pines might then return on their own. Or else—it makes little difference—we could plant them. At that point, our work would be done, and the pine forest could take care itself. It would take many decades, but restoring the Cathedral Pines would strain neither our capabilities nor nature's sufferance. And in doing so, we would also be restoring the congenial relationship between man and nature that prevailed in this place before the storm and the subsequent controversy. That would be no small thing.

Nature would not preclude more novel solutions for Cathedral Pines—other kinds of forest-gardens or even parks could probably flourish on this site. But since the town has traditionally regarded Cathedral Pines as a kind of local institution, one steeped in shared memories and historical significance, I would argue that the genius of the place rules out doing anything unprecedented here. The past is our best guide in this particular case, and not only on questions of ecology.

But replanting the pine forest is not the only good option for Cathedral Pines. There is another forest we might want to restore on this site, one that is also in keeping with its history and its meaning to the town.

Before the storm, we used to come to Cathedral Pines and imagine that this was how the New World forest looked to the first settlers. We now know that the precolonial forest probably looked somewhat different—for one thing, it was not exclusively pine. But it's conceivable that we could restore Cathedral Pines to something closely resembling its actual precolonial condition. By analyzing historical accounts, the rings of fallen trees, and fossilized pollen grains buried in the soil, we could reconstruct the variety and composition of species that flourished here in 1739, the year when the colonists first settled near this place and formed the town of Cornwall. We know that nature, having done so once before, would probably permit us to have such a forest here. And, using some of the more advanced techniques of ecological restoration, it is probably within our competence to recreate a precolonial forest on this site.

We would do this not because we'd decided to be faithful to the "state of nature" at Cathedral Pines, but very simply because the precolonial forest happens to mean a great deal to us. It is a touchstone in the history of this town, not to mention this nation. A walk in a restored version of the precolonial forest might recall us to our culture's first, fateful impressions of America, to our thoughts on coming upon what Fitzgerald called the "fresh green breast of the new world." In the contemplation of that scene we might be moved to reconsider what happened next—to us, to the Indians who once hunted here, to nature in this corner of America.

This is pretty much what I would have stood up and said if we'd had a town meeting to decide what to do in Cathedral Pines. Certainly a town meeting would have been a fitting way to decide the matter, nicely in keeping with the genius of *this* place, a small town in New England. I can easily imagine the speeches and the arguments. The people from the Nature Conservancy would have made their plea for leaving the place alone, for "letting nature take her course." Richard Dakin, the first selectman, and John Calhoun, the forest's nearest neighbor, would have warned about the dangers of fire. And then we might have heard some other points of view. I would have tried to make a pitch for restoration, talking about some of the ways we might "garden" the site. I can imagine Ian Ingersoll, a gifted cabinetmaker in town, speaking with feeling about the waste of such rare timbers, and the prospect of sitting down to a Thanksgiving dinner at a table in which you could see rings formed at the time of the American Revolution. Maybe somebody else would have talked about how much she missed her Sunday afternoon walks in the forest, and how very sad the place looked now. A scientist from the Yale School of Forestry might have patiently tried to explain, as indeed one Yale scientist did in the press, why "It's just as pretty to me now as it was then."

This is the same fellow who said, "If you're going to clean it up, you might as well put up condos." I can't imagine anyone actually proposing that, or any other kind of development in Cathedral Pines. But if someone did, he would probably get shouted down. Because we have too much respect for this place; and besides, our sympathies and interests are a lot more complicated than the economists or environmentalists always seem to think. Sooner than a developer, we'd be likely to hear from somebody speaking on behalf of the forest's fauna—the species who have lost out in the storm (like the owls), but also the ones for whom doing nothing would be a boon (the beetles). And so the various interests of the animals would be taken into account, too; indeed, I expect that "nature"—all those different (and contradictory) points of view—would be well represented at this town meeting. Perhaps it is naive of me to think so, but I'm confident that in the course of a public, democratic conversation about the disposition of Cathedral Pines, we would eventually arrive at a solution that would have at once pleased us and not offended nature.

But unfortunately that's not what happened. The future of Cathedral Pines was decided in a closed-door meeting at the Nature Conservancy in September, after a series of negotiations with the selectmen and the owners of adjacent property. The result was a compromise that seems to have pleased no one. The fallen trees will remain untouched—except for a fifty-foot swath clear-cut around the perimeter of the forest, a firebreak intended to appease the owners of a few nearby houses. The sole human interest taken into account in the decision was the worry about fire.

I drove up there one day in late fall to have a look around, to see what the truce between the Conservancy and the town had wrought. What a sad sight it is. Unwittingly, and in spite of the good intentions on both sides, the Conservancy and the selectmen have conspired to create a landscape that is a perfect symbol of our perverted relation to nature. The firebreak looks like nothing so much as a no-man's-land in a war zone, a forbidding expanse of blistered ground impounding what little remains of the Cathedral Pines. The landscape we've made here is grotesque. And yet it is the logical outcome of a confrontation between, on the one side, an abstract and mistaken concept of nature's interests and, on the other, a pinched and demeaning notion of our own interests. We should probably not be surprised that the result of such a confrontation is not a wilderness, or a garden, but a DMZ.

Man Killed by Pheasant

John T. Price

So I'm driving east on Highway 30, from our new home in Belle Plaine to Cedar Rapids, Iowa. It's a four-lane, and because I'm an eldest child, I'm driving the speed limit, around fifty-five, sixty miles per hour. I'm listening to Jimi Hendrix cry "Mary"—imagining, as usual, that I am Jimi Hendrix—when in the far distance I see some brown blobs hovering across the highway: one, then two. By the way they move, low and slow, I suspect they're young pheasants. As I near the place of their crossing I look over the empty passenger seat and into the grassy ditch to see if I can spot the whole clan. Suddenly, there is a peripheral darkness, the fast shadow of an eclipse, and something explodes against the side of my head in a fury of flapping and scratching and squawking. In an act of extraordinary timing, one of the straggling pheasants has flown in my driver's side window. And being the steel-jawed action hero I am, I scream, scream like a rabbit, and strike at it frantically with my left arm, the car swerving, wings snapping, Hendrix wailing, feathers beating at my face until, at last, I knock the thing back out the window and onto the road. I regain control of the car, if not myself, and pull over, undone.

That's the time I should have been killed by a pheasant. For reasons peculiar to that summer, I recall it often. It occurred, for one, while I was on my way to teach a technical writing course at a nearby community college, a summer job to help me through grad school. This "distance learning experience" took place exclusively by radio wave, with me in an empty room on campus and my fifteen students scattered at sites within a hundred-mile radius. The technology was such that my students could see me, but I couldn't see them. To converse we had to push buttons at the base of our microphones, so that each class felt like an episode of *Larry King Live: Judy, from Monticello, hello, you're on the air.* "The future of higher education" my supervisor called it. And I never did get the hang of the camera. I'd turn it on at the beginning of class and there, on the big-screen monitor, would be a super-close-up of my lips. I'd spend the next few minutes jostling the joystick, zooming in and out like one of those early music videos until I found the suitable frame. Sometimes my students would laugh at this, and I'd hear them laughing, but only if they pushed their buttons. If there was an electrical storm nearby, I wouldn't hear them at all.

On the way to such a displaced, bodiless job, a near-death experience had some additional currency. As did the larger natural disaster unfolding around me. It was the summer of the great Iowa floods, 1993, and the reason I was on

Highway 30 to begin with was that my usual route to campus had been washed out by the swollen Iowa River. This was a serious situation: People had been killed and Des Moines had been without water for over a week. "Nature Gone Mad!" was how the national media described it.

Although aware of the widespread suffering, I was privileged to watch the whole thing unfold more gently from the roadways of my rural commutes. And what I saw was a wilderness of birds. Bean fields suddenly became sheer, inaccessible places where herons stood piercing frogs in the shallows, where pelicans flew in great cyclonic towers, where bald eagles swung low to pick off stranded fish. Perched on soggy, neglected fence posts were birds I hadn't seen since early childhood, bobolinks and bluebirds and tanagers. Their color and song drew my eye closer to the earth, to the ragged ditches full of forgotten wildflowers and grasses—primrose and horsemint, big blue and switch—safe, at least for a while, from the mower's blade. The domesticated landscape of my home had gone wild and I was mesmerized by it.

Toward the end of the summer flooding, when the dramatic presence of wild birds dwindled, I thought a lot about Noah, about those end days on the Ark between the release of the raven and the return of the dove, between knowledge of a decimated landscape and faith in one that, through decimation, had become reborn. When it was all over, I thought I understood Noah's first impulse, once on dry land, to get drunk and forget. I'd lived my entire life in Iowa, the most ecologically altered state in the union, with less than one-tenth of 1 percent of its native habitats remaining. "Tragic" is what the ecologist Wes Jackson has called the plowing up of this prairie region, "one of the two or three worst atrocities committed by Americans." Not that I'd ever cared—it's hard to care about a wild place you've never seen or known. Yet in those short, flooded months of 1993, I witnessed a blurry reflection of what the land had once been: a rich ecology of wetlands and savannahs and prairies, alive with movement and migration. Alive with power. Under its influence, I felt closer to my home landscape than ever before. So when that power slipped from view, I was surprised to find myself longing to chase after it. Having spent most of my life wanting to leave the Midwest, where might I find the reasons to stay, to commit?

Death by pheasant didn't immediately come to mind. Although, in the wake of the floods, death was part of what I longed for. Or rather the possibility of a certain kind of death, the kind in which you become lost in a vast landscape and die, as Edward Abbey has described it, "alone, on rock under sun at the brink of the unknown, like a wolf, like a great bird." This had nearly been my fate on that cliff in Idaho, during our honeymoon, and in my mind it helped define that wilderness as a place worthy of respect, a place of consequence and a kind of fearful freedom. My German friend, Elmar, calls this freedom *vogelfrei*, which loosely translates into "free as a bird." Far from the positive spin we've put on this phrase, *vogelfrei* refers to the state of being cast out from the tribe, so free you'll die in the open, unburied, to be picked apart by birds. It's a state of fear and vulnerability and movement, one that might, especially here in the agricultural Midwest—a place seemingly without fang or claw or talon—make us more attentive to the natural world, more humbled by its power to transform us.

At first flush, my collision with the pheasant didn't seem to hold that kind of possibility. But it could have. If, for example, this had happened to me as a child or adolescent or as a member of a New Age men's group, I might have made something more of it. When I was a boy, some of my favorite comic book characters were mutations of man and animal—Mole Man, of course, and Spiderman and Captain America's ally, the Falcon. Imagine the comic book story that could have developed this time: A mild-mannered English professor is struck in the head by a wayward pheasant, his blood mingling with the bird's while, coincidentally, a cosmic tsunami from a distant stellar explosion soaks the whole scene in gamma radiation. Emerging from the smoldering rubble: Pheasant Man. No, *Super* Pheasant Man! As Super Pheasant Man, our mild-mannered professor finds he has acquired the bird's more powerful features—its pride and daring, its resilience, its colorful head feathers—learning to use them for the good of humanity while at the same time fighting the darker side of his condition, namely, a propensity for polygamy and loose stools.

But I was not a boy when I met that unlucky pheasant on Highway 30, which is too bad, because for a long time afterward I found nothing particularly uplifting about the experience. Instead, I saw my life, and death, made a joke. Imagine the regional headlines: *Iowa Man Killed by Pheasant; Mother Files for Hunting License.* Imagine the funeral, where, in the middle of "I'll Fly Away," one of my more successful cousins whispers to his wife, *You know, it wasn't even a cock pheasant that killed him. It was just a little baby pheasant.* Imagine the members of that hypothetical men's group, who, in their wailful mourning of my death, botch up the spirit animal ritual and condemn my soul to be borne not on the wings of an eagle or a falcon, but on those of a pheasant, stubby and insufficient, struggling to get us both off the ground, never getting more than maybe fifteen feet toward heaven before dropping back down to earth with a thud and a cluck.

No, thank you. I do not wish to become one with the pheasant, in this life or in the next. Yet seen through the history of the land, this bird and I have been colliding for centuries. Having evolved together on the grasslands of distant continents, we were both brought to this country by the accidents of nature and technology and desire. As Americans, the pheasant and I have come to share certain important historical figures, like Benjamin Franklin, whose son-in-law was one of the first to attempt to introduce the ring-necked pheasant, a native of China, to this country—an unsuccessful release in New

Jersey. Its introduction to Iowa over a century later was by accident, taking place during a 1901 windstorm near Cedar Falls that blew down confinement fences and released two thousand of the birds into the prairie night. They've remained here ever since, sharing with my people an affinity for the Northern Plains to which we've both become anchored by the peculiarities of the soil. This soil, loess and glacial till, is migrant and invasive, like us, having been carried here from ancient Canada by wind and by ice. Its rich, organic loam, black as oil, brought my farmer ancestors to the region and has, at the same time, held close the range of the ring-necked pheasant, lacing the bird's grit with calcium carbonate. Because the ring-neck requires an abundance of this mineral, it doesn't stray far, not even a few hundred miles south into the gray prairies of, say, lower Illinois.

So the pheasant and I have remained settlers in this region; watching as others of our kind move on. As such, we have come to share some of the same enemies, like the fencerow-to-fencerow, get-big-or-get-out agricultural policies of the 1970s and '80s. These policies, enacting yet another vision of migration, dramatically expanded agricultural exports and, at the same time, led the region to the farm crisis of the 1980s, to the flight and impoverishment and death of thousands of industrial and farm families. For the pheasant as well, despite set-aside programs, this fencerow-to-fencerow world has held its own kind of impoverishment, a destruction of habitat so thorough that two hundred pheasants have been known to crowd a shelterbelt only a hundred yards long. In such a bare-naked world a good blizzard, like the one in 1975— while I was honking truck horns with my grandfather—has the power to wipe out 80 percent of a local pheasant population in a single evening.

Yet, in sharing enemies, we have also been, together, the common enemy. To the prairie chicken, for instance—one of the many native citizens that had the unfortunate luck to precede us here in the "heartland." For almost a century European settlers hunted and plowed down prairie chicken populations in Iowa. But the ring-necked pheasant has also played a role, destroying the prairie chicken's eggs, occupying its nests, and interrupting, seemingly out of spite, its dancing-ground rituals. Some argue that restoring prairie chicken populations will have to coincide with significant reductions in pheasant populations. Reducing pheasant numbers around here, however, is about as easy and popular as reducing our own. The difficulties are partly economic: In Iowa, we hunt and eat this bird to the tune of about a million and a half a year. It's one of our biggest tourist attractions. But I wonder, too, if we don't see in this bird, at some unconscious level, a dark reflection of our own troubling history in the American grasslands, our role as ecological party crashers, as culture wreckers. Our role, ultimately, as killers and thieves. To question the pheasant's claim on the land is, in some way, to question our own.

It's unfair, of course, and dangerous to project our sins onto another species. When tossing around ethical responsibility, the difference between us, between instinct and intent, is significant. But the pheasants needn't worry about taking the blame. Hardly anyone around here gives them a second thought. That indifference was part of my problem when I finally began searching, while living in Belle Plaine, for reasons to care about my home landscape. In relation to that bird, as to most of the familiar, transplanted wildlife around me, I felt nothing. The pheasant was common, and the last thing I wanted to feel as a Midwesterner was common. Since early adolescence I'd been fleeing a sense of inadequacy shared by many in this region, a sense of self marked—as Minnesotan Patricia Hampl has said—by "an indelible brand of innocence, which is to be marked by an absence, a vacancy. By nothing at all." For Midwesterners like me, the complex, the worthy seemed always to be found elsewhere. Not here in this ordinary place, this ordinary life.

Not surprisingly, in the years immediately following the flood, I didn't seek that new relationship to the Midwest in the familiar land immediately around me, but by traveling to distant and, in my imagination, more exotic landscapes such as the Black Hills and Badlands in western South Dakota. What I discovered in those places did indeed transform me. Near Wind Cave, I saw for the first time elk bugling and mating at home on their native prairies. While sitting in a fly-plagued prairie dog town, I saw for the first time a bison bull wallowing in the brown dust. On the grasslands near Bear Butte, where Crazy Horse once sought vision, I saw for the first time a falcon stoop to kill a duck, the native cycles of predator and prey, of wild death, still lingering. Even *vogelfrei*, that fearful freedom—I felt it for the first time in this region while walking lost in the deep earth of the Badlands. My journey through these places toward commitment has been awkward, fragmented, and at times pathetic, even comic. Yet the significance of those experiences cannot be underestimated, how they have worked to cure a lifetime of ignorance and indifference. How, to use spiritual terms, they have filled what once was empty.

But if the spiritual journey to a place begins, as some claim, with mortal fear, then it was not the bison or the falcon or the Badlands that first drew me closer to the region in which I'd been raised. It was the pheasant, that particular baby pheasant—there on a highway in eastern Iowa—which almost, as my sister Allyson would say, rocked my world. In a sense, that's exactly what it did. It made me wake up, become more observant of what's lurking in the margins. What's lurking there, despite the rumors, is the possibility of surprise, of accident, of death. And if it's possible in this over determined landscape for a pheasant to kill a man, then why not also the possibility of restoration, renewal, and, at last, hope?

That's a romantic stretch, I know, and at the time of the incident itself I didn't feel particularly worshipful of its surprise. As I sat in the car, wiping my face, I just felt lucky—*Thank God it wasn't a two-lane!*—and then ridiculous. The whole thing was so absurd it might've been a dream. I carefully leaned my head out the window to see if the pheasant was still on the road. It wasn't. I thought about going back to see if it was injured, but decided against it—after all, it was only a pheasant. Besides, I was late for work, where in a few minutes I would be taking my own precarious flight through the airwaves, across the flooded land, to students I would never see, never truly know.

I started the car and eased back onto the highway. As I approached cruising speed I saw something move out of the corner of my eye. I jerked, swerving the car a little. A feather. An ordinary brown feather. Then another and another—there must have been a dozen—floating in the breeze of the open window. They tickled and annoyed me. Yet for reasons I still can't explain, I kept the window open, just a crack, enough to keep the feathers dancing about the cabin. And that's how I, the man almost killed by a pheasant, drove the rest of those miles, touched by its feathers in flight, touched by an intimacy as rare and welcome, in my tragic country, as laughter in a storm.

On Form

Lia Purpura

> *... It is the forged feature finds me; it is the rehearsal*
> *of own, of abrupt self there so thrusts on, so throngs the ear...*
> — Gerard Manley Hopkins, "Henry Purcell"

How does the guy with hooks for arms jerk off?

But it didn't come forth as a joke. Nor was the answer "very carefully."

More powerfully, there was his face, a face used to seeing questions like this in others' faces. How does a face like that look? It didn't shut me down. It didn't slam or ignore or isolate. But he recognized the question (hooks working the receipt into his wallet). He'd heard/seen it all before (outside the store, whoa, he drives a car with those things!) There was a shape to the question and it was a cliché to him. Thus, I felt seen, transparent. Naked. Looked through and turned inside out and found lacking. In imagination. Or just a beginner.

But neither did he see me imagining (the hooks unstrapped, the harness off) his arms on me: small of my back. Back of my neck.

Lifting my hair.

I'm practicing now.

Someone I know tilts her head to the side when looking hard at another. The gesture always annoyed me and seemed a contrived show of attention. Then I tried it. And it was like voices pouring in; it was like opening the front door and sweeping wide an arm for guests. Like kneeling in front of a child, eye to eye, to ease the confession. Inviting. Hospitable. I didn't know that.

I'll go on then, angled to the pour of these forms.

Though this may seem indecorous.

The hotel manager in Cambridge that afternoon was impatient with me. His name was Khalid. He was bald and had a large, flat forehead that shone. But his forehead was crushed in one spot, like a soda can gets dented. Or a garbage can. And the light lingered there, on the dent, and darkened as I asked—and asked again—for directions to the airport. Someone must run their hand over the dent and smooth it and know the dip of bone and hammock of skin as one knows the contours of a temperamental lock, how to jiggle and fit the key, first one way and then the other, unthinkingly. And though I repeated the words back—Red Line, Green Line, Blue Line, Shuttle—I was really, standing in front of him, jiggling the key. Hand on the tumbler plate, pushing to go in.

My child comes close to touch the imperfections of my face. Touches the flaws because they beckon. The white bumps and red bumps. Small scars. Dark spots. *Counter, original, spare, strange.* He touches because he can, because I allow it, though hiding back there (it's bubbling up, he's capping it, tapping it back down), is this: that thrill without a name. That weird package of love and revulsion, that "glad it's not me" layered over with real tenderness. Some forward sway. Some retraction. And him teetering on the line between. When he does this, all the soft, pink, round things, all the brown, scarred, pitted things that held me as a kid come back. I remember my own secretive glances at the compromised, familiar faces I loved as a child. The tiny, stiff hairs that made nets to catch me. How even as I twisted free, I wanted to be caught.

Here is a man fated to chew as if perpetually working an olive pit out of his mouth. There is a boy who spits when he talks and snuffles and is just too watery to make friends. And with the stem of a dandelion, cut, its bitter milk touched to the tongue, here I am, calling it "milk." Swallowing the bitterness so that an outward sign might match the inner atmosphere I carry with me these last, long days of fall. Swallowing makes me wince and contort. I feel my mouth tighten and take some more in. If it's poison, it's not enough to hurt me, I reason. And anyway, I'm testing. Making tests. Rehearsing ways a face can twist.
   I use a mirror for this.

I've been watching her run the bobbing-for-apples booth at the local Fall festival with her friends. After long minutes, I draw a horizontal line to see the way the girl would look if her jaw could be fixed, reinvented, if it weren't so lumpy and overgrown. I draw with a black line, in my head. And then, because I'm at a distance, staring, I squint and hold up a finger to nudge the line of her new jaw into place. But the new line doesn't work. Not at all. The next week, at a restaurant, in a booth across from me, is a younger girl with a half-sagging face and a bulging cheek. I go to work with my tools, sharp scalpel of sight, and pare her back to a simply chubby moon. I tack the sag up by her ear; I fix the slipped mouth. But her face is a soft curve of fine sand, a dune blown to an easy rise. It slips back into place and the fixing is wrong. The swell is like a velvet bag. *What lovely behaviour of silk sack clouds.* Throughout dinner she rested that cheek in her hand, as if she was thinking. Though I'm afraid she was hiding.
   "When the eye sees something beautiful, the hand wants to draw it," said Wittgenstein. And DaVinci wrote of the bodies he took apart to study, and to his colleagues inclined to work as he did "... if you should have a love for such things, you might be prevented by loathing ... and if this did not prevent you, perhaps you might not be able to draw so well as is necessary for such a dem-

onstration . . . or if you had the skill in drawing, it might not be combined with knowledge of perspective . . ."

And so forewarned, I'll try my hand: *Anthony touched my face with his stump.* We were 14. Anthony touched my face with his stump. I've said this phrase to myself for years. Sotto voce. Sometimes while walking. I say it in part because I like the beat, the variant anapests that beg another verse or want to break into hymn meter, and in part because that moment so impressed me. I hold the phrase itself up like an object of contemplation. His arm ended just below the elbow, this antic boy with raucous good humor, who played the trumpet and who, himself, called his arm "my stump." The sensation was like nothing else I knew. Not a head, not a nudge. Not a child's knee, not a ball. There was headlong force, texture, heat (this was summer on Long Island) and his unselfconscious desire, which instructed me.

In Botticelli's portrait of St. Sebastian, the one I've looked at most recently in my ongoing study of St. Sebastians, it's the outline of the arrows' shape, the many, whole arrowheads buried beneath the skin, lodged in the flesh and those slight hillocks there, where the tip entered and stuck that holds me. So well-focused and attended, it's more than a detail of the ecstasies of form: light, muscle, shadow. I think it's what Bottecelli wanted to paint most of all. The rise of flesh, *stippled, blue-bleak;* the body so changed and so reshaped, and how to praise that awful beauty—*pied. Plotted. Pierced.* I think this was the task he set himself.

At one time I would go so far as to get out of the tub to better hear my neighbors fighting. I'd reach, dripping and freezing, over the toilet and open the window to listen more closely. I'd wish away the noisy trains coupling down the street. I'd wish away my housemate talking in the driveway below so that I might log new accusations in their falling and rising cadences. I practiced seeing gestures, appointed gestures to their words in the steamy cold. Deformities of anger, gnashing twisted mouths, inner bile stirred and poisoning their postures. I wished them peace, I did. But when they screamed, I felt I could see the corners of mouths pull back. I felt the word "gnashing" freeze a mouth. Eyebrows slant like blades sharply down. They were real gargoyles perched and turned to stone.

All the better for sketching.

Sketching, I consider the line "These fragments I shore against my ruin"—from a time when so much was felt to be coming apart. But no. My fragments I shore to *reveal* my ruin. And all the similarities my eye is drawn to: flaw. Torque. Skew. I make a little pile by the shore: cracked horseshoe crab, ripped clam, wet ragged wing with feathers. I look because a thing is off, to locate the unlocatable in its features, forged as they are, or blunted, or blown. I look because the counter flashes its surprising grin.

My own deformities, of course, abound, but they are on the inside. I do not mean the flaws of reason, the insufficiencies of heart. I mean my spine fused and fixed in place with metal rods—all inside, except for the eleven months I wore a body cast. And then I was the walking ruin for all to see, the shore to keep in sight while sailing free.

The woman with the half-arm, no, a bit more than half an arm (it stopped below her elbow) stands chatting with her friends waiting for the bus. In a gesture she must have developed long ago, she rolls a magazine into a tube and slips her half-arm into it. How well and how long must the gesture have served, because, really, who hides an arm, a perfectly good arm, in a magazine? Whose, but a child's arm could be covered by a magazine, its length or its circumference?

One sees what one expects to see: "a magazine laid over the arm." But because I saw the arm slip in, I see instead her quiet strategy. And what does looking at her, what does knowing that teach me—since all along in here I've been practicing, letting the sight-of work on me. And recording, recording, recording. I am not her parent and so do not feel guilt. I am not her sister and so do not feel that dual reprieve/protectiveness. I call up the warmth of such an arm in my hand (I don't know if she says "stump"), the curve, the balance, its abrupt end and the ghost of its missing length. I feel, like a child, neither moral nor immoral saying this. I feel many things.

When the eye sees something beautiful the hand wants to draw it.

Or here's another way to say it: *a poem should not mean, but be.*

There is not, as many think, any air at all in a jellyfish, just organized cilia and bell muscles, a gelatinous scaffolding for hydrostatic propulsion. These simplest drifters are like bubbles of milky glass—and who doesn't want to see through to a thing's inner workings, the red nerves, and blood and poison with a clear pulse, circulating. And yet one scientist says "when thinking of jellies we have to suspend our bias towards hard skeletons with thick muscles and dense tissues." He means in order to see their particular beauty, to see *them*, we have to suspend our fear. We have to love contraction. Filtration. The word "gelatinous" too. The words "scull" and "buoyancy" are easy. We have to suspend "mucus web." And realize that their bioluminescence, which is a show to see at night, is used to confuse and startle prey. You can look right through them. As if into a lit front room when it's night outside.

Of course, we peer into houses at night not because they're beautiful, but because we want to see what's going on in there—illuminated, partial, and beckoning.

I've carried this image for a long time now: the port-wine birthmark on the girl's pale face. All that summer at the beach, the mark was like a harbor, or what I knew of the shore, growing up near the ocean as I did. Tidal, it crept up near her eye and stayed like a dampness. I felt I was supposed to separate that color—velvety, royal, berry-like—from its place: her face, where it shouldn't be. But I could not get the color to be unlovely. And I could not remove the mark from her face.

Magda, who worked at my favorite lunch counter in Warsaw, had the lovely plain face of a farm girl. When she laughed, her white teeth shone and the scar in the middle of her chin puckered. And when she looked past me, into the distance, one eye rolled to the side. Her left eye was fixed in place during our conversations as she ladled out the borscht with beans I ordered every day. And every day, I'd wait to see it slip away—the whiteness, the angle, the variation: the hand wants to draw it. If that which is beautiful is balanced and symmetrical, a "pleasing unity," then the unbeautiful's more a form of inter-ruption—like a gasp. A catch in breath. The unbeautiful's a form made of interruptions—a rough hand passed over wool's nap, snagging. And passed over again and again for the snag. It's a moment that catches your attention. It's a moment into which you fall, as when on a crowded bus, hot crowded subway, you forget yourself and enter some other, less populated world by an unexpected door: a woman's earlobe, deeply notched; the close back of a man's neck, oily and creased; a girl's cracked lip; a freckle; a boil; a split thumbnail with its crescent of dirt, next to which your own nail rests on the cool, aluminum pole.

Forest Beloved

Janisse Ray

Maybe a vision of the original longleaf pine flatwoods has been endowed to me through genes because I seem to remember their endlessness. I seem to recollect when these coastal plains were one big, brown-and-tan, daybreak-to-dark longleaf forest. It was a monotony one learned to love, for this is a place that, like a friend, offers multiplied loyalty with the passing years. A forest never tells its secrets but reveals them slowly over time, and a longleaf forest is full of secrets.

I know a few of them.

Longleaf pines are long-lived, reaching ages over five hundred years. As trees mature, their heartwood becomes so heavy and thick with resins that saw blades bounce away from it, and if saw teeth manage to enter the grain, they quickly gum up and dull. Heartwood mills a strong everlasting timber the color of ripe amber that earned longleaf the name "heart pine." Parcels of the tree, especially stumps and the area of the heart, are more heavily tamped with resin, and that wood is called "fat lightered," though people use the two names interchangeably, "heart pine" and "fat lightered," and sometimes they say only "fat," as in "Put another piece of that fat on the fire." It is so rich with concentrated, cured sap that it burns like a flare and has long been used, in very small pieces, as kindling; the resinous knots were early lanterns.

In the heart rests both the tree's strength and its weakness. After about ninety years, pines often are infected with red heart, a nonmortal fungus that makes the heartwood softer, more porous, and more flammable, and that often hollows out the pine and makes of it a refuge.

You don't think about diversity when you look at a longleaf. In a fully functioning longleaf woodland, tree diversity is low. A single species of pine reigns in an open monologue of tall timbers (except on sandhills where occurs an understory of turkey, post, and bluejack oak). The trees grow spaced so far apart in pine savannas, sunshine bathing the ground, that you can see forever; they are as much grassland as forest. The limbs of longleaf pine are gray and scaly and drape as the tree matures, and its needles are very long, up to seventeen inches, like a piano player's fingers, and held upright at ends of the limbs, like a bride holds her bouquet. In 1791, naturalist and explorer William Bartram, in his *Travels*, called the Southern pinelands a "vast forest of the most stately pine trees that can be imagined."

The ground cover, a comforter laid on the land, contains the diversity. *Wiregrass* dominates—it's a flammable, thin-leaved, yellowish bunchgrass that grows calf-high and so thick it resembles a mop head. From this sinewy matrix of wiregrass all manners of forbs, grasses, and low shrubs poke up. At every step, another leaf shape or petal form begs examination and documentation.

Meadow beauty. Liatris. Greeneyes. Summer farewell. Bracken fern. Golden aster. Sandhill blazing star. Goat's rue. Yellow-eyed grass. Purple balduina. Beautiful pawpaw. Pineland hoary pea. Wireleaf dropseed. Hair grass. Little bluestem. Lopside Indian grass. Toothache grass. Britton's beargrass. Gopher apple. Dwarf live oak. Low-bush blueberry. Blackberry. Runner oaks. Splitbeard bluestem. Honeycomb head. Croton. Clammey weed. Dog tongue. Rayless goldenrod. Narrow-leaf sunflower. Black-eyed Susan. Dwarf wax myrtle. New Jersey tea. Inkberry. Dwarf chinquapin. Cooley's meadowrue. Chaffseed. Sandhills milkvetch. Spurge ipecac. Wireweed. Sandwort. Blue lupine. Winter-flowering pixie-moss. Clasping warea. Pigeon wing. Toothed savory. Hairy wild indigo.

One hundred ninety-one species of rare vascular plants are associated with longleaf/wiregrass, 122 of these endangered or threatened.

When John Muir conducted what he termed his "floral pilgrimage" to the Gulf in 1867, somewhere on the fall line between Thomson and Augusta, Georgia, he described "the northern limit of the remarkable longleafed pine, a tree from sixty to seventy feet in height, from twenty to thirty inches in diameter, with leaves ten to fifteen inches long, in dense radiant masses at the ends of the naked branches.

"The wood is strong, hard and very resinous," he wrote. "It makes excellent ship spars, bridge timbers, and flooring." Later he added, "I thank the Lord with all my heart for his goodness in granting me admission to this magnificent realm."

What thrills me most about longleaf forests is how the pine trees sing. The horizontal limbs of flattened crowns hold the wind as if they are vessels, singing bowls, and air stirs in them like a whistling kettle. I lie in thick grasses covered with sun and listen to the music made there. This music cannot be heard anywhere else on the earth.

Rustle, whisper, shiver, whinny. Aria, chorus, ballad, chant. Lullaby. In the choirs of the original groves, the music must have resounded for hundreds of miles in a single note of rise and fall, lift and wane, and stirred the red-cockaded woodpeckers nesting in the hearts of these pines, where I also nest, child of soft heart. Now we strain to hear the music; anachronous, it has an edge. It falters, a great tongue chopped to pieces.

Something happens to you in an old-growth forest. At first you are curious to see the tremendous girth and height of the trees, and you sally forth, eager. You start to saunter, then amble, slower and slower, first like a fox and then an armadillo and then a tortoise, until you are trudging at the pace of an earthworm, and then even slower, the pace of a sassafras leaf's turning. The blood begins to languish in your veins, until you think it has turned to sap. You hanker to touch the trees and embrace them and lean your face against their bark, and you do. You smell them. You look up at leaves so high their shapes are beyond focus, into far branches with circumferences as thick as most trees.

Every limb of your body becomes weighted, and you have to prop yourself up. There's this strange current of energy running skyward, like a thousand tiny bells tied to your capillaries, ringing with your heartbeat. You sit and lean against one trunk—it's like leaning against a house or a mountain. The trunk is your spine, the nerve centers reaching into other worlds, below ground and above. You stand and press your body into the ancestral and enduring, arms wide, and your fingers do not touch. You wonder how big the unseen gap.

If you stay in one place too long, you know you'll root.

I drink old-growth forest in like water. This is the homeland that built us. Here I walk shoulder to shoulder with history—my history. I am in the presence of something ancient and venerable, perhaps of time itself, its unhurried passing marked by immensity and stolidity, each year purged by fire, cinched by a ring. Here mortality's roving hands grapple with air. I can see my place as human in a natural order more grand, whole and functional than I've ever witnessed, and I am humbled, not frightened, by it. Comforted. It is as if a round table springs up in the cathedral of pines and God graciously pulls out a chair for me, and I no longer have to worry about what happens to souls.

This Nature

Pattiann Rogers

Bach is nature, and the Marquis de Sade is nature. Florence Nightingale and the Iron Maiden are nature. Michelangelo's Pietà, the swastika, Penthouse magazine and solar flares are nature. Pedophiles and saints equally are nature. Ash pits, boggy graves, nuclear bombs, tubercle bacillus, Yosemite Falls, abortion, the polio vaccine, all are part of the sum total of everything that is and therefore nature. Nothing that is goes against nature, because nature is the way things are. Nature is what is, everything that is, everything that has been, and everything that is possible, including human actions, inventions, creations, and imaginations. This is my definition. This nature is the nature of roaches and cheetahs and honeysuckle, the nature of a Strauss waltz, the nature of the Ice Ages, the Black Plague, the eruption of Krakatoa, the nature of the slaughter of American bison, the nature of human sacrifice and bloody rituals carried out by Aztecs, Celts, Slavs.

Nothing that exists, including language, is outside nature. We do not know an "outside nature," because knowledge itself is an element of nature. Even the word "unnatural" is part of nature (how could it otherwise be here on this page?) and is therefore self-contradictory.

An ice pick through the chest or a soothing hand on the forehead, both are natural, both gestures of nature. Wild curly dock, malaria, exploding stars, continental drift, and the construction of Hoover Dam are natural, part of what is. Violent birth and violent extinction are older than we are and natural. We know a history of both. We have sometimes been involved in the nature of both. We cannot legitimately use the word "natural" as synonymous with the words "unsullied," "pure," or "righteous."

It is no more against nature for human beings to clearcut a forest than it is against nature for Mt. Vesuvius to erupt and eliminate the town of Herculaneum. Human actions may be judged moral or immoral, wise or unwise, cruel or benevolent, heedless or thoughtful, but those are other terms and other issues. I am speaking of nature. Everything that we name noble is nature, and everything that we name despicable is nature, and our attempt to distinguish between the noble and the despicable is nature.

Calculus, astrophysics, the automobile, the safety pin, and billboards were created by creatures born of the natural world and thus included naturally in the nature of everything that is. If we create justice, it exists in nature. If we act so as to bring compassion into existence, it is real within the natural world.

Divinity is of the universe, part of nature, when it is observed and noted and imagined and expressed by creatures born of nature with physical, blood-beating, light-snapping minds. We are thoroughly nature. To claim otherwise is to attempt to place human beings and everything we do in some rare unimaginable realm beyond the universe, thus rendering the power of our origins lost and our obligations vague.

Nature is everything that is. We are not and cannot be "unnatural." Our choices and our actions are never for or against nature. They are always simply of nature. Our decisions then involve determining what it is that we value among this everything-that-is, this nature. What is it we seek to preserve? to eliminate? to modify? to accept? to avoid? to cherish? to respect? to emulate? The decisions we make, how we justify and construct those decisions and the behavior that results, all these become part of the great milieu, and they have their effects in ways we may not always recognize. Our choices and our actions, whether based on aesthetic considerations, moral or spiritual considerations, economic considerations, or rational considerations, must be justified in some way other than by the claim that they are in accord with the natural world; for any behavior, even murder, even suicide, even war, even abuse of the young, can be justified by that claim. We may call these particular acts horrors, but they are horrors that are part of nature, part of everything that is, and they cannot be said to go against nature. They are horrors that are part of nature already replete with horrors. Perhaps these particular acts go against our sense of goodness or compassion, morality or beauty or justice, but they do not go against nature. Annihilation and creation are occurring constantly around us now, and they have occurred always, long before human beings came to be. Nature encompasses all contradictions.

This nature is not a single entity, not a consistent force that sanctions or condemns behavior, not a god-substitute that we can embrace or blame or escape. It composes the entire, complex myriad of ever-changing events and details, unpredictable, paradoxical, passing and eternal, known and mysterious. Nature is the vast expanse of abstractions and multiplicities; it is the void and the concrete presence, an unrestricted inclusiveness. The definition of the word "nature" even includes its own definition and the maker of its definition. It is self-referential.

I deliberately seek out the specific aspects of everything that is that I find ennobling, affirming, that engender in me hope, faith, action, and health, the chaos and mystery that energizes me. I select and cling to them. I choose to value and praise them. Just a few of these aspects, for me, are the words of Shakespeare, Dostoyevsky, Whitman, Melville, Twain, Faulkner, Roethke, Jacob Bronowski, Jesus Christ; the music of Chopin, Beethoven, Bruckner, Anne-Sophie Mutter, the Takács Quartet; the very existence of the body of preserved art, music, and literature that is my culture; the Magna Carta, the

Constitution of the United States and the Bill of Rights; arches, domes, and columns; the grace and order of an NBA basketball game; Jeremy Brett as Sherlock Holmes; the curiosity, facility, and complexity of the human mind that results in the revelations of science; the way sunlight appears—shifting its illuminations and colors on roofs and gardens and fields, making shadows of trees on the curtains—throughout the gradual coming of morning, throughout the patterns of evening, everyday, the gift of morning and evening; snow, that amazement; the surrounding great buffer of stars in which we are immersed; life in its unrelenting, ruthless, self-absorbed, tenacious grasp on being.

We are fortunate as human beings to have the opportunity to discern and to act, to recognize and experience ourselves in this welter of terror and beauty, to add our praise, gratitude, and testimony to the totality of everything that is, to place them as if we were placing seeds in soil into the flux and form of this nature.

Why She Won't Leave: My Mother's Blues

Sheryl St. Germain

My mother's sitting in her ruined backyard, the one haunted by the memories of children and swing sets, sandboxes, plastic pools, and Slip 'n Slides. Almost everything that wasn't knocked down, split in two, or uprooted by Katrina was drowned or damaged by the water that covered the yard for no one knows how many days. Skeletons of shade-giving pecan and avocado trees, hibiscus, bay leaf, holly, and the snaky vines of wisteria remind her of how vibrant this yard used to be. Once, there was even an addition to the house back here, a small room with large, screened windows and a ceiling fan where she and my father played card games late at night with friends, a room where he drank scotch and she drank wine and where they talked about the future.

My mother is sitting on a porch swing that is set on a cracked and roof-less cement floor, all that's left of that room she and my father added onto the house, and that was destroyed by another hurricane years ago. Her neighbor's house is empty, the tree that stabbed its heart still there, upside down, the treetop buried in the house, the roots reaching out to the sky. If she looks at it in just the right light, it almost looks alive, with the roots curling around like woody dreadlocks, like a living Medusa.

My mother is drinking a glass of wine and listening to music, a mix of New Orleans jazz and blues. She's not listening to anything intellectual or edgy, no Coltrane or Charlie Parker, not anything like what her daughter who doesn't live here anymore might listen to. No, she's listening to music she's always listened to, music that reminds her of people she loved who are gone, and her youth, which is gone, and her city, which also feels gone, and she's listening to music that deepens the sadness she already feels, and somehow the music's sadness combined with her own grief makes her feel exquisitely present in what has become her life in this city, and that's somehow weirdly better than actually feeling better. The music resonates with something ancient and animal inside her body, and she feels like the vibrating string of that resonance.

The music is coming from the back window of the living room, which she's left open, and she's turned it up loud because the cars on Williams Boulevard make lots of noise, and now that the airport, just a couple miles away, is back in business, the sound of planes often seems to speak for the sky, and the sound of planes is not music, will never be music, and even after almost fifty years of living in this house, the sound of planes still makes her feel helpless.

I don't know exactly what she's listening to since she's alone and I'm not there, but if I had to guess, I'd say she's listening to something with piano in it, since she loves piano: She's the one who insisted all five of her kids take lessons, who negotiated those free lessons from a neighbor. She was the one who scraped and saved to pay for a piano over many years, though she never touched it except to dust or move it.

She might be listening to Professor Longhair or Dr. John or Fats Domino or James Booker. She loves the way those New Orleans guys punch the piano, how they mix up blues and boogie-woogie and the parade rhythms of carnival, all sloppy and sexy-like. The piano also reminds her of her mother, who played by ear. *New Awleans*, Dr. John croons, *city of a million dreams, you never know how nice it seems when you way down South in New Awleans.*

My mother sips her wine, thinks of her life as a child growing up in the Quarter, *Yes it's true I got those Basin Street blues.* She thinks of JazzFest and seeing James Booker there years ago; she and her friends will go again this year even though her legs hurt more and more as she gets older and it gets more and more painful for her to walk. She doesn't want to think about that much, but she knows she probably only has a few more years where she'll be able to walk unaided.

James Booker. Only *he* sounds like this—that heartbroken, raw piano. Only someone who spent time in Angola, she thinks, could play like that. *I went down to St. James Infirmary, I heard my baby cry,* he sings, *I was so brokenhearted, she was gone somewhere, in the bye and bye.*

My mother is alone in her backyard because her parents are dead and her husband is dead and her two sons are dead and her sister and two brothers are dead and her two daughters do not live in this city that she will not leave. Her daughters live in nice Northern cities that are safe, with less crime than New Orleans, cities far from hurricanes and floods, but they are not *interesting* cities, in my mother's opinion, and this is still the most damning thing she can say about another city, that it's just not *interesting.* And besides, people talk different in those cities, and those cities are not *this city,* this city where she was born, this city where she had sex for the first and last time, this city where she married, then birthed and raised five children, this city where her sons, her husband, her mother and father and grandmother and grandfather and great-grandmother and great-grandfather and great-great grandparents and great-great-great grandparents are buried. Two hundred years of ancestors are buried in this muddy soil. She will not leave them; she will not desert them as her daughters have deserted her. *Down the road, came junco partner, he was loaded as he could be . . . knocked out, and loaded, and he was wobblin' all over the street.* Only here, she thinks, would we sing songs celebrating drunks, and she drinks a drink to my father, tilting her glass to the Medusa tree in her neighbor's yard.

Those cities her daughters live in don't have food like they have here, either, she thinks, no thick-rouxed gumbos and jambalayas and Creole sauces and crawfish and crabs and oysters and shrimp and red beans and rice, and roast beef po-boys, and they don't have *interestingly* named streets like *Desire* or *Tchoupitoulas* or *Melpomene* or *Humanity*, she thinks, and what can you say, really, about the imagination of cities that give their streets names like *Main* or *First* or *Second*, and what about cities that don't have King Cakes, or voodoo dolls or beads or Mardi Gras or crawfish festivals or rice festivals or oyster festivals, and those people in those other cities don't have the Mississippi *and* Lake Pontchartrain and they don't smell like this city, spicy and rank and full of color, and she's certain they don't even have a sense of humor, or *interesting* politicians, and she thinks that maybe people in those other cities might not even know how to dance, really, and they don't have the Saints or Al Hirt or Pete Fountain and now that I think of it, maybe that's what she's listening to as she sits alone in her backyard. Maybe she's listening to Pete Fountain's clarinet all high and sweet like a gladiola, and maybe she's singing along *when the saints go marchin' in, oh lord, I want to be in that number*, and how could she leave New Orleans now, now when the Saints are doing so well? She remembers when all the fans wore paper bags on their heads and called themselves the *Aints* because they were so embarrassed at how bad the team was, but they went to games anyway, and she remembers when Archie Manning wasn't yet the father of Peyton, but the redheaded hero of the Saints, and now that they're so good, it would be wrong to leave, all that time wasted on them when they were bad, and she drinks to that, and maybe it's trumpet she's listening to, maybe loungy Al Hirt, maybe he's blowing "Do You Know What It Means to Miss New Orleans?" She and my father used to go to his club on Bourbon, and she still likes to go now and visit his statue in the Quarter, touch his trumpet, and remember all that is gone.

My mother is sitting alone in the swing my brother gave her on Mother's Day the year before he died, the year before Katrina, and even though it's already rusted she thinks she will never not use it, she will never give it away, she will never move away from this swing. There's just room enough for her to sit comfortably on it without someone else and now she's swinging to the *drip drop drip drop* of Fats Domino, *I'm walkin' to New Awlins*, and she's thinking about music and sorrow and music and forgetting and music and remembering, and she's thinking of how important music is to this city and how it's not important in this way to any other city, and even though one of her daughters lives in a big city in the Northeast where she says there's lots of jazz, my mother knows in her bones it's not like it is here, music here is the voice of the city, but in this other city, where her daughter lives, she's certain the music is just some extra thing, some little curlicue, something nice—she's sure it's very nice—but it's not *necessary* like it is here, and she's certain this city would die if it couldn't sing, and she drinks to that. *Jackomo fe nan e', Jackomo fe nan e', you don't like what the big chief say Jackomo fe nan e'.*

She pushes herself in the swing and all of a sudden she realizes almost all the songs she loves from this city are riffs and "improvisations"—a word her daughter likes to use—on loss—*brother, brother, brother John is gone. . . When the levee breaks, I'll have no place to stay.*

How could she go to another city where music and food were not the breath and heart of it? She's sure she'd feel like an alien, living somewhere else, somewhere not here, with all her records and cookbooks and history books and Mardi Gras beads and colorful old-lady clothes and costumes; people would just see her as an eccentric old woman. Here, she thinks as she swings, here I am someone, here the earth knows me, the water loves me. Here I'm a native. I've lived here so long, she thinks, the air smells like me, the trees and the bushes sometimes look like me, and when I die I'll just switch one shape for another.

My mother is sitting alone in her backyard because she's sad, and it seems better to be alone when she's sad. I'm old, she thinks, I am an old woman, and who wants to look at an old woman? She has girlfriends, and she knows they don't care about how old she is. They have an informal club and they sometimes all wear purple like in that poem "When I Am an Old Woman I Shall Wear Purple." She could call one of her friends to come sit with her now, but most of her friends are sad, too, and she doesn't want to make them even sadder. *My grandma and your grandma, sittin' by the fire, my grandma told your grandma, I'm gonna set your flag on fire, talking 'bout hey now, hey now Iko Iko an de'.*

It's getting dark now, the mosquitoes are out, and she slaps at her arms and thinks about going in. Later maybe one of her friends will call her up and they'll go to a movie or out to listen to some music. They'll still be sad, though, because this city they love and will not abandon is so sick and broken and stinking. It's like a child, or a parent you love very much who is alcoholic or addicted or has been in a horrible accident and is now a quadriplegic, she thinks. Sometimes it seems to my mother that everyone who still lives in this city is depressed, although they are all trying not to be. They're sad because some of them are still living in trailers and some of them, like my mother, still have not had their houses repaired. The city is old, too, a gone pecan. *We're all gone pecans*, she says to herself, looking at the thousands of rotting pecans on the floor of the backyard. She's sad because it's hard for her to believe the city will ever be the same, and she wants it, she needs it, to be the same.

Maybe she's listening now to saxophone or clarinet, which she also loves. Maybe it's Lester Young's version of "Summertime," which she used to sing to me when I was a child, or "The Man I Love," a song that does not make her think of my father but rather of the boy she did not marry, the boy she didn't have a chance to fall out of love with. Or Sidney Bechet's "Black and Blue" or Louis Armstrong's. *What did I do to be so . . . .*

They call it stormy Monday, but Tuesday's just as bad. Lord and Wednesday's worse, Thursday's also sad. That's what it's like now, my mother thinks. Every day nothing's being done to help us and maybe soon I won't even remember what it used to be like, but she thinks if she keeps listening to the music, maybe it will help her remember.

My mother is sitting alone in her backyard feeling sorry for herself and not wanting to feel sorry for herself. She knows depression is a selfish thing, like a little cloud she carries around that keeps her from doing much for anyone, especially herself. She's sitting alone thinking of the last time she went out with one of her friends and of how they drove by the Lower Ninth and they saw again that the houses were still knifed into each other; and of how they went by the marina and Lake Pontchartrain where she loves to sit and dangle her feet in the water like she did when she was a kid and the boats were still all scrambled up. I'm seventy-five years old, she thinks, and maybe you just get more alone when you get older and maybe nothing will ever be fixed, and she thinks about how she's too old to fix anything, not even herself.

And as I write this I'm sitting here alone, like my mother, in my own bedroom in some Northeast city, listening to music, and it occurs to me all of a sudden that I'm not writing about my mother at all, that I'm writing about myself, my own loneliness and despair and love of the music she taught me to love, the music of our city, the city and music she won't leave, and I'm talking about *see that guy all dressed in green, Iko Iko an de'* and I'm talking about *Summertime and the livin' is easy* and I'm talking about *Brother John* and I'm talking about *I'm going back to Louisiana* and I'm talking about *Mama Roux!* and I'm talking about *way down yonder in New Orleans* and I'm talking about *I got my jambalaya crawfish pieya* and I'm talking about *when the levee breaks* and I'm talking about *I got nowhere to go* and I'm talking about I got *my saints marchin' in* and I'm talking about going down to *St. James Infirmary* and I'm talking about *I'm gonna be in that number* and I'm talking about *when junco partner comes down the road loaded* like my father, *knocked out, knocked out and loaded,* and I'm talking about my gone brother, I'm talking about *brother brother, brother* Jay *is gone* and I'm talking about *I know what it means to miss New Orleans.*

The Veil

Marjane Satrapi

THIS IS ME WHEN I WAS 10 YEARS OLD. THIS WAS IN 1980.

AND THIS IS A CLASS PHOTO. I'M SITTING ON THE FAR LEFT SO YOU DON'T SEE ME. FROM LEFT TO RIGHT: GOLNAZ, MAHSHID, NARINE, MINNA.

IN 1979 A REVOLUTION TOOK PLACE. IT WAS LATER CALLED "THE ISLAMIC REVOLUTION".

THEN CAME 1980: THE YEAR IT BECAME OBLIGATORY TO WEAR THE VEIL AT SCHOOL.

WEAR THIS!

WE DIDN'T REALLY LIKE TO WEAR THE VEIL, ESPECIALLY SINCE WE DIDN'T UNDERSTAND WHY WE HAD TO.

IT'S TOO HOT OUT!

EXECUTION IN THE NAME OF FREEDOM.

GIVE ME MY VEIL BACK!

YOU'LL HAVE TO LICK MY FEET!

OOH! I'M THE MONSTER OF DARKNESS.

GIDDYAP!

AND ALSO BECAUSE THE YEAR BEFORE, IN 1979, WE WERE IN A FRENCH NON-RELIGIOUS SCHOOL.

WHERE BOYS AND GIRLS WERE TOGETHER.

AND THEN SUDDENLY IN 1980...

ALL BILINGUAL SCHOOLS MUST BE CLOSED DOWN.

THEY ARE SYMBOLS OF CAPITALISM.

BRAVO!

WHAT WISDOM!

OF DECADENCE.

THIS IS CALLED A "CULTURAL REVOLUTION."

WE FOUND OURSELVES VEILED AND SEPARATED FROM OUR FRIENDS.

AND THAT WAS THAT...

EVERYWHERE IN THE STREETS THERE WERE DEMONSTRATIONS FOR AND AGAINST THE VEIL.

the veil! the veil! the veil! the veil! the veil!

freedom! freedom! freedom! freedom! freedom!

AT ONE OF THE DEMONSTRATIONS, A GERMAN JOURNALIST TOOK A PHOTO OF MY MOTHER.

I WAS REALLY PROUD OF HER. HER PHOTO WAS PUBLISHED IN ALL THE EUROPEAN NEWSPAPERS.

AND EVEN IN ONE MAGAZINE IN IRAN. MY MOTHER WAS REALLY SCARED.

HAVE YOU SEEN THIS?

DON'T WORRY, DARLING.

SHE DYED HER HAIR,

AND WORE DARK GLASSES FOR A LONG TIME,

299

I REALLY DIDN'T KNOW WHAT TO THINK ABOUT THE VEIL. DEEP DOWN I WAS VERY RELIGIOUS BUT AS A FAMILY WE WERE VERY MODERN AND AVANT-GARDE.

I WAS BORN WITH RELIGION.

AT THE AGE OF SIX I WAS ALREADY SURE I WAS THE LAST PROPHET. THIS WAS A FEW YEARS BEFORE THE REVOLUTION.

O' Celestial light!

BEFORE ME THERE HAD BEEN A FEW OTHERS.

A WOMAN?

I AM THE LAST PROPHET.

I WANTED TO BE A PROPHET...

BECAUSE OUR MAID DID NOT EAT WITH US.

BECAUSE MY FATHER HAD A CADILLAC.

AND, ABOVE ALL, BECAUSE MY GRANDMOTHER'S KNEES ALWAYS ACHED.

COME HERE MARJI! HELP ME TO STAND UP.

DON'T WORRY, SOON YOU WON'T HAVE ANY MORE PAIN. YOU'LL SEE.

LIKE ALL MY PREDECESSORS I HAD MY HOLY BOOK.

THE FIRST THREE RULES CAME FROM ZARATHUSTRA. HE WAS THE FIRST PROPHET IN MY COUNTRY BEFORE THE ARAB INVASION.

YOU MUST BASE EVERYTHING ON THESE THREE RULES: BEHAVE WELL, SPEAK WELL, ACT WELL.

I ALSO WANTED US TO CELEBRATE THE TRADITIONAL ZARATHUSTRIAN HOLIDAYS, LIKE THE FIRE CEREMONY,

BEFORE THE PERSIAN NEW YEAR, NOROUZ, ON MARCH 21ST, THE FIRST DAY OF SPRING.

ONLY MY GRANDMOTHER KNEW ABOUT MY BOOK.

RULE NUMBER SIX: EVERYBODY SHOULD HAVE A CAR.

RULE NUMBER SEVEN: ALL MAIDS SHOULD EAT AT THE TABLE WITH THE OTHERS.

RULE NUMBER EIGHT: NO OLD PERSON SHOULD HAVE TO SUFFER.

IN THAT CASE, I'LL BE YOUR FIRST DISCIPLE.

REALLY?

BUT TELL ME HOW YOU'LL ARRANGE FOR OLD PEOPLE NOT TO SUFFER?

IT WILL SIMPLY BE FORBIDDEN.

EVERY NIGHT I HAD A BIG DISCUSSION WITH GOD.

GOD, GIVE ME SOME MORE TIME, I AM NOT QUITE READY YET.

YES YOU ARE, CELESTIAL LIGHT, YOU ARE MY CHOICE, MY LAST AND MY BEST CHOICE.

EXCEPT FOR MY GRANDMOTHER I WAS OBVIOUSLY THE ONLY ONE WHO BELIEVED IN MYSELF.

WHAT DO YOU WANT TO BE WHEN YOU GROW UP?

I'LL BE A PROPHET.

HAHA! HAHA! HAHA!

SHE'S CRAZY.

MY PARENTS WERE CALLED IN BY THE TEACHER.

YOUR CHILD IS DISTURBED. SHE WANTS TO BECOME A PROPHET.

WHAT ABOUT IT?

DOESN'T THIS WORRY YOU?

NO! NOT AT ALL!

NONETHELESS, MY PARENTS WERE PUZZLED.

SO TELL ME, MY CHILD, WHAT DO YOU WANT TO BE WHEN YOU GROW UP?

A PROPHET.

I WANT TO BE A DOCTOR.

THAT'S FINE MY LOVE. THAT'S FINE.

I FELT GUILTY TOWARDS GOD.

YOU WANT TO BE A DOCTOR? I THOUGHT THAT...

NO, NO, I WILL BE A PROPHET BUT THEY MUSTN'T KNOW.

I WANTED TO BE JUSTICE, LOVE AND THE WRATH OF GOD ALL IN ONE.

303

Anniversary

Ruth L. Schwartz

Forty-five years ago today, my parents got married. My mother was a beautiful bride whose starched white dress hid her growing belly from all but the most careful observers. A naive, eager redhead from the wrong side of the tracks, she had just finished at Great Neck South High School two months before. "Lore the whore," some of her classmates had called her, though it wasn't true; she'd been a virgin when my parents met.

My father was a smart, insecure pre-medical student from Queens. He was short and had acne, but he also possessed a brash charm. On their first date he picked my mother up in his father's fifteen-year-old Chrysler, with classical music blaring incongruously from the stereo. His eagerness matched hers, and my mother's mother hissed, "Marry him! He's a good catch!" Years later, when my mother became a feminist, stopped wearing a bra, and wrote poems, she would write about my conception on the soiled corduroy couch in her parents' den. Years later, when my sister and I fought in the back seat of our parents' car, my father would remind us that we were both the products of *coitus interruptus*. "Stop being advertisements for birth control," he would say.

After the wedding, my father moved out of his dorm at Hobart-William Smith College—he'd wanted, badly, to join a fraternity, but none of them took Jewish boys then—and into a small apartment with my mother. Raccoons played cymbals with garbage can lids, the next-door neighbors' fights bled through the thin walls, and my mother cried every day for weeks—she'd never been away from her mother for that long before. She also got up early each morning, sneaking out of bed to put on just a little make-up before my father saw her.

They were kids together. She called him "Puppy"; he called her "Kitten." They bought an antique cradle at an auction, but they didn't know about burping babies, so I got colic, and wailed. My mother still tells how she sat down next to the cradle and sobbed along with me.

My parents were never truly hippies, but they had great disdain for the conventional. My mother wore fluorescent peasant dresses laced with rawhide; my father grew his sideburns long. They kept their television in the closet. They taught me the phrase "pecuniary canons of taste" when I was seven, the same year they bought me pet chickens for our urban back yard. They taught me to question authority, long before the bumper sticker came along. When my third-grade teacher hauled me from my seat and slapped me for talking back to her, they almost got her fired.

My parents' marriage lasted thirteen or sixteen years, depending on how you count. By year twelve, my father was throwing wine glasses at my mother, muttering that he was a slave under her whip. He was chewing up the insides of his mouth because he'd gotten hooked on amphetamines during his surgical residency, a year of long work hours and an even longer commute. My mother had gotten breast implants, done for free by one of my father's colleagues— "professional courtesy," it was called. She says my father shamed her into it by calling her Larry instead of Lorie, and telling her my breasts would soon be bigger than hers. My mother maintains to this day that she never wanted the surgery, she saw it as mutilation. My father maintains to this day that my mother's small breasts were just fine with him, he only arranged the surgery because she insisted on it. My mother says she did it in a last-ditch effort to keep him—she saw his eyes wander to the jiggle under other womens' blouses, she knew he'd had many affairs already, and would have more. My father says there was only one affair, only one.

By year thirteen, my father had moved out. He bought a Jaguar and a cottage in the woods, to which he brought as many women as he could. My mother dated younger men, wore tight shirts to show off her new breasts. Briefly they reconciled, took a trip to Mexico—where my father researched the red-light district, and my mother danced salsa with every guy in the bar. "You always half-try so damn hard," she wrote to him in a poem afterward. Puppy and Kitten had turned into Dog and Cat.

By year sixteen, my father had remarried—two weeks before my parents' divorce was actually final, as it turned out. His new wife was a dyed-blonde WASP who brought a red, white and blue jello mold to the picnic where we first met. My mother was being courted by a fat, bald, bossy brute who also happened to be another Jewish doctor. They married three months later, and I left home for good—in every sense of the word.

But this isn't what I wanted to say. This doesn't say it at all.

What if I could say it differently—let all the streams of beauty and damage pour out from me and over me, a fountain strewn with pennies and wishes, littered with cigarettes? What if I could say how hopeful she was, how shy and bold and full of longing— how ardent he was, how frightened and filled with bravado and need? What if I could cut through the sludge of my anger and heartbreak at who they became, my grief at what they suffered in the becoming—and finally embrace my parents, those unwise gods?

The summer my mother was six, her parents left her alone at sleepover camp. They snuck away without saying goodbye—that was, they explained later, what the camp counselors had advised. My mother panicked. She cried so long and hard she couldn't eat or sleep. She wrote her mother daily—anguished six-year-old epistles—but the counselors never mailed the letters.

At eight, my father was a musical prodigy. He could sit down at the piano and play a song, any song, even if he'd heard it just once on the radio. His mother pounced on this gift, forced him to practice every day. Her efforts backfired; my father rebelled, the music withered inside him.

My mother's grade-school teachers missed her dyslexia, diagnosed her as slow, told her she "wasn't college material." She spent her childhood hearing her parents say, "Helen is the smart one, Lorie is the pretty one." Though she'd later complete all the coursework for a Ph.D. in English and, later still, publish six books, she would always believe her looks were all she had.

My father was the apple of his mother's eye, the golden boy who could do no wrong—even when he showed up at my grandmother's doorstep so broke she had to pay the cabbie, and went into withdrawal on her sofabed. And it was hard work being golden, and doing no wrong. He needed the uppers to keep going when it wasn't human to keep going, and then the downers, afterward, so he could finally sleep. He was an E.R. doctor, a good one. He wrote a textbook that defined the field. He saved lives. And he destroyed his own.

My mother was terrified of loss, and of the shame she'd felt when she couldn't match the clothes and hairstyles of the rich girls at Great Neck South. So she married the bossy brute with money, stayed with him through over twenty years of cruelty and humiliation. I was her "Child Sister," as she addressed me in a poem once, and her confidant. So I could tell you what he said and did to her in bed. I could tell you about the times he knocked her down, or how he shot the fuzzy ducklings that paddled like toys in their swimming pool, while my mother cried.

Forty-five happy years, say the websites, when I google "anniversary." The traditional gift is sapphires, but blue flowers may be given instead. And what is "happy," anyway, and where does this story end? My mother never broke it off with the brute, but took a lover instead. He has no money, is neither Jewish nor doctor, but he is good to her. All those narcotics prescriptions caught up with my father; he lost his medical license last year. Now, on the phone from his mother's condo in Florida, slurring his words, he still maintains he was framed.

And which stories do I choose to tell, and which do I leave out? Why haven't I said my father always kept a bottle of champagne in the trunk of the car—because, he'd say, "You never know when you might need to celebrate"? Why don't I say my mother loved sex, and taught me to love it, too? Why don't I say that every time I see a "No Trespassing" sign, I remember how my father would say impishly, "But it doesn't say *Absolutely* No Trespassing," and keep walking?

I learned many things from my parents. They taught me the subjectivity of truth; they made it impossible for me to ever arrive at a single, definitive version of anything. They showed me the traps minds make for themselves, the way the early wounds can calcify and weaken, warp and deform the eager, ardent child-brides and grooms in all of us. I look at my father and vow to embrace my fears, rather than go down in his stubborn flames. I look at my mother and vow to take risks, rather than suffocate in her luxurious prison.

Forty-five years ago today, my parents got married. I want to say something that honors all of the truths. I want words faceted as sapphires, words that hold blue flowers in their arms.

Pissed Off at Three Years and Four Months

Lawrence Sutin

One theory of life development is that we are designed never to understand ourselves. Those who think they come to any final understanding are merely sedated, however crystalline their reasons or bloody their faiths. Under this theory I would have no idea why at a very early age, as far back as I can remember there being a me, I was uneasy, easily angered, cognizant of the rankness of adult human odors. I never liked it when adults had a story for me that wasn't from a book. It meant they wanted me to believe something they believed. I couldn't have said it this way then but I knew that my mind was the field of play between us. I was jumbled inside between theirs and mine and only quiet could make it stop. I didn't want to talk back. I was too angry already for that. I wouldn't come out to meet company in the living room if they offered fruit or sugar cookies. I would if they offered chocolate. I would if it was my birthday or Hanukkah and they had presents. I would if my parents came looking for me and insisted. Craven as I was, my parents would kindly give in after I'd made my brief hellos and how are yous and let me hide in the basement where I learned to make sparks pounding nails into the concrete floor hard.

Tower of Silence

Lawrence Sutin

Returning home after dealing with people, I have the sense of silence rushing at me as I unlock the door. There is the same brief echo of turmoil as with water just gone down the drain, and then nothing except for my own noises that I don't hear. There is the hot silence of summer with the windows open and the curtains lifting now and then like idle hands reaching for an apple, a magazine, a smoke. There is the cold silence of winter in which the frost webs the panes and the telephone shivers as it rings unanswered. The deep, daily silence of single life seldom survives the decision to marry. That was the loss for me, not monogamy. A couple reading together in a room is a comfort, not a silence. Being a parent and loving your child means giving up silence when the child needs to break it. You cannot recover your silence through anger, a corrosive. Stepping back into silence is now a fantasy, as in the old tales when one stepped into Faery unawares, nothing changed so much as lit from within. I've often contemplated climbing the steps to the lasting Tower of Silence but then grown afraid. I fear that it would be weakness—evading the world. I fear I would contract what the monks called *acedia*, dryness. I fear I would worship my own hallucinations. I fear that one night I would jump the wall and hire a whore with coins stolen from the alms bowls of my brethren.

Tower of Silence, Bombay.

Young Man with Rifle, Black Dog and Dead Ducks

Lawrence Sutin

Because my parents survived the Holocaust as Jewish partisans hiding and fighting in the woods, it was important to me to prove myself in the woods as well. Not to them, but to me. I arranged for immersions, spans of ten days or longer in which I was carefully, minimally equipped for wind, sun, rain, the wet of the northern Minnesota Boundary Waters—ceaseless intricate chains of lakes ranging in shape from Australia to fallen leaves. The only problem was that if I'd tried such trips by myself I would have died. I had no idea how to pack, paddle, portage, pitch camp, produce potable lake water, plot an ultimate course. My friend Greg knew all these things and more. He could balance on the gunnels of a fully loaded canoe in the middle of a lake on a windy day and arc a pee away from us. He could scout the depths and shallows of a rocky shoreline to find a safe site to dive into naked over and over, cutting through the throbbing sun of July into water that was ice only two months before. He'd been going to the woods since boyhood and had a feeling for it I stole from. He loved to bathe in the lake with biodegradable Dr. Bronner's eucalyptus soap while the morning sun was still caught in the trees and a tiny cassette player floated out Northumberland pipes or the Grateful Dead. I'd ask what should we do today, he'd say, "Let's get lost."

Island

Rhett Iseman Trull

We wake to the rumor that started in the night while some of us slept or tried to sleep, and others stumbled back to the dorms from the Dock House bar across the water—coming in at all hours in the final groups in which they'd found themselves, each in various states of intoxication, someone always leaning too hard on the others, and me in my bunk afraid to let myself go like that but feeling some sort of vicarious thrill in being awake as the wilder, freer students returned, as I was rocked at last to sleep on their sloppy waves of laughter from the hall—we wake to the rumor that a whale has beached itself.

It's the middle of the first summer session on Pivers Island, home of Duke University's Marine Lab, near Beaufort, North Carolina. I'm not sure what I'm doing here. I came here to squeeze in my last science requirement so that I can graduate early in December, partly to save my parents tuition, and partly—maybe mostly—because I am exhausted. These last five years have felt like one long emergency and aftermath. I need an easy fall semester, followed by a spring at my parents' beach house, where I'll work at the discount movie theater to save money for whatever my next step might be. But I don't belong, an English major on this island of science students, all of whom seem to know one another. They clique up easily. They roam in packs. I feel alone, even as word of the whale courses through campus and we gather, crowding onto the beach for a glimpse of the stranded animal and its eager rescuers.

My first night in the hospital, less than two years ago, they sent my friends away at the close of visiting hours, but let my mother stay a while longer. My father, needing to be at work in the morning and, I think, unable to handle feeling helpless, had left already for the drive home, leaving Mama behind to spend the next few days by my bed. We rarely spoke. I was catching up on sleep now that I could let go of the fight, now that others were watching out for me at last and giving me medicine to stop my convulsing, though Mama told me years later that my body continued to shake in my sleep. Eventually, the nurses asked her to leave. I kept my eyes closed, though I felt her linger in the doorway. Then she was gone, heading for my empty dorm room, in the middle of a block of sorority girls whose party noise would jar her throughout her restless night, while I floated in the starched sheets, safe at last and too relieved at that moment to feel guilty for the pain I'd caused my loved ones by letting my situation get so extreme.

But I hadn't known how to ask for help when the trouble started. I didn't even know what was wrong with me or what I needed. Though the truth is, my silence was more complicated than that. How does someone suffering from a condition that makes her self-destructive seek salvation? One moment I would be throwing myself head first down the stairs in the middle of the night, not exactly trying to die but hoping for some sort of oblivion and release—unconsciousness, maybe; the next moment, I'd be curled up in some dark corner, begging God to fix me, please, somehow fix me, praying out loud through sobs, half-hoping for a stranger to pass by and hear. But to ask someone for help? The minute I'd try, my mind would turn against itself and lock away the words. For years I walked around with a war inside, the will to live and the desire to die tangled in my every motivation.

In the end, my body did the speaking for me, though I tried the direct approach first. Sometime in the fall of my sophomore year, with more courage than I'd ever managed to muster before, from my friend Lucy's dorm room, while she held my hand, I called my parents and told them, as calmly as I could, that I thought I might be losing my mind.

"Maybe I should be in a hospital, you know, or something," I managed to get out, my teeth starting to chatter.

"Why do you think that, Rhett?" Mama's tone was careful, drenched in worry. I'd heard it before, in high school, when I was suicidal. The fear in her voice made me want to clam up again, to push her away as I'd done before, out of the path of my destruction, to spare her from having to watch and to allow myself room to break down as necessary.

And it was necessary. I was barely holding my mind together. I needed to let go of the pieces, let someone else pick them up. I was afraid I was going to die. And this time, I didn't want to. This wasn't like the depression that had taken me over at sixteen, when I hated being alive and wanted out. I'd been depressed all fall, yes, but something was different this time. It was as if the zippers in my brain were coming undone, the stuffing falling out. The first signs were slight: forgetting a meeting, trouble concentrating. Then the lapses got bigger. I would forget what day it was, not just for a moment but for hours at a time, unable, no matter how hard I thought, to remember, frantically trying to find a paper with the date or guessing which class to go to based on one of the notebooks in my backpack, and sometimes guessing wrong. Or I would be reading a textbook, say *Ancient Myths of the Near East*, and would glance up to discover, to my shock, that it had taken me three hours to get from the top of a page to the bottom.

"This is just stress, honey," Daddy was saying, before I could figure out how to explain what was happening. "It's the end of the semester. Once you get through it, you'll feel much better. Don't you think?"

"I don't know. It's not . . . I don't know."

"You just work too hard. Can you try to finish the semester and then, if you still feel this way, we'll talk about it?"

Seemed reasonable. "Okay."

But the lapses got worse. I'd find myself in the middle of the quad at two in the morning in pouring rain, wearing nothing but a thin T-shirt but unable to feel the winter cold and unsure how I ended up outside. I starved myself, but not on purpose; I simply forgot to eat for days and didn't realize it until stomach cramps woke me. I dropped to less than a hundred pounds. I walked out of the shower and forgot I was naked, walked right down the hallway of my coed dorm all the way to my room before I realized I had no key, I had no clothes, I was dripping, exposed. Sometime that November the shaking started, little tremors at first, then whole body convulsions beyond my control—not like a seizure, more like the steady shivering of every bone.

My dorm room was a single, so no one was there to witness the details. But by December, friends noticed that something wasn't right. A senior I admired confronted me at one point to ask if I had a drinking problem. "What? I'm not drunk," I told her. "I think I'm losing my mind." Days later—or hours later?—I somehow wound up on her couch. I think I spent two days there, drifting in and out of awareness. I know I never was left alone. My friends took shifts at my side. I slept hours at a time, which I had not done in quite a while, feeling watched, feeling safe. At one point a group of them sat on the floor, someone's hand on my head, talking about what to do with me. I didn't mind. On the contrary, it felt good to let someone else make the decisions. I turned my brain off. I went numb with peace.

Only that next night, in the hospital, once my mother had gone and I found myself alone again for the first time in days, did my fear begin to return. But before it could take root, a nurse pulled a chair up to my bed and handed me a Styrofoam cup of chipped ice and Ginger Ale.

"My name's Barbara," she said. I turned to look at her, stationed in the chair. She was tall, with graying hair, and something rugged but kind about her. "I just want you to know that I worked as a nurse in a psychiatric ward for thirteen years before coming here, so I can relate a lot more to you than these kids with the flu."

As if on cue, my roommate launched into a phlegmy series of coughs. Barbara closed her eyes and shook her head, smiling, "We'll see what we can do about getting you your own room, okay?"

The next day I was given a single at the end of the hall, nearer the nurse's station and across from the showers. I lived there in the student infirmary section of the hospital for two weeks. Since I wasn't suicidal, the Duke counselors had decided it was safe to let me stay and try to finish the semester, even though my teachers had given me extensions. With Klonopin to stop my shaking, and with others telling me when and what to eat, taking care of basic needs, I was able to focus. My parents brought my old laptop from home, an early word processor on its last days, but it served me fine. I wrote an exegesis on a chapter of *Exodus* and a thesis paper on Shakespeare's *The Tempest*. Somehow I aced both, though as soon as I'd finished, I couldn't remember a word I'd written.

My room became a gathering place and a study hall, friends drifting in throughout the day. Jill was pre-med and chronically stressed, but she liked to study in the quiet of the hospital, and I think, liked it near me where she felt needed. Sometimes she would bring her guitar and sing songs she'd written and was too nervous to play for anyone but me. Both afraid of me living alone, we decided we would room together next semester. Everything was looking up. My friends, who had been rocks during this difficult time, seemed relieved. Along with the nurses, they were a calming presence, always near. After the first week, even my parents seemed to be in good spirits when they visited.

We all thought the worst was over.

The beached whale is a juvenile pygmy killer, around six feet long. I work my way to the front of the onlookers, some of whom are dispersing as more arrive. The water is calm on this side of the island and laps gently against the sides of the whale, which sometimes moves, jostled by the drift of the current but held upright by the net slung underneath it. The graduate students and professors work in shifts, standing sentry six at a time, water up to their thighs and waists, hands on the whale to keep it from rolling. When it breathes, a jet of spray releases from its blow hole, and the rescuers groan and lean away from the stink. As the morning goes on, they learn to anticipate these moments and brace themselves. Had the whale energy, it might slip away easily, but it hardly moves, just an occasional thrash to let us all know that yes, it lives, and is unhappy.

Most of the students lose interest after a while. A pick-up game of basketball is starting at the hoop near the dining hall. Someone's organizing a drive to Atlantic Beach. Some straggle back throughout the day to check on the whale's status, but it's Katey and I who stay the longest, keeping vigil. We don't know each other well, but as we sit on the sand, speaking in whispers, concern and fascination connect us.

Two of the marine lab staff are bending to the whale's mouth to work wet towels inside with a sawing motion. It's difficult work, and the whale comes to life a bit, uncooperative, though not strong enough to fight them off. Someone shouts a warning about not getting bitten. Sweat stains mix with water stains on their T-shirts and tank tops. It takes time, but finally, the towels are in place. Two people pull up on the top towel while two pull down on the bottom one, prying the mouth open enough for a woman to work a tube inside. She coaxes the whale with soft words as she tilts the tube deeper, then attaches a funnel through which they force it to eat.

"He doesn't seem to have any fight left, does he?" I whisper.

Katey shakes her head. It doesn't look good for the whale, but neither of us wants to admit it. Katey is a graduate student, a few years older than me and married, a fact that makes me a little awestruck and jealous; I am beginning to yearn for romance, now that my life no longer seems in danger every other moment. Katey misses her husband. Perhaps it's that longing that puts her closer to my wavelength than the other, more carefree students. We both wished to be off this island until we saw the whale. Now we can't imagine being anywhere but here.

Many theories circle the island as to why the young whale beached: sickness, problems with its echolocation system, something humans have done to change the environment. But the rescuers are too busy trying to keep the whale alive to worry about what went wrong out at sea. They pour cold water over it, between feedings, to keep its blubber from overheating, and there is talk of getting it moved to deeper water that will support it better before it suffocates under its own weight.

I am trying to live differently, more openly, so that night in my room when Katey asks what pill I'm taking, I toss her the bottle and tell her the truth. I'm surprised by how easy it is.

When I started college three years ago, I vowed none of the friends I was about to make would get close enough to learn about my depression. I hid my Zoloft behind a box in my closet. I pretended, for awhile, that I was happy. Only to Nathan did I tell the truth. I met him on the Internet. We emailed every day and wrote letters by post each week. He lived in Australia, half a world away, a safe enough distance for honesty. And perhaps putting the difficult truth into words to him was what helped me begin to let a few of my college friends in, as well, though I tried to limit what I told them.

Even after ending up in the hospital December of my sophomore year, after letting my friends get close enough to carry me through the suffering, I returned to campus in January—well-rested and on a new antidepressant— and, as soon as I found myself in trouble again, resorted to the same old tricks, the mask of *I'm fine* held tightly in place. My friends were relieved; some never thought I'd make it back to school. I didn't want to burden those whom I'd put through so much just months ago.

When Katey, all curiosity no alarm, asks when and how I was diagnosed with manic depression, I continue my new policy of honest nonchalance. But I don't tell her everything. It will be years before I'm ready to divulge the details. I give her the medical explanation, that bipolar disorder can begin as depression in the teenage years and sometime around a person's twenties, the chemicals transition into more of a manic depressive state. In some people, without treatment, the mind becomes susceptible to psychosis. The antidepressant I was on made my encroaching mania worse that first semester after the hospital. My in-flux chemicals, combined with stress, which was accelerated by my refusal to admit to anyone that something still seemed to be wrong with me, led to a psychotic break from reality.

"I did some messed up stuff. And after that, they tested me: a Rorschach test and a big four-hundred question true or false test. And after several hours of that, they came up with the right diagnosis and put me on the right medicine, Depakote. And it worked." I tell Katey the science, not the story, which I don't fully understand myself.

What I do know is that because I would not let myself cry for help, my mind found a way to do so in spite of me. It constructed convincing drama: Someone was trying to kill me. Death threats were left on my answering machine. Then my friends began getting the phone calls, "I'm going to kill Rhett." Of course, it was me making the calls, but at the time, I didn't know. Or, part of me didn't know. I heard the threats and believed them. I was terrified. I called the campus police and filed a report. They put a trace on my phone line to figure out from where on campus the calls originated. It was as if my brain had divided itself into two sections, the one that made the threats and the one that received them. Most of the time these sections remained disconnected. I could have passed a lie detector test; I honestly thought someone was after me. But there were, during each day, moments of clarity in which the two parts of my brain communicated and I knew what I had done. I didn't know why, didn't even ask myself. I just knew I was doing this somehow and needed to stop. But I couldn't. I had gone too far, put something into motion that was rolling now on its own momentum. It didn't matter that, in my few moments of clarity, I knew what I was doing and wanted it to end; I had lost control of the part of my mind that was taking over. I would lie awake in a sweat, trying to calculate how many more calls I would need to make in order finally to stop, as if by calling a magic number of times, everything would somehow be okay again. But by the time I made and received the calls the next day, I wouldn't know again that it was me. All I knew was terror: someone was going to kill me.

And someone was, after all. I was. My mind had buckled against itself. It was working in opposite directions: stay quiet and don't burden anyone versus scream and plead for help. I was falling apart, after everything, still falling. In my determination to make no more waves for everyone, I was going to get myself killed. My brain knew that, somewhere deep inside, and did what it had to do to short-circuit my commands and find a way, through metaphor, to let everyone know its destruction was imminent.

When Lucy confronted me about the phone calls and told me my friends had been meeting for weeks to decide what to do, some wanting me sent to a mental institution, some thinking that drastic move unnecessary, I ran: across West Campus, across the gardens. This would be my life now, running. Everyone knew what I had done. Soon my parents would find out, too. There was no going back to any of them. They would hate me forever. It was criminal, what I had done. I hadn't even known I was doing it, most of the time. But how could anyone understand that? I couldn't even understand, though at last clarity held: I did know I had done it.

Unable to face any of my friends again, I made a tape, confessing and trying to explain, as best I could. I left the tape by Lucy's door, then drove to an Arby's parking lot and turned off my car. I would sleep here tonight and leave town in the morning. I would drive west until I ran out of gas and money. I would find a job in a diner somewhere—but no, I'd have to give my social security number for that, an identity that wasn't me anymore—maybe I'd beg in the streets instead. Or maybe I'd live in a barn on some ranch and work the land for food. I would miss my family, but my old life was over. I had ruined it. There was no going back.

Lucky for me, it was winter. After the sun went down it began to get cold. I pulled my arms inside my sleeves but continued to shiver. It wouldn't do to get sick the night before I was to leave. How would I get medicine on the run? I decided to go back for a blanket, then return to the car to sleep. But when I opened the door of my room, Jill was there, pacing, the phone in her hand. Before I could run, she threw her arms around me. She was crying. I couldn't believe she was touching me. How could anyone still love me after all I had done? How could anyone want me?

I don't tell Katey these details, and to my relief, she doesn't ask for them. She wants to know what the Rorschach test is like, what are the side effects of Depakote. These are easy to explain. Facts are easy. But how could I explain how real a mind's fictions can be? Or the breaking point of friendship?

Though most of my friendships continued to deepen after I confessed to the phone calls, got help, and began the long work of healing, some friends never spoke to me again. I couldn't blame them. What I had put them through was difficult to understand (even my father insisted what I had done was simple, immature prank calling). Ironically, it was because of my recovery that my relationship with Jill unraveled. During our junior year, while Depakote and weekly therapy did wonders for me, Organic Chemistry was, as Jill put it, kicking her butt. "I wish all I had to do was read books and write papers," she'd say so often I began to avoid her. Our room bristled with tension. I think we'd grown so close during my illness, building our friendship through crisis, that now that I was getting well, we didn't know how to relate to each other.

At one point I came into the room to find her crying on her bed. "I went to visit my lab partner in the infirmary today," she said, drying her cheeks with the back of her hand, "and I was riding up that rickety elevator and I just thought about you and what it must have been like for you."

I didn't know how to comfort her, aware even then that she was crying not so much for what I had gone through as for what she went through watching it happen.

"But you're okay now?" Katey's asking.

I hesitate, holding the unfamiliar truth in my mind before letting it out: "I'm the best I've ever been."

In many ways, life is miserable on the island. I usually feel at home on the coast, but despite nightly walks on the beach with Katey, I am lonely and out of my element. I have to work twice as hard as the other students in my class. All science or pre-med majors, they are used to dissection tests and hypothetical theory questions. If a crab were divided into paragraphs and stanzas, I could take it apart and put it back together in my sleep, too, but this type of lab work and analysis, I'm not used to. In grade school and high school, I was at the top of my class in science, but I'm a different person now.

Therefore, when not in class, I'm studying or reading my thousand-plus page textbook with its tiny print and dry sentences. I've staked out a spot for myself on the bank overlooking the waterway between our island and the city of Beaufort. The grass is sharp, sandspurs pricking the tops of my feet above my flip-flops. Each afternoon, I read for hours, highlighting until each page bleeds neon, distracted often by students laughing near the dock and boats passing by.

I want to be reading fiction. It's summer. I should be on a sandy beach, lulled deeper into the plot by breaking waves. What a dusty, cool library does for some booklovers, a long stretch of shoreline does for me. Growing up, I lived for the summers, for the moment I could prop my little blue chair into the sand and dig into the beach bag for whatever book I was reading. It's impossible to think of those books now—*The Cricket in Times Square, Communion, Misery*—without remembering where I first read them, situated happily on the edge of the continent, my mother distant but still visible on one of her long walks, my brother building in the sand, and my father beside me, working on the latest Ludlum. He'd read all the classics, too, many of them the summer he was seventeen and ordered to stay on the couch while he healed from myocarditis and pericarditis, muscle damage and inflammation of the heart that had nearly killed him at a Junior Civitan retreat. When I get away from this marine lab, that's my plan: to go to Myrtle Beach and read in the sun until the sun goes down, then read for as long as I can as the dark comes on and the tide creeps in.

My mother is at Myrtle now, waiting for me. For a long time, for most of these last five years, I've been avoiding her, avoiding my whole family. Home was uncomfortable while I was sick, my parents walking carefully into a room I occupied, glancing down my arm for fresh cuts, trying out words in their heads before speaking, their fear palpable, their worry unspoken, dominant. I found excuses to escape, to slip their searchlight. Sometimes I walked our town for hours, thighs going numb, sweat collecting into a salty cake on my skin, just to be anywhere but home.

But the time has come for home again, it seems. I yearn for my family. In fact, my first Saturday here, I drove five hours home for my brother's high school graduation. I was there less than a day, but the trip was an oasis of connection in these weeks of solitude, a reminder of who I am, despite the trials and changes of the last five years, who I will be always: sister, daughter.

My mother and I are friends again. I call her every night and write her letters each day between chapters. My homesickness surprises me, though I know it's fueled partly by the fact that I'm too exhausted to study as much as I'm having to here. According to Katey, I've chosen the hardest class on the island. The science majors knew this going in, but there was no one to prepare me. I simply chose what sounded interesting: Marine Invertebrate Zoology. I wanted to know more about what lives in the sea.

And it is interesting. It's hands-on. We are picking up new creatures every day, turning them over, touching the parts that look like they should sting or pinch. I become addicted to handling the horseshoe crabs, and each day after class, on my way to my spot on the bank, I walk by the big water tanks to watch them. Sometimes I get lucky and catch one flipped over. Then I drop my bookbag and prop my elbows on the edge of the tank to study how the crab uses its long tail—which I have learned is called a telson—to hoist itself up as it rocks side to side on the back of its shell, until it can get a claw-hold and right itself.

My favorite classes are the field trips, usually to gather samples for observation or dissection. We might dig for clams in the oyster beds, pluck barnacles off the dock, or take the boat to trawl for specimens in deeper water. I'd thought the boat trips would be my favorite excursions—thought I belonged on the open sea—until our farthest venture. It was fun at first, the wind and spray refreshing. Then we stopped to drop the nets overboard. The water was rough, rocking us. Some of my classmates grew sick and were sent below deck to lie down, their groans rising up the narrow stairwell each time we lurched. After several minutes, our professor and a few of the boys pulled one of the nets in, heaving it with a clatter into the middle of the deck, where we gathered to see the bounty. I'd gotten just close enough to glimpse several large crabs climbing over each other, confused, when my professor put a hand on my shoulder.

"Are you okay?" he asked.

"I'm fine."

"Whoa," a student to my right whispered, backing quickly away. Others followed his example, wide eyes on me.

"I'm fine," I repeated.

"I think you're sick. You should go lie down," said my professor.

"Your face is green," added one of the girls.

Only as she spoke did I feel my stomach churn. "But I don't get seasick," I said. I had been in plenty of boats and never felt sick. The sea was my element. I tried to step closer to the net, and my insides rolled. I motioned toward the stairs. "I'd better . . . "

"Go. Go lie down right now."

"I'm not seasick," I insisted, wobbling across the deck. "I've never been seasick."

But the rest of the class had returned their focus to what squirmed in the net.

My father's visit on the third weekend is my favorite part of the summer session. By the time he arrives, I'm in dire need of escape. I was burned out before I started class at the lab, and I've been pushing myself harder and harder to read each chapter and pass each test. Maybe it's my imagination, but I never see anyone else studying. I see them shooting hoops or canoeing or heading to the beach or the bar. They must do their work at some point, but I work all through the day and into the night. Maybe, as science majors, it's that much easier for them.

Meanwhile, everything around me has fallen into disrepair. The laundry machines eat quarter after quarter, each load needing at least two wash cycles to get the soap out and three cycles to dry. My car window is stuck in the down position. When it rains, I trudge to the parking lot with a garbage bag and bricks to hold it in place. Worst of all, my computer is dying. It's hooked up in the lab, where I steal away each evening to write a few pages, the one hour a day I can feed the creative part of my brain. The grad student who runs the lab spent hours erasing programs to get my word processing working again. Now I'm afraid that every time I turn it on will be the last.

If it weren't for this daily escape into fiction, I don't know what I'd do. Even TV isn't an option here; the lounge in the boathouse is infested with roaches. Turn on the light and dozens skitter up the walls and into the furniture. But the other, larger lounge is packed with students who stare uninvitingly the few times I try to join them. Besides, they watch sports. I need a show with plot. One night I'm so desperate I brave the roach-house for an episode of *Friends*, but I'm miserable, marooned on the coffee table because roaches hide in the couch cushions. When one starts to crawl up the table's leg, I turn off the television in the middle of a joke. My need for at least thirty minutes of sitcom to help me wind down at the end of a long day is a practice I learned from my father, who would come home from work with his mind still running full speed. He'd open the mail—his and everyone else's—still in his suit and tie, and eat dinner so quickly one would think his food still alive, wiggling off the plate. But in the evenings, every evening, we would sit on the couch and watch our shows—lights off, he insisted, despite Mama's protests that she couldn't see her magazine—and all of our lives slowed down.

I know when Daddy comes to the island, he'll understand my need to get away, and he does. After a quick tour including, of course, my demonstration on how to pick up a horseshoe crab, my father, true champion, whisks me off, first to explore the Civil War cannons of nearby Fort Macon, siege of which gave the Union control of the North Carolina coast; then to a seafood dinner; and then, at last, to the movies.

I've been plot-hungry for three weeks, sated ever-so-briefly last Sunday when Katey and I watched *Hope Floats* in the local theater—one of those small-town, been-there-for-decades cinemas with permanently sticky floors and a handful of screens—finding escape for two hours in other people's stories. This weekend, Daddy takes me to *A Perfect Murder*, based on Hitchcock's *Dial M for Murder*, which Mama and I rented years ago, the summer we devoted to Hitchcock and musicals; so that in a way, watching this movie with my father connects me to my mother, as well. I feel pleasantly nostalgic, even as the violence unfolds. And that night, in Daddy's hotel room, I don't even mind his snoring, a sound from the childhood I once thought I'd left behind forever.

It's nice to think fondly of my past and my home, but I am, for the first time in a long time, trying to live in the present. I am learning to let go of regret. Okay, I once wanted to die. Okay, I cut myself. As for the friends I hurt and lost, well, much of what I did was beyond my control at the time; and while the mistakes were costly, they did lead to the help I needed. Today I feel steadier. I look without dread to the future.

More and more, moving to Los Angeles after college, to study screenwriting, seems like something I could handle. With my mother's encouragement and support, I will begin, soon, to plan for that next step of my life. My father will have the most trouble with this. In fact, at one point, he will forbid me to go. And I will learn to disobey him for his own good as well as mine. He will be the last of us to let go of his fear.

It is this fear that brought him to visit me on the island, I will realize later. He heard misery in my voice when I called home and has come to attempt to distract me and reassure himself I'm not returning to a dangerous mental state. At first I think his curiosity about the island brought him here, but toward the end of the summer, when I'm back home asking him about the possibility of a trip to Australia, the motives that drive all his decisions about me these days will become clear.

Part of my new attitude of hope includes, for the first time in many years, thinking I could be capable of being in a relationship. I think I could look outside myself and love someone. To reward myself for graduating early, I want to go meet Nathan, face to face at last. He has invited me, and I want to go. It's a ridiculous idea, of course. I met him on the Internet. I'm still such a kid. I certainly don't have enough money to pay for the trip by myself. But my father's protests will have nothing to do with those logical objections.

"I can't have you across the world from me," he will say, tears in his eyes, once we've stopped fighting, he and Mama sitting on the edge of my bed. Then he will drop the bomb, "If I thought you were better, maybe, but—"

"What does that mean?"

"You're still depressed. I don't know what you might do. I can't have you that far away, where I can't get to you if . . ."

Mama will look at him with both anger and pity, her hand on his knee.

"But I'm not depressed anymore. I'm better. On the Depakote, I'm much better. And therapy's been helping."

"You say that, but you still seem unhappy to me. Until I see that you're happy, you can't take any big trips."

"But that's not fair. I may never be happy. I'm not sick anymore, though. I'm not *un*happy. Look at these books." I gesture to the walls of my room. "They're not about being happy. That's—that's not what life is about. It's about pain and, you know, figuring out how to live, how to get through it. It's life. Life's not happiness."

"I think she has been doing much better," Mama will agree.

"I don't see it." Daddy will say. "In Beaufort this summer you were miserable."

"What? No. I mean, that was like a normal miserable. Everybody felt that way. We were stressed out and the living conditions weren't the best and, well," I will add softly, "I was homesick."

"You don't know what it's like for a parent." He won't look at me anymore. "I cringe every time that phone rings."

And I will understand. While I have been healing, while I've begun to concentrate less on survival than on living itself, he has remained rooted in the horrors of a past in which his daughter could lose her will to live and her grip on reality at any moment. I know that fear. I know how difficult it is to move beyond that fear's control.

I trap three horseshoe crabs, for my independent study this summer, in a chicken-wire enclosure on the beach. I set up this cage at different times of day and measure how long it takes the crabs to burrow in varying consistencies of sand. In dry sand they do not move and, afraid I might be killing them, I return them to their tanks after fifteen minutes. In mud and mud covered with water, they burrow within seconds. In wet sand, with a little water coming in, they burrow only after spending ten minutes trying to escape their fencing, trying to follow the retreating tide back to the sea. I name the crabs Sylvester, Tom, and Jerry, and with my final paper on the project, turn in a poem, a poorly written parody of Poe's "Annabel Lee," with lines like: "And neither the scientists in labs up above / Nor those working down under the sea / Can dissever my soul from the burrowing souls / Of Sylvester, Tom, and Jerry."

After my paper, the last hurdle of the summer is our final identification exam. Dissection trays line the tables, little numbered pins flagging each specimen. Though I have studied and memorized for days, I feel queasy, ill-prepared. The class moves among the trays in silence, except for one boy, pre-med, who begins, mid-way through the hour, laughing loudly and proclaiming things like, "Oh, this is too easy! Piece of cake!" I look up. No one else looks up. No one asks him to be quiet. He continues, bouncing from tray to tray, saying, "I thought this was supposed to be hard! This is nothing! Nothing!" At one point he tosses his pen from hand to hand in a little dance and sings, "Easy, easy, easy." Not until ten years later will it occur to me I may have been hallucinating. By then, I will know of two other visual and auditory hallucinations during times of stress and exhaustion, one of them during finals the semester after my summer at the marine lab. Of course, hallucinations seem real at the time, so I may have had more that I didn't catch; it's only when I realize the absurdity of what I'm witnessing and have a chance to reality test it, asking others present if they see or hear the same thing, for instance, that I can confirm whether the event is happening or not. Thus, a decade will pass before I think to wonder, could the boy in my class have made such a commotion? Was everyone else ignoring him? Was our professor in the room? Surely, if so, he would have said something, wouldn't he? I suppose, in the end, it doesn't matter whether I'm hallucinating or not: I score the second highest grade on the exam, a B before the curve. Sole non-science major, I not only pass the hardest class on the island, I ace it.

Before I leave, I walk the campus one more time, saying goodbye to the horseshoe crabs in their water tanks; goodbye to Cape Lookout in the distance, one of many lighthouses that, though restored now, were destroyed or dismantled during the Civil War by retreating Confederates attempting to darken their coast against attack; goodbye across the water to the wild horses of Shackleford Banks, possibly descended from horses who survived a shipwreck during the early days of exploration; and finally, goodbye to the whale. I stand on the spot where he beached, where the marine lab staff and graduate students worked in shifts throughout the day and into the night until he was strong enough to be air-lifted, while the rest of us slept, to Panama City. I don't even know if he made it back out to sea. If he did, what are his chances for survival?

I know that sometimes a whale is rescued only to get stranded again on the same beach, or to die of toxins that built up in its body while on land. But some of them must make it. Some of them—I'm sure of it—go on to live long lives in the deep. And do they remember their time on the beach? Maybe. Maybe they think of it—of us—from time to time, wondering if it was real or a dream from which they never fully will wake: the struggle to breathe, the wash of the tide, the hands that held them.

Let's Pretend

Tom Varisco

IF YOU WANT COFFEE WHEN YOU VISIT JUST FOLLOW YOUR NOSE BUT REALLY
IT IS EASY JUST STAY ON I-10 EAST UNTIL YOU GET TO THE ESPLANA
DE AVENUE EXIT WHICH IS RIGHT AFTER THE VIEUX CARRE EXIT WHEN
YOU COME TO ESPLANADE TURN RIGHT AND AFTER A FEW BLOCKS YOU
WILL COME TO RAMPART STREET AND YOU WANT TO CROSS IT PLEASE
DO NOT TURN LEFT BECAUSE RAMPART TURNS INTO SAINT CLAUDE
WHICH WILL LEAD YOU TO THE NINTH WARD WHICH WAS DESTROYED BY
FLOOD WATERS IT IS REALY AN AWFUL SIGHT AND IF YOU END UP THERE YOU
MAY NOT BE IN THE MOOD FOR COFFEE SO DO NOT TURN LEFT BUT
DRIVE STRAIGHT AHEAD UNTIL YOU GET TO DECATUR STREET
WHICH IS AFTER CHARTRES AND RIGHT BEFORE THE RIVER SO
THEN YOU TURN RIGHT AND DRIVE A FEW BLOCKS PAST THE
JOAN OF ARC STATUE AND REALLY A BLOCK OR SO LATER
TO YOUR LEFT IS CAFE DU MONDE WHERE YOU CAN FINAL
LY RELAX WITH A CUP OF OUR VERY BEST COFFEE AND

PRETEND NOTHING EVER HAPPENED

Into Africa

Margaret L. Whitford

A friend once referred to my husband Tom's and my service with the US Peace Corps as "Margaret's folly." I let the comment pass, but it stung—because he was not entirely off the mark. Tom and I were in our thirties and had been married for seven years when we accepted teaching assignments in Kenya. We departed for Africa intending to stay for at least two to three years, and were open to the possibility that we'd remain overseas indefinitely, our lives unfurling as expatriates. We arrived in Nairobi in September 1989. We left six months later in early April.

Although our family and closest friends supported our decision to go to Kenya, I doubt they understood. Anyone looking at our lives from the outside would have seen little to justify so dramatic a change. We were each doing well professionally and on paths to capitalize on our MBAs. I worked as an administrator for a major university. Tom, as the youngest senior vice president in his company's history, seemed destined to achieve prominence in his field. We'd purchased our first home in the Philadelphia suburbs, a 1930s stone house with detached garage, flower beds, and basketball hoop. We had a growing network of amusing friends. Our life glowed with privilege and promise, yet I could not fully commit to it. I cannot explain all the reasons why. In one sense, I wanted simply to be elsewhere.

At sixteen, I'd spent a summer in Europe and had longed to live overseas ever since. For a variety of reasons, especially paternal pressure, most choices had failed to move me closer to that dream. By my thirties, the frustration was such that I could no longer repress it. And so, blind to other considerations, I began searching for opportunities to work abroad, hopeful that the force of my desire would carry Tom along with me.

But Tom was not carried along; instead, he chose to encourage me. He wasn't unhappy, except to the extent that my discontent affected him. And the professional risks he assumed by supporting my quest were substantial. Once he decided to join me, though, he did so wholeheartedly.

Our Peace Corps assignments took us to Kenya's Western Highlands, to the Moi Institute of Technology (we liked referring to it as MIT), a trade school about twenty-five miles southwest of Kisii, the hill town that serves as the region's transportation hub.

MIT's agreement with the Peace Corps required the school to provide us with a house, yet after repeated delays, we learned that Mr. Nyasoro, the headmaster, had given our lodging to friends of his. He tried to persuade us to share a house with another teacher, but we refused. We appealed to the local Peace Corps representative, who intervened, threatening to remove us from the school. Shortly thereafter, Mr. Nyasoro's friends moved elsewhere, along with the electric cooker we'd been promised.

Although I'm not sure what I had been expecting, our new home wasn't it. The house's dirty, mustard-colored walls were cracked and peeling, the floors caked in mud, and trash strewn everywhere. One bedroom was padlocked. And a hen was roosting in one of the kitchen cabinets.

"You've forgotten your hen," I said to Sarah during one of her visits to check on the locked bedroom. "Please take her with you."

"Your hen, there's a hen in the cabinet," I persisted in response to Sarah's blank look.

"But she's sitting on eggs. I can't move her."

Why on earth would you let a hen roost in the kitchen? I thought. *And why is that now my problem?* But I didn't say any of this. I just stood there and watched Sarah depart.

We tried living with this hen for a week or so, tried to be culturally sensitive, but the hen made me mad. We'd already dealt with the rat population (dozens of them, discovered our first night in the house), and had learned to co-exist with the roaches (enormous, could fly, and emerged at night to blanket the walls).

But the hen intimidated me. She looked unnaturally large and somehow threatening. Whenever I approached, her red feathered body expanded over her eggs like a protective cloak. And the smell, well, it was like a pungent fog had enveloped the kitchen, emphatically discouraging us from cooking there.

We purchased paint and cleaning products, intending to make the house habitable once again. We scrubbed the floors and wiped down walls. Tom spent a day painting the kitchen and hallway, the areas in the worst condition. I followed with an arsenal of cleaning compounds. The combined odors of powerful chemicals and oil-based paint polluted the air. At first, the hen seemed unaffected, but that proved temporary. From another room I heard a commotion in the kitchen and entered to find the hen flapping her wings and hopping about in a kind of hysteria. Seeing my chance, I guided her toward a window and she flew out. I'd like to say that I gathered the eggs carefully and moved them to the hen house, and that she recovered them, but I don't think that's what happened. I *did* move the eggs, but I doubt that saved the unborn chicks.

Our house had indoor plumbing, so we assumed we had running water, until we realized the pipes didn't connect to a water source. The bathtub, toilet, and sink were for display purposes only, having been installed by MIT's student plumbers as part of a training exercise. Our water came from a bore-hole about a half-mile away, and from rainwater. To avoid intestinal problems, we boiled and filtered the well water for drinking and cooking, and used rain-water for everything else.

It surprised me how quickly we learned to conserve. "Bucket baths" re-placed my long hot showers. Each night I set a stool in the bathtub and Tom placed a large basin of heated water on top. Using a ladle, I poured just enough water over my head to get wet, then massaged shampoo into my scalp, and slid a bar of soap over my body. I rinsed off the same way, with ladles of water, until all traces of soap were gone. Bathing felt like a small blessing at the end of the day.

Every night as I got started, a visitor appeared. A single dark, graceful leg emerged from between the window frame and wall, then another, as the spider gradually side-stepped his way out. He clung to the wall in what felt like companionable silence until I had finished my bath, and then returned to his hiding place. Tom never reported seeing him (and for some reason, this pleased me).

Our house stood in the midst of fields planted in sugar cane and corn, waves of emerald fire in the wind. In the afternoons we walked red dirt roads winding through lushness, attentive to the sky in anticipation of rain. Dark, heavy clouds would accumulate on the horizon and roll toward us. The rain moved across the land like a dense gray curtain, obscuring what lay behind it. Timing our return home became a kind of game. Dashing indoors just as fat, cool drops of water started to fall, we felt triumphant. The rain battered our house's tin roof until its din was the only sound we heard. It stopped as abruptly as it had begun.

I loved the light in Kenya, the way it changed throughout the day. In the early morning, sunlight muted the land's hues and edges to reveal our sur-roundings with quiet grace. Our bodies grew long shadows. At midday, light held a dazzling, metallic edge. We wore hats and long-sleeved shirts in re-sponse to its force. The sun seared our skins, its brightness almost blinding. And by late afternoon, light seemed playful, preoccupied with rain clouds, illuminating them from within. They moved across the sky like burning ships. Wet leaves glowed as though green were a newly discovered color. Perhaps sunlight entranced me because of its dramatic sense of timing. Kenya sits on the equator where day does not linger. Dusk brings a brief softening and blush to the sky, and then night falls suddenly.

Our bread came from a local woman who sold it out of a wooden shack near our home. It was dense and moist, but only lasted one to two days in the heat. For everything else, we traveled to Kisii. We always headed out early, walking two miles along a dirt path to the main road where we waited for transportation. Although Kisii was relatively close, the round trip could take more than six hours, depending on how long we waited for a vehicle. Our first stop was a small grocery store.

As we departed, laden with packages, a little girl would stop us with bags of roasted peanuts for sale. She generally wore the same sleeveless cotton shift and flimsy sandals. Her braided hair stood out like branches from her delicate head. She was relentless, trying to hand us bags of peanuts while we shook our heads and attempted to move on. At first, her behavior irritated me, but eventually I came to admire her tenacity and looked forward to visiting with her. I doubt Wanjiko attended school, because she had not mastered Swahili or English, Kenya's official languages. She spoke Luo, one of the country's many indigenous tongues, so we communicated mostly through gestures. Tom would count off fingers to show her we wanted ten small bags of peanuts; then, after paying, he would return two for her inventory. She always responded with a smile that transformed her small face and made me regret my annoyance. I occasionally wondered about her life, about whether she got to keep any of her earnings, if she had siblings, what she did when she wasn't selling peanuts. Eventually we brought her a Frisbee, the only toy we had packed for the journey.

From the store, we continued uphill to Kisii's center, where adjacent to the chaotic bus depot stood a crowded open-air market. The variety of fruits and vegetables never failed to delight: tiny eggplants, leafy greens, carrots, onions, and tomatoes. We bought fragrant pineapples and whole stalks of creamy finger bananas. Custard apples, with their pudding-like texture and honeyed flavor, looked like exaggerated grenades. My favorite, passion fruit, had an intense sweet-tart taste. Once, I dropped a piece of fruit pulp on my jeans; it left a brown-orange stain that never washed out.

As we entered the market, the smell of diesel fuel gave way to the clean earth scent of fresh produce. The cries of drivers recruiting passengers and the tinny noise of radios faded, replaced by the market's song, a sound like birds calling to each other. Women wrapped in colorful fabrics sat on the ground, their fruits and vegetables displayed on cloths before them.

Going to the market always involved bargaining. Tom relished it (as a game of strategy, I think) so I deferred to him. We had learned there were two prices, one for Kenyans and a much higher one for "mzungus," white people in Swahili. Tom believed a fair price was a reasonable premium over what a native Kenyan would pay.

"Jambo, Mama," he liked to say as he strolled among the women, surveying the produce, finally pausing in front of one or two vendors. Never revealing his opinion, he would pick up an onion or tomato and roll it in his hand. At this point, the vendor usually called out a price, always a hefty percentage over what a Kenyan would pay. Tom responded with a much lower figure and started to walk away. He was always called back. He opened his palm to display the few coins he held and negotiations continued. By now, several women would be paying attention. Sometimes, if he couldn't get the vendor to reduce the price for the two or three items we wanted, he scooped up an additional vegetable or piece of fruit, effectively reducing the price that way. The conversation grew more animated. Eventually, having arrived at a compromise, amid smiles and handshakes, Tom completed the transaction.

Our encounters with other Kenyans were rarely as satisfying. Once, a woman I had never seen before stopped me on the street, pointed to my hair ornament and said, "Give me that."

A similar incident involved a routine visit to a bank. We were there to cash our checks from the Peace Corps. As usual, it took an incomprehensible amount of time. After a wait of two and half hours, the bank clerk cashed the checks but charged us a three-percent fee. He insisted that the fee was justified because the bank's main office had neglected to send a form authorizing our transactions with the Kisii branch. In fact, the bank had sent the form several weeks before. Nevertheless, we paid the fee, took our Kenyan shillings, and went off to eat lunch at a nearby Indian restaurant. While we were seated at a table the same bank teller came up to us.

"Jambo. How are you?" he said, smiling.

We were surprised to see him, but responded, "Fine, and you?"

"Very fine. Please give me $100." He extended his palm, as though our acquiescence were a foregone conclusion.

"No, we can't do that," Tom explained, straightening in his chair.

A shadow of disappointment and exasperation colored the teller's face for a moment, and then he departed. In addition to behaving as though he were entitled to the money, he assumed that as Americans we would have an ample supply of US currency on hand for such demands.

We grew accustomed to strangers asking us for money; requests from teachers and students were a different story. Several students approached Tom and asked him to finance education in the US or simply to hand over some cash. Mr. Guda, head of the school's building program and one of our closer colleagues, didn't ask us for money; he just wanted our camera.

A missionary we came to know in Kenya explained, "Kenyans will ask for a lot of things, because even if they don't get what they ask for, they may get something." At the time, his comment struck me as narrow-minded and possibly racist. Yet it came from a man who had grown up in Tanzania, spoke Swahili fluently, and had lived in Kenya for years with his family working to establish a Baptist church in Kisii. When his prediction came true, I resented it. The sense that we were valued primarily for the possessions we could give away gnawed at me and gradually wore me down.

Wherever we went, we attracted attention. Children, especially, were fascinated. On our daily walks, they called out in singsong voices, "mzungu, mzungu," and continued their chanting, punctuated by giggles and insistent waving, until we were out of sight.

When we ventured outside to do some household chore, children arrived to watch. On a weekly basis, we burned our trash on a bare patch of earth a few yards from our front door. If something seemed salvageable, we gave it away, only burning what we viewed as worthless.

As we started the fire, our small neighbors would gather around, standing solemnly at a discrete distance, their patient dark eyes following the fire's progress. Later, after we had gone and the ashes were cool, the children sifted through them in search of some gem we might have overlooked.

One late afternoon I was standing at the kitchen sink peeling carrots. Just beyond the kitchen's window stood a small nondescript tree, its branches bare. On this day, though, the tree's limbs looked as if white flowers had blossomed overnight. Once outside, it took me a moment to see the ornaments for what they were: Today Sponges, my chosen method of contraception. Each salvaged sponge had been carefully attached to a branch.

Several smiling children, who had obviously retrieved the sponges from the embers, were gathered in a loose semi-circle at the edge of our yard watching me. Only their bare feet, shifting in the dirt, betrayed their excitement, as they waited for my reaction. I returned their smiles, because I didn't know what else to do. Here were the most intimate of objects, believed destroyed, adorning a tree. These kids could not possibly have known what the sponges were, so despite my embarrassment, I sensed they were offering us something.

"Tom, could you come outside?" I called. He waved to the children as he joined me.

"Notice anything?" I asked.

"What are those things?" he replied.

"You don't recognize them?" I persisted.

A smile spread slowly over his face. He grinned at the children, and then we retreated.

After they had departed for the day, we carefully removed each sponge, returning the tree to plainness.

Now, years later, I still wonder about those children. Perhaps they saw a chance to create something pretty. Maybe it was a game, a way to experiment with bits of foam and elastic, but they could have done that without making us participants in their play. Unlike the adults, these children never asked us for anything, yet they had so little, certainly no toys or much of anything beyond the minimum required for survival. Our attention was the only thing they seemed to want.

They must have been delighted when they uncovered the sponges. I assume they wondered at our carelessness and lack of imagination, since we'd discarded something with such potential. I once saw a Kenyan child turn a cardboard tube into a boat, so who knows what magic foam and elastic could yield. But instead of keeping their recovered treasure, they gave us a gift.

MIT's business program, our official reason for being in Kenya, ostensibly prepared students for national exams aimed at establishing professional credentials in accounting at one of three levels, ranging from basic bookkeeping to the more demanding Chartered Public Accounting degree. The school accepted anyone who could afford the tuition.

The apparent appeal of an accounting certificate did not translate into high enrollments. When we started, the business program had thirty students and ten teachers. Tom's commercial arithmetic class had seven students, a crowd compared to my two students in business law. At our first faculty meeting prior to the start of classes, we talked to the teachers who had taught our courses during the previous semester. Tom's predecessor had covered two-thirds of the text, but the students had not mastered the material and had difficulty completing basic math problems in a timely way. Numbers less than one were incomprehensible and word problems overwhelming. To his six hours of scheduled class time, Tom added another four in which to do remedial work and practice exams.

Surprisingly, my predecessor had accomplished even less.

"How much did you cover?" I inquired.

"Fifty pages," he responded, without a trace of embarrassment, even though the textbook numbered some 300 pages.

Having examined the text beforehand, I realized the fifty pages to which he referred included the introduction and two chapters on the history and nature of law.

"You only covered two chapters?" I asked.

"Yes," he responded, puffing his chest. "And they know them very well."

With that ludicrous foundation, I launched into torts, contracts, partnerships, and other business law essentials. In addition to coping with the complexity and volume of the material, I found that my two students needed remedial work in English composition.

I sometimes dreaded facing these students, in part, because I was fairly sure they would have preferred a male teacher. Also, unlike Tom who is skilled in math, I had to teach myself the relevant law subjects in advance of each class.

My students were never discourteous in a direct way, but their passivity bordered on rudeness. I would greet them as I entered the classroom and receive only mumbled replies. When I asked a question, for example: "Can you explain the nature of this contract?" I got blank stares. "OK, who are the contracting parties?" Still, no response, but they began fidgeting in their seats. Sometimes, I read the case examples aloud in class, and then asked questions. Nothing worked. I didn't know how to engage them, but I persisted.

As we learned more about MIT, we realized the school took advantage of students in several ways. Instead of teaching a course in a single semester as other schools did, MIT extended the course over an entire academic year. One could argue that this allowed students sufficient time to learn difficult material, but our students fared worse on the national exams than those at other schools. Classes were often cancelled to free students to harvest corn grown on MIT's land; they were not compensated for their work. Mr. Nyasoro shortened the semester by a couple of weeks, without any commensurate reduction in tuition.

When not on foot, we generally traveled by matatu. Matatus were privately-owned and operated, average-sized, enclosed trucks with benches lining the sides for passengers. Before getting in any vehicle, Tom would examine it for relative soundness. Worn and damaged tires were a common problem. When concerned about safety, we would choose another matatu, ignoring the protocol of taking the first available vehicle. We couldn't evaluate the driver's competency, but the majority drove aggressively at dangerously high speeds. We could do little except hold on. I always tried to sit between Tom and the window to avoid the press of strangers' bodies and get some fresh air. I fixed my gaze on the landscape spinning past.

Occasionally, we took Nissan vans. These vans resembled vintage Volkswagen buses. In the event of an accident, the windshield and about one-quarter inch of metal were all that protected the driver and passengers in the front seat. For this reason, the Peace Corps urged volunteers to sit in the third or fourth row. We ignored this once.

We were returning from a weekend visiting friends in Eldoret, a day's trip from our home. It was Valentine's Day and we wanted to stop in Kisumu, Kenya's third largest city situated on the shores of Lake Victoria. Although the front row was available, we sat in the van's third row with three other passengers. It was painfully cramped; three people would have been crowded in the humid, sour-smelling space and we were five. I sat half on Tom's lap during the three-hour ride, my arms pinned to my sides. He was equally uncomfortable. We arrived in Kisumu safely, but stiff from having sat in one position for so long.

That night we splurged on pizza and wine at the Imperial Hotel, the most luxurious in the city. Sitting on upholstered chairs at a table set with white linens and silver, eating by candlelight, we felt like indulged tourists on a romantic getaway.

The following day, we continued our journey to Kisii. We chose a Nissan van again and this time sat in the front with the driver. About an hour or so into the trip, we saw a large truck ahead gradually beginning a left turn onto a dirt road. Initially, I thought nothing of it, because our driver had plenty of time to slow down. He did not reduce his speed; instead, he started honking his horn. The truck continued its ponderous turn. "Slow down," we yelled, but our driver continued to fly down the road, leaning heavily on his horn. At the last moment, he swerved to the right. The van careened off the road, bounced over a two-foot high cement island, and came to a stop in a market crowded with people. None of the shoppers were hurt. Tom was thrown against the roof of the van because he'd leaned over to protect me. I can still feel his weight pushing me down on the seat, trying to shield me from the expected impact.

I grabbed Tom by the arm, unaware he'd been injured, yanked our luggage out of the van and lurched off, dazed and angry. We left the driver in the midst of women yelling and waving their fists. Later, our missionary friend told me that had our driver injured someone in the crowd, the mob might have killed him.

I suffered only minor bruises, but for several months feared taking public transportation. After initial worry that Tom had fractured his neck, doctors diagnosed a severe case of whiplash. He wore a cervical collar for a few weeks to keep his head and neck still, but he recovered. Had the van hit the truck, as it was within inches of doing, we would have been killed. That knowledge haunted us.

After the accident, we started weighing the costs of staying in Kenya against our desire to honor our commitment as volunteers. We had so few students and little confidence that this would change in the next semester. Mr. Nyasoro had told us he wanted to convert our home into student housing and that we would have to move. Given the work we'd done on the house, his decision felt manipulative. Living in Kenya required us to travel by public transportation, putting us at risk for injury. Finally, our work at MIT didn't amount to much, as the school's administration fostered a culture that exploited rather than educated the students. Tom and I were mere window dressing, our purpose to enhance Mr. Nyasoro's stature. We completed the semester and then resigned as Peace Corps volunteers.

We returned to the United States in April 1990 and began remaking the fabric of our lives with intent, increased clarity, and gratitude. Tom went back to his former employer, now a considerably larger institution, and is still with them today two decades later. Although he might not admit it, he has indeed achieved prominence in his field. He handles it with humor and grace.

I asked him recently how his experience in Kenya had affected him as a manager and leader. He said Kenya taught him patience. Tom would not be characterized as a patient person, but he is more so now, more willing to let people and situations reveal themselves to him. He is also brave, and this attribute serves him well in both his professional and personal life. Tom did not acquire courage in Kenya. He was reminded he possessed it.

Rather than return to academic administration, I took a job with a start-up nonprofit group focused on community development, the field I had hoped to enter in Kenya. I spent more than ten years with the organization, helping to build its credibility and effectiveness. Although I have moved on to other ventures, I continue to regard that work as enormously satisfying. At the beginning, the gap between the organization's ambition and competence was so large, I should have been discouraged. I wasn't, because my ideas about work and risk had changed.

Our six months in Kenya were a great disruption. We gave up jobs, our home—so much that was familiar—in pursuit of another life without considering the consequences. In that sense, our friend's assessment of our time in Africa as "folly" is understandable. That said, what he failed to appreciate is that this upheaval laid the foundation for a richer life. Before we went to Africa, we were both at risk of being seduced by the material comfort and conventional success of our lives, even though neither of us could have articulated that at the time. Eventually, our choices would have been driven by the need to preserve the status quo. For us, this would have been a hollow existence.

Today, our life has many luxuries and its share of success, but neither of us believes we are defined by or bound to these things. We let go of them once. I think we could remember how to do it again.

Whose War

John Edgar Wideman

Nobody asked me, but I need to say what I'm thinking in this new year in New York City, five months after the Twin Towers burned, after long stretches of fall weather eerily close to perfect—clear blue skies, shirtsleeve warmth—through December, a bizarre hesitation, as if nature couldn't get on with its life and cycle to the next season, the city enclosed in a fragile, bell-jar calm till shattered by a siren, a plane's roar overhead.

I grew up in Homewood, an African-American community in Pittsburgh where people passing in the street might not have known each other's names but we knew something about each other's stories, so we always exchanged a greeting. We greeted each other because it feels good but also because we share the burden of racism, understand how it hurts, scars, deforms, but yes, it can be survived, and here we are, living proof meeting on the ground zero of a neighborhood street. The burning and collapse of the World Trade Center has conferred a similar sort of immediate intimacy upon all Americans. We've had the good luck to survive something awful, but do we truly understand, as Homewood people are disciplined to understand by the continuing presence of racism, that it ain't over yet. There's the next precarious step, and the next down the street, and to survive we must attend to the facts of division as well as the healing wish for solidarity.

Staring up at a vast, seamless blue sky, it's hard to reckon what's missing. The city shrinks in scale as the dome of sky endlessly recedes. Piles of steel and concrete are whims, the vexed arc of the city's history a moment lasting no longer than the lives of victims consumed in the burning towers. The lives lost mirror our own fragility and vulnerability, our unpredictable passage through the mysterious flow of time that eternally surrounds us, buoys us, drowns us. Ourselves the glass where we look for the faces of those who have disappeared, those we can no longer touch, where we find them looking back at us, terrified, terrifying.

A few moments ago I was a man standing at a window, nine stories up in an apartment building on the Lower East Side of New York, staring out at a building about a hundred yards away, more or less identical to his, wondering why he can't finish a piece of writing that for days had felt frustratingly close to being complete, then not even begun. Wondering why anybody, no matter how hard they'd plugged away at articulating their little piece of the puzzle, would want to throw more words on a pile so high the thing to be written about has disappeared. A man with the bright idea that he might call his work in progress "a speech to be performed because no one's listening." Like singing in the shower: no one hears you, but don't people sing their hearts out anyway, because the singing, the act itself, is also a listening to itself, so why not do your best to please yourself.

And the man standing at the window retracts his long arms from the top of the upper pane he's lowered to rest on as he stares. Then all of him retracts. Picture him standing a few moments ago where there's emptiness now. Picture him rising from a couch where he'd been stretched out, his back cushioned against the couch's arm, then rising and walking to the window. Now visualize the film running backward, the special effect of him sucked back like red wine spilled from the lip of a jug returning to fill the jug's belly, him restored exactly, legs stretched out, back against the couch's cushioned arm. Because that's who I am. What I'm doing and did. I'm the same man, a bit older now, but still a man like him, restless, worried, trying to fashion some tolerable response with words to a situation so collapsed, so asphyxiated by words, words, it's an abomination, an affront to dead people, to toss any more words on the ruins of what happened to them.

I, too, return to the couch, return also to the thought of a person alone singing in a shower. A sad thought, because all writing pretends to be something it's not, something it can't be: something or someone other, but sooner or later the writing will be snuffed back into its jug, back where I am, a writer a step, maybe two, behind my lemming words scuffling over the edge of the abyss.

I'm sorry. I'm an American of African descent, and I can't applaud my president for doing unto foreign others what he's inflicted on me and mine. Even if he calls it ole-time religion. Even if he tells me all good Americans have nothing to fear but fear itself and promises he's gonna ride over there and kick fear's ass real good, so I don't need to worry about anything, just let him handle it his way, relax and enjoy the show on TV, pay attention to each breath I take and be careful whose letters I open and listen up for the high alerts from the high-alert guy and gwan and do something nice for a Muslim neighbor this week. Plus, be patient. Don't expect too much too soon. These things take time. Their own good time. You know. The sweet by-and-by. Trust me.

I'm sorry. It all sounds too familiar. I've heard the thunder, seen the flash of his terrible swift sword before. I wish I could be the best kind of American. Not doubt his promises. Not raise his ire. I've felt his pointy boots in my butt before. But this time I can't be Tonto to his Lone Ranger. Amos to his Andy. Tambo to his Bones. Stepin to his Fetchit. I'm sorry. It's too late. I can't be as good an American as he's telling me to be. You know what I'm saying. I must be real. Hear what I'm saying. We ain't going nowhere, as the boys in the hood be saying. Nowhere. If you promote all the surviving Afghans to the status of honorary Americans, Mr. President, where exactly on the bus does that leave me. When do I get paid.

When can I expect my invitation to the ranch. I hear Mr. Putin's wearing jingle-jangle silver spurs around his dacha. Heard you fixed him up with an eight-figure advance on his memoirs. Is it true he's iced up to be the Marlboro man after he retires from Russia. Anything left under the table for me. And mine.

Like all my fellow countrymen and -women, even the ones who won't admit it, the ones who choose to think of themselves as not implicated, who maintain what James Baldwin called "a willed innocence," even the ones just off boats from Russia, Dominica, Thailand, Ireland, I am an heir to centuries of legal apartheid and must negotiate daily, with just about every step I take, the foul muck of unfulfilled promises, the apparent and not so apparent effects of racism that continue to plague America (and, do I need to add, plague the rest of the Alliance as well). It's complicated muck, muck that doesn't seem to dirty Colin Powell or Oprah or Michael Jordan or the black engineer in your firm who received a bigger raise than all her white colleagues, muck so thick it obscures the presence of millions of underclass African Americans living below the poverty line, hides from public concern legions of young people of color wasting away in prison. How can I support a president whose rhetoric both denies and worsens the muck when he pitches his crusade against terror as a holy war, a war of good against evil, forces of light versus forces of darkness, a summons to arms that for colored folks chillingly echoes and resuscitates the Manichaean dualism of racism.

I remain puzzled by the shock and surprise nonblack Americans express when confronted by what they deem my "*anger*" (most would accept the friendly amendment of "*rage*" or "*bitterness*" inside the quotes). Did I see in their eyes a similar shock and surprise on September 11. Is it truly news that some people's bad times (slavery, colonial subjugation, racial oppression, despair) have underwritten other people's good times (prosperity, luxury, imperial domination, complacency). News that a systematic pattern of gross inequities still has not been corrected and that those who suffer them are desperate (*angry, bitter, enraged*) for change.

For months an acrid pall of smoke rose from smoldering ruins, and now a smokescreen of terror hovers, *terror* as the enemy, terror as the problem, terror as the excuse for denying and unleashing the darkness within ourselves.

To upstage and camouflage a real war at home the threat of terror is being employed to justify a phony war in Afghanistan. A phony war because it's being pitched to the world as righteous retaliation, as self-defense after a wicked, unwarranted sucker punch when in fact the terrible September 11 attack as well as the present military incursion into Afghanistan are episodes in a long-standing vicious competition—buses bombed in Israel, helicopters strafing Palestinian homes, economic sanctions blocking the flow of food and medicine for Iraq, no-fly zones, Desert Storms, and embassy bombings—for oil and geopolitical leverage in the Middle East.

A phony war that the press, in shameless collusion with the military, exploits daily as newsy entertainment, a self-promoting concoction of fiction, fact, propaganda, and melodrama designed to keep the public tuned in, uninformed, distracted, convinced a real war is taking place.

A phony war because its stated objective—eradicating terrorism—is impossible and serves to mask unstated, alarmingly open-ended goals, a kind of fishing expedition that provides an opportunity for America to display its intimidating arsenal and test its allies' loyalty, license them to crush internal dissent.

A phony war, finally, because it's not waged to defend America from an external foe but to homogenize and coerce its citizens under a flag of rabid nationalism.

The Afghan campaign reflects a global struggle but also reveals a crisis inside America—the attempt to construct on these shores a society willing to sacrifice democracy and individual autonomy for the promise of material security, the exchange of principles for goods and services. A society willing to trade the tumultuous uncertainty generated by a government dedicated to serving the interests of many different, unequal kinds of citizens for the certainty of a government responsive to a privileged few and their self-serving, single-minded, ubiquitous, thus invisible, ideology: profit. Such a government of the few is fabricating new versions of freedom. Freedom to exploit race, class, and gender inequities without guilt or accountability; freedom to drown in ignorance while flooded by information; freedom to be plundered by corporations. Freedom to drug ourselves and subject our children's minds to the addictive mix of fantasy and propaganda, the nonstop ads that pass for a culture.

A phony war but also a real war, because as it bumbles and rumbles along people are dying and because like all wars it's a sign of failure and chaos. When we revert to the final solution of kill or be killed, all warring parties in the name of clan tribe nation religion violate the first law of civilization—that human life is precious. In this general collapse, one of the first victims is language. Words are deployed as weapons to identify, stigmatize, eliminate, the enemy. One side boasts of inflicting casualties, excoriates the other side as cowards and murderers. One side calls civilians it kills collateral damage, labels civilian deaths by its opponents' terrorism.

From their initial appearance in English to describe the bloody dismantling of royal authority during the French Revolution (Burke's "thousands of those

Hell-hounds called Terrorists . . . are let loose on the people") the words *terror* and *terrorist* have signified godless savagery. Other definitions—government by a system of coercive intimidation—have almost entirely disappeared. Seldom if ever perceived neutrally as a tool, a set of practices and tactics for winning a conflict, terror instead is understood as pure evil. Terror and terrorists in this Manichaean scheme are excluded even from the problematic dignity of conventional warfare.

One side's use of *terrorist* to describe the other is never the result of a reasoned exchange between antagonists. It's a refusal of dialogue, a negation of the other. The designation terrorist is produced by the one-way gaze of power. Only one point of view, one vision, one story, is necessary and permissible, since what defines the gaze of power is its absolute, unquestionable authority.

To label an enemy a terrorist confers the same invisibility a colonist's gaze confers upon the native. Dismissing the possibility that the native can look back at you just as you are looking at him is a first step toward blinding him and ultimately rendering him or her invisible. Once a slave or colonized native is imagined as invisible, the business of owning him, occupying and exploiting his land, becomes more efficient, pleasant.

A state proclaiming itself besieged by terrorists asserts its total innocence, cites the unreasonableness, the outrageousness, of the assaults upon it. A holy war may be launched to root out terrorism, but its form must be a punitive crusade, an angry god's vengeance exacted upon sinners, since no proper war can exist when there is no recognition of the other's list of grievances, no awareness of the relentless dynamic binding the powerful and powerless. Perhaps that's why the monumental collapsing of the towers delivered such a shocking double dose of reality to Americans—yes, a war's been raging and yes, here's astounding proof we may have already lost it. It's as if one brick snatched away, one sledgehammer blow, demolished our Berlin Wall.

Regimes resisting change dismiss challenges to their authority by branding them terrorist provocations. In the long bloody struggles that often follow, civil protests, car bombings, kidnappings, assassinations, guerrilla warfare in the mountains, full-scale conventional military engagements, blur one into the other. At first the media duly reports on the frightening depredations of terrorists—Algerian terror, Mau Mau terror, Palestinian terror, Israeli terror, South African terror—then bears witness as fighters from the Mau Mau, the Palmach, the PLO, emerge to become leaders of new states. George Washington, inaugurated as America's first president only a few blocks from the ruins of the World Trade Center, would have been branded a terrorist if the word had been invented in 1775. Clearly not all terrorists become prime ministers or presidents, but if and when they do they rewrite the history of their struggle to attain legitimacy. This turnabout clarifies the relationship between power and terror. Terrorists are those who have no official standing, no gaze, no voice in the established order, those determined by all means possible to usurp power in order to be seen and heard. Some former terrorists survive to accomplish precisely that. Others survive long enough to decry and denounce the terrorist threat nibbling at the edges of their own regime.

The destruction of the World Trade Center was a criminal act, the loss of life an unforgivable consequence, but it would be a crime of another order, with an even greater destructive potential, to allow the evocation of the word *terror* to descend like a veil over the event, to rob us of the opportunity to see ourselves as others see us.

The terror that arises from fear of loss, fear of pain, death, annihilation, prostrates us because it's both rational and irrational. Rational because our sense of the world's uncertainty is accurate. Rational because reason confirms the difference between what is knowable and unknowable, warns us that in certain situations we can expect no answers, no help. We are alone. Irrational because that's all we have left when reason abandons us. Our naked emotions, our overwhelmed smallness.

Terror thrives in the hour of the wolf, the hour of Gestapo raids on Jewish ghettos, of blue-coated cavalry charges on Native American villages. Those predawn hours when most of us are born or die, the hour when cops smash through doors to crack down on drugs or on dissidents, the hour of transition when sleep has transported the body furthest from its waking state, when our ability to distinguish dream from not-dream weakens. Terror manifests itself at this primal juncture between sleep and waking because there we are eternally children, outside time, beyond the protections and consolations of society, prey to fear of the dark.

To a child alone, startled from sleep by a siren, the hulking bear silhouetted in the middle of the dark room is real. The child may remember being assured that no bears live on the Lower East Side of New York, may know his parents' bed is just down the hall, may even recall tossing his bulky down parka over the back of the chair instead of hanging it neatly in the closet like he's been told a million times to do. None of this helps, because reason has deserted him. Even if things get better when his mother knocks and calls him for breakfast, the darkness has been branded once again, indelibly, by agonizing, demoralizing fear, by a return to stark terror.

For those who don't lose a child's knack for perceiving the aural archaeology within the sound of words, words carry forward fragments, sound bites that reveal a word's history, its layered onomatopoeic sources, its multiplicity of shadowed meanings. *Terror* embeds a grab bag of unsettling echoes: tear (as in rip) (as in run fast), terra (earth, ground, grave, dirt, unfamiliar turf), err (mistake), air (terra firma's opposite element), eerie (strange, unnatural), error (of our ways), roar-r-r (beasts, machines, parents, gods). Of course any word's repertoire is arbitrary and precise, but that's also the point, the power of puns, double entendre, words migrating among languages, Freudian slips, Lacan's "breaks," all calling attention to the unconscious, archaic intentionality buried in the words.

But the word *terror* also incarcerates. Like the child pinned to its bed, not moving a muscle for fear it will arouse the bear, we're immobilized, paralyzed by terror. Dreading what we might discover, we resist investigating terror's source. Terror feeds on ignorance, confines us to our inflamed, tortured imaginings. If we forget that terror, like evil, resides in us, is spawned by us no matter what name we give it, then it makes good sense to march off and destroy the enemy. But we own terror. We can't offload it onto the back of some hooded, barbaric, shadowy other. Someone we can root out of his cave and annihilate. However, we continue to be seduced by the idea that we might be able to cleanse ourselves of terror, accomplish a final resolution of our indeterminate nature. But even if we could achieve freedom from terror, what would we gain by such a radical reconfiguration of what constitutes being human. What kind of new world order would erase the terror we're born with, the terror we chip away at but never entirely remove. What system could anticipate, translate, or diffuse the abiding principle of uncertainty governing the cosmos. Systems that promise a world based on imperishable, impregnable truth deliver societies of truncated imagination, of history and appetite denied, versions of Eden where there is no dreaming, no rebellion, no Eros, where individuality is sacrificed for interchangeability, eternal entertainment, becalmed ego, mortality disguised as immortality by the absence of dread.

Power pales (turns white with terror—imagines its enemies black—invents race) when power confronts the inevitability of change. By promising to keep things as they are, promising to freeze out or squeeze out those not already secure within the safety net of privilege, Mr. Bush won (some say stole) an election. By launching a phony war he is managing to avoid the scrutiny a first-term, skin-of-its-teeth presidency deserves. Instead he's terrorizing Americans into believing that we require a wartime leader wielding unquestioned emergency powers. Beneath the drumbeat belligerence of his demands for national unity, if you listen you'll hear the bullying, the self-serving, the hollowness, of his appeals to patriotism. Listen carefully and you'll also hear what he's not saying: that we need, in a democracy full of contradictions and unresolved divisions, opposition voices.

Those who mount a challenge to established order are not the embodiment of evil. Horrifically bloody, criminal acts may blot the humanity of the perpetrators and stimulate terror in victims and survivors, but the ones who perpetrate such deeds are not the source of the terror within us. To call these people terrorists or evil, even to maintain our absolute distinction between victims and perpetrators, exercises the blind, one-way gaze of power, perpetuates the reign of the irrational and supernatural, closes down the possibility that by speaking to one another we might formulate appropriate responses, even to the unthinkable.

Although trouble may always prevail, being human offers us a chance to experience moments when trouble doesn't rule, when trouble's not totally immune to compassion and reason, when we make choices, and try to better ourselves and make other lives better.

Is war a preferable alternative. If a child's afraid of the dark, do we solve the problem by buying her a gun.

Suggestions for Further Reading

Abbey, Edward. *Desert Solitaire.*

Acimen, André. *False Papers: Essays on Exile and Memory.*

——————, ed. *Letters of Transit: Reflections on Exile, Identity, Language and Loss.*

Adnan, Etel. *In the Heart of the Heart of Another Country.*

Allison, Dorothy. *Two or Three Things I Know For Sure.*

Baca, Jimmy Santiago. *Working in the Dark: Reflections of a Poet of the Barrio.*

——————. *A Place to Stand.*

Barns, Kim. *Hungry for the World.*

Berry, Wendell. *Sex, Economy, Freedom and Community: Eight Essays.*

Bottoms, Greg. *Fight Scenes.*

——————. *Angelhead: My Brother's Descent into Madness.*

Boully, Jenny. *The Body: An Essay.*

Courturier, Lisa. *The Hopes of Snakes: And Other Tales from the Urban Landscape.*

D'Agata, John. *Halls of Fame: Essays.*

De Botton, Alain. *The Art of Travel.*

Deming, Alison and Lucinda Bliss. *Anatomy of Desire: The Daughter/Mother Sessions.*

Derricotte, Toi. *The Black Notebooks: An Interior Journey.*

Dillard, Annie. *Pilgrim at Tinker Creek.*

Dixon, Terrell. *City Wilds: Essays and Stories about Urban Nature.*

Doty, Mark. *Still Life with Oysters and Lemon.*

Dubus, Andre. *Broken Vessels.*

——————. *Meditations from a Movable Chair.*

Eggers, Dave. *A Heartbreaking Work of Staggering Genius.*

Ehrlich, Gretel. *The Solace of Open Spaces.*

——————. *The Future of Ice.*

Elliott, Stephen. *The Adderall Diaries: A Memoir of Moods, Masochism, and Murder.*

Flynn, Nick. *Another Bullshit Night in Suck City.*

Galeano, Eduardo. Tr. Cedric Belfrage. *The Book of Embraces.*

Gass, William. *Finding a Form: Essays.*

Gawande, Atul. *Complications: A Surgeon's Notes on an Imperfect Science.*

Gessner, David. *Sick of Nature.*

_____. *Return of the Osprey: A Season of Flight and Wonder.*

Griffin, Susan. *Made from this Earth: An Anthology of Writings.*

Griffiths, Jay. *Wild: An Elemental Journey.*

Haines, John. *The Stars, the Snow, the Fire: Twenty-five Years in the Alaska Wilderness.*

Hampl, Patricia. *I Could Tell You Stories: Sojourns in the Land of Memory.*

Hickey, Dave. *Air Guitar: Essays on Art & Democracy.*

Hoagland, Edward. *The Courage of Turtles.*

hooks, bell. *Remembered Rapture: The Writer at Work.*

Hogan, Linda. *Dwellings: A Spiritual History of the Living World.*

Hurd, Barbara. *Entering the Stone: On Caves and Feeling Through the Dark.*

_____. *Walking the Wrack Line: On Tidal Shifts and What Remains.*

_____. *Stirring the Mud: On Swamps, Bogs, and Human Imagination.*

Jakiela, Lori. *Miss New York Has Everything.*

Karr, Mary. *Lit: A Memoir.*

_____. *The Liars' Club.*

Kincaid, Jamaica. *A Small Place.*

_____. *My Brother.*

Kooser, Ted. *Local Wonders: Seasons in the Bohemian Alps.*

_____. *Lights on a Ground of Darkness: An Evocation of a Place and Time.*

Lamberton, Ken. *Wilderness and Razor Wire: A Naturalist's Observations from Prison.*

Legler, Gretchen. *On the Ice: An Intimate Portrait of Life at the McMurdo Station, Antarctica.*

Lopate, Phillip. *Getting Personal: Selected Writings.*

Lopez, Barry. *Crossing Open Ground.*

_____. *Of Wolves and Men.*

Lorde, Audre. *Zami: A New Spelling of My Name.*

McPhee, John. *The Control of Nature.*

McMahon, Bucky. *Night Diver.*

Mairs, Nancy. *Waist-High in the World: A Life Among the Nondisabled.*

_____. *Carnal Acts*

Marquart, Debra. *The Horizontal World: Growing up Wild in the Middle of Nowhere.*

Martone, Michael. *The Flatness and Other Landscapes.*

Matthiessen, Peter. *The Snow Leopard.*

Miles, Kathryn. *Adventures with Ari.*

Miller, Brenda. *Season of the Body: Essays*

_____. *Blessing of the Animals.*

Monson, Ander. *Neck Deep and Other Predicaments: Essays.*

Mora, Pat. *House of Houses.*

Nabhan, Gary Paul. *Cross-pollinations: The Marriage of Science and Poetry.*

Nelson, Richard. *The Island Within.*

Norris, Kathleen. *Dakota: A Spiritual Geography.*

Nye, Naomi Shihab. *Never in a Hurry: Essays on People and Places.*

Orlean, Susan. *The Orchid Thief.*

Pollan, Michael. *Second Nature: A Gardener's Education.*

——————————. *The Botany of Desire.*

Price, John T. *Man Killed by Pheasant: And Other Kinships.*

Purpura, Lia. *On Looking: Essays.*

Rankine, Claudia. *Don't Let Me Be Lonely: An American Lyric.*

Ray, Janisse. *Ecology of a Cracker Childhood.*

——————————. *Wild Card Quilt: The Ecology of Home.*

Reichl, Ruth. *Comfort Me with Apples.*

Rodriguez, Robert. *Days of Obligation: An Argument with My Mexican Father.*

Rogers, Pattiann. *The Dream of the Marsh Wren: Writing as Reciprocal Creation.*

Rosenthal, Amy Krouse. *Encyclopedia of an Ordinary Life.*

St. Germain, Sheryl. *Swamp Songs: The Making of an Unruly Woman.*

Sanders, Scott Russell. *Writing from the Center.*

——————————. *Secrets of the Universe: Essays on Family, Community, Spirit, and Place.*

——————————. *Hunting for Hope: A Father's Journeys.*

Satrapi, Marjane. *Persepolis: The Story of a Childhood.*

Schwartz, Ruth L. *Death in Reverse: A Love Story.*

Sebald, W.G. *The Rings of Saturn.*

Selzer, Richard. *The Exact Location of the Soul: New and Selected Essays.*

Shepard, Paul. *Thinking Animals: Animals and the Development of Human Intelligence.*

Silko, Leslie Mormon. *Yellow Woman and a Beauty of the Spirit: Essays on Native American Life Today.*

Slater, Lauren. *Lying: A Metaphorical Memoir.*

Slovic, Scott. *Going Away to Think: Engagement, Retreat, and Ecocritical Responsibility.*

Solnit, Rebecca. *A Field Guide to Getting Lost.*

Spragg, Mark. *Where Rivers Change Direction.*

Steingraber, Sandra. *Having Faith: An Ecologist's Journey to Motherhood.*

Sutin, Lawrence. *A Postcard Memoir.*

Tevis, Joni. *The Wet Collection.*

Theroux, Paul. *The Old Patagonia Express: By Train through the Americas.*

Thomas, Abigail. *Safekeeping: Some True Stories from a Life.*

——————————. *A Three Dog Life.*

Turner, Jack. *The Abstract Wild.*
Vowell, Sarah. *Assassination Vacation.*
Weisman, Alan. *The World Without Us.*
Wideman, John Edgar. *Hoop Roots: Basketball, Race, and Love.*
——————————. *Brothers and Keepers.*
Williams, Terry Tempest. *Desert Quartet: An Erotic Landscape*
——————————. *Refuge: An Unnatural History of Family and Place.*
Wolff, Geoffrey. *The Duke of Deception.*
Wolff, Tobias. *This Boy's Life.*

Anthologies, Craft Guides

Aaron, Jane. *40 Model Essays: A Portable Anthology.*
Atkins, Douglas. *Tracing the Essay: Through Experience to Truth.*
Atwan, Robert, series editor. *Best American Essays* series.
Barnhill, David Landis. *At Home on Earth: Becoming Native to Our Place.*
Bergon, Frank. *The Wilderness Reader.*
Birkerts, Sven. *The Art of Time in Memoir.*
——————————, ed. *Tolstoy's Dictaphone: Technology and the Muse.*
Bradway, Becky and Doug Hesse, eds. *Creating Nonfiction: A Guide and Anthology.*
Bradway, Becky, ed. *In the Middle of the Middle West: Literary Nonfiction from the Heartland.*
Butrym, Alexander J., ed. *Essays on the Essay: Redefining the Genre.*
Calvino, Italo. *Six Memos for the Next Millennium.*
D'Agata, John, ed. *The Next American Essay.*
——————————, ed. *The Lost Origins of the Essay.*
DiYanni, Robert. *The Essay: An Introduction.*
Doty, Mark. *Open House: Writers Redefine Home.*
Ducornet, Rikki, Bradford Morrow, Robert Polito, and Rick Moody, eds. *Conjunctions: 46, Selected Subversions: Essays on the World at Large.*
Elder, John. *The Norton Book of Nature Writing.*
Epstein, Joseph, ed. *The Norton Book of Personal Essays.*
Fiffer, Sharon Sloan and Steve Fiffer, eds. *Home: American Writers Remember Rooms of Their Own.*
Folger, Tim, series editor. *The Best American Science and Nature Writing.*
Forché, Carolyn and Philip Gerard, eds. *Writing Creative Nonfiction.*
Foster, Patricia and Mary Swander, eds. *The Healing Circle: Authors Writing of Recovery.*
Good, Graham. *The Observing Self: Rediscovering the Essay.*
Gutkind, Lee, ed. *The Best Creative Nonfiction,* Vol. 2.
Halpern, Daniel and Dan Frank. *Nature Reader.*

Heard, Georgia. *Writing Toward Home: Tales and Lessons to Find Your Way.*
Holzer, Burghild Nina. *A Walk Between Heaven and Earth: A Personal Journal on Writing and the Creative Process.*
Lanham, Richard. *Revising Prose.*
Lazar, David, ed. *Truth in Nonfiction: Essays.*
Le Guin, Ursula K. *The Wave in the Mind: Talks and Essays on the Writer, the Reader, and the Imagination.*
Lopate, Phillip, ed. *The Art of the Personal Essay: An Anthology from the Classical Era to the Present.*
Maso, Carole. *Break Every Rule: Essays on Language, Longing, & Moments of Desire.*
Miller, Brenda and Suzanne Paola. *Tell it Slant: Writing and Shaping Creative Nonfiction.*
Moore, Dinty W. *The Truth of the Matter: Art and Craft in Creative Nonfiction.*
Nelson, Victoria. *On Writer's Block: A New Approach to Creativity.*
Nguyen, B. Minh and Porter Shreve. *Contemporary Creative Nonfiction: I & Eye.*
Oates, Joyce Carol, ed. *The Best American Essays of the Century.*
Perl, Sondra and Mimi Schwartz. *Writing True: The Art and Craft of Creative Nonfiction.*
Root, Robert L. and Michael Steinberg. *The Fourth Genre: Contemporary Writers of/on Creative Nonfiction*
Shields, David. *Reality Hunger: A Manifesto.*
Wilson, Jason, series editor. *The Best American Travel Writing.*
Yagoda, Ben. *Memoir: A History.*

Journals and Magazines

The American Scholar
Ascent
The Atlantic
Bellingham Review
Black Warrior Review
Brevity
The Chattahoochee Review
Colorado Review
Crab Orchard Review
Crazyhorse
Creative Nonfiction
Diagram
Ecotone: Reimagining Place
The Florida Review
Flyway

Fourth Genre: Explorations in Nonfiction
The Fourth River
The Georgia Review
The Gettysburg Review
Granta
Harper's Magazine
Harvard Review
Hawk and Handsaw
Iowa Review
ISLE (Interdisciplinary Studies in Literature and Environment)
Isotope
The Journal
The Literary Review
Louisiana Literature
Memoir(and)
Mid-American Review
The Missouri Review
Narrative Magazine
The New Yorker
The Ninth Letter
Orion
Passages North
The Pinch
Ploughshares
PMS poemmemoirstory
Prairie Schooner
River Teeth
Salmagundi
The Seneca Review
Southern Humanities Review
The Sun
Swink
Tiny Lights: A Journal of Personal Narrative
Vanity Fair
The Virginia Quarterly Review

Contributors

DOROTHY ALLISON

Dorothy Allison is the author of: three novels, *Bastard Out of Carolina*, a finalist for the National Book Award; *Cavedweller*, a *New York Times* Notable book of the year; and *She Who*; a short story collection, *Trash*, winner of two Lambda Literary Awards and an ALA prize; and a chapbook of poetry, *The Women Who Hate Me*. *Bastard Out of Carolina* and *Cavedweller* have been adapted into movies. Allison received the 2007 Robert Penn Warren Award for Fiction.

JIMMY SANTIAGO BACA

Jimmy Santiago Baca's semi-autobiographical novel in verse, *Martin and Meditations on the South Valley*, received the American Book Award for poetry in 1987. His poetry collections include *Selected Poems* (2009), *Set This Book on Fire*, and *Black Mesa Poems*. Baca is also the author of a memoir, *A Place to Stand: The Making of a Poet*; a collection of stories and essays, *Working in the Dark: Reflections of a Poet of the Barrio*; a play, *Los Tres Hijos de Julia*; and a screenplay, *Bound by Honor*, which was released by Hollywood Pictures in 1993.

JOHN BIGUENET

John Biguenet wrote *The Torturer's Apprentice: Stories* and the novel *Oyster* as well as the award-winning plays *The Vulgar Soul, Rising Water*, and *Shotgun*. He edited or co-edited *Foreign Fictions, The Craft of Translation* and *Theories of Translation: An Anthology of Essays from Dryden to Derrida*, and *Strange Harbors*. An O. Henry award winner for short fiction and *New York Times* guest columnist as well as past president of the American Literary Translators Association, he is the Robert Hunter Distinguished University Professor at Loyola University in New Orleans.

TOM BISSELL

Tom Bissell is the author of *Chasing the Sea* (a travel narrative), *God Lives in St. Petersburg* (a story collection), *The Father of All Things* (a hybrid work of history and memoir), and *Extra Lives* (a work of criticism about video games). He lives in Portland, Oregon.

GREG BOTTOMS

Greg Bottoms is the author of a memoir, *Angelhead*, a documentary narrative, *The Colorful Apocalypse*, and two prose collections, *Sentimental, Heartbroken Rednecks* and *Fight Scenes*. He is an Associate Professor of English at the University of Vermont.

JOY CASTRO

Author of the memoir *The Truth Book*, Joy Castro has published fiction and creative nonfiction in journals including *North American Review, Quarterly West, Texas Review, Afro-Hispanic Review, Fourth Genre, Seneca Review*, and *The New York Times Magazine*. Her essays appear in anthologies including *Breeder, Without a Net, An Angle of Vision*, and *The Other Latino*. Named a Best New Latino Writer of 2009 by the editors of *Latino Boom*, she teaches English and Ethnic Studies at the University of Nebraska-Lincoln.

TOI DERRICOTTE

Toi Derricotte is the author of a memoir, *The Black Notebooks*, and four books of poetry, *Tender, Captivity, Natural Birth*, and *Empress of the Death House*. She has received numerous awards, including a fellowship from the Rockefeller Foundation, a Guggenheim Fellowship, two fellowships in poetry from the National Endowment for the Arts, and two Pushcart Prizes. *The Black Notebooks* received the Anisfield-Wolf Award and was a *New York Times* Notable book of the year. She is the co-founder of Cave Canem, the historic workshop/retreat for African American poets.

BRIAN DOYLE

Brian Doyle is the author of nine books: five collections of essays, two nonfiction books (*The Grail* and *The Wet Engine*), and two collections of "proems," most recently *Thirsty for the Joy: Australian & American Voices*. Doyle's essays have appeared in publications such as *The Best American Essays, The Atlantic, Harper's*, and *The American Scholar*. Honors for his work include two Pushcart Prizes, the Catholic Press Association Book Award, and a 2008 Award in Literature from the American Academy of Arts and Letters. He edits *Portland Magazine*.

GRETEL EHRLICH

Gretel Ehrlich is an essayist, novelist, and poet whose books include *The Solace of Open Spaces, A Match to the Heart*, and *This Cold Heaven*. Her work has appeared in such publications as *Best Essays of the Century, Best American Essays, Best Spiritual Writing, Best Travel Writing, The Nature Reader, Harper's, The Atlantic*, and *The New York Times Magazine*. She is the recipient of numerous awards and honors including an NEA Fellowship, a Whiting Foundation Award, and a Guggenheim Fellowship.

JANE FISHMAN

Jane Fishman is a former high school English teacher, speechwriter, and public relations specialist. She has owned a laundromat and a Middle Eastern vegetarian restaurant. After leaving restaurant work she entered journalism, first as an obituary writer, then a feature writer, then, for the past 20 years, as a columnist for the *Savannah Morning News.* Her collection of essays from the newspaper, *Everyone's Gotta Be Somewhere,* appeared in 2001. She is a gardener who does not plant in rows, a Northerner at heart who lives in her adopted city, Savannah, and a former resident of Chicago, Eureka Springs, Arkansas, and Key West, Florida.

MELANIE DYLAN FOX

In addition to receiving a notable mention in the *Best American Essays* series and an AWP Intro Award, Melanie Dylan Fox's work has previously appeared in the journals *Fourth Genre, Flyway,* and *Bayou Magazine* and in the anthologies *American Nature Writing* and *Figuring Animals: Essays on Animal Images in Art, Literature, Philosophy, & Popular Culture.* She teaches in Chatham University's low-residency MFA program and currently makes her home at the confluence of the Blue Ridge and Appalachian Mountains in rural southwestern Virginia.

DAVID GESSNER

David Gessner is the author of six books of literary nonfiction, including *Sick of Nature, Return of the Osprey,* and *Soaring with Fidel.* His recent essays have appeared in *The New York Times Magazine, Best American Nonrequired Reading,* and on NPR's "This I Believe." He has taught Environmental Writing as a Briggs-Copeland Lecturer at Harvard, and is currently a Professor at the University of North Carolina at Wilmington, where he also edits the literary journal of place, *Ecotone.*

DEREK GREEN

Derek Green is the author of *New World Order,* a collection of short stories about American expatriates living abroad in the age of terror. A veteran traveler who has worked in 22 countries on six continents, his fiction and nonfiction have appeared in many publications. He lives in New Haven, Connecticut with his wife and two sons.

JOHN HAINES

John Haines has published over ten collections of poetry, including *At the End of This Summer: Poems 1948-1954,* and *New Poems 1980-88,* for which he received the Lenore Marshall Poetry Prize and the Western States Book Award; a collection of essays, *Fables and Distances;* and a memoir, *The Stars, the Snow, the Fire: Twenty-five Years in the Alaska Wilderness.* Former Poet Laureate of Alaska, his honors include two Guggenheim Fellowships, an Amy Lowell Travelling Fellowship, an NEA Fellowship, and a Lifetime Achievement Award from the Library of Congress.

LINDA HOGAN

Linda Hogan's works include *Seeing Through the Sun,* winner of the American Book Award; *The Book of Medicines,* a finalist for the National Book Critics Circle; and *Mean Spirit,* a Pulitzer Prize finalist. Recent publications include *Rounding the Human Corners: Poems* (2008), *People of the Whale: A Novel* (2008), and *The Inner Journey: Views from Native Traditions* (editor, 2009). She has received the Oklahoma Book Award, the Colorado Book Award, the Mountains and Plains Booksellers Award, an NEA grant, a Minnesota Arts Board grant, a Lannan Award, and a Guggenheim Fellowship.

BARBARA HURD

Barbara Hurd is the author of *Walking the Wrack Line: On Tidal Shifts and What Remains, Entering the Stone: On Caves and Feeling Through the Dark* (a Library Journal Best Natural History Book of the Year), *The Singer's Temple, Stirring the Mud: On Swamps, Bogs, and Human Imagination* (a Los Angeles Times Best Book of 2001), and *Objects in This Mirror.* She has received an NEA Fellowship for Creative Nonfiction, the Sierra Club's National Nature Writing Award, and two Pushcart Prizes. She teaches creative writing at Frostburg State University and in Stonecoast and Chatham University's low-residency MFA programs.

ROBERT ISENBERG

Robert Isenberg is a writer and stage performer. He has contributed essays to *Mental_Floss, MSN.com, Storyscape, The New Yinzer, Conte,* and *Pittsburgh Love Stories.* As a journalist, he has earned a Keystone Award and a Golden Quill Award. As a playwright, his scripts have been staged by the Pittsburgh New Works Festival, the Pittsburgh Pride Theatre Festival, B.U.S. 24-Hour Play Festival, New Plays on Penn, and Duquesne University. Isenberg is also creator of the Pittsburgh Monologue Project. His first book, *The Iron Mountain,* was published in 2009. Isenberg teaches playwriting at Duquesne University.

LORI JAKIELA

Lori Jakiela's essays and poems have appeared in *DoubleTake, River Styx, Creative Nonfiction, The Pittsburgh Post Gazette, The Chicago Review, 5 AM,* and elsewhere. Her chapbook, *The Regulars*—a collection of poems and essays—was published by Liquid Paper Press and was awarded first prize in Nerve Cowboy's 2001 chapbook contest. Her memoir, *Miss New York Has Everything,* was published in January 2006. She is the director of the writing program at The University of Pittsburgh at Greensburg.

JAMAICA KINCAID

Jamaica Kincaid's books include the novels *Annie John, Lucy, The Autobiography of My Mother*, and *Mr. Potter*, the book-length essay *A Small Place; My Brother*, a memoir; and *At the Bottom of the River*, a book of short stories. Kincaid explores her love of horticulture in *Among Flowers: A Walk in the Himalaya, My Garden Book*, and *My Favorite Plant* (editor). *Talk Stories*, a collection of writings from her time at *The New Yorker*, was published in 2000. The recipient of numerous awards and honors, she is a Professor of Literature at Claremont McKenna College.

ELIZABETH KIRSCHNER

Elizabeth Kirschner has published five volumes of poetry, most recently, *My Life as a Doll*, published by Autumn House Press in 2008 and *Surrender to Light*, brought out from Cherry Grove Collections in 2009. She taught at Boston College for many years, and now resides in Kittery Point, Maine.

AMANDA LESKOVAC

Amanda Leskovac is the 2009 nonfiction prize recipient from the *Bellevue Literary Review*. Her work has also appeared in *Calyx, The Sylvan Echo*, and *The Chimeara*. She lives in Pittsburgh, where she teaches composition, literature and creative writing. She is currently finishing her memoir, *Cock-Eyed View*, and celebrates her 14th year in a chair this year.

PHILLIP LOPATE

Phillip Lopate has written three personal essay collections, *Bachelorhood, Against Joie de Vivre*, and *Portrait of My Body*; two novels, *Confessions of Summer* and *The Rug Merchant*; two poetry collections, *The Eyes Don't Always Want to Stay Open* and *The Daily Round*; a memoir of his teaching experiences, *Being With Children*; a collection of movie criticism, *Totally Tenderly Tragically*; an urbanist meditation, *Waterfront: A Journey Around Manhattan*, and a biographical monograph, *Rudy Burckhardt: Photographer and Filmmaker*. In addition, there is a Phillip Lopate reader, *Getting Personal: Selected Writings*. He has been a recipient of numerous awards, including a Guggenheim and two NEA grants.

BK LOREN

BK Loren has worked as a truck driver, ad-woman, candy factory dipper, naturalist, ranch hand, large predator tracker, and many other things to support her writing habit. Her essays and stories have been published widely in periodicals and anthologies including *Orion Magazine, Parabola, Women on the Verge, The Future of Nature, Best American Spiritual Writing*, and others. She is grateful to the Mary Roberts-Rinehart Foundation, Colorado Council on the Arts, Ucross Foundation, Colorado Art Ranch, and all the folks who have generously offered her fellowships. Her first book, *The Way of the River*, came out in 2001.

JO MCDOUGALL

Jo McDougall is the author of five books of poetry, *Woman in the Next Booth, Towns Facing Railroads, From Darkening Porches, Dirt* and *Satisfied with Havoc*. She is completing a memoir, *Daddy's Money*. A native of DeWitt, Arkansas, she lives in Leawood, Kansas.

DEBRA MARQUART

Debra Marquart is a Professor of English in the MFA Program in Creative Writing & Environment at Iowa State University. Her books include two poetry collections—*Everything's a Verb* and *From Sweetness*—and a short story collection, *The Hunger Bone: Rock & Roll Stories*. Marquart's memoir, *The Horizontal World: Growing Up Wild in the Middle of Nowhere*, received the 2007 PEN USA Creative Nonfiction Award, the Elle Lettres Award from *Elle Magazine*, and a *New York Times* Editors' Choices commendation. Marquart has received a Pushcart Prize, the Shelby Foote Nonfiction Prize, and an NEA Fellowship.

KATHRYN MILES

Kathryn Miles is an award-winning writer whose recent essays have appeared in *Ecotone, Editor Unleashed, Terrain, The Bioregional Imagination, PMLA*, and *Best American Essays*. She is also the author of *Adventures With Ari* (2009) and the long-running "Backcountry Bistro" column. She has lectured at Harvard, Antioch New England, Green Mountain College, and Orion Society workshops. Miles currently serves as director of the Environmental Writing program at Unity College, as editor of *Hawk & Handsaw: The Journal of Creative Sustainability*, and as a scholar-in-residence for The Maine Humanities Council.

BRENDA MILLER

Brenda Miller is the author of *Blessing of the Animals* (2009), *Season of the Body*, and co-author of *Tell it Slant: Writing and Shaping Creative Nonfiction*. Her work has received five Pushcart Prizes and has been published in *Fourth Genre, Creative Nonfiction, Brevity, The Sun, Utne Reader, Georgia Review*, and *Witness*, among other journals. She is a Professor of English at Western Washington University and serves as Editor-in-Chief of the *Bellingham Review*.

ANDER MONSON

Ander Monson is the author of a host of paraphernalia including a decoder wheel, several chapbooks and limited edition letterpress collaborations, a website, http://otherelectricities.com, and five books, most recently *The Available World* (poetry, 2010) and *Vanishing Point: Not a Memoir* (nonfiction, 2010). His work has appeared in *The Best Creative Nonfiction 2* and *The Best*

American Essays 2008. He lives and teaches in Tucson, Arizona, where he edits the magazine *DIAGRAM* and the New Michigan Press.

DINTY W. MOORE

Dinty W. Moore's memoir *Between Panic & Desire* was winner of the Grub Street Nonfiction Book Prize in 2009. His other books include *The Accidental Buddhist, Toothpick Men, The Emperor's Virtual Clothes,* and the writing guide, *The Truth of the Matter: Art and Craft in Creative Nonfiction.* Moore has published essays and stories in *The Southern Review, The Georgia Review, Harper's, The New York Times Sunday Magazine, Gettysburg Review, Utne Reader,* and *Crazyhorse,* among numerous other venues. A professor of nonfiction writing at Ohio University, Moore edits *Brevity,* the journal of concise literary nonfiction.

MICHELE MORANO

Michele Morano is the author of the essay collection *Grammar Lessons: Translating a Life in Spain,* and her essays have appeared in anthologies and literary journals such as *Best American Essays, Fourth Genre, Georgia Review,* and *Missouri Review.* Her work has been honored by the Rona Jaffe Foundation, the Illinois Arts Council, the American Association of University Women, and the MacDowell Colony, among others. She is associate professor of English at DePaul University.

NAOMI SHIHAB NYE

Naomi Shihab Nye's books of poetry include *You and Yours, 19 Varieties of Gazelle: Poems of the Middle East* (a finalist for the National Book Award), *Fuel, Red Suitcase,* and *Hugging the Jukebox.* She has received many awards including a Lannan Fellowship, a Guggenheim Fellowship, a Wittner Bynner Fellowship, the Paterson Poetry Prize, and four Pushcart Prizes. In 2010 she was elected to the Board of Chancellors of the Academy of American Poets.

JOYCE CAROL OATES

Joyce Carol Oates has written more than 50 novels, over 30 collections of short stories, eight volumes of poetry, plays, innumerable essays and book reviews, as well as longer nonfiction works. Her novel *them* won the National Book Award in 1970, and her novels *Black Water, What I Lived For,* and *Blonde* were nominated for the Pulitzer Prize. Oates received the 2009 National Book Critics Circle Ivan Sandrof Lifetime Achievement Award. She teaches at Princeton University.

ALICIA OSTRIKER

Alicia Ostriker's most recent collection of poems is *The Book of Seventy.* Her 1980 anti-war poem sequence *The Mother/Child Papers* was recently reprinted by the University of Pittsburgh Press, and her chapbook *At the Revelation Restaurant* is published by Marick Press. As a critic, Ostriker is the author of *Stealing the Language; the Emergence of Women's Poetry in America* and other books on poetry and the Bible. She teaches in the MFA program of Drew University.

MICHAEL POLLAN
Michael Pollan is the author of *In Defense of Food: An Eater's Manifesto*, winner of the James Beard Award, and *The Omnivore's Dilemma*, which was named one of the ten best books of 2006 by *The New York Times* and *The Washington Post.* It also won the California Book Award, the Northern California Book Award, the James Beard Award, and was a finalist for the National Book Critics Circle Award. Other books include *The Botany of Desire, A Place of My Own, Second Nature,* and most recently, *Food Rules* (2009). Pollan is the Knight Professor of Journalism at UC Berkeley.

JOHN T. PRICE
John T. Price is the author of two environmental memoirs, *Not Just Any Land: A Personal and Literary Journey into the American Grasslands* and *Man Killed by Pheasant: And Other Kinships*, which won the 2009 *Orion Magazine* Readers' Choice Award. The recipient of an NEA fellowship, his nonfiction has recently appeared or is forthcoming in *Orion, The Iowa Review*, and *Hawk & Handsaw: The Journal of Creative Sustainability.* He teaches at the University of Nebraska at Omaha and lives with his family in the Loess Hills of western Iowa.

LIA PURPURA
Lia Purpura is the author of two collections of essays, *On Looking*, a National Book Critics Circle Award finalist and winner of the Towson University Prize in Literature, and *Increase*, winner of the AWP Award in Creative Nonfiction; three collections of poems, *King Baby* (winner of the Beatrice Hawley Award), *Stone Sky Lifting* (winner of the Ohio State University Press Award), and *The Brighter the Veil*; and a collection of translations. She has received NEA and Fulbright fellowships and two Pushcart Prizes. She is currently Writer-in-Residence at Loyola College in Baltimore.

JANISSE RAY
Writer, naturalist, and activist Janisse Ray is author of three books of literary nonfiction, *Pinhook, Wild Card Quilt*, and *Ecology of a Cracker Childhood*, and numerous poems and essays. She is on the faculty of Chatham University's low-residency MFA program, and is a Woodrow Wilson Visiting Fellow. In 2007 she was awarded an honorary doctorate from Unity College in Maine.

PATTIANN ROGERS

Pattiann Rogers has published twelve books, including *Wayfare* (2008), *Generations, Song of the World Becoming: New and Collected Poems, 1981-2001*, *Firekeeper: New and Selected Poems*, which was a finalist for the Lenore Marshall Poetry Prize, and *Eating Milk and Honey*. She has received two NEA Grants, a Guggenheim Fellowship, a Lannan Literary Award in Poetry, and a Lannan Poetry Fellowship. Her poems have been awarded the Tietjens Prize, the Hokin Prize, and the Bock prize from *Poetry*, the Roethke Prize from *Poetry Northwest*, the Strousse Award from *Prairie Schooner* twice, and five Pushcart Prizes.

MARJANE SATRAPI

Marjane Satrapi is the author of the autobiographical graphic novel *Persepolis*, winner of the Angoulême Coup de Coeur Award among other honors. It was adapted into an animated film of the same name that won the Jury Prize at the Cannes Film Festival and was nominated for an Academy Award for Best Animated Feature Film. Subsequent publications include *Embroideries* and *Chicken with Plums*, recipient of the Angoulême Album of the Year award. Satrapi is also the author of several children's books, including *Monsters Are Afraid of the Moon*.

RUTH L. SCHWARTZ

Ruth L. Schwartz is the author of four award-winning books of poetry, including *Edgewater*, a 2001 National Poetry Series selection, and *Dear Good Naked Morning*, winner of the 2004 Autumn House Poetry Prize. Her memoir, *Death in Reverse: A Love Story*, was published by Michigan State University Press. She is on the faculty at the low-residency MFA Program at Ashland University, and teaches private workshops on the theme of The Writer As Shaman, and other topics which bridge creativity and spiritual growth.

LAWRENCE SUTIN

Lawrence Sutin is the author of two memoirs, *Jack and Rochelle: A Holocaust Story of Love and Resistance* and *A Postcard Memoir*; two biographies, *Divine Invasions: A Life of Philip K. Dick* and *Do What Thou Wilt: A Life of Aleister Crowley*; a historical work, *All Is Change: The Two Thousand Year Journey of Buddhism to the West*; and a novel, *When to Go into the Water* (2009). He lives in Minneapolis and teaches in the MFA program at Hamline University and the low-residency MFA program at Vermont College.

RHETT ISEMAN TRULL

Rhett Iseman Trull won the Anhinga Prize for Poetry for her first book, *The Real Warnings* (2009). Her poems and essays have appeared or are forthcoming in *The American Poetry Review, Best New Poets 2008, Georgetown Review, Prairie Schooner, The Southern Review*, and other publications. Her awards include prizes from the Academy of American Poets and the Dorothy Sargent Rosenberg Foundation. She and her husband publish *Cave Wall* in Greensboro, North Carolina.

TOM VARISCO

Tom Varisco is sole proprietor and creative director of Tom Varisco Designs, a full service, award-winning design/branding studio in New Orleans. In 2007, Tom was awarded the first "Fellow Award" by the New Orleans chapter of the American Institute of Graphic Arts for "making a significant contribution to raising the standards of excellence in practice and conduct within the local or regional design community." He has two self-published books: *Spoiled*, about the refrigerators left out after Hurricane Katrina, and *Signs of New Orleans*, a design and photo book that serves as a brief record of the city's "sign language."

JOHN EDGAR WIDEMAN

John Edgar Wideman's novels include *Sent for You Yesterday* and *Philadelphia Fire*, both of which won the PEN/Faulkner Award for Fiction. He is also the author of several works of nonfiction, including *Fatheralong*, a finalist for the National Book Award, and *Brothers and Keepers*, a finalist for the National Book Critics Circle Award. His short story collections include *Damballah, Fever*, and *All Stories Are True*. Wideman has received the Rea Award for the Short Story, the American Book Award for Fiction, the Lannan Literary Fellowship for Fiction, and the MacArthur Grant. He teaches at Brown University.

Acknowledgments ‖

This book would not exist without the generosity of the writers collected between its covers. We are grateful both for their words and for their willingness to accept low fees or in some cases donating their essays. It would also not exist without the help of people like Jayne Adair, Christy Diulus, Lori Jakiela, Debra Marquart, Dawn Marano, Dinty W. Moore, and Mike Simms who suggested selections to us. Ruth L. Schwartz, John Biguenet, Derek Green, and Peter Oresick read early drafts of the introduction, and we thank them. It would not exist without the determination and skill of Caitlin Clarke, our editorial assistant, who tracked down writers and publishers and did the hard work of negotiating for rights. It would not exist without Adrienne Block, who compiled bios and proofed, Libba Nichols and Gina Olszowski who also proofed, or Linda L. Marasti who scanned and converted numerous essays into the electronic format we needed. And it would not exist without a host of Chatham University MFA students and alums who read and responded to many of the essays included here over the years in workshops taught by Sheryl.

We would like to thank our husbands, Teake Zuidema and Tom Whitford, for their unfailing good spirit and support during the extended period of work on this anthology.

Credits

Title Index

About the Editors ‖

Sheryl St. Germain

A native of New Orleans, Sheryl St. Germain has taught creative writing at The University of Texas at Dallas, The University of Louisiana at Lafayette, Knox College, and Iowa State University. She currently directs the MFA program in Creative Writing at Chatham University where she also teaches poetry and creative nonfiction. Her work has received several awards, including two NEA Fellowships, an NEH Fellowship, the Dobie-Paisano Fellowship, the Ki Davis Award from the Aspen Writers Foundation, and most recently the William Faulkner Award for the personal essay. Her books include *Going Home, The Mask of Medusa, Making Bread at Midnight, How Heavy the Breath of God,* and *The Journals of Scheherazade.* She has also published a book of translations of the Cajun poet Jean Arceneaux, *Je Suis Cadien.* A book of lyric essays, *Swamp Songs: the Making of an Unruly Woman,* was published in 2003. Her most recent book is *Let It Be a Dark Roux: New and Selected Poems,* published in 2007.

Margaret L. Whitford

Margaret L. Whitford has a background in community development finance and organizational development. After earning an MBA from the University of Pennsylvania's Wharton School, she spent nearly twenty years in the not-for-profit field before returning to graduate school for an MFA in Creative Writing. Her essays have appeared or are forthcoming in the anthology *Good Dogs Doing Good, The Pittsburgh Quarterly, MARY Magazine,* and *Brevity.* She divides her time between homes she shares with her husband in Pittsburgh and the south of France.

Autumn House Press Anthologies

The Autumn House Anthology of Contemporary American Poetry, 1st edition, edited by Sue Ellen Thompson

Joyful Noise: An Anthology of American Spiritual Poetry, edited by Robert Strong

When She Named Fire: An Anthology of Contemporary Poetry by American Women, edited by Andrea Hollander Budy

The Working Poet: 75 Writing Exercises and a Poetry Anthology, edited by Scott Minar

Keeping the Wolves at Bay: Stories by Emerging American Writers, edited by Sharon Dilworth

The Autumn House Anthology of Contemporary American Poetry, 2nd edition, edited by Michael Simms

Between Song and Story: Essays for the Twenty-first Century, edited by Sheryl St. Germain and Margaret L. Whitford

Design and Production

Cover and text design by Kathy Boykowycz
Cover photograph by Holly Brubach

Set in Lucida fonts, designed in 1987 by
Kris Holmes

Printed by McNaughton & Gunn on Nature's
Book, a 30% recycled paper